People Skills at Work

People Skills
at Work

Evan Berman and Dira Berman

CRC Press
Taylor & Francis Group
Boca Raton   London   New York

CRC Press is an imprint of the
Taylor & Francis Group, an **informa** business

CRC Press
Taylor & Francis Group
6000 Broken Sound Parkway NW, Suite 300
Boca Raton, FL 33487-2742

© 2012 by Taylor & Francis Group, LLC
CRC Press is an imprint of Taylor & Francis Group, an Informa business

No claim to original U.S. Government works

Printed in the United States of America on acid-free paper
Version Date: 2011921

International Standard Book Number: 978-1-4200-9385-8 (Hardback)

Library of Congress Cataloging-in-Publication Data

Berman, Evan M.
    People skills at work / Evan Berman, Dira Berman.
        p. cm.
    Includes bibliographical references and index.
    ISBN 978-1-4200-9385-8 (hbk. : alk. paper)
    1. Psychology, Industrial. 2. Interpersonal relations. 3. Interpersonal communication.
I. Berman, Dira. II. Title.

HF5548.8.B3934 2012
650.1'3--dc23   2011033931

Visit the Taylor & Francis Web site at
http://www.taylorandfrancis.com

and the CRC Press Web site at
http://www.crcpress.com

Contents

Preface

Every day millions of people go to work. How well they interact with others often determines what work gets done, how well the work gets done, and how much they enjoy doing it. Getting along with people is a central task of the workplace, affecting the quality of work that gets done and one's sense of well-being and career. We come across many different people: employees, program clients, customers, superiors, citizens, and so on. Many of these people are easy to work with and get along, but there are those who are difficult and test our patience and abilities to get the job done. Almost every workplace offers a mix of people—a reflection of humankind—and it is important to get along well with everyone.

Our people skills are defined, in short, as our ability to deal with people. A longer definition is our ability to deal with people in different situations, to recognize these situations, and to have a broad set of skills and to know when and how to skillfully use these skills with regard to impacts on job performance, well-being, and career. The ultimate point of people skills is to smooth the process and better deal with the people issues that inevitably come up. While we cannot control others, we can surely anticipate different situations that might come up, and we can be prepared for them.

The need for a book on people skills today is as large as it has ever been. People act in friendly ways, but support, friendship, and camaraderie seem increasingly harder to find. Even though people spend many hours together, they sometimes know little about the person whom they work with. The person next door is sometimes little more than the stranger next door. Globalization implies that we often deal with others who come from quite different countries and cultures. People also often know little about themselves and their coping abilities to deal with others until they actually experience different people and workplace situations. The consequences of the thinning of human relations at work include reduced communication, commitment, and help working through problems with others.

People skills are not an abstraction or body of knowledge only but the ability to assess and address a broad range of situations. Numerous job issues come up at work such as setting expectations with supervisors and coworkers, putting one's best foot forward in job interviews, dealing with issues of social manners, overcoming problems of communication, understanding ethics, managing one's network, finding a mentor, dealing with difficult bosses and coworkers, and handling the many strategies and tactics for furthering one's career. People have little tolerance for those who have a poor ability to get along with others, yet we need good skills to navigate the maze of people issues at work.

There is good payoff from mastering the situations in this book. In general, this book examines the impact of people skills in four major areas:

- achieving better work results,
- advancing one's career,
- surviving at work, and
- balancing work with personal well-being.

This book has three main parts that go successively deeper into the subject matter. The first main part, "Social Skills in a Modern World," discusses critical social skills that address respect giving, communication, conflict, emotions, how to get along, and assessment—all in practical ways and with many specific examples that provide guidance. The second main part, "The Professional Self," examines topics related to career advancement and professionalism, such as networking, professional commitment statements, interviews, and psychological contracts at work as relating to professional and career development. It also addresses matters of ethics. This part has in-depth, practical advice for advancing one's career and building on work that we developed. The third main part, "The Human Condition Explored," deals with topics that relate to well-being, survival, and the nature of useful personal self-knowledge. It examines how different stages of one's career affect major tasks and challenges, which in turn affect key issues and relations with others. This part also examines growing awareness of the impact of mental health at work. This broad and deeper section completes the book.

People skills are increasingly in demand, in the public and private sectors alike. For example, people in the public sector often have significant responsibilities, and how well they get along with others matters greatly for outcomes. Their work often involves dealing with many people, not only citizens and customers but also those in other agencies, levels of government, and private companies who partner with them in delivering services and project development. Many of these people deal with hundreds of people every day from all walks of life and some with a great deal of power and expertise. In such settings, good people skills are simply a must. Of course, the same can also be said of people in other organizations and in private and nonprofit organizations too. Very few people can escape the reality that their success usually requires having good people skills.

In our experience, people skills do not always come easy, at least not for everyone. Most people show up at work with very little preparation for dealing with other people. People are put together and expected to make it work out. Seldom do schools and colleges offer courses that teach people to hone their people skills and work better with others. Parents and life experiences provide valuable lessons, but not everyone shares equally in these lessons. Most people stumble through trials,

> *"You can always find people with hard skills, but success or failure often depends on the softer, people skills; these are more difficult to find."*

figuring out some ways that work for them, frequently picking up skills along the way. Frustrations in dealing with others are rampant and common at work. As one manager states, "You can always find people with hard skills, but success or failure often depend on the softer, people skills; these are more difficult to find."[1]

Misconceptions abound about getting along with others, and here we would like to set a few straight. First, having good people skills is not only or always about being liked and being popular. Being well liked surely matters, and it is important—it builds confidence and provides support and help in doing one's job. But those with good people skills will sometimes want to speak up. Many people join public organizations because they want to make a difference. People skills also involve getting support for one's positions and knowing how to put visions into practice. But people at work are also apt to sometimes disagree with each other, and people skills are needed to help people with those who are far from their sense of propriety. In such instances, the measure of people skills is about how people handle disagreement and, sometimes, separation. The measure of people skills is surely more than just being popular.

A second misconception is that getting along well with others is a matter of traits with which people are endowed. Research shows that childhood experiences, culture, and personality profiles have a strong, formative impact on skills that are honed and later put into practice. Some people come out of young adulthood with better people skills than others, for sure. But parents and culture do not provide all the essential knowledge and orientations for dealing with others. People learn to improve their people skills. People are constantly adapting to new people at work, and they deal with a broad range of cultures and expectations too. Almost everyone recognizes the need to improve their ability to work with others. People skills are learned, and people often continue to refine their skills throughout their lifetime.

Knowledge and insight matter deeply for mastering people skills, but people don't master people skills by reading many books or by memorizing a finite list of knowledge points or doing well on exams. People skills are mastered in practice; it is a contact sport. By analogy, mastering people skills is more akin to doing a driving license road test than to doing a driving license theory test. People skills can be improved by theory and insight, but they are not a theory-based exam. This book helps by providing (1) a clear description and analysis of the complexity of many important work situations, (2) straightforward frameworks and heuristics that can be put in practice, and (3) empirical detail and observations that prompt the development of insight. We go for depth analysis in these matters, as oversimplification and pithy adages alone seldom produce satisfactory development and application. Each chapter reflects this and provides the following:

- balance between broad themes, specific issues, and detailed examples;
- a description of real-life cases with details of important guideposts;
- clearly written and illustrated heuristic strategies;
- mindfulness of gender and cultural differences, as well as of an increasingly global world;
- an accessible writing style;
- use of a broad range of knowledge sources, including research-based evidence (and sources with which readers may be less familiar);
- neither an overly optimistic nor pessimistic depiction of the workplace; and
- ideas to stimulate readers' own insights and applications.

We think and hope that this approach will further readers' insight and appeal to their needs in a wide range of areas. We think it is consistent with the nature and complexity of the subject matter. Surely, people vary in their situations, and some will find some sections more relevant to them than others. But whatever situation or experience one has, there is always improvement to be had. People skills are a lifelong learning project, and we hope this book can help readers in their journey.

With reference to our academic colleagues, we note that this book goes beyond those books currently available. This book is grounded in four major, diverse knowledge sources. First, it acknowledges the heritage of organizational behavior (OB) and industrial psychology, which created an awareness of these matters in the 1960s and 1970s that continues through the present. Staple OB topics include communication, conflict, teamwork, job satisfaction, and leadership, which are major, expected foci in business and public administration teaching programs today. Yet these studies often focus on employer rather than employee interests, and the implicit promise in these fields of illuminating matters of individual psychology and well-functioning and human experience at work is often unfulfilled. Also, as science has advanced, so the domain of OB has become increasingly too broad for meaningful coverage and treatment. A need now exists to target selected, specific aspects or themes and to infuse these with knowledge from other fields. Readers will recognize the selection of topics in the section "Social Skills in a Modern World" as reflecting many mainstream OB interests.

Second, humanism and ethics are essential in human relations. People are far more than the sum of their legal or economic rights and responsibilities, and the renewed attention to ethics has shown to be more than a passing phenomenon. The ability to tap into the essential humanness of people has shown great practical value as being an essential key to smoothing conflict, ensuring cooperation, increasing motivation, and furthering loyalty and high performance. The ability to connect with others is much praised. Though problems of alienation and bureaucratic structure are well discussed in the older literature,[2] recent studies have also made great progress on human development. A new focus is now available to discuss human connection. We think that the next twenty years will see much growth in this area and reshape current OB research.

Third, we developed new material that helps people develop and market their professional identity. Doing so has become essential as the way through which people impact their world. Organizations are a means through which people affect their world, and organizations increasingly seek those who have a vision to do so that can be aligned with the organization's mission. For example, public service motivation is to be translated into specific roles and purposes through which that motivation becomes manifested. Increased global competition and varying economic outlooks have further increased the need for effective self-expression of one's purpose in the world and of the ability to connect with others and their organizations to make that a reality. The section "The Professional Self" addresses this aspect.

Fourth, in recent years, elements of mental health and psychopathology have become increasingly mainstream in U.S. society and relevant to the workforce and interacting with others. Whereas a generation ago mention of depression or bipolar disorders would be unknown or met with high stigma, today these terms are mainstream, especially for younger Americans who, along with their friends, are increasingly familiar with psychotropic medication. Depression and anxiety affect more than a quarter of the population and have consequences for how people behave toward others. This knowledge also contributes insights into human fulfillment and differentiation (or "complexity"). Awareness and comfort with these topics are now the new dividing line between generations. Also, while many people in other countries are often still behind this uniquely American trend, it is likely that they too will benefit from this literature. It is time to bring this literature into our mainstream; it is discussed in the latter part of this book.

Finally, this book is also shaped by our experiences. We are a husband–wife team. We grew up in vastly different cultures (the Netherlands and Brazil), established careers in the United States, and have advanced degrees from the United States. As a distinguished and chair professor in the United States and Taiwan, Evan Berman has taught courses in human resource management (HRM) and OB and has researched and published extensively on these topics. He is an author of a best-selling textbook, *Human Resource Management in Public Service* (4th ed., Sage, 2012). Dira (pronounced *Dee-ra*) Berman, a psychotherapist, has dealt extensively with the impact of mental health on workplace relations and performance. In the past few years, we have lived in East Asia, where people skills are both different and highly important. We are well aware of the impact of Buddhist and Confucian thinking on human relations. This book reflects our professional and personal integration of many different sources of knowledge and experience.

We thank the many, many people in our life who, through their interactions with us, contributed to the development of knowledge and insight that is reflected here. All encounters are opportunities for learning and reflection, and many people contributed without intending to do so. We are indebted and grateful.

Evan and Dira Berman
Taipei, 2011

Biographies

Evan M. Berman is currently university chair professor at National Chengchi University in Taipei (Taiwan). He is also past chair of the American Society for Public Administration's (ASPA) Section of Personnel and Labor Relations, senior editor of *Public Performance & Management Review*, a Distinguished Fulbright Scholar, and past editor in chief of ASPA's Book Series in Public Administration and Public Policy. His areas of expertise are human resource management, public performance, local government, and international public governance. He has published in all the leading peer-reviewed journals of the discipline and serves on many editorial boards. He is a coauthor of the leading textbooks *Human Resource Management in Public Service* (4th ed., 2012) and *Essential Statistics for Public Managers and Policy Analysts* (3rd ed., 2012). Other recent books include *Public Administration in East Asia: Mainland China, Japan, South Korea, and Taiwan* (2010) and *Public Administration in Southeast Asia: Thailand, Philippines, Malaysia, Hong Kong, and Macao* (2011). Prior to joining National Chengchi University in 2008, he was the Huey McElveen Distinguished Professor at Louisiana State University. He has assisted numerous local jurisdictions on matters of team building, strategic planning, and citizen participation. Evan Berman has received awards for his work and is recognized as one of the top scholars of his generation. He can be reached at evanmberman@gmail.com.

Maria (Dira) Berman is a psychotherapist and current international student counselor at National Chengchi University in Taipei (Taiwan). She is responsible for providing mental health assistance to and improving the well-being of the large number of international students at NCCU. She is a member of the Office of International Cooperation and of the Counseling Center at NCCU. She has extensive experience providing therapy, crisis management, and counseling, including educational and therapeutic services, to employees and their families and corporations. She has provided psychiatric evaluation, assessment, and diagnosis treatment for anger management, anxiety, depression, behavioral self-control, social skills, sexual issues, adaptation for multicultural populations, geriatric issues, women's issues, and many other problems. She has provided services through employee-assistance programs for several major government agencies and private corporations. Prior to joining National Chengchi University, she had private practices in Florida and Louisiana. Dira Berman is a native of Rio de Janeiro (Brazil). She can be reached at diraberman@gmail.com.

Section

One

Setting the Stage

1

Common Sense Is Not Enough

An Introduction

So, my supervisor said, "It's just simple, common sense." But I still don't know what to do.

What is expected of us? What should we do? These are common questions that almost everyone has, especially at the beginning of new jobs. When asked, people may be told to "stay out of trouble," "do what you are told to do," or "treat others with respect." Some may also be told to "behave yourself professionally," "don't make waves," and "do some good." There is a fair amount of common sense that is assumed to guide us in what we do.[1] Beyond doubt, these are useful orientations for people to have as they figure out what to do, and this advice is given to new employees and senior managers alike. Such advice often stays with people throughout their careers.

Popular expressions and pithy adages often contain kernels of truth and wisdom, but more is needed as well. Common sense is often defined as widely held beliefs that are considered as valid, prudent, and sound by some group and assumed to be adopted or followed by group members and newcomers. Common sense helps guide decisions and understanding. Adages are often popular expressions of some of these beliefs.[2] However, any sentence or phrase containing the word *should*, such as "people should behave professionally," is typically indicative of what often or at least sometimes is not. If it were otherwise, we wouldn't have to remind them, or as Voltaire (1694–1778) once said, "Common sense is not so common."

Let's do a little reality check here. Everybody knows not to steal—that seems common sense. Yet according to the University of Florida 2005 *National Retail Security Survey*, employee theft is responsible for 47 percent of store inventory shrinkage.[3] People also take in other ways, such as using an excessive amount of work time for personal matters, online shopping, chatting, or investing; they spend many times more than the 40 to 50 minutes per day that most people do.[4] As a further example, almost everyone knows instances where the adage "to act professionally and treat others with respect" is not followed at work.[5] One book discusses that women, in competition with other women, often shy away from direct confrontation and engage in competition by talking behind backs, spreading gossip, and sabotaging others.[6] Competition involving men is also often neither respectful nor professional. "We have people that backstab and make it their duty to slaughter certain coworkers just because they don't like or get along with them," states an employee.[7]

As related to equal treatment and performance, some people are promoted based on their friendships with others, and when they turn out to have deficient skills and achievements, their friends and bosses continue to support them and encourage others to "not make waves" and "wait their turn." Some managers give very difficult assignments to those they personally dislike and pass them over for desirable assignments that would prepare them for promotion. Studies show also that people who are perceived as handsome or attractive are more likely to receive employment offers and promotion than those who are not, which not fair with regard to merit.[8] In many workplaces these patterns are very common, not the exception, and people experience them.

As a further example of adages that do not exactly describe reality, almost everyone knows that they should avoid improper decorum and that sex and alcohol in the workplace are clear examples of inappropriate, unprofessional conduct. In a nationwide sample of

1,522 employed U.S. adults aged 18 and over, 17 percent have secretly dated someone from work, 37 percent have flirted with a colleague, and 8 percent currently have a secret crush at work.[9] According to one survey, by the American Management Association, of 390 managers and executives, 30 percent said they had dated a coworker and 44 percent of office romances led to marriage.[10] In yet another survey, 31 percent stated that while they did not date their boss or another superior, they would be willing; "I have fantasized about it, that's for sure," says one respondent. Other surveys report higher numbers.[11] President Bill Clinton's tryst with Monica Lewinsky might be among the more famous, but it is by no means the only.[12] And alcohol and illicit drug use occurs, too. According to one study, workplace alcohol use and impairment directly affects 15 percent of the U.S. workforce (19.2 million workers) every year, and 3.1 percent of employed adults use illicit drugs while at work.[13]

We are not arguing that it is OK to have sex, engage in favoritism, or treat others unkindly, of course—we merely state some facts about the workplace, because it is important to deal with reality as it is. Immoral behavior can certainly get a person fired or passed over for promotion. Rather, the point is that it is difficult to know exactly which adages are widely held as common sense in organizations. Even though some managers seem to rely on them, we do well to assume that adages and common sense do *not* necessarily reflect practice at work. It is paradoxical to say that if people behaved according to common sense and adages, there would be little need for pointing them out; adages often deal what *should* be. Moreover, as people try to improve their workplace and make it more professional and effective, they necessarily confront a good deal of behavior that is not so. The road to professional progression and advancement inescapably requires dealing with reality that is not fully described by pithy adages and popular expressions alone.

Given the extent of the above problems, we might ask why common sense, adages, and axioms do not have greater effect on behavior.

The issue is not that common and sage advice lack merit. Common sense and adages often point to standards of what should or should not be done. Values and moral principles guide like a lodestar and provide standards for evaluating what goes on around us today. They are surely needed. Let's look a bit closer at some adages and common sense expressions that are used at work. Consider the following examples of common sense expressions that may be heard around the workplace:

- Treat others like you would like to be treated yourself (Golden Rule).
- All is fair in love and war (and at work, too).
- Cream rises.
- It's not what you know, it's who you know.
- Always act professionally, and don't lie or cheat.
- "It's very important to live your life by an internal yardstick … rather than relying on the affirmation of others" (Warren Buffet).
- Give an honest day's work for an honest day's pay.
- Always look out for #1 (which is yourself).
- Speak softly but carry a big stick.
- The squeaky wheel gets the grease.
- Don't makes waves.

These expressions clearly contain kernels of wisdom and important truths. They represent conclusions and lessons from past situations, and there are many situations today in which these same lessons can apply. The art is to know when these conclusions can be applied and to which circumstances to apply them—a bit later, we show specific instances where they are useful. But these adages also have serious limitations that should prevent readers from seeking to relate to others by following them indiscriminately or as omnipresent truths, which they are not.

First, many adages contradict each other. For example, "Cream rises" suggests that merit is recognized and rewarded, while "It's not what you know, it's who you know" suggests that merit alone is not enough to be rewarded. "Speak softly" suggests that it is unwise to "make waves" and cause aggravation, but "The squeaky wheel gets the grease" suggests quite the contrary, namely, that causing some aggravation for others can get you what you want. These adages don't all contradict each other, but many do, and sufficiently so that the need for additional information such as about the context in which they are to be applied becomes quickly needed.

Many situations are handled by using multiple adages, even those that contradict each other. Let's take the Golden Rule, which is often held as immutable. For example, if you want others to treat you nicely, it might be good to treat them nicely too.[14] But it is also true that having a big stick helps to get others to treat you nicely. Moreover, if you are always nice to people, then why do they need to be nice to you? They could treat you crappy, and you would still be nice to them, hoping for better. So, in dealing with people, it seems that sometimes the Golden Rule might be applied, while in other instances some other adage might be better. Even the Golden Rule does not always or universally lead to favorable outcomes. Nor do individual adages apply as broadly some people think. Does the Golden Rule imply that those who push work off onto others would welcome others doing that to them too?

This also means that there is almost always a common sense expression to justify one's point of view, right or wrong, in some way. Ample adages and truisms exist that can be applied. For example, people can say that you did not get what you wanted because you spoke up and also because you did not speak up enough. Some people are veritable masters at justifying their actions, sometimes projecting confidence and superiority over others (e.g., "If you had just used common sense …"), sometimes justifying the impossibility of obtaining better outcomes.

> **There is always a common sense expression to justify one's point of view.**

Second, beyond this, people also struggle to make sense of competing values and expectations, which sometimes reflect choosing between adages. When is less than full disclosure intentional misleading? How much do you want to tell your boss or customers about problems with an approval or product? Most of these decisions are made quickly, sometimes in just split seconds. Leading organizations increasingly recognize the need for specificity. Answers depend on specific facts and circumstances, as well as on the application of guidelines. Training is increasingly about making employees and managers aware of specific situations and helping them make the right decisions. The fact that organizations do so is testimony to the limits of relying on existing common sense and adages alone.[15]

Yet organizations cannot foresee the thousands of different ways in which new situations come up; we need to work through many problems ourselves. Consider the following example. A twenty-five-year-old sales coordinator is told by his supervisor not to use text-messaging abbreviations in e-mail to clients, because "doing so is rude."[16] In response, the young employee asks, "How is GL, TY, BRB, and YW rude?" and then proceeds to explain to the manager that these abbreviations stand for good luck, thank you, be right back, and you're welcome.[17] One way to view this is as a rather harmless, innocent misunderstanding by the manager, whose technical unfamiliarity should be addressed; it is time for management to get with it. Yet another view sees this as an oversight in people skills—the employee fails to grasp that communication must project professional demeanor, be understood, and put others at ease. Some clients may not be familiar with these abbreviations, and ignorance of electronic ways could unknowingly embarrass them. The abbreviations also are not commonly accepted and professional English, and allowing their usage is tantamount to condoning unprofessional conduct in the organization. However minor this instance seems, it could sow undesirable seeds of doubt in future business relations or amplify already existing concerns that the employee is unaware of. The supervisor could be pointing to broader purposes. "TY" may be acceptable in some situations, but not in all.

Most situations are far more consequential than this example. People are told by their bosses to "stay out of trouble," but what "trouble" should they try to avoid? What does "professional" or "respect" mean, especially for someone raised in another country or coming from a different industry? A graduating student asks, "I'd like to know what we can do to make a smooth transition into the working world. What are the qualities we fail to acquire through the traditional education system? I'm confused. Are we undisciplined and careless? Are we blind careerists? Our elders seem to be telling us we're doing everything wrong."[18] People need specificity and answers. Common sense and adages do not help enough. They stimulate a little awareness and insight, but they are not a reliable guide to correct answers.

Common sense also fails to address some important organizational processes and realities. Whatever these are called, there are many bureaupathologies. For example, the Peter Principle[19] states that people are promoted to their highest level of incompetence; had they been competent in their current position, they would be further promoted. In our experience, quite some managers are unable to move their departments along, and if not for their secretaries and one or more staff who hope to be promoted, their units would have even worse performance. Many managers are truly mediocre, sometimes borderline inept, yet such people exist with alarming frequency in many organizations. Common sense can scarcely begin to explain how such persons came into their positions and why their superiors tolerate their mediocre or poor performance. Common sense also provides little guidance to their employees on how to deal with them, which is of utmost need for them.

Common sense or pithy adages scarcely provide a basis for assuming what these processes and their main characteristics are. Newcomers might believe that merit is a key factor in hiring and promotion (e.g., "do well and good things will happen"), but that is not always or even necessarily a preeminent feature—it may be only a necessary but not sufficient condition. People are sometimes also promoted because of their loyalty to those above them ("he is reliable") or so they won't expose compromising information. Common sense also does not tell people what to do on the job. Organizations in which most people merely "follow orders" and "do what is their job" often produce highly mediocre and, for stakeholders, unacceptably poor results. Though people often need to do more than just their job, "just following orders" does not adequately tell people when they should do what.

As a management strategy, common sense also has its limits. For example, when crisis strikes, managers and leaders often fall back on common sense or their version of it. While the above adages may provide some guidance, they seldom do so adequately—such as in the face of employees failing to forward critical messages, when key office personnel threaten to resign, and when key Web sites are inoperable for several days at end. When people are overtaken by events, they need to get "waist deep" into circumstances, events, and facts and be all over what is happening and present like "gravy over rice."[20] People are sometimes seen to address crisis through rigid application of one or more adages, sometimes even citing biblical and religious dicta as guiding strategies, without fully understanding the facts and specific circumstances, which can cause poor or even dangerous outcomes to result.

Common sense also does little to help people with inevitably emotional moments at work. Frustration happens. How does common sense help us deal with physical symptoms of stress and intruding, negative thoughts of others? Physiologically, the evolutionary purpose of discomfort is to push us into action to deal with these threatening and unpleasant situations, but that does not mean that we have the tools for doing so very well. What should you do? "Not rock the boat?" "Act professionally?" "Love thy enemy?" "Save face?" Accept that "this is just how it is"? These give conflicting advice, none of which is specific enough to act on. Not surprisingly, many people often suffer long when they are confronted by such moments, and some people prefer not to work or seek happiness elsewhere than to engage in work and confront these matters for which they do not have adequate preparation. We need a better way.

Common sense also does little to explain how personal well-being and emotions affect decision making. Consider this quote from an Internet blog:

> A young employee resigned after completing a costly six month company training program. She said the industry wasn't right for her and that she had a new job with better pay, but when the manager pushed back on her reasons for leaving and found flaws in her story, the employee started crying and admitted she didn't have another job, she was just quitting because she didn't get enough praise from the manager and was feeling like a failure. Thus, she was moving home with her parents.[21]

This is hardly an aberration. The generation gap is sometimes understood as younger workers giving more value to the Pleasure Principle (which states that people seek to experience pleasure and avoid pain) and older workers following the Reality Principle in their choices (i.e., people are able and willing to defer present gratification for future gains).[22] Emotions drive and affect choices in many ways; modern management theory and practice have gaping holes dealing with the role of emotion and well-being. Generation X workers often work out of loyalty to their bosses, because they make them feel good about themselves, not their organizations, and they follow their managers when they can.[23] All human beings want happiness and contentment. As one IT manager states, "People don't quit jobs; they quit managers."[24] Even people who don't care about personal well-being in the abstract do care about it when it affects them. In Japan, *Karochi* refers to death from overwork; who wants that?[25]

Common sense and management adages are also thoroughly devoid of the impact of mental health on choices that people make. Such adages as "keeping your troubles to yourself" are increasingly inconsistent and harmful to dealing with the reality that, according to the U.S. Department of Health and Human Services, "an estimated 26.2 percent of Americans ages 18 and older—about one in four adults—suffer from a diagnosable mental disorder in a given year."[26] In addition, many more have proclivities and behaviors that do not constitute a "diagnosable mental disorder" but nonetheless affect workplace interactions. Also, about 6 percent of the population older than age twenty-five years reported illicit drug use in the past month.[27] Indeed, mental health problems and addiction are often found to lie at the heart of behavior mentioned at the beginning of this chapter relating to sex, substance abuse, and stealing. Many young people are quite comfortable discussing mental health; in groups, they often readily self-identify with problems: "yes, that is us—depression! anxiety! attention deficit!" No surprise here; according to the U.S. Centers for Disease Control, antidepressants are the most prescribed drug in the United States.[28] Yet older workers, some of whom are managers of younger workers, are ill informed about mental health, as they themselves often go undiagnosed and treated for these problems. Unaware of medical advances, their attitudes often embody the fear and stigmatization of mental health instead of allowing them to see these as partly reflecting physical realities too. It is obvious that knowing about mental health conditions and how they affect people doing their work and relating to others matters.[29] Later chapters discuss these connections. What you don't know about yourself and others can hurt you.

It is paradoxical that those who live by pithy adages and axioms often fail to find the sound practical judgment and results that are promised. Yes, common sense, axioms, and adages help by suggesting standards to be strived for. Who is against the Golden Rule and principles of justice in the world, at least in theory? No one, of course.

> It is paradoxical that those who live by common sense often fail to find the practical judgment and results that are promised.

But common sense is often also inconsistent, confounding, and in need of the specificity of context and experience. Those who use it well often have decades of experience that they also bring to the table. Sound application of common sense requires this, as well; without this, common sense and adages are a liability or error waiting to happen. And some aspects of reality are beyond common sense, such as those dealing with mental health, compulsions, and emotional well-being. Common sense can be a useful pointer, but not always. In short, common sense is needed, but more than common sense is also needed.

Section

TWO

Social Skills in a Modern World

2

"Welcome"

What goes around comes around.

—Popular expression

When a group of human resource professionals was asked, "In general, how important are good manners in advancing a person's career in your department and/or organization?" 65 percent stated *extremely important*, and 30 percent stated *somewhat important*. Only 5 percent stated that good manners are either *somewhat unimportant* or *not at all important*.[1]

Why are social manners so important? Many people at work are strangers to each other, to more or lesser degree, and social manners help smooth interactions. Social manners are an invitation for working together and an initial starting point or basis for dealing with many issues that work inevitably brings up. Social manners alone are not enough for being successful at work, but without them, people do not get much beyond first base. Poor social manners cause concern about one's ability to get along with others. They draw attention to people with whom we do not want to work, especially when there is choice to be had among people. A consensus exists that people with effective social skills are more likely to be successful, get favorable responses from others and support from their environment, and are more likely to feel good about themselves.

We define *social skills* as the "capacity for situation-specific, interpersonal behavior that is effective to achieve desired outcomes." This is consistent with other commonly used definitions.[2] *Social manners* are loosely defined as a subset of social skills that are commonly taken as customary ways of behaving and interacting, typically for the purpose of getting along in some basic way. All groups have norms of what is expected and what works for getting along, and modern workplaces are no different. This short opening chapter identifies some essential social manners that are an invitation for others to want to work with us and, at times, to continue to do so. Without others wanting to work with us, we do not get very far.

Social manners are the most basic of social skills and generally concern ways in which people show themselves to be courteous, welcoming, respectful, effective, and able to connect with others. The point here is not about old-fashioned etiquette or stylized ways of high society from a bygone time (globalization and diversity have broken many of those down) but rather about basic, courteous, and effective ways of relating to others at work. Expectations about social manners in the United States have surely become relaxed in recent years, and informality in workplace relations is increasingly seen. Yet this does not mean that "everything goes." The vast majority of people want to work with others who are seen as friendly and cooperative, and they like to avoid those who are seen as difficult or unfriendly. It is paradoxical to think that by foregoing and debunking some old-fashioned forms of courtesy and interactions, people now face the more challenging task of figuring out for themselves how to use these basic values of being courteous, welcoming, respectful, and so on in the myriad daily interactions in which they find themselves. Instead of applying a known but long list of actions, they now must create their own.

The record to date does not suggest that U.S. employees and their managers are doing very well. The lack of well-defined ways of interacting with each other is seen to bring conflict, stress, and incivility to the U.S. workplace. As we discuss later, it also affects performance and competitiveness. When asked, "Compared to twenty or thirty years ago, do you think people are more rude, less rude, or about the same?" 69 percent stated *more rude*, 26 percent stated *about the same*, and only 4 percent stated *less rude*. Among baby boomers and Gen X workers, respectively, only 17 percent and 24 percent described millennial coworkers as being respectful of coworkers; among millennials, only 55 percent described other millennials as being respectful of other coworkers. The social graces of new employees are perceived as weak or uneven, but many younger workers find their older bosses uncaring and unsupportive. In a 2009 poll, 75 percent of adults said Americans are becoming ruder and less civilized,[3] and quite some foreigners agree.[4]

Of course, few people knowingly violate social manners; many more are simply not conscious of them or apply them in less than skillful ways. "I would identify a 'nonrespectful' attitude—as contrasted with a 'disrespectful' attitude—as the single greatest problem in the workplace," stated one manager. Few people are intentionally rude (though some are, for sure!), but a lack of mindfulness and skillfulness exists. Work life consists of hundreds of interactions, and the above values have numerous ways of being applied—or not. People come to work late, are unshaven or improperly dressed, prepare poor work, and address others in nondeferential ways. People take others for granted and do to others what they would not like others to do to them. At job

> "I would identify a 'nonrespectful' attitude as the single greatest problem in the workplace."

interviews, people show the ability to forge connections and to be courteous and professional—or not. Informality is one thing, but not showing the intention to be respectful or courteous is quite another. Such behavior often has its consequences.

It is widely agreed that it is time to polish up manners. This first chapter on people skills discusses essential, basic (even baseline) behaviors for getting along with others. We also focus on respect and effectiveness, which, in recent years, have sometimes become problematic.

✳

All groups have social manners or, more accurately, a repertoire of manners that their members are expected to follow. These behaviors usually span a range of acceptable behaviors, fit to different situations. Determining what that repertoire is inherently an imprecise task, as these expectations are seldom stated on any exact list; a challenge for all newcomers is to find out which social manners they are expected to follow. But it is obvious that society has some general expectations for how people should behave at work, and some assumptions or good guesses are to be made about what behaviors are likely expected at work that are courteous, welcoming, respectful, and effective and show our ability to connect with others. Some people and workplaces make these a bit more explicit, but few do.[5]

Table 2.1 shows foundational values of social manners at work. No definitive list exists, and while these values are widely accepted, readers might add a few additional ones. Workplace values often vary from general values in important ways—the same word means something different.[6] For example, *respect* is usually, in everyday use, defined as holding something in esteem or high regard, but its workplace usage is defined as giving thoughtful consideration to the opinions, feelings, or rights of others. Likewise, *courtesy* has general meanings that include companies giving someone something for free (e.g., a courtesy shuttle service), but its application in the workplace is more specific: showing, considering, or extending help to others with regard to their needs or circumstances. Workplace practices and need lead to modification. As regarding respect, it is quite obvious that we cannot always hold someone's opinion in high esteem, such as when the opinion is wrong, but we should give people respect by providing them an opportunity to express their opinion, giving their opinion full consideration, and providing them with feedback or a response that acknowledges their basic dignity, rights, and role in the organization. These examples show well that workplace adaptations are indeed a bit different.

People skills are not about philosophical discourse or agreement but about behaviors that signify or show one to be respecting, acting

Table 2.1 Basic Values in Social Manners

Values	Definition at Work	Key Examples
Courtesy	Showing consideration or extending help for the needs or circumstances of others, acting in polite or kind ways, showing a little allowance or generosity despite the facts	Ensuring people are comfortable, helping others in kind or polite ways, allowing a client extra leeway
Respect	Giving thoughtful consideration to the opinions, feelings, or rights of others	Not making disparaging remarks, ensuring that everyone's opinion is heard
Welcoming	To greet or be (initially) accepting of people and their ideas	Encouraging others, being friendly
Effective	Being able to produce results in appropriate ways or at desired standards, being able to work with others	Being the go-to person for certain issues, being someone that others can work with
Able to connect	Having behaviors that facilitate and do not push away contact and communication with others	Responding to others in appropriate ways, maintaining correct distance, not sending weird or off-base verbal or nonverbal messages

Note: Authors' adapted definitions. General definitions are based on the Merriam-Webster dictionary (http://www.merriam-webster.com/dictionary/).

with courtesy, welcoming, able or willing to connect, and effective. The key examples in Table 2.1 spell out specific behaviors, which can be listed in this way:

- greeting people in courteous or friendly ways (saying "hello") and ensuring that other people are comfortable;
- being respectful of others' opinions and feelings and getting to know others' interests and goals;
- being deferential (especially to customers and those in higher authority) and not making disparaging remarks;
- being mindful of how one's work affects that of others and the reputation of the organization;
- following standard protocols (e.g., not interrupting others in meetings);
- being effective in one's work;

- ensuring that interpersonal relations are consistent with law, rules, professionalism, and ethics (including not sending weird or off-base verbal or nonverbal messages);
- respecting the personal boundaries and spaces of others; and
- maintaining hygiene and professional appearance at work.

These are rather basic practices, indeed, and most seasoned professionals that we know would agree that these are guidelines that should be followed. Various authors mention one or more of these in connection with career management, too.[7] Indeed, it is easy to see that people who act in the above ways would indeed be people with whom others would probably want to work—they would be showing themselves to be courteous, welcoming, respectful, effective, and able to connect with others.

However, these practices are not always followed or followed well. Nonprofessionalism points to what happens when people act in ways that are not mindful of the above guidelines. To a large extent, interest in the above matters is born from myriad practical experiences of what happens when people act with little or no regard to, for example, "acting with courtesy" or "being mindful of how one's work affects the reputation of the organization." The concern is not with applying them wrongly but rather with hardly applying them at all. In a previous era, subsequent discussion would have focused on how to apply the above values correctly in specific situations, but the present discussion is about getting people to apply them in any form. Consider the following example from a workplace blog:

> At work, I've chewed out a few new entry-level engineers. … For example, I'm in a meeting with an aircraft parts supplier discussing a multi-million dollar deal, and one of my counterpart engineers answers his cell phone and proceeds to loudly talk about going to Quizno's for lunch and how his kids are doing. He doesn't even bother to walk outside and do it. What does that say to me? "I care infinitely more about my lunch and social life than I do about you and your aircraft parts." It's become such a problem that we've actually had informal training on portable electronics etiquette. People have to be told to not scream on the phone, don't interrupt clients to answer calls about business stuff unless it's a red-hot emergency. And don't fiddle with your palm pilot during meetings.[8,9]

This example shows how a lack of mindfulness leads to unintentional and unacceptable perceptions of rudeness. In the modern and competitive world, people may not wish to accept more than one or two of such instances before they move on. In public life, they might complain or become cynical. Organizations may not be able to tolerate too many of such nonrespectful episodes from their employees, even if some employees, when confronted by negative feedback, might respond with disbelief and search for another job where people are less critical and more appreciative of their efforts. The need for emphasis of respect, courtesy, and effectiveness is increasingly important, and there is broad convergence about this.

As a second example, applications to *listening* show how attention to the above guidelines not only avoids problems but also brings advantage. Listening is widely regarded as the preeminent opportunity for forming connections, putting others at ease, and learning about others' goals and needs. Unhappily, listening often is ill performed at work; it is also an example of missed opportunity. An Internet poll asked, "What is the worst quality of your boss?" and 23 percent of respondents stated, "doesn't listen."[10] Listening is an activity that requires a high degree of giving respect to others, showing courtesy, and being welcoming to what others have to say. Listening provides the opportunity to practice these values. It shows up in not interrupting and engaging others in dialog, for example. Among strangers, the lack of respect is often seized in minutes, if not snap judgment, through how someone listens and greets.[11] Those who practice listening with inadequate respect and courtesy often find other opportunities not occurring for them. However, those who listen well will more likely find misunderstanding avoided and opportunities created for forming connections. How people listen matters.

As a third example, consider application in the increasingly well-established area of net-etiquette. Values of respect and effectiveness would lead one to abstain from certain behaviors; being fun or cool are not the only guiding values. Not all e-mail and electronic communication are created equally, and what goes on at work needs to pass the propriety test. We are well beyond the era of sending e-mail in caps (which is considered yelling), but we now must also avoid e-mail that is personally embarrassing or inappropriate. It is not cool to write things in e-mail that are derogatory, regardless of the legality of them. It is also not cool to send an e-mail with many attachments that take people a long time to digest. People have many things to do, and many people receive fifty to seventy e-mails a day, excluding junk. A certain brevity is appreciated. People who have the above values in mind may not need to wait until the latest "electronic decorum guidelines" have been passed around; they have already thought of many things themselves.

In short, there are many ways in which being courteous, welcoming, respectful, effective, and able to connect with others show up. The challenging task today is for people to be relatively expansive in applying the above values in the everyday course of their work life; that is, occasionally thinking about whether they are handling their situation in a way that is respectful, courteous, and so on. Appendix B shows forty specific behaviors in four main areas of work:

- Greeting and Acknowledging Others
- Speaking and Listening
- Work Performance
- Respecting Boundaries

For example, Item 10 is "being polite and helpful to people in subordinate positions"; getting some people to be considerate to others is already a significant improvement. The subsequent chapters in this book address numerous specific examples. A basic conclusion from the above is that people, at a minimum, will need to demonstrate ways of showing respect.

Because at work we often deal with strangers and unfamiliar settings, a certain restraint or conservatism is expected that increases the need for mindfulness. We cannot know what others may find acceptable, and the point of first encounters is to pave the way for future ones. The exact degree of formality of behavior in these instances varies and is a reminder that the old styles of the past are not yet totally gone. When meeting the company president or agency director for the first time, one is expected to behave in a certain way that shows respect by not breaking the decorum of the event such as by making jokes. In an extreme example, even pop stars like Madonna curtsy before the British queen. President Bush received instructions on etiquette when receiving the British queen, but he made a faux pas when he winked at her, and the British queen visibly showed her displeasure at this.[12] In some cultures, some stylized ways are still important; for example, it may be inappropriate to shake another's hand or look too much into the eyes of someone of the opposite gender. While these are not everyday situations for most people, they do happen, and people are judged on their performance in them.

We see global convergence on the matter, and people are expected to tune in to the comfort of others. In global settings, one routinely hears people discuss how they are showing respect and courtesy for another and how their actions could be taken a wrong way. People "bend over backward" to avoid unintentional disrespect, sometimes asking beforehand whether a certain behavior might cause discomfort. Overattention rather than a lack of attention is the norm. At the slightest hint of discomfort, people step up and proactively query about its source. The price of dealing with more people and a greater sense of diversity is heightened sensitivity to such values as being courteous, welcoming, respectful, effective, and able to connect with others. Consider the following dialog:

A: Is everything all right?
B: Yes, why?
A: You look a bit upset or disturbed about something.
B: No, I am not.
A: I hope my comment about Mr. Azziz did not upset you. If I caused any upset for you, I apologize. I only wanted to draw attention to the problem of performance, because I want all to be happy in the end.
B: It was not that, really not.
A: Well, if it is something that I said, please let me know. I am very committed to this working out.

People find offense in the smallest of things, but the job of social manners is to address that. The continuation of the above dialog is likely that "B" calls "A" in a few days to talk about what it was that did upset.

The task of people to find application of these basic values allows self-expression and differentiation. People with strong social skills at work are sometimes described by others as having an uncanny ability to be liked by others. When we study such people, we see that they demonstrate *continuous consideration* toward others in highly skillful and consistent ways. Seeking out new ways of showing respect and courtesy is apt to bring forth innovation. Some people develop their own ways of being courteous, welcoming, respectful, effective, and able to connect with others. There is self-expression and individuality involved in deciding how to bring the above essential values into the world. Consider the following:

> Here is a person who is always helpful and makes sure the workplace is full of smiles and happiness. This in spite of the fact we are competitors. When I was sick and off work, she saw my clients and took good care of them. If someone was having a problem, she would always be there to help them and not expect anything in return. Another point to show her kindness and character was the birthday of one of our registrars and we were pleasantly surprised to see a bouquet and a huge cake waiting for him to cut! Way to go. Wish everyone had, starts having a colleague like this, and world would be a much better place to live, work, and enjoy.[13]

People have their unique strengths and past experiences that likely shape these behaviors, and this example is surely not relevant to everyone. As one example, we routinely host foreign citizens in a Chinese-speaking culture. Local custom is to provide translation of speeches, and personal guides and translators to guests. This little extra touch helps visitors better enjoy their experience. It is about our showing respect and consideration for their experiences of others. There are hundreds and hundreds of ways of showing a little extra respect and courtesy in ways that others feel are appropriate and desirable. The above is all very basic, but people don't get beyond first base without putting respect and courtesy in practice. They need to be continuously there in some shape or form.

Of course, not everyone that we deal with plays by the same rules. While there surely are some very rude people, many others act in ways that we consider rude but they think are acceptable. The lack of consideration and interest taken by some managers toward younger workers can surely be seen as a form of rudeness, even though the former are unlikely to define it as such. But people obviously do well to not define themselves by the lowest common denominator. Rather, we need to be people whom others want to work with.

Social manners are not only about getting along but also a matter of work effectiveness. These two matters are related in many ways. The sloppiness of one person, which can be viewed as poor social manners in a work setting, affects the job performance of another. Being accessible to others increases communication and sharing that provides unexpected support. Respectful listening helps improve communication and awareness and invites others to listen better to us. Avoiding unkind words about others may cause less unkind words to be said about us. Being polite and helpful to subordinates is surely also a matter of reciprocity and self-interest, as people typically depend on the politeness and helpfulness of others for their performance. People sometimes work as if their activities are unconnected to those of others, but they are not.

The balance between performance and respect can be a core challenge to one's social skills at work. Those who seek higher performance often know well the value of good social manners. Improving performance usually involves the support of others in some way. It is hard to go very far when others are actively opposed to what someone wants to do; getting cooperation, or at least nonresistance, often is essential. Social manners lay the groundwork for communication and consensus building at work, which we will discuss further. Those who push for excellence in the absence of social manners often find their efforts thwarted by those who do not have the skills or interest for what is being proposed. It is hard, if not impossible, to improve performance in a workplace that is filled with people with poor social skills or with entrepreneurs who lack social manners. Some may even lose their job in the process.

Indeed, many modern performance strategies involve processes that include an element of social manners; research shows that high-performance organizations often have a culture that includes commitments toward ethics and communication.[14] Being attentive to others helps people find opportunities for improvement. Listening to others helps people take the suggestion of employees seriously. Performance requires communication and social skills to avoid misunderstanding. Performance involves change, and people are more likely to embrace that when they feel treated well. Social manners at work emphasize respect and effectiveness, which further whatever change and improvement is contemplated. Surely, emphasis on social manners alone is not sufficient for performance (e.g., incentives also matter), but performance without social manners is unlikely to go very far either, and this book contains numerous examples of this.

However, the concerns at the beginning of this chapter speak of a shortfall of social skills at work that may affect how one connects with others and, hence, performance. As noted in the preface, "You can always find people with hard skills, but success or failure often depend on the softer, people skills; these are more difficult to find." Authors argue various reasons for the current concerns with social skills at work. Some argue that parents and schools do not sufficiently emphasize or instill the core values shown in Table 2.1; there is merit and evidence to suggest that learning to be polite and say "thank you" is learned early and continued later in life. Others argue that children spend more time alone, watching TV and sitting in front of computers, rather than engaging with others where patterns and norms of social interaction occur. Still others note that growing pressure has made the workplace more competitive. The hurried office is a common experience, and when people are anxious and overworked, little instances of rudeness and inconsideration creep in and become commonplace. Though it is nice to have people who, as in the above quote, take extra care to look after people, even that may not be enough.

Even though the extent of social skills at work is uncertain (research is scarce), the above discussion does have implications for employees and managers. For employees, the implication is one of self-improvement. The lack of organizational attention to the problem of social manners and even rudeness does not mean that it is unimportant. Indeed, those with good social manners will likely find a competitive advantage that improves career development (e.g., Chapter 9). But only a few organizations, in a few jobs, give useful and specific feedback, sometimes 360-degree feedback involving employees, superiors, and coworkers, but not many. Rather, vague and imprecise feedback is used on annual appraisals (e.g., "needing to improve interactions with others"), or people are simply passed over for promotion or attractive assignments, and other reasons are then usually offered than their social skills. Indeed, even when others are asked for feedback, they often are hesitant to tell us the truth and may have little more to say than "Yes, sometimes you should try to be a little bit nicer." People do well to be open to feedback and signals that suggest areas for improvement, because in many settings they may not get much more than some hints about their social skills.

A challenge is that, psychologically, people tend to overestimate their own performance in this area. The saying that "we judge ourselves by our intentions, and others by their actions" is also used to imply that we judge ourselves by a lesser standard than we do others. People are more willing to overlook their own infractions ("Surely, she understood I did not mean it that way.") than those of others ("How could she have said that!"). Culturally acceptable patterns may be unacceptable to others (e.g., spitting). It is also readily observed that some people have significant barriers to improving their social skills, such as heightened anxiety, a lack of work experience, and disinterest in people. Social manners are habits, and these can be difficult to change; sometimes the lack of manners points to other problems discussed later. We are probably not as nice as we think we are and certainly not as nice and pleasant as we hope others experience us. People like to have people around who show a good sense of respect and ability to get along and also perform; it is always time to polish up on a few manners.[15]

For managers, the implication is that setting standards for workplace conduct is likely to shape performance in many settings. Just emphasizing a few examples, whatever they are, of respect, courtesy, communication, or consideration for the work of others could have a significant and broad impact on work performance. The basic managerial strategy is to model examples, ask employees to follow them, monitor performance, provide feedback, and address deficiencies. There is surely nothing wrong, and much appropriate, with efforts to increase the climate for consideration and communication among coworkers.

All groups have social manners or, more accurately, a repertoire of manners that their members are expected to follow. Workplaces are no different, even though it is a bit hard to know exactly what these sometimes are. Social manners are increasingly more than etiquette or stylized behaviors and include a broad range of behaviors that focus on such activities as greeting, speaking and listening, working, and respecting boundaries between people at work. In these instances, showing social manners is especially about showing ways of projecting respect, courtesy, welcoming, connecting, and effectiveness in relation with others.

A consensus exists that people with effective social skills are more likely to be successful, get favorable responses from their environment, and feel good about themselves. We see anecdotal evidence in Asia, North America, South America, and Europe of growing convergence on these matters. People come from different cultures and have different perspectives on things, yet they deal with differences by falling back on common concerns for respect, courtesy, and effectiveness. Good manners do not always speak for themselves, and increased communication seems to go hand in hand with increased diversity and tolerance for a broader range of manners at work. At the very least, by showing *respect*, *listening* to others attentively, and showing a heightened *concern for the comfort* and discomfort of others, a minimum of social manners is put in place for getting along with others at work. Without these, people usually don't get very far. They are quite basic to that which follows, such as communication, which is discussed in the next chapter.

3

Communication

The Rule of Three is this: People only hear what has been said three times.

—Berman[1]

Everybody loves to complain about communication. Workers who repeatedly disappoint in their performance are sometimes described as poor listeners: "He just doesn't listen to what I tell him." Supervisors are also said to be poor listeners who don't listen to their employees. According to a U.K. study, nine out of ten graduates say they feel well prepared for the workplace, but employers disagree, with about half saying that it is hard to find graduates with good communication skills.[2] Many of these skills concern writing, speaking in public, and getting along with others. In another survey, 64 percent of working adults state that poor communication between management and workers keeps them from doing their best job.[3] There seems to be room for improvement.

One study concludes that misunderstandings between workers and managers cost firms $37,000,000,000 a year.[4] The largest category of losses is "unplanned downtime" caused by employees who misunderstand, misinterpret, or are misinformed about policies, business processes, or their job duties or functions. The fundamental point is that communication is not about talking but about being understood, of course. People fail to gauge the importance of words, and even mishear them. People fail to pick up on nuances or urgency or on the importance of doing things in a particular way, for a particular purpose, and so on.

The importance of good communication for maintaining good relations at work is hard to overstate. When people misunderstand things, consequences arise that include customer complaints, unacceptable performance, and accidents. People are compelled to confront others with their acts, which, no matter how tactfully done, eventually leads to resentment and finger pointing. In airports and other public spaces, businesspeople are often overheard, talking on their cell phones, attempting hard to correct some action that caused someone upset: "No, that was not said," "She told me later," "You did not say it was urgent," and so on. Such conversations not only point to inefficient business practices but also take a toll on human relations. Poor communication at work contributes sharply to poor human relations.

Human communication includes many opportunities for misunderstandings. The fact that misunderstandings are ubiquitous suggests that communication problems are not readily avoided; they seem inherent to interactions among people. We talk a lot, but communication is no better for it. This chapter looks into many sources of miscommunication and concludes that the potential for misunderstanding is vast; people do well to assume misunderstanding. This chapter also suggests a rather straightforward way of avoiding

> People do well to assume that they misunderstand each other.

much miscommunication: slow down, repeat, verify what was heard, and follow up. Think broadly about who needs to know what. It is human, but wrong, to think that what was said once is understood or even heard. It often is not.

Communication is a big topic that includes many facets. Here, the focus is on avoiding deterioration of what are otherwise good working relations. Other dimensions are discussed later in this book, such as what might be said to repair bad relations, nonverbal communication, and how to deal with people who are difficult in some way.

A classic theory of communication sees it as a process in which there is a "sender" and "receiver" of information. Almost all authors agree that information requires verification of some kind. Especially when important or critical information is involved, a typical, albeit rigid form of communication is (1) for the sender to transmit the information to receiver, (2) then ask the sender to paraphrase or summarize the information received, (3) then identify ambiguities ("cross-check") and improve clarifications, and finally, as relevant, (4) agree on a timetable or process for follow up or any further action.[5] This clearly shows the feedback loop that is intended to ensure mutual understanding and alignment.

Some communication misunderstandings occur because of genuinely sloppy or unclear instructions and a failure to cross-check for a common understanding. This is a cause of the infamous Tenerife (1977) airplane crash of two 747s, resulting in 583 deaths—the deadliest in aviation history. Both parties wrongfully assumed to have a mutual understanding. In this case, one of the planes involved a KLM pilot using the nonstandard phrase "We're at take-off" to which the control tower responded with "OK." The KLM pilot inferred that this meant he was cleared for take-off, while the Tenerife control tower understood the KLM pilot to be stationary at the end of the runway, awaiting take-off clearance. The KLM pilot then commenced accelerating for take-off and crashed into a Pan Am 747 that was on the same runway but invisible because of heavy fog. People are tightening up their protocols for giving and acknowledging instructions, especially in instances where outcome can be critical. As a result of this accident, standard phrases in aviation are now required; the phrase "take-off" is now spoken only when the actual take-off clearance is given, and key phrases of air traffic instruction are now read back rather than acknowledged with a mere "OK" or "Roger."[6]

The government's response to Hurricane Katrina was also fraught with employee misunderstandings and errors of judgment. The following is just one of many typical examples of judgment errors that can be given:

> A key communication error occurred when a FEMA forward observer surveyed the levee breaches from the air on the afternoon of August 29th and the White House was not informed of the breach because the Department of Homeland Security's Operational Center viewed this as an unconfirmed eyewitness report. Thus, the White House did not have confirmation of levee failure until … some eight hours later. The importance of this communication failure point cannot be overstated. A levee breach was understood to require a complete evacuation of New Orleans, necessitating immediate allocation of federal assets (U.S. House of Representatives, 2006).[7]

People routinely make errors when judging the importance of information, and it does point to the need for redundancy of several people being involved in cross-checking both the information and the conclusions drawn from it.

The need for cross-checking is not because people are sloppy or not rational, though some are. Psychological processes also affect communication. It is said that while the average person speaks about 125 to 250 words per minute, the average person listens to and comprehends up to 600 words per minute and can think about 1,000 to 3,000 words per minute. Some disagreement exists over these numbers,[8] but the point is that the mind leaves ample time for the listener's mind to be distracted. People normally find their mind wandering off, being easily distracted and filling in down time with thoughts of its own that are not always relevant to the topic at hand. Also, people's tunnel vision and preexisting assumptions or agendas cause them to overlook what is actually said or done; for example, even though people carefully spell check and read e-mail before sending them, they can still contain many errors. We also send e-mail to the wrong people or with the wrong attachments. People also make "Freudian slips," slip of the tongues whereby people unintentionally say one thing but mean another, sometimes hinting at some deeper meaning. For example, people might "mistakenly" call a client by the name of another client whom they dislike and who befell some misfortune. All people are subject to these errors (or conditions) of the mind.

Technology also contributes to communication misunderstandings. Continuing the above Tenerife case, another problem was radio interference, a phenomenon in which simultaneous radio communications cause each other to become jumbled and inaudible. A moment after the control tower said "OK" to the KLM flight, it added "Stand by for take-off, I will call you" to avoid misunderstanding, as it knew that the Pan Am flight was on the same runway. Yet at the exact same moment, the Pan Am flight radioed "We're still taxiing down the runway."[9] Interference of these messages made both inaudible, including to the KLM pilot, who, if he had heard either message, could have aborted take-off and, hence, avoided collision. Technology also causes other misunderstandings, such as e-mail messages that land in people "junk e-mail" folders and are, hence, not read. This happens often in some office settings.

Linguistics is also a cause of misunderstandings. Homophones are words that sound alike but have different meanings: *ate* and *eight*, *buy* and *bye*, *cent* and *scent*, *do* and *due*, *earn* and *urn*, *facts* and *fax*, *grate* and *great*, *here* and *hear*, *it's* and *its*, *karat* and *carrot*, *lacks* and *lax*, *mail* and *male*, and so on.[10] People depend on the context to infer (or guess) at the right meaning, hence, creating the possibility of error. People use expressions such as "We need to get on the same page" or "Let's take a blue-sky approach" without fully specifying what is intended—sometimes the vagueness is intended as a tactic for moving on. People also use abbreviations or jargon ("We're on a three-way street here" or "After we do the JABR, we need to pay attention to the CDX and bring DGZ into the picture, right?"), as well as references to people or events, that are unknown or not fully understood to others. While this is sometimes done to impress others, communicating in ways that others don't understand is also considered rude.[11]

Still other problems stem from foreign language uses. In advertising, the Parker Quink pen was advertised in English as "won't leak and embarrass you," which was translated in Spanish as "the Quink pen won't *embarazar* you" (make you pregnant). A pharmaceutical company wanted to call a new weight-loss pill "Tegro" in English, but in French the word is phonetically similar to *t'es gros*, or "you're fat."[12] Nonnative pronunciations also give rise to misunderstandings. In Korean, for example, the English letters *p, f, b,* and *v* can be made by the same letter, having approximately the same sound.[13] Hence, one foreigner recalls asking for directions in a library to its copy machine, only to be sent to its coffee machine. "It also explains my perplexity when a Korean colleague said she was upset over her pizza (i.e., her visa)," stated one English-speaking native in Korea.[14] Whether any of these examples are funny or serious depends, of course, on the context and its consequences.

E-mail and text messaging have significant communication limitations that warrant attention. "Because of our reliance on written communication—e-mail and texting, for example—much of our visual clues as to meaning are lost," stated one reviewer. Nonverbal clues are an important part of the information that people use to interpret and understand what is communicated. "Non-verbal cues like attire, eye gaze, smiling, posture, distance, listener responses are just as important as choosing the right words—sometimes more so," wrote Knap and Hall.[15] E-mail is devoid of opportunities for obtaining this nonverbal information, of course. Another problem with all writing is that it requires a certain parsimony of words that in speech is not as constraining. It is not possible to communicate as much as we might want to about the context, things to watch out for, and so on in our e-mail and text messages. This is compounded by e-mail etiquette, which is to keep e-mail brief; many people already receive about thirty to sixty substantive e-mails daily. E-mail and text messaging is fraught with partial and incomplete communication.[16]

It is important to note that all of the above examples show instances in which the speaker *does not knowingly* engage in unclear communication. It is not necessary to be sloppy or vague in order to cause misunderstanding; misunderstandings can occur with no one being at fault. People intend to say one thing but say it unclearly or say something else. People assume knowing what someone will say, without carefully fact checking what has been said. Sometimes people catch errors but not always. Sometimes they see the error but don't speak up. In the recent book *Outliers*,[17] Malcolm Gladwell noted from studying airplane accidents that "the typical accident involves seven consecutive human errors. … It's not that the pilot has to negotiate some critical technical maneuver and fails. The kinds of errors that cause plane crashes are invariably errors of teamwork and communication. One pilot knows something important and somehow doesn't tell the other pilot. One pilot does something wrong, and the other pilot doesn't catch the error. A tricky situation needs to be resolved through a complex series of steps—and somehow the pilots fail to coordinate and miss one of them." The failure of communication is almost always present when things go wrong.

This means that asking for feedback and read back are indeed essential and necessary techniques to ensure mutual understanding. They are necessities, not niceties or etiquette. Having more rules, procedures, or checklists alone seldom reduces errors of communication; in fact, it may well increase them as it gives people more to talk about and thus to misunderstand. Relatedly, Winston Churchill said, "If you have ten thousand regulations you destroy all respect for the law."[18] The point is not to talk about more things but to verify and validate what was said: "The desire to communicate effectively is probably as important, if not more important, than all of the behavioral prescriptions we might employ."[19] We might as well assume misunderstanding and then work to find what miscommunication occurred. It is important to deeply appreciate this insight. Table 3.1 includes some helpful phrases to reduce miscommunications.

In the case of e-mail, one rule is to pick up the phone and talk about recent exchanges and interactions after every four or five e-mail exchanges. The purpose of calling is to uncover the misunderstanding that is assumed to exist and to address it. Speaking allows everyone to talk and say things that cannot (or should not) be put in e-mail. There are no more excuses for not fact checking and talking; even international calls are now almost free, thanks to advances in broadband technology.[20] So four or five e-mails and then talk—that's the rule to avoid misunderstanding getting out of

Table 3.1 Practicing Task-Oriented Communication

Ten helpful phrases:

1. "Can you repeat that please, so we don't have a misunderstanding?"
2. "Do you have any questions or thoughts about this?"
3. "I will send you an e-mail to acknowledge our understanding."
4. "Can you/we do this? How will you/we do this?"
5. "By when will this be done?"
6. "Will you need any help?"
7. "The due date is very important."
8. "Please let me know immediately if you see any problems that would prevent you from meeting the deadline."
9. "I will ask for a progress report three days from now."
10. "I really appreciate that you will do this."

hand and causing damage. Or immediately call if the subject is very important. Assume misunderstanding.[21]

A common lament is also that "people hear what they want to hear." This describes the phenomenon that people mishear or misconstrue what is said in order for it to conform to what they would like to hear. Public hearings are often recorded so that people can go back to what originally was said or agreed to, in the event that later different versions arise and circulate. A common way in which this occurs is that people take speakers' sentences or phrases out of context of what was said and instead put it into their own context, often reflecting their interests. News reporters are especially notorious for doing this, sometimes intentionally, thereby creating controversies where none exist.

In one example, during the 2008 U.S. presidential primary elections, Michelle Obama, the wife of then-contender for the Democratic Party's presidential nomination Barack Obama, used the phrase "If you can't run your own house, you can't run the White House." Reporters took this as Michelle Obama making a swipe at Hillary Clinton, who was competing with Barack Obama for their party's nomination and referring to Hillary Clinton's well-documented marital problems with Bill Clinton. It made for headlines. However, the context of Michelle's comment, in her own words, was her husband's ability to balance competing demands of managing family life and running a campaign, such as finding time to read books to their children at bedtime and attend family events. The comment had to do with good qualities of her husband, not about Hillary Clinton's past. People hear what they want to hear.[22]

Cognitive dissonance is the name of a well-known psychological theory that states that people modify or interpret information, or even their beliefs, to make conflicts among inconsistent information disappear. The reason that people want to make conflicting or inconsistent information disappear is, well, because people want to avoid negative feelings associated with ambiguity or conflict. All people want to experience positive emotions. So people twist, filter, and downplay information that is either internally inconsistent (containing contradictory information) or externally inconsistent (conflicting with other beliefs, priorities, etc.) in order to feel good. The expression "People don't want to hear bad news" contains much truth. In the above example, a news reporter hears what gets said through the lens and filter of deadlines and newspaper circulation; any "sensational" news bite will do that reduces the pain of not meeting deadlines and circulation targets. Other ways in which negative feelings are avoided is by postponing (e.g., procrastination), denying ("Oh, I don't recall you saying that."), and pushing them off onto someone else ("Why suffer? I can get John to do this for me.").

Having tunnel vision, hearing what people want to hear, avoiding cognitive dissonance, and wanting to feel good can come together in sometimes catastrophic or fiery ways. Consider the following exchange:

> When the Dean said it was possible, what he meant was "maybe." When the psychology professor heard that it was possible, she took it to mean "yes." So when the Dean came back the following week and said "no," the Professor took it as betrayal and reacted accordingly; the Dean took her anger as inexplicable and therefore unprofessional. The Professor called the Dean a liar, which she believed to be true and he believed to be false. A single ambiguous word led to a major clash.[23]

This example points not only to these problems but also to emotions, often negative emotions, affecting what gets thought and said.

All emotions, both positive and negative, affect judgment and how we express ourselves. Negative emotions in particular often lead to snap judgments that are inaccurate and to statements that we later would like to take back. Little is gained by calling one's boss a liar, but the professor probably felt good in the very moment when those words were spoken. The release of negative feelings feels good. (Of course, it is advisable to control oneself, and an apology seems due, which, we hope, the dean will accept.)

People need to be aware of their emotions and know how they affect their judgment, behavior, and communication. The final contributing element to the Tenerife airport disaster was a tired cockpit crew under deadline pressure. Earlier, planes bound for Las Palmas were diverted to Tenerife because of a terrorist bomb threat and explosion at Las Palmas. The KLM and Pan Am planes were two of many planes waiting to continue their journey from Tenerife to Las Palmas, but the KLM crew was at the very end of its regulated duty time; any further delays would have meant that KLM would need to send a new crew or the crew would need to wait out its mandatory off-duty time. The passengers were tired, as was the crew, and the pilot was anxious to get on with it. The copilot voiced concern about whether the Pan Am plane was off the runway, which was indeterminate in the heavy fog, but the pilot proceeded with take-off. He was tired and irritated.

Wanting to feel good heavily affects workplace communications. Many people avoid communication when doing so could bring negative emotions such as embarrassment or conflict. There is wisdom in that as a tactic for survival in the long term—no one gets very far by making enemies or stoking negative feelings in others. People withhold information in the hope that it will not bring suffering to others, but it does not always lead to the right communication or decision in the moment. The lack of communication and information is almost inherent in work. People need to work hard to ensure that they get the information they need.

❊

To further add to the above complications, people have different styles of communication that get misinterpreted. Men and women have different styles of communication that are almost universally noted. Men tend toward direct and assertive styles of communication, whereas women tend to be indirect and less vocal. While the latter is usually called a passive style of communication, a more descriptive label is "affiliative." Deborah Tannen, who is noted for her research on sex-based language differences,[24] notes that from an early age, girls will use affiliation-oriented language that maintains social harmony and avoids conflict; "let's play house," for an example. When they want something that might disturb social harmony, they ask "Let's play shopping, OK?" By contrast, boys assert themselves, bragging, taking, and instructing others what to do. They are direct and assertive, and when there is conflict, well, they fight it out. They use an assertive, aggressive, and direct style of communication. Girls can be aggressive too, but they are more prone to using methods of passive-aggression, such as avoidance and gossip that avoid direct confrontation.[25]

In recent years, some scientists have tried to apply research from brain research to begin explaining these differences. While biology does not dictate outcomes, it does shape how people behave. The argument is that during pregnancy, a huge testosterone surge occurs in boys that kills off some cells in the brain's communication centers and increases sensitivity to stimuli associated with sex and aggression.[26] This does not occur for girls, thereby unaffecting their hippocampus that is key to language and reading emotions in others. At birth, girls experience a temporary surge in estrogen that stimulates neural connections, while boys experience another surge in testosterone. Correspondingly, girls speak sooner and are more attuned to reading emotional expressions than boys.[27] Then at puberty, ovarian estrogen stimulates oxytocin and dopamine production. Dopamine stimulates the desire for pleasure, and social bonding that includes talking triggers oxytocin, which leads to pleasure. Among boys, seeing, experiencing, or thinking aggressively stimulates the release of dopamine that leads to pleasure.[28] Boys tend toward "aggression nurturance," a system based on competitiveness and helping each other move up hierarchies. When someone has a weakness, "males will try to make you perform better," while girls tend toward empathy nurturance: "How are you? I'm going to hug you and make you feel better."[29] Though some of the above inferences from biology to behavior are contested,[30] biology does seem to be in the background of some gender differences, even as science has yet to provide a full and accurate explanation of them.

What's the point? We all like to feel good, and gender affects how we do so, triggering neurohormones in different ways. None of this means that people can't practice a broader range of communication styles (assertion vs. affiliation), but research (specifically brain research) is making these biological gender differences and proclivities increasingly clear. Even as scientific consensus is likely to alter the above in some fundamental ways in coming years, few people would be surprised to find some biological differences between men and women that affect their proclivities in some ways, to some degree.

These gender differences affect workplace communication. Men are apt to speak their mind, even interrupting as necessary, but women are apt not to interrupt or speak directly, concerned that doing so increases separation. Thus, men often interpret a lack of response or argument as a sign of agreement and comprehension, whereas for an indirect and less vocal person, a lack of response could signal nothing whatsoever, disapproval, reservation, a lack of understanding, disagreement, or simply the desire for more time before responding.[31] Even a "yes" might not mean that they agree and understand, only that they heard being spoken to. We easily misread people when we read them through our style, which is what most people

> **Even a "yes" might not mean that people agree and understand.**

instinctively do. It seems very hard not to do this.[32] In this regard, it does appear that women do need to speak up and take responsibility for clear and direct communications. There is no other realistic way of working together with people across different cultures, generations, and countries in the cyberage. We need to be clear in our communications.

Beyond gender, there are other communication style differences too. People vary *how* they show caring and respect. Some people have preferences for using words, whereas others have preferences for actions.[33] When a request is made, some people acknowledge it in words and talk about it, whereas others say nothing, only to deliver the result in positive ways some time later. This difference is not necessarily gender related.[34] A word-oriented person is apt to take the silence of an action-focused person as disinterest or rejection, considering such a person rude and socially inappropriate. Miscommunication can occur also because too little is said. Chapter 1 showed that older workers, baby boomers, and matures often suppress talking about their feelings, which younger workers interpret as inadequate consideration and rapport with them, up to the point that they quit their jobs. Cultural norms sometimes promote these styles; East Asian countries in particular tend to adopt action-oriented approaches, and some officials do not answer or return phone calls until an action can be given. Westerners are apt to interpret the absence of verbal responsiveness as rudeness.

National, social-economic, and cultural differences also give rise to other misunderstandings. For example, cultures vary greatly about the meaning of the word "yes." Consider the following posting:[35]

J.J. Ngulube: There are a lot of unwritten business rules and this varies from West Africa to East Africa even within.

Robyn Curnow: Like what?

JN: How you communicate. For example when somebody says "yes." When a West African says "yes" you have to understand what that means.

RC: What does it mean?

JN: Is it "yes I hear what you are saying"? Is it "yes I agree"? Or is it "yes I'm politely agreeing but I'm not happy with what you're saying"?

RC: So, it basically means no?

JN: Exactly. So even that "yes," you have to be able to interpret and body language is everything. It's so easy for a non-African to go away thinking "I met those guys and they agreed with everything I said."

A similar use of "yes" is common in East Asia, too, where it often means no more than "yes, I heard and understand what you said" in order to avoid disagreement or even confrontation with another person. Cultures vary in how people interpret and form the context and the exact meaning of what was said. Clarifications are often needed in communications among people from different cultures.

Language also expresses where we come from, through which others infer positive or negative stereotypes.[36] Discrimination exists, and communication styles can trigger it. For example, some will readily assume that people who say "yo" are associated with hip-hop culture, which is prone to being dangerous and unprofessional. In an antiracist stance, some young people use interesting language and mix different dialects. Organizations also vary in how they express decisions and processes, especially those in other countries. Officials' expressions of excitement and engagement often signal commitment in the United States, but in some Asian countries they may signal nothing more than pleasantries and no commitment whatsoever. In the United States, "the check is in the mail" can have the opposite meaning, but in some countries, the equivalent expression is "the contract has been signed," which is apt to cause misunderstanding among Americans.

Communication styles exist. Our tendency to avoid cognitive dissonance leads us to want to ignore these different styles or make "everyone just like us." But it is not to be—it is biologically impossible and culturally almost so. Together with cognitive dissonance, we are almost certain likely to misread others' intentions, purposes, and efforts. It seems that we are destined to misunderstand each other.

The problem of communication is that, in the end, all communication is partial. Our words can only partially express what we mean and intend to express, and our listening is clouded by our frameworks and desire for feeling good. In addition, technology exacerbates the potential for misunderstanding. Recall the Tenerife disaster, the government's response to Hurricane Katrina, and the limits of e-mail, and *assume misunderstanding*.

Not all problems of communication are mentioned above, either. Organizational problems with communication are, for example, office and departments that do not share information with other departments, and leaders making decisions for others without getting their input. Either way, information flows are limited, and decisions are made with insufficient knowledge. Others may have assumed that more information was available and thus different decisions are made. In organizations, less than optimal decisions are to be expected, before even considering other factors that further detract from good decisions. But as this book focuses on people skills, we do not focus on these problems here. Assume misunderstanding, even as we do not always know its origins.

There is a connection here with manners, the topic of the previous chapter. If miscommunication exists, we do well to be gentle with others in the face of alleged performance deficits or relationship disturbances. Misunderstanding could genuinely underlie it. We do well to first assess the possibility of miscommunication, misunderstanding, or inadequate information before jumping to more negative conclusions. Social manners suggest that we inquire into these possibilities first and insist that others do so as well when they have problems with us. We can do so in appropriately kind and constructive ways.

In the end, the solution to the communication problems is clear: we need to have communication and feedback about what each of us understands. Speakers need to ask for feedback, so that they can cross-check what they hear and assess that against their intentions and goals. Listeners need to focus on providing feedback, sometimes as read back, and take the opportunity to articulate their interests. Yes, some people do need to speak up, and others need to give space for others to do so. Communication is a cause of misunderstandings, as well as a pathway for identifying and minimizing these misunderstandings. People need to, well, talk in order to reach clarification too. Practicing people skills is to insist that these necessary processes occur in respectful and effective ways.

4

Getting Along

You may not like all your co-workers, but you must learn to work with them. Realize that any unfriendliness you encounter probably isn't personal. For instance, some people will forget you're new and expect you to know certain things. Others think giving newcomers a hard time is a rite of passage. Still others have personal problems that have nothing to do with you. Your only concern is learning to work with these people.[1]

The above advice given to a new employee reflects the basic fact that while we do not choose our coworkers, we do need to get along with them. What does it take to get along with others? It sometimes is said that three behaviors are key to getting along with others at work: being nice to others, following orders, and doing your job well. This advice has a great deal of merit. We all like people who are pleasant, and not following orders will surely get people into trouble. But as the above vignette suggests, being nice does not guarantee that others will also be nice to us. A bit more is often needed.

So how do we get along with people at work? A useful starting point is to consider that many people at work are strangers to us and to each other. Regardless of our accomplishments and efforts, there are limits to what they will put up with. Getting along requires attention to the "comfort zone" of others. The concept of a comfort zone is defined as a situation or condition in which a person feels secure, comfortable, or in control.[2] It is a state in which tasks and goals are comfortably achieved. People have different comfort zones for different types of things, such as what they can deal with in others, what minimum of planning and security they need, how they separate their professional life and personal life, what types and levels of competition they can comfortably deal with, and so on. Pushing people out of these comfort zones often produces anxiety or resentment, as it makes them face a new situation or a situation that they experience as unpleasant. To get along is to not push others too often or too much beyond their comfort zone.

When people lament that newcomers, after some months, have failed to fit in, get along, or be liked, they use these somewhat ill-defined and often puzzling terms to describe that someone has pushed others once too often out of their comfort zone. For example, a typical problem of newcomers is their telling others how they might do things better. Though this often is done with the best of intentions to improve the organizations, others often experience this as disrespecting the boundaries of jobs and roles for which others are responsible. It also ignores stress and extra work that intended changes may require. Another example of a cause of frustration and resentment is newcomers' distracting the concentration of others with (what others perceive as) unnecessary chatter. To be often interrupted or questioned produces resentment. It is hard to be liked or appreciated when you are associated with negative experiences. People may not always know it, but they do monitor the comfort zone infractions by others.

By contrast, those who do fit in have not brought forth negative emotions—and they also do their job and provide support for others too. Though fitting in requires more than being mindful of others' comfort zone (such as also being effective and agreeing with others on performance tasks—see Part 3), doing so is an essential element. In reference to the vignette, a focus on doing one's job, showing alignment (being helpful and supportive), and avoiding resentment is usually enough to turn most people around in due time. Being pleasant is certainly intended to keep people in their comfort zone.

The concept of a comfort zone is a broad and useful pointer, but it is lacking in specificity. People vary hugely in the challenges to their comfort zone and how they react to those challenges. Some people have a narrow set of circumstances that keep them in their comfort zone. According to one survey, 29 percent of working adults state that they have a great deal of stress in their jobs, and another 41 percent state they have a moderate amount of stress.[3] Stress lowers peoples' tolerances.[4] People also vary in how easily they adapt and what they regard as their comfort zone. While we know little of these matters about other people when we first meet them, we can make and act on some reasonable assumptions. Then as we get to know others better, we better understand their comfort zone. There is wisdom to taking things slow with people.

> People at work are usually strangers to us and to each other. How do we get along with them?

Getting along is more than just putting on a pleasant face—some real substance is often needed. The following passages focus on six core areas. The multitude of different ways in which people can fail to get along also explains why people often have such varying experiences. The following includes a mix of things that are both job and people oriented.

1. *Doing your own job well, on time and reliably.* While at first glance doing one's job seems unrelated to getting along with people and their comfort zone, when one person fails to do his or her job, it causes work or problems for others. The purpose of working is also to work. In a recent Randstad/Harris poll about thirty coworker traits, the most important trait according to workers is being competent (70 to 81 percent).[5] Jobs are interrelated, and when people fail to do their job, it causes more work and, hence, stress for others. Even worrying about whether other people will show up and do their job can be too much, and not considering how our performance affects others is a sign of disrespect or nonrespect. Numerous bosses tell

their employees that they will accept a lot but "not any surprises." An adequate job performance often leads to one's becoming the subject of bad talk and gossip and being socially excluded from interactions—typical precursors of negative performance appraisals later. We need to be considerate of how our job affects others.

Some people are just unreliable. Work needs to get done, and no one likes dealing with employees who have perennial excuses. Unreliability is a worldwide issue, and U.S. workers are no exception to being creative in finding excuses for a lack of performance. Finger-pointing and blame shifting are common tactics ("I did my job—it was Sarah who performed late."), including involving inanimate objects ("My car didn't work this morning—I had a flat tire."). The law of unintended consequences now adds growing support for family–work balance as a newly acceptable reason: "My child (or babysitter) is sick" or "I have to care for my aging parents." Whether these excuses are true or false (which boss is going to fact-check?), the reality is that either someone else needs to do the work or someone else has to worry about unmet performance targets. Bosses respect your family up to a point, but the job must get done.[6] People with too many excuses will eventually be seen as being just too unreliable.

2. Being pleasant. Getting along obviously requires being pleasant, nice, and friendly to others. This matter was previously discussed in Chapter 2 as showing good social manners and respect. Greeting people; making small talk; occasionally bringing small gifts to the office; respecting hierarchy, rank, and seniority; talking well about others and the office; and thanking people sincerely for their help are all things that should be done daily. "It's the small things that count" is an expression that signifies the importance of being nice. Failing to do these things will surely irk some folks, which, when combined with any other problem (and we all mess up sometimes), may be just too much for some. Good social manners are not enough for getting along, but they are necessary. Unhappily, quite some people overestimate their "likability factor" and do need to be told of specific things that they need to stop doing or begin doing, including mentioning such things on formal performance appraisals or in conversations;

for example, "unless you behave a bit nicer to others, your future is not going to be very bright." We do not have much to add to the obvious point that people need to be at least a little bit pleasant at work.

3. *Supporting others doing their job.* We all have a job to do, and we all like people who support us in some way. The point here is surely not about a busybody who interferes with the work of others but rather about someone who understands what others are trying to do and conducts himself or herself in a way that is supportive of others doing their job. This may involve occasionally voicing support and appreciation of their efforts or supporting a new idea that helps them in some way. In the same Randstad/Harris poll, 67 to 77 percent said that being respectful of coworkers is important. Well, that shows up in many different ways, of course, including refraining from doing or saying things to others regarding their work that puts them out of their comfort zone. Examples include not only talking loudly or being messy but also making or supporting proposals that curtail resources for their work or add additional work for them. A good colleague is someone who does not add to the troubles of others.

One aspect of this is also understanding the broader purposes or ramifications of one's job. Just doing one's job may not be enough. The following is fairly typical of the kinds of trouble that may result, causing additional work for others:

> Jim said he knew what to do, and when I asked how it was going, he said "fine," or something like that. Well, next thing, I have Helen of DoE on the line asking me "what the heck I think I'm doing." I have no idea what she is talking about, of course, but it turns out that Jim installed the new version of the program without providing instructions or backup for Helen's staff. Of course, Jim says that he was never asked to do either by Bill, but Helen is claiming that her staff has lost important data.

Such events are distractions that add to the workload of others (in this case, Jim's supervisor, who needs to address the matter). In today's world, many stakeholders are increasingly outcome oriented, and they expect others to be that way too. People want to deal with others who understand that and go the extra mile to avoid problems. Failing to do so can bring trouble that is interpreted as those people not getting along. Ironically, people can do their job and still fail to do the job that is needed.

4. *Avoiding hot buttons.* Everyone has hot buttons, yet people are different, and surprises are likely. There is wisdom in the dictum of not talking of politics, religion, gender issues, and sex in the workplace—these topics tend to be highly value laden, and people often have strong opinions about them to which they are sometimes emotionally and inflexibly attached. Few people are able to take their own strong views with a dose of humor and relativism—most don't. Some people "go off" when they feel that their religion or politics are being attacked or disrespected. Academic discussions about abortion and labor unions can be had with some, but for some these involve highly emotional issues. While some people like to provoke others into taking positions on sensitive topics, it is wise to parry such inquiries in diplomatic and respecting ways (see below). Little good comes from unintentionally pushing peoples' hot buttons. People can be quite unforgiving of others who press their hot buttons, and grudges can be held for years on end.

The broader issue is that we need to get to know other people. The above paragraph is not about the topic but about other people's sensitivity to it. Someone who has had a child seriously injured by a car may have strong feelings about safe driving. Someone who has been passed over for promotion three times is likely disinclined to view management in a kind way. Someone whose father has a serious medical condition may be sensitive about health care policy and insurance. Someone who has been sexually abused is likely to have strong feelings on topics of gender. We need to understand other people's comfort zone. We do well to tread gently until we have gotten to know people and their sensitivities a bit better.

5. *Going gently with excellence.* The excellence of others also often challenges the comfort zone of others. As one quote puts it, "The sad truth is that excellence makes people nervous."[7] According to a Randstad/Harris poll, the *least* important employee trait is "being demanding" (7–14 percent). Those who do their work extra well often find that doing so causes social distance with others. Excellence puts others out of their comfort zone because, by definition, it sets results and standards for what most others cannot or do not wish to attain;

"You will make people feel bad about themselves and jealous of you, which will make them resent you."[8] Others cannot or do not want to match the level of excellence, and some people just don't understand it. Professionalism is often used in reference to conduct and minimum performance but much less as commitment to standards of excellence these days. Beyond a minimum level of competence, excellence becomes a hot button for many. A bad colleague is sometimes described as someone who brings out negative feelings in us, such as envy or resentment—that's what excellence does.

Describing excellence as annoying is certainly not politically correct or the standard treatment of the topic, but in most workplaces, people ask only that subordinates and colleagues do their job and don't make trouble. Newcomers often wrongly assume more commitment to excellence than exists among work-group members, perhaps reflecting the marketing hype of the organization or job interview. People can be a little innovative, but being too innovative or having ideas that are too big is quickly seen as annoying.[9] Even offering others to help with their work only adds to making others aware of shortcomings. Someone who persists with being excellent or innovative often is seen as troublesome, perhaps even as a troublemaker who "is not the right material for promotion" or who should be fired. Those who get ahead often figure out what others or the system needs, and they make producing these needs their priority; no more, no less. Of course, there are always exceptions, but people who wish to pursue excellence do well to find the right workplace for them. Some studies suggest that no more than 10 to 20 percent of workplaces have excellence as a common or expected pursuit, depending on how excellence and its acceptance are defined, but even in those workplaces people will need to have good people skills.[10] Excellence is more often spoken about than pursued—there is wisdom in the advice of going slowly and softly with it, unless there is compelling evidence to the contrary. We need to figure out what the system wants from its people and then decide whether or to what extent we want to give that.

Poignantly, the importance of getting along was recently noted in an article about hiring at General Electric, the technology giant:

> We need to figure out what the system wants from its people.

"To get hired at the Batesville (Miss.) plant, applicants must first take a reading, math and problem-solving test administered by the state employment agency. Candidates who do well are then invited for interviews at the plant and are evaluated in team settings. For example, they are placed in groups of four and told to assemble a Lego helicopter in 15 minutes. We want to see how they interact, how they work together," says Terry Collins, the plant's human resources leader. "We don't give a heck about making the helicopter."[11] Even at GE, one cannot assume that excellence is the key feature, or the only feature, or a sufficient feature that people are looking for. It is not.

6. *Dealing well with difficult situations, tasks, and people without making too many waves.* One survey finds that 46 percent of employees mention "troublesome or uncooperative colleagues" as that which keeps them from doing their best job;[12] the rest of the problems come from work itself. There are some difficult people and situations at work, for sure. No good estimates exist of the number of difficult people at work, and a lot depends on definitions. Our own experience is that about one in seven to one in ten coworkers is a reasonable estimate of people with whom one might have trouble in some way. Other estimates, based on mental health and substance abuse (discussed in Part 4), suggest that about 10 to 15 percent of the workforce have a strong propensity for being inconsiderate or incapable of respecting the needs or feelings of others,[13] and the earlier mentioned survey finds that 20 percent state the people whom they work with are a source of stress. Another 10 percent report their boss. In short, most work groups of ten to fifteen people will have one maybe even two or more persons who are difficult or even nasty. While the empirical foundation is shaky, it is consistent with the experience that a small but important minority of people exists at work that causes a good deal of suffering. The above vignette also hints at this; as Jean-Paul Sartre succinctly stated, "Hell is other people."[14]

A bit of diplomacy can go a long way to keeping others, and ourselves, in their comfort zone. As an example, during the 2010 FIFA

World Cup, the Dutch coach Bert van Marwijk substituted a star player, Robin van Persie. While coming off the field, van Persie reportedly said to his coach that another star player, Wesley Sneijder, should have come off the field instead. Not wanting to create a distracting incident, the coach told the media, "If he said that, he said that. Everyone is entitled to having an opinion. If he was disappointed, everyone is allowed to feel that, too."[15] The team later met to discuss the matter, after which it was put aside. Van Persie is said to have a history of being a bit difficult, and a certain discomfort between these star players is known to exist. Every group has a few. People and groups need calm and focus too, and they respect others who work hard to maintain that for others. Diplomacy has its place, helping people to get to a larger picture of performance and group peace. Diplomacy often is needed between people because they have very different ideas of what is right or what needs to be done.

Tactically difficult situations are plenty at work.[16] Some people challenge others on their commitments and loyalties: "Where do you stand on the issue of X," where X polarizes two groups in an office and makes any substantive response a no-win situation. How to respond? Table 4.1 shows some diplomatic phrases that can help. The point is to sidestep the matter as presented and instead focus on a bigger issue or value that is of obvious and great importance too or to point to undesirable or problematic parts of the plan that any

Table 4.1 Ten Diplomatic Phrases for Work

1. "Everything is possible."
2. "Many roads lead to Rome."
3. "We need to keep our eye on the big picture, too, which …"
4. "It sounds like a reasonable and even a good idea, but I haven't heard the other side yet."
5. "I support all my colleagues."
6. "I'd like to, but doing so will cause trouble for both of us and that is not worth it."
7. "It is possible, but we should discuss it with the boss/others/the work group first, as it involves others too."
8. "I can support this if others do."
9. "This is not a big deal for me, but can you do (something very big) for me?"
10. "It's an interesting idea. How would you deal with (something very big and impossible that the idea implies)?"

reasonable person would want to see resolved first.[17] Beyond this, people in the public sector often get a good deal of criticism and feedback that sometimes is simply over the top. Some citizens gripe or have an ideological vendetta against government, and elected officials in public hearings sometimes give public servants a grilling that is undeserved and for political benefit. While negative emotions arise (and also, is there another shoe about to drop?), in such situations it is well to remember that those are others' words, not those of oneself. Getting along in such situations requires remembering that one is in it for the long haul. Another day, another battle. It is wise to pause and consider getting input from others over the upcoming days: "You're saying a lot here. I'd like to talk it over with others first before responding." Not every spoken word has to be taken on face value on the spot.

By way of another example, some of the above examples come together in the matter of competent or even excellent employees dealing with bosses whom they perceive as having a lack of leadership or competence. Most competent employees know more than their boss about the specifics of whom they are dealing with and the details of their job, but bosses make up for the lack of detailed knowledge by providing employees with supportive supervision, stability of employment, growth opportunities, and period rewards. Hence, a partnership between competent employees and competent bosses readily suggests itself, and such relations often play out in this way, usually in fulfilling and rewarding ways. But challenging situations arise when employees regard their bosses as lacking vision, leadership, competence, support, or rewards. In addition, employees may have more vision and drive that is not appreciated or understood by the boss. While such situations inevitably require employees to keep their tongue in check (expressing negative opinions about one's boss will inevitably come to be seen as a lack of support and disloyalty), eventually employees either will come to accept lower standards of others and often themselves ("I guess the organization does not want excellence.") or must seek out better employment elsewhere, as mentioned a few paragraphs before. Yet even intending to leave requires that in the interim, people remain supportive of others and their boss and exit in a graceful and respectful way, hopefully on their own terms. Getting along with incompetent and mediocre bosses is not always easy for competent employees; it requires a good deal of demonstrated diplomacy and tact (see Chapter 16, "The Search for Happiness and Fulfillment"). Leaving one's job is not always for lack of people skills, but it should not be because of it.

Being confronted with difficult situations and issues are part of working. Dealing with them in a way that does not distract group efforts is expected and appreciated.[18]

Of recent interest is heightened respect of personal boundaries in getting along. Boundaries exist in all human relations, if only because limits need to be set on what we are willing to endure from others. Cultural diversity and global migration patterns have surely increased the presence at work of people with beliefs, customs, and practices that are different from our own. Yet many matters that affect getting along have little to do with cultural diversity; they are foremost about respecting the physical space and working conditions of others. People vary greatly in their attachments to the following, yet they also have blind spots for the attachments of others. We sometimes cannot imagine that something could be such a great deal for others.

Boundaries are especially important in cultures that emphasize individualism, such as the United States. Examples of common privacy violations at work are hovering around (e.g., looking over someone else's shoulder), interrupting people when they are in conversation with others, and looking at someone else's computer. Some people also share too much of their personal life with others; many people don't want to hear about others' personal or medical problems. People need to respect the desire of others to not want to talk about personal, nonprofessional matters, and there is risk in sharing one's intimate details with strangers and coworkers. Looking at someone's e-mail and taking something from someone's desk without asking are also considered disrespectful violations of privacy, regardless of

BOX 4.1   POSTHIRING ADJUSTMENT

The problems described in this chapter often arise as people adjust to their new workplace. New employees experience unfamiliar work processes and colleagues. Though the first few days at work are often a bit boring, quite soon people are given assignments that have unknown or unfamiliar protocols. New colleagues come by and introduce themselves, making subtle hints at expectations that may leave new employees uncomfortable or worried. It is easy to say or do the wrong thing in the first few months on the job—almost everyone does, to some degree.

Most people describe success in the first few months in a new job as not having done too many wrong things and not having upset too many people. Just surviving is sometimes more than enough and also lays the groundwork for actual performance results in the next six months. For existing colleagues, however, the measure of fitting in often is whether newcomers' responses show consideration for the comfort zone of the office and individuals and whether the newcomers have a sense of performance and personal ethics. Those who do not fit in may have rubbed people the wrong way, once too often.

The first few months on the job is usually a busy time getting to know the expectations and comfort zones of others.

employers' rights to do such things. People have spheres of privacy, and these need to be respected.[19]

Sound is a common privacy violation. According to a CNN.com article, "Saying the Unsayable to Your Co-worker,"[20] among the top common workplace etiquette complaints are laughing loudly, talking loudly, checking voice mail on a speaker phone with the office door open, drumming pencils, playing CDs without headphones, whistling or singing, not programming voice mail to intercept calls when you're away from your desk to avoid long ringing, and having group meetings in the hallway or other open spaces. Noise is very distracting to some people, and one way of showing courtesy and respect to coworkers is to not unnecessarily distract them. Not everyone is easily distracted by sound, but a social standard is to speak low in public places, and this applies in the workplace as well.

Personal grooming and food also cause boundary violations. These are more than just distractions; these violations say, "I expect you to put up with my personal preferences." Food smells awaken the appetite of others and thus distracts, and a few foods, sometimes ethnic foods, are experienced as foul smelling by some.[21] Heavy perfume not only distracts but can also give others headaches and incite allergies. Hygiene standards matter too. Body odors distract and show a lack of respect for others. Respiratory etiquette is that one should cover one's face when sneezing; it bothers many people when sick coworkers sneeze or cough and then touch common surfaces without covering their face or cleaning their hands first. People should wash their hands well after using the toilet, of course.

Personal grooming or dress code is also related to getting along. At issue are not showering, wearing baseball caps and other articles that reflect an insufficient professional demeanor, and, for women, wearing clothing that for different reasons makes people uncomfortable. It is now well established that women should wear clothing that is nonrevealing and nonprovocative (and, hence, appropriately professional), but there are other situations too:

> I dress in very professional business suits and dresses that are no shorter than knee length with business heels every day, and I have worked hard and enjoy wearing designer clothes (Dior, Prada, etc.). I was told that I needed to tone it down and think about wearing jeans, etc. because I was dressing too professionally and that coworkers had complained that it made them uncomfortable. They then continued that donning designer shoes/bags/dresses makes my coworkers feel like I think that I am better than them. I was told that this is Wyoming and business is casual.[22]

A variety of surveys support the above concerns. For example, a 2010 survey of one thousand U.S. workers of the top five workplace pet peeves ranked messiness in communal spaces as third, loud noises as fourth, and potent scents as fifth. Overuse of personal electronic devices ranked sixth. Other issues were gossip (second) and various issues regarding time, such as meetings that run over time, meetings without structure, meetings that cut into personal time, and people who take excessive work breaks, which are grouped as "time management" issues and ranked first.[23]

Indeed, another area is respecting others' time. Many people are really very busy. There is a lot to do and so little time. In the United States, some people are paid by the hour, and time then really is money. In addition, they have often have families and children who depend on them, not only for money but also for time. Thus, keeping conversations to the point and not piling on extra work, especially just before the weekend, are usually greatly appreciated as a sign of consideration. Showing up on time and respecting the time of employees is among the most basic forms of respect. A survey of one thousand employed U.S. adults finds that the top two workplace pet peeves involve people with poor time management skills (43 percent): they waste the time of others or do their own work in an untimely manner that also affects others.[24] (Yet cultural practices do differ, and in South America time is not seen in this way. People are often paid on a monthly basis, and what they are paid is not very much or correlated with how much they do. Hence, time does not have the same connation, and being rushed might be seen as violating other social mores. Meetings are not always expected to begin on time. These differences can put others out of their comfort zone, of course.)

The above is hardly exhaustive, and many variations exist on respecting others' boundaries. It is impossible to regulate and foresee all of the ways in which people may disturb others, but experience shows that a little communication goes a long way toward reaching reasonable accommodations among those who seek to get along. U.S. laws give supervisors and their organizations authority to take reasonable measures to promote work activity ("efficiency") in ways that do not trample on the rights of others (or violate other well-known laws of discrimination). Sick workers can be asked to show respect by staying home and not making others sick, for example. Strong smelling foods and perfumes do not need to be used at work, and people can be asked not to do so. Some of these matters make it in the news because of lawsuits, and these lawsuits may provide a way of norming some behaviors. But laws do not exist that deal with everything that can come up at work, and people will need to sort things out. Respecting boundaries is not enough to get along, but failing to do so makes getting along much more difficult.

Getting along with others is an important matter that can be discussed as identifying and respecting the comfort zone of others. People vary in what makes them comfortable, and there is good sense in going slow and taking time to get to know others. Still, there are some general assumptions that can be made about what others are likely to find important about others so they fit in and get along:

- doing one's own job well,
- being pleasant,
- supporting others doing their job,
- avoiding hot buttons,
- going gently with excellence, and
- dealing with difficult people in diplomatic ways.

It is paradoxical that those with orientations toward people will lose those people relations if they don't also develop adequate technical skills and show commitment to organizational goals, while those with strong technical skills will fail to realize their projects and reach organizational goals if they don't have good people skills. People have a multitude of ways in which the above problems can show up, and they will need different strategies and effort to ensure that they respect the comfort zones of others. Getting along helps people establish a baseline from which they can then pursue other goals.

5

Connecting

We don't accomplish anything in this world alone.

—Sandra Day O'Connor (U.S. Supreme Court Justice)[1]

Almost all of us who have had a good career have had someone to help us in some way. Coworkers provided support and resources for doing our job better. Supervisors showed us new and better ways of doing our work and provided cover when we needed it most. Friends and powerful acquaintances provided access to influential people and opened doors for us to obtain favorable assignments and positions. All these people went the extra mile for us and often overlooked our flaws and emphasized our positive qualities to others. Close connections make the work experience better and easier.

"It's not what you know, it's who you know" is a popular expression emphasizing the importance of having close connections. Well, it surely matters that people are competently able to do their job well, but who you know is what gives the critical, extra edge to get ahead.[2] Some people are born into very well-connected families whose access, know-how, and resources provide an almost unstoppable formula for success. But there is also much that other people can do to make their own destiny. We meet many people along the way, and sometimes it is an eighteen-year-old environmental activist whose uncle is the state senator who can be asked for help. We

> It is wise to make a few friends at work.

need to know how to take advantage of fortuitous contacts and then forge some close connections. It is wise to make some connections and a few friends at work. This chapter is about forming such connections.

Connecting is part of the human survival instinct, as it is for many animals, bringing emotional support, well-being, and instrumental gains. These are positive experiences, and at the foundation of connecting lies *pleasure*. It feels good to have support and feel less alone at work and in one's career. The Pleasure Principle states, succinctly, that people are predisposed to pursue things that bring pleasure, and connecting and its benefits are among those. Of course, in the very big picture, people rely much more on their family and friends to meet their needs for belonging and support, but there is no doubt that having a few work-related friends makes the workplace a decidedly better place. Having a few friends increases fun and support at work. Effective work teams often produce a sense of belonging and camaraderie among members. A Gallup research poll shows that close friendships at work boosts employee satisfaction by almost 50 percent,[3] and a survey of U.S. city managers finds that the most prevalent outcomes of workplace friendship are obtaining mutual support (84 percent agree or strongly agree), improving the workplace atmosphere (78 percent), improving communication (76 percent), making difficult jobs better (72 percent), and helping employees to get their jobs done (70 percent).[4,5]

Connections at work often involve a mix of personal enjoyment and instrumental motives or exchanges, and people vary in how freely they talk about this aspect of workplace connections. We associate with different people in different ways, but we seldom know exactly how these associations are going to play out. Some people make us feel good about ourselves or keep us company during lunch and breaks. Some of them have connections that, unbeknownst to us, one day we actually need. With others we enjoy good conversation or working through work problems, creating new solutions. Some of these also provide valuable support when needed, not only in adversity but also in making opportunities available. Connections at work usually have a mix of pleasure and instrumental gain.

How much to connect with others in the workplace is subject of considerable debate. No one denies that having some supportive relations helps one do one's job and often maintain one's peace of mind, but not everyone believes it is wise to have close friends at work. While being friendly and getting along with people is important, there are risks of betrayal, gossip, and favoritism. Much of the debate is framed as workplace friendship and friendliness, and many concerns are about the former. Those who report having a close friend at work also report keeping their guard up in some ways: "I think it's important to keep some boundaries and not totally drop your guard with colleagues." Yet the above survey of city managers does not report friendship problems very high. The most frequently mentioned risk is gossip (53 percent), followed by developing an office romance (26 percent), being distracted from work (18 percent), undermining merit-based decisions (15 percent), and being a threat to the line of command (8 percent). Like other things, these problems benefit from skillful management. We need some close connections at work, but we must also manage these well. People with close connections do well to be aware of these problems and to work toward openly addressing these and other matters as they may come up in closer relations.[6]

Generational and cultural differences exist regarding workplace friendship. Young people are more likely to seek close friends at work. This may reflect a "phase of life" with a stronger desire for support and belonging caused by starting new careers and moving away from one's parental families, causing significant stress. Young people also may have less experience with the downsides of workplace friendship (betrayal, gossip, and favoritism). Cultural patterns also exist. British and American cultures emphasize sharp distinction between private and professional life aspects. However, in Asia and South America, people readily mingle and know each other quite well outside work, forming friendships that transcend employment. Sharing in life dramas, sports, hobbies, drinking, and caring for children creates and strengthens bonds, and they see nothing inherently out of bounds with this. Indeed, in some cultures people are not ready to do business with outsiders until they have been fully accepted as part of a group or unless someone of the group is willing to vouch for them. In this regard, some foreigners perceive Americans as friendly (i.e., easy to get along with) but cold and unable or unwilling to develop close friendships. They may have a point. In 1985, the average American had only three people to whom to confide matters that were important to them. By 2004 that number dropped to two, and 25 percent of respondents had no close confidants at all.[7] Americans do not see much need for close connections beyond a few, and that affects their workplace relations too.

People usually hone their connections skills by experience, but not everyone has good experiences or skills dealing with people. Not everyone experiences pleasures in connecting. The above focus on workplace friendliness or friendship goes only so far, and we need a bit deeper understanding about the nature and range of connections at work. We also need to have skills in making connections and knowing how to make them last and be successful.

Connections at work often start from a minimum of interaction and relations. It's a basic fact that we are hired by others to do a task, get along with others in the process, and provide a sense of contribution or support for others. We appreciate the plumber who fixes our toilet, but we may not know anything or much about the plumber. Yet we appreciate the service and are likely to want to use the service again. We appreciate the store clerk who helps find the shirt that is right for us and the printer who produces our brochures on time and with good quality. These minimum connections are related to these basic purposes; they are based on the service, not the person.

These are not very deep interactions, but they provide a necessary starting point for increasing connections. People like to work with others who bring good things to them, but to connect with others also requires sharing a bit of ourselves in the process. One way is to go the extra mile, going beyond that which is required as a minimum service. When that is done with consistency, deeper feelings of appreciation may develop. Showing this side of oneself is also a reflection of what may be deeper things that a person cares about and about which others may feel a sense of mutual connection of appreciation. Forming deeper connections is about having things in common and about enjoying others in some way as relating to that.

Going the extra mile is an obvious way of showing commitment to another, but in and by itself it may not always include sufficient sharing of oneself. People find positive appreciation for additional things they have in common, such as shared pursuits or interests, shared ways of interacting, shared past experiences that lead to common outlooks, shared ways of taking breaks, and so on. Connecting is always about finding something of oneself in another. Once both people have shared a little of themselves, then it is only a small step from having such shared dimensions to enjoying exploring these with another person and to finding a heightened sense of support and pleasure at work. Things in common include not only sharing a commitment to office goals but also sharing hobbies, keeping company during breaks, bringing interesting news to each other that improves their life in some way (e.g., notice of upcoming leisure or professional events), and so on. People can find connection in many things. Consider the following example:

> Quarterback Favre tutored Keller, helping the rookie tight end throughout last season. They spent countless hours studying third-down films. "More than most people do. I think doing that extra film work and speaking about it a lot, that's why we had that good connection. He helped me a ton." Favre's lessons sped up Keller's maturation process. "When a Hall of Famer takes you under his wing like that and teaches you," fullback Tony Richardson said, "you can't put a price on that. Dustin is much further along by having a guy like Favre around last year."[8]

or

> Sarah was one of the best employees I ever had. She always did her job on time and above expectation. If there was a problem, she would ask. If there was an opportunity, she would bring it to us. If there was

a new colleague, she would help that person learn the ropes. When I needed some extra time from her, she would give. I wish I could have kept her, but she decided to go back to move away, to another area. We even offered a scholarship to keep her.

From these quotes, we do not know exactly what bonds were established, but it seems quite likely that some special bonds were indeed established. For example, it is likely that Keller came to feel a special connection with Favre as a result, and vice versa. One can also imagine that between studying film, they might have explored and established additional fragments of commonality, perhaps over the course of a shared meal after hours of working together.

A sense of satisfaction with each other's performance and social manners often is a necessary condition. One can surely maintain friendly relations with those who provide services with which we are not happy about, but at some point the matter is likely to come to a boil in ways that require resolution. Sloppy performance or inappropriate social manners cannot be tolerated for too long. Sometimes people work through performance issues and thereby actually strengthen connections ("We even work through difficult issues together."), and sometimes another person's limitations are accommodated by office reassignments. But if after repeated efforts performance or social skills remain unsatisfactory, further relations may be stunted. One may ask whether Favre would have spent so much time if he had these concerns about Keller, and in some instances the person may even be let go ("I like you, but this just is not working out."). Satisfaction with others' performance and social manners is usually a prelude to deeper connections at work.

Sharing a bit of oneself is required, as it is the basis for appreciating others and feeling a connection with them. We can't feel connected with those we know little about, and thus others need to share a little too. Friends and good colleagues do little or big favors for each other, and people can find ample opportunities for giving expression of this in daily activities. There are opportunities for going out for lunch or dinner, sharing an online article, suggesting a leisure activity together, remembering someone's birthday or special event, bringing someone's favorite food or candy, or sharing information

Table 5.1 Ten Ideas for Building Closer Relations

1. Sending someone an article in his or her area of interest
2. Sharing a coffee break together and exploring interests
3. Inquiring into others' interests or hobbies
4. Sharing a bit of your own interests or news
5. Bringing something to work for the benefit of others
6. Consistently getting along well
7. Avoiding making comments or doing things that irritate others
8. Keeping confidences
9. Bringing back materials from conferences or seminars for the benefit of others
10. Inviting someone to your personal event

on an upcoming event. Friendship requires nourishment and a little time and money, and this is demonstrated too. Robert Brault states, "I value the friend who for me finds time on his calendar, but I cherish the friend who for me does not consult his calendar." Table 5.1 lists a few more items that might be regularly done in combination that show support and contribution to positive feelings in others. It is a bit of a "chicken and egg" question as to what comes first, the connection or the activity. People go to lunch because they have something in common, and over lunch they discover more things in common.

Going a bit deeper still, the ability to be concerned for another requires the ability to understand or imagine their interests and concerns. Indeed, one could be tragically mistaken to assume that others care as much about office goals or work as someone else might. We need to know what others are interested in, how they perceive things, and how current conditions or circumstances affect them. We need to know how to bring others some pleasure. This capacity to perceive others requires a bit less than empathy, which Berger defines as "the capacity to know emotionally what another is experiencing from within the frame of reference of that other person, the capacity to sample the feelings of another or to put oneself in another's shoes."[9] While it obviously helps to be able to feel what someone else is feeling, at the very least we need to know what they are feeling and how can we contribute to their happiness. Even when our guesses are wrong, people are likely to welcome our sincere intention of showing support and caring for them.

Trust, acceptance, and dependability are indeed the currency and foundations of stronger bonds, and a common tactic is feeding trust. Women tell each other secrets, and men who drink together often say things that they shouldn't. Doing so is an intentional exercise in trust building, providing someone else the chance to hold secrets in confidence. Trust is also built up by allowing another to correct a mistake and then hold that act in confidence. As Laurence J. Peter said, "You can always tell a real friend: when you've made a fool of yourself he doesn't feel you've done a permanent job."[10] Those who keep friendships going find ways to point out what they like about another, and they are dependable in their opinion and availability. "Lots of people want to ride with you in the limo, but what you want is someone who will take the bus with you when the limo breaks down," said Oprah Winfrey, a media celebrity. People solidify their relationship by taking the bus and being there for others.

The above also deals with the sustainability of connections. It is not enough to connect with others; one must sustain the relationship as well by continuing to find nice things to bring for others and otherwise nourish it, by dealing with performance shortfalls or other work-based disagreements in ways that do not threaten those areas that are in common, and by dealing with adversity when it strikes. Sometimes we need to be forgiving in areas where people do not perform very well—diplomacy has a place here too. People respect and treasure their important relations at work.

Of course, sharing vulnerabilities has its risks, and almost everyone who has done so has been burned at some time. It is this aspect that raises concern and caution. As one person noted, "Maintaining a friendly relationship is key in the workplace, but do not misconstrue 'buddies' or 'colleagues' with friends. If you do, you'll be in for a rude awakening when one day…" It is wise to give people some time to show us who they really are, and building relationships up from basic ones, as described at the beginning of this section, is therefore common. The point is not to be best buddies with everyone but to connect with people in different ways, to different degrees. Also, reaching out to others is a probabilistic exercise; how others respond to us is uncertain at best. Some people are not given to sharing of themselves, and some people who appear nice may not be so.

With this in mind, many people seek to make relations with those outside of their immediate workplace. Within organizations, committees and sport activities are common places for first meeting other people, and there people may inquire about others' hobbies, interests, and so on. Outside organizations, professional associations and local and national meetings provide additional avenues for meeting people. Professional associations and meetings also have key instrumental value for networking and career development, and these are further discussed in Chapter 9. Putting oneself in a situation to meet others is necessary for developing connections.[11] Agreement exists that making close connections requires following up on conversations and taking an active hand in creating the possibility of finding mutual interests or ways to support others.

The point is to establish a few close connections at work so that we have more support and can improve our work experience. Sometimes the connection is little more than supporting each other in meetings for our different projects. Some of these connections are with coworkers, but others are with supervisors or more experienced professionals outside our department. You never know how someone else will respond, but if we try enough people, we then hope, along the way, there may also be one or two close friends and loyal supporters as well.

People form connections about all kinds of things. Here we explore some of the common deeper ones. It might be noted that while instrumental gains are also present in close connections, the following is directed toward the person. We would like the person even if he or she did not work with us, and we would be motivated to engage with the person outside of the work context. We care about the common interest, as well as the person.

Common passion for common interests. What is it about sports that bind men? And what is it about talking about families that binds women? People often connect on the basis of deep-seated passions and interests, indeed. Sports touch men, relating to matters of physical honing and dealing with strategic issues that resemble the game of life. Talking about families touch women, relating to bonding and security through connections and pleasures. Talking and sharing among men is also more common in group-oriented cultures such as India,[12] rather than the United States. The question "What do you do outside of work?" is often directed toward identifying new common interests. When people participate in common interests, they may understand each other's pleasures and feed these, thereby improving each other's positive experience and creating a positive cycle of increased pleasure. People enjoy themselves more in the presence of another, which also causes them to want to spend time with each other. Pleasure is indeed at the heart of sharing common interests.

Clicking work styles. Some people naturally complement at work where it matters and have commonalities in other areas. Not many words need to be spoken among them, but they surely enjoy each other:

> Michael and I just naturally click and complement each other. After working on so many projects, we almost know what the other is thinking before it is said. We complement each other's strengths and compensate for each other's weaknesses in doing certain things. We also have much the same attitude toward getting things done in planned and professional ways. We also find good things to bring to each that strengthen our joint abilities. For example, Michael found a new software program that really helps us. It's just a joy coming to work knowing that Michael is there. The odd thing is that, personally speaking, we have fairly little in common. Our politics are different, we are of different generations, he has a large family to which he is very devoted, I have travelled a lot. We are just very different, but, gosh, do we work well together!

This example also shows that commonality does not need to extend to all areas or that people always need to agree with each other. Plutarch said, "Friendship is not about always agreeing—I don't need a friend who changes when I change and who nods when I nod; my shadow does that much better." People who have areas of connection are freer to speak honestly and with less reservation to each other than among strangers. Friends tell you not only what you want to hear but also what you need to hear.

Similar pasts, perspectives, and personalities. People sometimes have similar pasts or personalities that bond them together. There is a past of shared experiences and travails, such as having majored in similar subjects or attended similar schools, having lived in the same towns, or even having parents in similar endeavors. Whether these matters bond depends largely on shared important meanings. Yet, for example, those who started a career in environmental engineering and later moved into human resource management and have spouses from the same foreign country are likely to have some similar travails and experiences. People also connect based on similar personalities, which points to certain ways of seeing the world and interacting with others. Some people have distinctive personalities that are a bit different from what is often found, and when they meet people with similar, distinctive personalities, they may bond in some ways based on similar views, type of humor, interests, and so on. These are deep matters about which people may have a common understanding and perspective. Indeed, people sometimes sense that they have such commonalities before knowing what these are.

As an aside, such connections are not always positive. People may connect with others who add little to their positive development or to a positive office climate. People who like to abuse others may connect with others who have similar interests. People who are fatalistic and negative may feel much akin with others who share these outlooks. In addition, psychopaths and some others with major personality disorders (discussed in Chapter 17) often have very keen insight of the needs and pleasures of others, hence attracting others to them, but they use this information for the control, manipulation, and detriment of other people. This negative side is seldom mentioned in the workplace literature, but it is a common enough occurrence at work. Thus, people do well to double-check with whom they are associating. Not everyone with whom we would like to connect is necessarily good for us.

Common major life circumstances. People facing similar life circumstances often experience similar pathways and obstacles; sharing these experiences sometimes creates special, deep bonds based on sincere appreciation of each other. Examples include caring for older parents or family members with similar chronic and difficult diseases. People having children of similar ages with similar issues (e.g., special needs, cancer, etc.) creates multiple opportunities for shared support and sharing of information and experiences on treatment, doctors, school issues, and so on. These are very deep-seated matters that resonate and define part of a person's life.

Strong support for the passion of others. Some people deeply respect the passion of others. Art lovers may fully and passionately support the passion of artists. This is more than just about the artistic product; it is also about understanding and supporting the person who does it. As Maria Cavall said,[13]

> We have emotions because we care about what happens to us, and care about things in the world as they relate to our vital interests. Caring is implicit in all the emotions: If we didn't care about what we do, about how people treat us, about who we are and about things and people in the world, we wouldn't feel emotions.

At work, we may admire the dedication of the person who tirelessly aims to do the best that can be done. Such admiration can also start new relationships; mentoring (see Chapter 13) is a classic example. In mentoring, a senior person helps the junior person learn the ropes, and the senior is rewarded by seeing the junior person grow. Often the junior person contributes to work projects of the mentor in an example of mixed altruistic and instrumental motives. There is great pleasure in helping others, including gratitude in giving and receiving.

Deeper connections often involve deeper interests. It should be noted that most of the above discussion involves matters that are somewhat given for people; we may click or have common pasts, but if we don't, it is difficult to modify oneself. Statistically, we don't often bump into such others, even when we are open to exploring deeper connections. A few, at best. As one person said, "In my 22 years of gainful employment (i.e., career-grade employment) I have made

BOX 5.1 SMALL TALK

What is it about small talk that is so difficult for some people? Small talk is the art of exploring common bases and a foundation from which to go deeper into conversation. "Small talk is the pathway to big talk," and without small talk, there is not big talk. It is essential to do small talk well.

Topics appropriate for small talk are often introductory and noncontroversial. Introductions point to places ("I am from San Francisco, but I grew up in Paris.") that may provide an opportunity of further exploration ("Really? My daughter lives in Paris these days."). Small talk also includes discussing current events ("The art in this room is interesting. Have you heard of the Van Gogh exhibition that is coming to town?") and finding ways to tie them to things that others are interested in ("You are not so interested in that? What kinds of things do you like?"). The point of small talk is to find a few common interests before moving on.

Being nervous or shy in the presence of others stymies the flow of conversation and may cause others to wonder whether anything is wrong. Controversial or provocative answers make people cringe at the thought of what else might come out or wonder how someone might really deal with controversial answers. Hanging around someone too long also shows a lack of etiquette; you can always follow up in the days ahead if there is something valuable to share. Getting small talk just right is a valuable asset in establishing connections.[16]

3 friends, of which, only one do I still stay in any contact with."[14] This may be a bit extreme, but it is not atypical of the low prevalence of deep connections at work. Aristotle once said, "Friendship is a single soul dwelling in two bodies."[15] Well, in the modern world, sadly, we don't come across that too often, but it does make the point. But here is one major exception: mentoring is a relationship that people can search for and develop, and it is strongly related to career advancement.

There is another exception too. People who make many connections often have a wide range of interests. They read up on many subjects and engage with others in small talk in which these interests are explored. We don't always know what we will find interesting, and it is useful to be open to the interests and hobbies of others. Some may be very interesting to us, indeed.

Close connections are surely not always found among one's immediate colleagues, but having a few close relations is important for experiencing a sense of support at work, improving one's well-being, and gaining important advantages in getting ahead. Everyone who has gotten ahead has benefitted at some point from their relations with others. While there is wisdom in being cautious and taking things slowly, people do well to establish commonalities and connections with others. It often is not enough to just do one's job well.

Some people are veritable masters at establishing relationships and keeping relationships going. People do well to show engagement with and commitment to others, such as by going the extra mile and also by showing something of themselves. All relationships require giving a little of ourselves, showing what we like and are motivated by, as well as being able to understand the needs of others and being able to improve their pleasure in some way. Having an interest in others and being able to support the interests of others help us to get along and find new areas in common.

It is wise to make a few friends at work. Surely, there are risks of close connections, but connections are vital for getting ahead.[17] As one person said, "They don't teach this in management school, but learning how to build and maintain friendships in the workplace is a skill that can take you a long way in your career."[18] It is also a source of pleasure.

6

We Need to Talk

People, I just want to say, you know, can we all get along? … I mean, we're all stuck here for a while. Let's try to work it out.

—Rodney King (1992)[1]

No matter how well we try to get along, conflict at work is a reality that cannot be avoided. People are apt to have disagreements over policies, interests, or strategies. Some people get under our skin. Even the best of colleagues are apt to have disagreements, and many believe that a certain clash of ideas is useful in developing better programs and policies. Yet disagreements can spill over into conflict, and some people even seek conflict as a way to advance their interests. One key point is to use people skills to prevent disagreements from becoming full-blown conflicts. Though people should try to prevent disagreements from becoming conflicts, another key point is also to be prepared for when they do occur.

> **Conflict at work is a reality.**

A conflict is generally defined as a clash of people who are locked in a struggle over resources, interests, goals, or values.[2] Conflicts are to be distinguished from disagreements, which are defined as differences of opinion. People can have disagreements without being locked in a personal struggle; they can test and harmonize the veracity of statements and then move on. They can find better solutions. Indeed, it is commonly heard that differences can be functional (though not necessarily pleasant or easy) when differences are used to improve work efforts and outcomes. Each contributes to a better outcome. By contrast, conflict is more akin to warfare that comes in different shades. Conflict produces winners and losers—and sometimes only losers. At work, some conflicts are open (known to many), whereas others are known to only a few (only insiders) or not even known to those who are the target of the struggle ("I had no idea that she had it in for me."). Some involve individuals, and others involve cliques (factions) or entire departments pitted against each other. Some conflicts are active, whereas others are dormant or temporarily put aside (e.g., a truce), only to erupt at some later time.

The cost of conflict is high. Conflict produces stress, frustration, anxiety, and sometimes a loss of sleep. Good employees do not stay on in conflict-laden environments; they move to better locales. Not only individuals but also organizations are becoming concerned about the high costs of conflict. Conflict lowers employee productivity, causes people to take additional sick days, and takes up managers' and others' time listening to employee venting. According to one estimate, this cost is about $8,000 to $12,000 per incident, but beyond this, conflict increases employee turnover, and the cost of recruiting each professional employee is about $20,000 to $30,000 for recruitment, training, and diminished department performance during the recruitment process (though it could be more; according to some accounting firms, the cost of hiring and training a new employee can be 1.5 times a departing worker's salary).[3] In addition, conflict can lead to litigation, which can easily cost $50,000 to $100,000 and up in legal fees and settlement costs and be a distraction for several years. Conflict and turnover damage the reputation of departments, which can result in a loss of business, grants, or standing in dealing with others.[4] The point is clear: the cost of conflict is high.

Organizational life provides many opportunities for disagreement and conflict, and being aware of them is a first step. Some disagreements over priorities do not have easy compromises or many logical right–wrong positions, and disagreements over new priorities and direction of agencies often spawn ideological battles. Disagreements over values easily spiral into conflict (we need say nothing about religious wars in the world), especially when they are perceived as being an injustice or as causing harm. Conflicts also occur when people overstep their boundaries or authority, such as when people project their interests and responsibilities. Conflicts further result from ignorance and confusion, as people may misinterpret statements as final positions rather than as something less. Conflict thrives on ambiguity.

But people's own minds also contribute to disagreement and conflict at work. Studies show that people have abundant negative thoughts and that such negative thoughts tend to be judgmental and fuel negative emotions. Negative emotions fuel conflict; for example, one way is to knock off the person causing negative emotions—hence, fueling conflict. People ought not to kill the messenger, but it seems a fairly universal reaction to want to do so. Beyond this, being greedy and wanting to get ahead breed gamesmanship and inconsideration that also bring conflict. De Tocqueville's concept of "self-interest properly understood" is sometimes reduced to "it's a dog eat dog world."[5] Some people also see conflict and injustice in everything, generating conflict wherever they go. People also judge others by a higher standard than they do themselves. As one common expression has it, "We judge ourselves by our intentions and others by their impact." The human minds brings ample fuel that incites conflict.

In short, many opportunities exist for conflict and disagreement to arise. Conflict at work is a reality that cannot be avoided. Though some people are prone to being combative or fighting with others, a valuable lesson from the animal world is that longevity is ensured by avoiding conflict not by engaging it. People who fight get hurt, or as the saying goes, people who "live by the sword die by the sword." It takes a good deal of mental acuity to avoid conflict. People often signal when, for them, disagreement is about to become conflict, and that may be a wise moment to think twice, take a breather, and perhaps back off—using a respite to think of other ways to achieve one's goals. Not only are negative emotions associated with conflict unpleasant, but prolonged exposure to them is bad for one's health and well-being. Negative emotions, such as anger and anxiety, cause sleeplessness and trigger a variety of specific substances (e.g., epinephrine and norepinephrine) and processes (e.g., hypertension) associated with heart disease.[6] Negative emotions also compromise the immune system, such as the release of the antibody immunoglobulin A (s-IgA), considered the first-line of defense against the common cold. Long-term stress reduces other abilities to fight disease too, including cancer.[7] Conflict has direct and indirect losses for people involved, and people have multiple reasons for disliking people who cause them grief.

Vigilance is needed to avoid conflict, but people also require good skills in dealing with conflict when it cannot be avoided. This chapter discusses both.

Some conflicts follow a stage model that can be described as developing from (1) vaguely perceived dissatisfaction to (2) positions of disagreement and (3) hardened positions of dislike, which eventually lead to (4) conflict and its (5) aftermath. We first discuss the first three stages, with an emphasis on trying to avoid conflict by nipping it in the bud.

In the first stage of dissatisfaction, people often have a feeling of something being not quite right. There is reason for their being not wholly satisfied or even dissatisfied. Things are not quite measuring up to expectations or standards. Perhaps others are starting to take note too. Consider the following:

> Sarah's work was never the best, but lately it has considerable errors and is done late too. She has many excuses, some valid, others questionable. Most are somewhat reasonable, but when pushed, such as when asked for her records, she gets defensive. "Don't you trust me?" Well, in truth, I don't fully trust Sarah, but there is still too little evidence to draw her out or to make a case of it.

Some people refer to dissatisfaction as the "latent" stage of conflict. People are dissatisfied, and it is time to increase communication about standards and performance. Others may not know what standards apply or may not know that work has been deficient because it has not yet been made an issue. The dissatisfied person may not know of the circumstances under which work has taken place. Dissatisfaction can be found in many things, such as performance, how work is done, how people interact with others, and specific things such as comportment, keeping promises, and the failure to make promises. Whatever the object of dissatisfaction, it is time to get more information and dialog about what is going on.

A constructive attitude and approach goes a long way. Speech matters. This is also where getting along with others and having some diplomacy pay off, and insight into the importance of avoiding negative emotion also pays off. Negative and blaming words increase fear and defensiveness. A constructive dialog focuses on the facts of the performance or behavior rather than on motive or personality. There are few quicker ways to escalate an issue than by using language that blames and responses that avoid, deny, stonewall, or project helplessness. The task is to stay focused on achieving positive outcomes, and specific tasks or actions that lead to them, and to avoid stepping into blaming, fearful, or derogatory linguistic traps. Language is I focused or problem focused rather than other focused and blame focused:

- Instead of saying, "You make too much noise," we say, "The others and I have difficulty concentrating and working when you talk loudly on the phone."
- Instead of saying, "You don't seem to get it," we say, "I'd like to show you how this affects us."
- Instead of saying, "You are always late," we say, "We need to be sure that you are here to cover your duties."
- Instead of saying, "Your work is shoddy," we say, "I am concerned about your performance lately" or "Your work contains these specific problems and errors."
- Instead of saying, "Can't you get this right?" we say, "Let's work together to get this right."

The customary "performance talk" is exactly of this nature. This is a delicate matter, because these employees may be good or needed in other ways, and we may be loath to see them go. There may also be equity issues ("Do others perform better?") or special circumstances and many employees we don't want to see leave. To some, we owe a debt of gratitude for long service and key contributions in the past. This is also where getting along with others and having some diplomacy pay off; having other office workers also agree that things are not right can get people to accept the reality of the situation and embrace the need for change.

The typical approach is to make the behavior objective and to focus on the behavior rather than on the person. Yes, the person may have undesirable characteristics (lazy, sloppy, etc.), but the behavior is the topic and focus of discussion. The behavior and performance have been documented so that it is undeniable. The discussion is about reaching agreement on the existence of the behavior, on the negative consequences of the behavior, and on agreement of working with the employee to get it to stop. The unproductive behavior must stop, and productive behavior must occur. Many managers fear the conflict of a performance talk (confrontation), but the point is to reach agreement. Some further guidelines are shown in Table 6.1.

Difficult people are a different situation. Some people take pleasure in being contrary and getting under our skin. They use daily interactions to oppose all that we offer or suggest. Of course, some people do not intend to be nasty or difficult but are experiencing an "off day," which includes using unfortunate and abrasive language, but that is not always the case. Some people are often or almost

Table 6.1 Guidelines for Performance Talk

1. Never accuse. Minimize using the word *you*.
2. For every negative, find a positive contribution.
3. Speak just the facts.
4. Keep the conversation light but serious.
5. Reduce discomfort of the other.
6. Agree or state specific performance or behavior standards that are adequate improvement.
7. Be short, but let the other person talk as long as he or she wishes.
8. Have your facts documented.
9. Document the talk.
10. Send a copy of the talk to the employee.

always nasty with others. They remember their grudges and sometimes remind others of them. They are sometimes proficient at getting their way, but they don't care much whether work gets done or whether customers or the public is better off. They use being difficult as way of staking their territory and avoiding interactions and thus being asked to do their share. Dealing with such people is obviously mentally disturbing. It is the kind of work stuff that people bring home and discuss with significant others and friends.

The challenge in dealing with such people (and almost every workplace seems to have at least one such person) is to prevent interactions with them from escalating from dissatisfaction to disagreement to conflict. If the above suggests that people can change, the reality is that not everyone can or will. So after trying the above tactics of reasonableness, we might need other tactics. Sometimes we can avoid interactions or at least reduce interactions to a bare minimum and only when they are really needed. Less interaction surely reduces dissatisfaction, and we can also try reducing our work for them to a minimum. In addition, as the expression goes, "Give people a long enough rope and eventually they will hang themselves." All people trip up sometimes, and such moments may be duly and publicly noted, sometimes with implication for their performance appraisal.

The above objective approach is well-known and almost universally accepted, but taking emotions fully out of the picture may be culturally biased and not always appropriate. Being objective does not mean being coldhearted too. For example, East Asian cultures are very much duty based, and having a shortfall pointed out by one's supervisor is tantamount to a personal failure of not having put adequate dedication and effort forward. This personal failure often is felt as embarrassing, shameful, and emotional. Giving some emotional support going forward may be expected from a good boss, including being lenient in subsequent performance appraisals. Americans too may feel the need for support in the face of the social embarrassment of being pointed out. Improvement may be tough, and giving support is consistent with working together toward improvement. Discipline is a tough matter, but it is not without heart and consideration.[9]

BOX 6.1   HUMAN RESOURCES MANAGEMENT AND CONFLICT

This is not a book on human resources management (HRM), but there are a few instances in which HRM is relevant to the subject matter. Conflict is one those instances.

One instance of conflict is disobeying workplace orders. Supervisors have far-reaching authority to issue work orders, and workers cannot disregard them or perform in unsatisfactory ways without having concern for adverse action, which can include unsatisfactory performance evaluation, reprimand, suspension, transferring, and dismissal (termination). The use of orders is usually a last resort (see Chapter 11). Typically, supervisors use a process of "progressive discipline," defined as an escalation of performance orders, documentation of unsatisfactory employee performance, and the use of increased severity of punishment to obtain either compliance or separation of a person. These punitive tools are thought to be reasonable to achieve the aims of workplace organizations.

The implication is that conflict with supervisors has limits and should not include disobedient behavior. For supervisors, documentation is key to progressive discipline. The lack of documentation opens up the possibility of worker retaliation through grievances, Equal Employment Opportunity Commission complaints, and even litigation, but well-documented actions often ward these off. While termination is said to be more difficult in the public sector, because of civil service protections, termination in the private sector also requires careful documentation for any subsequent litigation. Oftentimes, the threat of being transferred may be sufficient to get worker compliance. Disobeying a workplace order is a serious matter.

Another instance deals with workplace violence, which has become a hot topic in recent years. Employers have adopted strict policies on workplace violence to avoid it. No one wants to see another instance of workers "going postal," and threats of violence, as well as violent acts, are taken extremely seriously. Conflict and disagreement are not to escalate to include threats of physical violence. Making workplace threats, when reported to superiors, would likely result in formal actions, including possible investigation, sending the individual home, mandatory counseling, suspension, and others acts.

The lines of disobedience and physical violence and threats are not to be crossed.[8]

The second stage of conflict is disagreement, a difference of opinion. Parties have gathered facts and formed divergent opinions; rather than agreement, there are contrasting opinions and perspectives. Differences have become crystallized. When the issue involves office matters, then factions may begin to form. Meeting agendas induce considerable premeeting maneuvering, adding to the tension.

A variety of suggestions are offered for deescalating and finding common ground.[10] Emphasizing common goals, common methods, and positive-sum gains is often useful. Disagreements are put in context or subjected to trial and error ("Can we try this for a little while before we agree on it?"). Misunderstandings and incomplete information are brought to light and resolved. People are made to feel appreciated for their contributions, avoiding or minimizing further negative emotions, and people are encouraged to work collaboratively toward common solutions. Some horse-trading and quid pro quo may help ("If he gives a little, how about you?"). Emphasizing what each has to lose if disagreement continues may help ("We will all stay here until midnight until this is resolved!"). Withholding a point of view that is useful does not build common ground—why highlight differences? At times, it may be helpful to bring in third parties who also have stake in the argument and who are willing to force consensus.[11]

Yet consensus is not always reached. There are process traps to be avoided, lest disagreement escalates. Prematurely closing off discussion allows disagreements to fester and reappear later. Voting is common in group settings, but using it prematurely is often seen as a tactic to close off valid arguments, which then creates opposition. Suggesting that a proposal be made to some other department or committee is usually taken as a deliberate construction (we've been there before ...). Withholding and avoiding discussion are sometimes passive-aggressive tactics that aim to sabotage problem solving, though some withhold opinions because they don't want to offend others. People can perceive when others dig in and are being less than helpful.

Sometimes it is wise to take a breather in interactions. People often signal when they are experiencing negative emotions, and pushing beyond that in such moments may result in things being said, or certain tones of voice being used, that irreversibly cause hardened dislike and conflict. People show their negative emotions through their body posture, their tone of voice, their withholding of thoughts, a frown or tightening around their eyes or mouth, and so on. Taking a step back is useful to reflect and digest what has been said ("Let's take a break and deal with this in a few days.") Perhaps the matter can be recast and even mutual gain outcomes suggested. Alternatives might come to mind later, and sometimes it is wise to bring others into the picture. At the very least, it is wise to give oneself more time to deal with conflict and war, if that is what it is going to be. It is useful to cool things down and then decide on one's options and next steps.

Yet when disagreements are not resolved, the third stage of dislike may be reached. Positions are hardened, and communications become a bit more aggressive, replete with repartees, verbal provocations, sarcasm, and openly aggressive or passive-aggressive behavior. Negative emotions fill the air. Disagreement is made personal by ascribing personal motives, such as hankering for power or seeking personal gain, or such intractable personal characteristics as "a difficult character," "a lack of collegiality," and "unprofessional conduct." The psychological basis for escalation into the personal realm is usually explained as a fundamental attribution error, which occurs when people cast blame on others' character or values rather than on their circumstances.[12] Simply put, after failing to address misunderstandings and disagreements early on, people have become convinced that there is something fundamentally wrong with the other person that "just doesn't do."

Once dislike has been established, it is difficult to reverse, and the next stage of conflict may be inevitable. Sometimes people seek to move on by insisting that people should get along, but after character and values are impugned, prospects for agreement and collaboration are diminished. Sometimes a third party, such as a manager, becomes a bridge between such parties, pointing out that the other person is not all bad and makes positive contributions and enjoys support from others ("You know, Jim is not really all that bad. Just last week he …"). Managers can also insist on professional conduct between parties, and once people change their communication patterns, the next step of finding reasons to appreciate others becomes more possible. They can even force the issue: "I know you two haven't gotten along lately, but I need the two of you to put your differences temporarily aside and do what is in the interest of the office. I need you to work together on this, and please tell me tomorrow how you plan to do that." But personal dislike is hard to overcome, and none of this may be successful.

Dealing with disagreement at an early stage is often essential before it further escalates into dislike. Postponement often makes resolution more difficult.[13]

The pathway to conflict is not always through escalation. Sometimes people want to clash in order to knock people or their efforts down. They want to win, and there is no misunderstanding that lies at the basis of such conflict. People use misunderstandings as a pretext to fight, disobey, or engage in passive-aggressive behavior. Sometimes people want to clash with those whose behavior is seen as inappropriate or those who cause them to experience envy, resentment, or anger. There is no end to reasons and pretexts for engaging in

> **Sometimes people want to clash in order to knock others down.**

conflict, including because someone is more fortunate; is pretty; has different values or priorities; has either more children or fewer children; has black, yellow, or white skin; and so on.

Conflict is sometimes unavoidable. Strangers at work are a reflection of society, and some people really like to fight.

Books on the subject of office politics exist by the hundreds, and the stated purpose of most is to inform how people can win or survive politics. But the reality is that people have numerous ways of inflicting damage on others, and people cannot always adequately prepare themselves for what is coming. Conflict is a form of war, and surprise is a legitimate warfare tactic. Not everyone is a very smart or original Machiavellian. (Chapter 18 discusses difficult behaviors in more detail.) Here are some basic tactics with which everyone should be familiar.[14]

From supervisors toward a subordinate:

- giving difficult, impossible, conflictual, or dead-end assignments to those they want to see fail;
- passing employees over for advantageous assignments on which future promotions or rewards will be based;
- denying credit for work done, or giving credit to self or someone else;
- blowing up and publicly announcing small mistakes;
- pairing people up with nonperformers or troublemakers;
- spreading information that pits people against each other;
- delaying critical decisions that cause projects to fail; and
- favoring other employees, thereby sending the message that something is wrong with others.

Among coworkers:

- spreading gossip behind the back of others, some true or exaggerated;
- tricking people into disclosing personal or professional embarrassments, which are later used against them (sometimes also as gossip);

- sabotaging a colleague's work by giving cooperation that is too late or too little;
- sabotaging a colleague's work by withholding information or giving misleading information;
- leaving coworkers out of important decisions or meetings;
- forming factions that lobby against the project or initiative of an employee; and
- using sexual incitement to lead someone on and then threatening embarrassment or legal action to obtain advantage (e.g., getting a promotion or salary raise, having someone else do their work, etc.).

Again, sometimes a little warning signal tells others that something is not quite right. Adversaries seldom tell their targets that they are scheming against them; avoidance, distance, and cold relations may be such clues. When confronted with the above tactics, adversaries might explain unfair assignments as "paying one's dues" or "giving Martha a break." Being paired with a troublemaker might be explained as "acting in the best interest of the organization." Confronting someone with gossip might be met with denial and disbelief. Being left out of a key meeting or decision is explained as an "unfortunate oversight that won't happen again." At some point, the coincidence of too many of these events may be just too much to ignore.[15]

It is often necessary to build a case in one's own mind or with others that the above tactics are in fact being used. Once the facts are established, bringing them into the open may cause others to back off. Asking why you are given a more difficult assignment than someone else shows that you are aware of this fact, are willing to speak about it, and will possibly even speak up about it too. Confronting unreliable or untimely information shifts blame to where it belongs. Dealing with misleading information is an opportunity to seek clarification of it. Confronting gossip directly challenges its credibility and directs others to come out in the open for a discussion about it. While there are no guarantees, openness and the threat of exposing systematic, adversarial efforts that are neither collegial nor professional often cause bullies and others to stop and search for easier victims.

Yet some very skillful adversaries successfully preempt the above by creating early vulnerabilities for their targets. They compromise their targets into embarrassing or wrongful conduct, such as encouraging their target to overcharge their expenses, to accept inappropriate gifts from clients, to tell a lie, or to engage in compromising or even sexual conduct. As discussed in Chapter 1, sex is quite common at work; undoubtedly, some of it is used for blackmail later. These liabilities are later used to preempt targets from striking back by making them conscious of their own vulnerabilities. New employees are especially vulnerable to these tactics, as they may be unable to distinguish sincere colleagues from false ones. Because of such tactics, Buffet's admonition that "it's very important to live your life by an internal yardstick ... rather than relying on the affirmation of others"[16] acquires even further merit in one's effort to avoid becoming compromised.

> Some adversaries successfully compromise their targets into embarrassing or wrongful conduct.

All of this is stressful for most people, to say the least, and people experiencing this find much value in having some close connections at work. Yet not everyone is bothered by the stress, notably not the person who is inflicting it. Indeed some people really enjoy being able to inflict stress on others, as they experience the joys of power and control. In the face of the above, many employees in the United States are tempted to threaten legal action, but doing so is expensive, stressful, and hazardous to one's career. Those who threaten litigation also make poor candidates for promotion, and people are hesitant to hire those who sue. Sometimes inappropriate action is not illegal action, and people do not have sufficient basis for litigation. For example, in wrongful discharge, there must be clear evidence that an employer failed to follow its own discipline or termination processes, failed to investigate allegations of harassment, or retaliated against an employee for exercising a right. These facts are not always easily or sufficiently established.

Conflict is best avoided by addressing nastiness at a very early stage. Those who let it prolong may find that addressing it becomes more difficult. Not every conflict has a happy outcome, and many people are left with little else but to severely reduce their expectations and begin looking for another job.

People at work are apt to have different opinions about things, and that can be constructive when they work together to find common solutions and better strategies. But conflict exists, and dealing with it is a basic people skill. Most people experience conflict as very stressful, and for this reason it is best addressed as soon as possible, head-on with a measure of openness. Disagreements require an open and positive tone, focusing on performance rather than on the other person and seeking to reach consensus. Strangers need to get along, and conflict is not a sign of that. It is hoped that dealing with conflict is not an everyday occurrence, but it is an important people skill.

7

Assessment

I refuse to join a club that would have me as a member.

Groucho Marx

The need to assess others is a constant one. We meet new people all the time at work, and we know from experience that not everyone is as competent and gracious as we would like them to be. When joining a new group, we really cannot know what to expect. Reading others is an imprecise art at best, prone to errors, misjudgment, and deception, but it is also unavoidable and necessary, as we try to identify those who are easy, pleasant, and effective to work with. Getting along also requires that we know some specific things about others, such as their working styles and preferences. It matters that we are able to make accurate and rather quick observations and assessments of others.

There is little evidence that those with titles and degrees, high accomplishments, and expensive rings or cars are any easier to work with than those without. Van Gogh was a highly accomplished artist with severe mental health issues, and Lisa Nowak was a NASA astronaut who famously drove one thousand miles in a diaper to attack a romantic rival.[1] The list goes on, and these behaviors are not exceptional. A degree from Harvard says nothing about a person's job skills, ability to work under pressure and uncertainty, and ability

to get along with others. Top universities puts out many poorly qual-
ified employees and managers—we have interviewed and counseled
a few. The point is clear: assessment needs to be about more than a
person's titles and pedigree.

In fact, we do well to assume that people we meet are representa-
tive of the population at large. It is hard to get exact facts about the
workforce, but some reasonable "guesstimates" are the following:
about 2 to 3 percent of people have severe personality disorders
that are highly toxic and often ruin any sense of team cohesion;[2]
about 10 to 15 percent have significant anxiety or depression in
ways that limit their capacity to fulfill their work duties,[3] and an
additional 5 percent have other mental health issues; about 5 to
8 percent abuse substances or are alcoholic;[4] 20 to 25 percent are
disinterested in working and contributing;[5] and only 10 to 25 percent are guided by strong commitments to professional excellence.[6]
While other facts could be added, the implication is this: among
any group of, say, twelve people, there is a 25 to 30 percent chance
that a highly toxic person prevents any group spirit, two or three
people have limited functionality because of substance or mental
health issues, two or three people are disinterested and unmoti-
vated, one person may also have a personal or medical issue that
prevents engagement, and only one or two people are truly extraor-
dinary in their motivation and skills. About six to eight people will
do just enough to keep their jobs, keep their boss happy, and get an
occasional promotion.

It can be naive and dangerous to ignore these realities or to assume
the best in people. The textbook model of the "high performance
work team" is an oversimplification that borders on Hollywood
deception. It is an ideal at best, seldom a reality. Some readers may
have better experiences, but our experience indeed puts the above
numbers as average for the workplace. Assessment often focuses on
the performance, commitment, and people skills of others, and the
point is to improve the odds of making a right or better choice for
us. Quite obviously, we want to identify those people with whom we
do want to work, provide some distance from those who bring problems, and, among those with whom we do work, make an assessment

of their working styles and quirks that lays the groundwork for a best possible working relationship with others. Organizations also ask managers to alert them of behavioral problems that may signify more serious issues.[7]

Assessment is necessary and unavoidable, but it also is not a crystal ball or magic. It is about getting information and making initial assessments and, as more information is obtained, revising these assessments. Assessment is akin to a preliminary diagnosis. This chapter examines assessment in three situations: (1) first impressions, (2) assessments related to forming a working relationship, and (3) specific working style preferences and quirks of others to which we may need to adapt when working with them. These are common situations that almost everyone has. Assessment of others is imprecise, but it can be done in ways that reduce unpleasant surprises and increase the chances of better workplace connections. This is the key point.

First impressions are unavoidable, even as we know that getting to know someone takes time. When we meet someone, we make an assessment of that person. People may object to putting others in categories or boxes, but we use first encounters to get an early read on whether people may be helpful or harmful to us in some way, now and down the road. From an evolutionary perspective, we need to know whether someone is dangerous or safe. At work, this line of thinking continues; having a sense that someone might be dangerous, incompetent, or difficult to get along with is valuable. Our mind is destined to make judgments. A large volume of research supports this and also shows how first impressions guide what we later see and want to see about others.[8]

Of course, the reliability of first impressions varies, which is a key point. The Chinese expression "don't be overly self-confident with your first impressions of people" speaks to the incompleteness and error of initial impressions. Consider the typical business introduction. In first encounters, people often are assessed in three main areas. First, we need to know what broad area people are working in and get a sense of what their involvement or goals are (e.g., "I work with the Department of Transportation in their IT application divisions. I work on electronic applications that make driving safer. Safety is a big interest of mine."). Second, we want to know something about a person's specific interests or competencies ("I graduated in electrical engineering and enjoy systems development."). Quite often, people will involve or drop a few names of famous others or institutions through which additional credibility is given ("I graduated from Malaysia's top technical university, and I worked with Professor Smith from USC."). Third, people project their people skills by being friendly and appropriate to the context. Being friendly is often seen as being personable, smiling, being mindful of others ("Do you want to sit down?"), and connecting with them in some way; many of these behaviors reflect good manners (Chapter 2) and connecting (Chapter 5; for example, "I also visited France. I much enjoyed it and also worked with a client from France."). Being appropriate means keeping a good distance, not telling off-color jokes, keeping conversations to the right length (not too short, not too long), being appropriately dressed and groomed for the setting, and otherwise giving people little to object to.

This often is a game. People know what others are looking for in first impressions, and many are eager to provide that. There is good reason to applaud more relaxed interactions so that performance and people skills can be shown in broader range. Yet it is also well-known that people overstate their qualifications and show a friendliness that may not be present later; they may be less accommodating when the chips are down and disagreements occur at work. As a reminder of the above Chinese expression, people who are known to others from conferences and professional interactions for many years have turned out to be jerks later ("It is like he has Janus face, two different personalities. I had no idea. He impressed everyone so well."). Many people work hard to make favorable first impressions. People say one thing, but we cannot know what the reality will turn out to be.

As first impressions go, it can be difficult to distinguish between the real deal and the con artist—except that the con artist likely works harder to leave a more favorable first impression.[9] Good first impressions cannot be taken as a sign of good things to come. As an expression states, "Behind

> Good first impressions cannot be taken as a sign of good things to come.

welcome smiles hide some unkind hearts." A good deal of literature focuses on detecting lies and danger in first encounters. While seldom conclusive, the literature signals the possibility of a red flag, focusing on areas for subsequent follow-up. A book by the title *The Gift of Fear*[10] shows how feelings may provide advance warning of danger by tuning into things that are just not quite right. Language or grooming that is just a bit too polished and the feeling that, after an hour talking with someone, you still don't really know the person's goals, past, or skills are important signs. These can trigger the emotion of something being not right, even before people are conscious of these facts. But feelings and intuitions can be wrong (they can be culturally biased), and thus empirical observations are also made to validate one's early warning signal. Gladwell,[11] in the best-selling book *Blink*, shows that people often make good decisions when using their instincts, but they are more likely to do so when they are familiar with the subject matter and have a record of success.

People seek out additional information. Paul Ekman, in *Telling Lies*,[12] discusses how concealment and lies have "leakage" that is shown by such behaviors as clasping hands and making nanosecond expressions of anger or fear, which signal that something is not quite right. Questions are asked to probe someone's depth of expertise: "What was your involvement with the sensors?" "Where did you learn that skill?" "Which books do you most like on that subject?" and so on. Having in-depth knowledge obviously helps to tease out inconsistencies. But assessments are often incomplete, and people differ in what they observe (some make faulty observations). At work, it is common for people to discuss their opinion after meeting others. By sharing different information or signals that they picked up, people form a more complete picture, however incomplete. Some people also follow up their first impressions by finding a bit more evidence on the Internet or from their circle of acquaintances. In one such instance, misgivings were matched by a newspaper report of a person's various lawsuits, though in another case a person was found to have additional rewards and accomplishments that were unknown. A good first impression was strengthened, but it remained just an initial assessment. No more, no less.

There is also a problem of misleading first impressions. Psychologically, strong desires, aversions, or beliefs are more likely to overlook information from first impressions that contradict them. Strongly believing that someone is a credible expert in an area and seeing what are believed to be signs of achievement (a fancy office, good-looking clothes) may cause one to overlook warning signs ("I don't understand what he said, but he is obviously successful, so let's give him the benefit of doubt."). One of the more widespread and interesting self-deceptions that people have is they believe that people from well-known universities are especially smart and suitable for leadership positions; we often see this in selection and appointment processes ("We are very glad to have Mary. She is from Harvard.") So what? The person may or may not have the needed skills. Conversely, strong belief biases (e.g., racial, religious, political) are likely to cause questioning and skepticism of a person's abilities or achievements (e.g., "I just can't believe that a person with her background would really be that charitable. There must be some ulterior motive, I'm sure."). Our dispositions color our impressions of others, sometimes strongly so.

Finally, it is well worth noting that people in public settings deal with many others, people who are strangers whom we do not know very well and more than likely never will. It is important that we deal well with strangers; many have connections and information that they may be willing to share. When asked, they may help us. In truth, none of us know how many convicted criminals and people with disagreeable predispositions have helped us, such as by giving us correct directions or making a useful introduction or comment for us. We might not have allowed ourselves to be helped by them if we had known. It is important to neither understate nor overstate the case for detecting danger and lies in first impressions. We need to get along with strangers, and first impressions are just a part of that equation.

Assessments are also made when people join a new workplace. Newcomers face the challenging task of not only making a favorable impression on their new boss and coworkers but also assessing their boss and coworkers as well. Not everything that is told during a job interview is the full truth. People often talk up the importance and functions of their office, the opportunities that exist, how easy and collegial people are to work with, and how they expect excellence. No matter what people have learned about their new organization and workplace, it is common that people know very little about the people who work in the office that they join. What is the assessment to be made?

The relationship with one's supervisor is key to one's success and happiness. Getting along well with one's supervisor often brings support, calm, and further growth opportunities to the extent that they can be given, while getting along poorly and not seeing eye to eye on important matters bring stress, dissatisfaction, and uncertainty. Assessment is always multidimensional, and one aspect concerns the goals and tasks that are expected of oneself. The assessment that is to be made is based on the assumption that one's supervisor is responsible for performance to his or her supervisor and, as such, is dependent on the performance of his or her staff. There are likely some things that the supervisor expects. It is necessary to know what these things are.

Some supervisors have a style of asking very little from people and seeing what they proactively undertake. Sometimes a person joins an office during a "low spell," and while little is currently being done or asked, more will come later. In our experience, when supervisors ask little, they could later be disappointed that certain things were not done. There are expectations even when they go unstated. By contrast, some supervisors ask a lot but vary in how much support and direction they give. Some supervisors let people figure out for themselves, whereas others are micromanagers. Some people like to know about progress, but others only want to see a final result. It is important to know what the supervisors' style of task giving and reporting is. Almost no manager likes to be blindsided; when there are problems in getting an assignment, it is important to let one's manager know and work on solving the problem.

A second dimension is the people aspect, specifically, the extent that we can expect support, encouragement, and a bit of mentoring in the beginning. People offer this in a few different ways. Some people are more people oriented, whereas others are more task or analysis orientated. Working for a people-oriented person helps one to feel almost immediately supported and appreciated, and it may be easy to establish rapport with such a person. Support will probably be readily forthcoming, but that does not mean that it is always effective. As discussed in Part 4, it also does not mean that such people will later do the kinds of things that one would like them to. But for the first few weeks or months, any such support is welcome.

Other people are more task or analysis orientated; they aren't immediately warm, but they are not uncaring or unsupportive. They fully support their staff when they run into problems, and they are very fair. One may need to approach such persons for help or orientation, and the response may be telling. Some people readily offer to be helpful; they understand well the stresses of the first few weeks or months at a new job. Others, however, may be too busy or not available and make no provision that others do help out. First experiences may not always be indicative, but some people are just not very helpful and supportive. We need to know what we are dealing with.

A third dimension is hard to assess immediately and usually becomes known only after a few months. While we defer the following to Chapter 18, some people are given to nastiness, indecisiveness, manipulation, bullying, and narcissism. There are odds of having such a supervisor, but it is almost always impossible to get such information from job interviews. Superficially and first impressions of such people are almost always great or fine. Sometimes an insider can give additional information ("Don't come work here!"), but that information is not always available. Any such information will eventually come out, usually in a few months, if not sooner. Colleagues and coworkers are assessed in much the same way, in the same dimensions. We need to know their expectations of a new coworker. Some may expect some help from you, whereas others will just let you do your thing. Some may welcome that you ask them for help, but others will not. Most coworkers just want a person to get along with them, as mentioned in Chapter 4, by doing one's job, being pleasant, helping others when asked, learning what the hot buttons are and avoiding them, being good but not too excellent, and dealing well and diplomatically with difficult situations. Perhaps, in time, one or two might even become a friend of sorts. Rather, the problem of assessing coworkers lies in numbers; though the chances of one person being prone to nastiness, indecisiveness, manipulation, bullying, and narcissism is not too big, the odds of a group of twelve people having people with troublesome behavior is a near certainty. The question is not whether there is a difficult or troublesome person among one's coworkers but rather who it is and whether there is even more than one.

While we defer to Chapters 17 and 18 for dealing with this matter, the implication is to not jump too quickly to conclusions about coworkers. There is wisdom in the advice that is often given that people who come up to a person in the first few days or weeks to be friends may have baggage that you do not want to share. The problem of assessment is that these serious matters usually take a few months to become apparent. Thus, the first few months on the job can often be a bit lonely or rocky when one is being taken for a ride.

Assessment is always tentative and given to change as new and better data of a person or group become available, but it is unavoidable and necessary to figure out what others want from us and how we can get along with them.

Beyond the above, getting along with others often includes adapting a bit to the working styles of others and, hence, assessing these styles. If we want things to go smoothly, we need to know how others get things done and be considerate and accommodating of that. We sometimes need to change our style a bit. There is little gained from being seen as having a working style that others just can't put up with.

Several authors suggest that there are fundamental preferences or proclivities that give people their unique working style and contribution.[13] People's working styles have their place in the world. Some people are more detail oriented than others, and others are great at making people feel great and at ease. Some are greatly focused on details, things, and perfection and must make decisions carefully if they are to be successful workers. Others act with bold strokes, seeing the big picture and key directions, and enjoy dealing with people while delegating the details to others. People who are successful leaders often need to have these skills. Being a good architect, counselor, or primary school teacher requires other skills. A psychological insight is that people often develop these orientations at an early age, and they are deeply ingrained. Specifically, there are some basic ways in which peoples' working styles differ:

- Information preference (verbal, e-mail, memo, meeting, etc.)
- Response to stress
- Speed of working and decision making (fast or slow)
- Decision-making preference (single or group, open or closed)
- Focus on the big picture or focus on details, rules, and regulations
- Support emphases (people, group harmony or achievements)

This does not mean that people are fixed in these styles, of course; we can all adjust a little the way we do things. When a scientist and politician need to work together, each will find plenty not to like in the other's work style, especially as they are more extreme in their ways. A political leader who thinks only about the great vision will be very annoyed by someone who focuses on the small details and why something may or may not be problematic in the future. If they are to work together, the scientist should get quicker to the point and relate to the big idea, and the political leader needs to take a bit more time to look at the details. Getting in sync with others' styles requires adapting our styles a bit. Adjustment is especially important when the other person is one's boss or key client.

The following are some areas where some accommodation may be needed. Assessment is sometimes straightforward—a matter of making observations, asking others, and paying attention to feedback. Some of these may be evident from first or second impressions.

Information preferences. Some people like to get information from others by e-mail and memo; they do not operate with an open door policy, and verbal comments are not remembered as well as written ones are. Others prefer talking to more fully understand the point, which may or may not include any follow-ups at a later date. Still others want just a thirty-second sound bite, and they are clearly fidgety with discussions that go beyond three minutes. Some people don't want to talk about anything. Different people have different styles, and it is well advised to get to know them for one's own information or point to have any effect. Often it is useful to have a few alternative ways of communicating information. (This is a bit basic, but it can get complicated; see also Chapter 18.)

Decision-making style. Some people like to make decisions in groups, whereas others like to make them alone. There is good reason for having group decisions (consensus), but group decisions are not always the best. People who prefer group decisions sometimes find that those made individually are just as good and also reflect any input that was offered. If we want to influence decisions, we need to know how others make them.

Focus. What do people look at when making decisions? Many people look to rules and regulations as the basis for decision making, perhaps reflecting a propensity for safety ("I was just following the rule.") and common sense ("Rules exist for a reason, yes?"). Yet others are impatient with that approach and prefer to focus on the big picture and on the intent of things. They see rules as a barrier to change and progress that are needed. Still others make decisions based on science and facts. Rules may be wrong or not applicable in a particular setting because of the facts at hand. All three approaches are needed, yet people can get very emotional and frustrated when their style is not followed. Those who need to work with others do well to accept the need for alternate styles and justify their preference within that.

Work and decision speed. Some people are real pacesetters, working fast and furiously (e.g., Type A personality; see Chapter 15). Others like to take it slow. Some people make decisions quickly, perhaps on even fragments of evidence, whereas others are deliberative and prefer to make a decision after they have mulled things over and over. People with greatly divergent styles find a lot of friction when working with each other, not understanding why someone is taking so long or how someone can make a decision on little more than a hunch. Some adjustment and consideration are often needed. Some need to pick up the speed, while others do well to dial back and take a walk to smell the roses. Literally.

Support. While everyone should respect other people, people do differ fundamentally in what they support or respect in people. People look to different things in people, and it is important to know what one is respected for. People who like to be personally appreciated for their effort often feel a bit down and underappreciated when that is not given. Some people are very results oriented and focus heavily on the contributions that people make to tasks and projects. Sometimes we can ask to get a bit more appreciation for things that we value, though this often requires constant reminding for some time. These are very fundamental ways of dealing with the world that people have developed over time.

Response to stress. People do not like to experience more stress than they are comfortable with (see Chapter 4 regarding comfort zones), and it is important to know the signs of stress in others. Yet people respond differently to stress, and it is important to know any characteristic pattern. Some people when pushed or stressed go into avoidance and postponement, perhaps with little communication ("Oh, I'll get to that."), while others simply give in ("No problem, you got it."). Still others go for the quick dictatorial decision ("I decided that's just the way it is going to be.") or start attacking ("See how angry you make me!"). Bolton and Bolton note that people often have primary and secondary ways of dealing; they start with one of the above modes, and when stressed further they change their style.[14] It is important to know the warning signs of people experiencing stress and to use some diplomacy in bringing a person back from stress.

People do have different work styles, and we do well to adjust to them. People come in many shapes and sizes, and we do well to know what approaches work best with them and what ticks them off. Having social skills is about the ability to assess these differences and to adjust to them.

People vary, and we need to assess them. Assessment is preliminary, subject to later additional knowledge that comes as we get to know people better. Here, assessments are discussed regarding first impressions, job candidates, and working styles. First impressions can be very unreliable and deceiving, especially of people who leave us with positive ones. An adage states that "first impressions are often the truest," but not always, and so we do well to be wary of overly positive impressions that we may have. When making assessments of job candidates, one would do well to get information from those who have worked with them. The popular belief that people will not share information that is negative about others is not accurate. We need to know what to ask for and how to listen to what is being said or, rather, not said.

Assessments are also made of others' working styles, which is often of paramount importance for getting along. Working styles vary with regard to information and communication preferences, response to stress, the speed of work and decision making (fast or slow), how people prefer to make decisions, people's ability to focus on the big and small pictures, and what others tend to support—people, group harmony, or achievements. That's a long list, and it usually takes some time to observe these things and figure them out. We do well to adapt to the styles of others or at least take these styles into account, for the sake of getting along.

It should be stated that other assessments also exist. For example, assessments are also to be made of job candidates; this is discussed in Chapter 9. Assessments can also be made of the organizations, such as its past and future goals, its operating styles, the achievements that get people rewarded and promoted, and the industry or political trends that affect future prospects.

Assessment represents a progressive deepening of social skills. People first deal with the basics, showing respect, using social manners, and dealing with the challenges of communication. Then they confront the challenge of getting along and making a few friends, as well as dealing with conflict and organizational policies regarding that. Addressing these challenges often brings special attention to careful assessment, as an approach to minimizing conflict and getting off on the right foot. Assessing others is the first thing we do when we meet others, but, paradoxically, assessing them well usually requires considerable experience and reflection of prior interactions. Even so, assessments are always preliminary.

Section

Three

The Professional Self

8

What's Your Commitment?

Eighty percent of success is showing up.

—Woody Allen

David Rye tells the story that several years ago, former senator Edward Kennedy was trying to capture the Democratic Party's presidential nomination. During an interview with newsman Roger Mudd, he was asked why he wanted to become the president of the United States. "It wasn't that he came up with a poor answer, he couldn't find any words at all."[1] It made it seem that he didn't have a clear sense of purpose or an appropriate motivation. "The public blasted him and … shortly after the interview, his campaign was disbanded." The hard truth is that we are not much interested in what others want for themselves—we are far more interested in what others can do for us.

In broader context, this chapter is about career development and professional identity.[2] People skills are more than our interpersonal ways of relating with others. A good deal of how people communicate, get along, and deal with disagreements, as discussed in the previous chapters, is rooted not only in how well they manage these situations but also in the commitments and contributions that they seek to make. The commitments and contributions of others are an essential part of how we know them at work. Through their commitments, people express themselves to the world and in the world. People need to know what we stand for, and what we stand for and seek shapes how we relate to others, what we look for in them, and how others come to see us. It is part of our professional identity.

People choose to be an engineer, a financial manager, or an artist, and they also decide what they make out of being one. The point of Woody Allen's quote about success is that people must show up not only in body but also with spirit. People decide what they make out of their circumstances and the opportunities offered to them.

> Our commitments and contributions are an essential part of how others know us.

Formal job descriptions define only the basics, and while our supervisors might tell us a bit more, what people make of any job also depends on them. Managers and their organizations can encourage and reward motivation, but it is an act of self-expression and self-leadership by employees to show up with motivation and commitment, which no one can really force.

To quote from the senator's older brother, the former president Kennedy, "Do not ask what your country can do for you, ask what you can do for your country" or community or employer as the case may be. This is not an altogether altruistic matter. People like to work with others who bring good things to them, and people want to know what that will be.

Articulating our commitment has become increasingly key in career development, as few organizations now offer a guaranteed lifelong tenure and a guaranteed track of promotions. Sector switching and job hopping is a way to get broader experiences and sometimes a quicker promotion and salary raise too. Individuals are now apt to find themselves a bit more often on the job market than in past generations. The average number of jobs in the United States held among those between ages eighteen and forty-four is now about 11,[3] and though no data exist for older workers, a reasonable estimate might be about 15 jobs held for those through age sixty-four,[4] up considerably from 10.5 in 1993.[5] We do not know how many different employers people will have, but a reasonable estimate is probably 7 to 10.[6] Those who can readily articulate their commitment and contributions will find it easier to be selected and rewarded. Even when people stay longer within the same organization, promotion is as much based on past performance as it is on the need for future contributions and commitment. We need to know what others stand for, and with that comes opportunity.

Yet defining one's commitment does not always come easy. For people in their twenties, knowing what contribution they want to make can be daunting in the face of limited job experience. About 20 to 25 percent of the population is said to chronically procrastinate, and self-leadership is obviously difficult for them.[7] Some people wishfully hope that good performance will somehow be rewarded by promotions or that a degree will somehow result in job offers. These things do happen, but explaining to others what we can do, along with a little networking, increases the odds. Most people do not know at an early age what they later want to be or did not have parents like those of Tiger Woods (golf) or the Williams sisters (tennis), who shaped their choices at a very early age. For people who have lost their job in midcareer, redefining oneself to match one's skills and abilities with the new realities of the marketplace can be a daunting and nerve-racking task. Self-expression is then also tempered by the realities of providing for one's family and not wanting to uproot it by moving to new locations.

This chapter looks at our commitments and, hence, an important dimension of our professional identity—who we are and how we want others to know us. This is seldom about choosing an ideal job or about having far-flung dreams of becoming CEO or agency director one day. Rather, what follows below is shown as building on a realistic sense of one's strengths and interests and then crafting a broad range of jobs that is consistent with the difference that one would like to make, now and in the immediate future. A popular expression is "be careful what you ask for, because you might get it." It is time to express that.

Successful people often have an enduring commitment to a cause or skill set that they enjoy. People do not become excellent overnight. There is trial and error in discovering something that we really like doing and in recognizing that one has a talent or predisposition for doing it well enough to make a living from it. Then it often takes years of practice and dedication to master one's skills. Modern jobs often require professional-grade skills that are grounded in education and training and take time to acquire and master. Malcolm Gladwell writes that successful superstars like the Beatles or Tiger Woods often practiced as much as 10,000 hours before they achieved their first famous successes.[8] These people are extreme examples as regarding their popularity, but they demonstrate the general pattern of finding a relatively narrow area in which people work hard at applying their talent and mastering skills. Recent book titles such as *Talent Is Overrated* highlight social and other skills as relevant factors, but they do not deny the importance of talent, ability, and practice too.[9] People need to know what they are good at and enjoy doing and then seek out opportunities to practice and develop their skills—whether one is a scientist, lawyer, carpenter, or anything else.

To seek out such opportunities is a measure of commitment. Commitments are often in rather defined areas of practice that in the modern world are increasingly narrow. This is not only because people need to know the specific problems of an area (such as writing country pop songs or practicing maritime law) but also because they need to establish relations with people in these areas. This takes time, sometimes a few years. Different industries have different social networks within which people are to be accepted, and many networks exist at local levels too. People need to know whether others are as good as they might say and also whether they are pleasant and effective to work with. These data often come from people's experience with them and comments made by others too. Recommendations are the key to success in almost every line of business. It is who knows you that also matters.[10]

Modern professional commitments, which we define as a range of professional activities people would like to be involved in, often are highly specific and reflect the backgrounds and talents of people themselves. Some typical examples are making contributions to information applications in urban planning, doing marketing for hospice services, finding financial solutions for municipalities, or teaching science to underprivileged children. Each activity shows commitment to a skills or knowledge area of application. Such commitments are specific but also provide *a path* that is broader than any particular job. Professionals look for jobs that allow them to express their commitments, and at any point in time, several jobs and several organizations may be appropriate. It can be said that while recruiters look for suitable persons to fill their jobs, professionals look for suitable jobs to fill their commitment.

These notions can come together when describing what people do and why, focusing on (1) an area of strength, (2) how people came to enjoy doing what they do, (3) sustained commitment to developing an area, (4) patterns of successful accomplishment, and (5) people they know in the field. For example, when asked, "What do you do?" people may be able to give a fairly specific discussion of how they came to be committed to, for example, teaching science to underprivileged children, how they are currently giving expression to this, and how these efforts can possibly develop in the future. Indeed, people have a personal discussion about their commitment, how they came to embrace it, and why ("I did many internships in urban planning and focused my courses on it."). People in school often underestimate the individuality of their curriculum choices; not everyone chooses to study or make a career in, say, public administration or geology, and these choices can be explained.

In working with professional-degree students for over a decade, we developed an exercise called the *professional commitment statement* that captures these qualities. Students, who range from ages twenty-six to forty-five years, are asked to write a few short paragraphs about (1) what kinds of activities (or career path) they would like to be involved with; (2) their past and present experiences that are consistent with their motivations for having this commitment; (3) the strengths that are required to be successful in their line of work, including some past accomplishments or successes and evidence of having these strengths; and (4) their current efforts to improve their skills and abilities to be successful in their line of work.

Though it is just a few paragraphs, this is a challenging assignment. It typically takes students about six to eight weeks to complete (about half a semester). Some students have little job experience or self-knowledge about what they want to do. Some also hope that a graduate degree will answer these matters for them in the shape of a job, and for others graduate school is refuge from dealing with these issues. Because people usually lack specific knowledge about the types of jobs they think they would like to have, we send them into the field to conduct interviews with those who have jobs that they might like to have. By talking to these jobholders, including those who hire, students can ask specific questions about the nature of these jobs, what is required to be successful, and how people make their hiring decisions for these specific jobs. (As a practical matter, people often ask how students get appointments with people they don't know. Well, most students ask their acquaintances for relevant referrals and introductions, and some also make cold calls. Few people are denied a request to talk for a few minutes with others about their future.)

For most students, this becomes an eye-opening experience about the specific requirements and possibilities in a line of work. It often results in their rethinking and sharpening their current efforts and the way that they articulate their interests. Another outcome is also profound appreciation for the benefits of networking with others in this way (e.g., "I never expected that such a busy person would spend such time with me. She was so helpful."). This activity also helps to shape and give expression to key elements of professional career commitments. These elements are as follows:

- an area (or line of business) in which people want to work;
- a range of activities or skills that people want to apply in this area, giving shape to a range of specific contributions that people would like to make;
- a pattern of prior experiences that shows development of these skills or commitment to this type of contribution;

- current job or other experiences that apply or further develop these skills; and
- an indication of involvement in the near future showing growth consistent with expected experiences, skills, and qualifications.

By way of example, the following is a short commitment statement, articulated after this exercise:

> Throughout my life, I have been privileged to mentor several disadvantaged and underprivileged young men reach high levels of success. I want to continue mentoring young men that may have single parents, uninvolved parents, low economic statuses, and/or poor educational systems available. I have a few years experience in related social programs and working with nonprofit funding, sometimes working as a volunteer, too. My next goal is to begin a program that mentors male high-school juniors and seniors as well as college undergraduates, who will in turn mentor younger boys. Mentoring will consist of being and providing examples of strong, educated, ambitious men that will cause the student to reach and surpass his potential. I am currently talking with different funding agencies about establishing such a program in our city. Perhaps one day I might run my own nonprofit organization. My hope is to develop an effective mentoring method and extend the program throughout the nation and to females, as well.

Goals may change, but this brief statement clearly shows purpose; a history of relevant experiences; skill sets related to mentoring, program management, and development; and an eye toward future progressive achievement. (The importance of stating a commitment is valid at every level of work. This person is only twenty-five years old with very little job experience, but commitment is also relevant in the previous story of former senator Kennedy.) Appendix C provides more detailed examples, including the full-length example from which the above is based.

Commitments are surely not set in stone, and they vary over the course of one's career. People change and grow, and they often stumble through happenstance onto what they enjoy doing. The roles of happenstance and chance encounters cannot be ignored when one is finding one's commitment. Few know from an early age what they want to do, and most people come about it by chance. Many people in their early twenties know only school, and that is not where they want to be. Then internships, participation in "service learning" courses, and talks with people who work in jobs they might consider often provide the detailed experiences and information that they need to find something to which they are attracted. Getting out there also provides people with a valuable lesson in how networks do lead to chance encounters that can change one's career life.

It is hard to deny the value of having a clear pathway that is expressed in this way. It gives structure, purpose, and meaning to one's career life, expressing in practical ways what contribution one seeks to make. It provides clear communication to others and is also eminently helpful in interviews and networking, as discussed in the next chapter. Indeed, some people develop two or three of such commitment statements, suitable for different purposes. It is also helpful for communicating with superiors about the next steps in one's career, focusing on the kinds of contributions that one would like to make. It can be delivered in a flexible way, providing one's organization with a range of opportunities for which one would like to be considered, or as a dialog or conversation about opportunities that may be available in the future. It is through expressions of commitment and purpose that others also get to know us, indeed.

Discussing commitment leads, willy-nilly, to matters of identity and professionalism too. In psychology and sociology, *identity* refers to a self-image (or mental model) that people have of themselves. Having a positive self-image is important, as it reflects someone who is able to commit to and master a set of skills. The professional commitment statement contributes to developing empowering self-images that are grounded in one's experiences and goals. Making positive contributions and having achievements associated with these commitments also reinforce a positive self-image and build self-confidence.

Today's emphasis is increasingly about people being able to fulfill a positive role and make positive contributions.

Yet identity is sometimes also understood in another way. Some organizations, especially in the past, strongly encouraged people to self-identify with an organizational role. Yet, identity is sometimes also understood in another way. Some organizations, especially in the past, strongly encouraged people to self-identify with an organizational role. Others want to see us in some way, but to take on such a job-based identity is to effectively live someone else's or a fantasy life. We can play the role of the effective public manager, but it is quite another to *be* the public manager. Doctors, lawyers and Wall Street stock brokers are some archetypical examples of occupations where people sometimes fully live in the role that they or their employer script. Doctors are expected to be patient and altruistic, even when some are not. Adaptability is good, but living in a theatric script is not. Some adaptation is necessary in the world, but it is necessary to remember that we have our own past, our own strengths, our own weakness, our own sense of humor, etc. We can contribute to the world without becoming fully defined by it. We are more than the roles that others ask us to play. [11]

Professionalism and ethics are further elaborate on one's commitment. Commitments are to be fulfilled in certain ways, meeting certain expectations. *Professionalism* refers to the notion that members of an occupation practice their trade in accordance with certain technical and ethical standards. Professional norms and ethics are not always specific but rather about giving direction and consideration, and it is not very difficult to elaborate on one's commitment by giving consideration to them. Professional societies and educational programs have a long history of articulating standards and ethics that tie to apprenticeships, guilds, unions, and professional associations issuing norms of conduct pertaining to its members. Past generations made major contribution to this, which still guide today. As regarding the above bulleted list of items that make up professional commitment statements, we now add the following:

- standards or evaluation criteria pertaining to one's commitments and achievements, and
- ethics and professional norms or roles by which people are guided in their work activities.

For example, codes of ethics from professional associations such as the ASPA provide a range of standards and consideration that usefully informs one's professional commitment in public service. Typically, such codes cover the following elements: (1) working for the public interest and respecting the employer's interests; (2) knowing the state-of-the-art knowledge and standards of one's field and applying them in one's work; (3) promoting honest, effective, and innovative organizations; (4) knowing and respecting the law in one's field; (5) respecting the roles of governing boards, elected officials, and democratic processes, as well as giving due process and allowing dissent; (6) endeavoring with compassion, benevolence, fairness, and optimism; (7) being honest, forthright, and trustworthy; (8) avoiding improper conduct and the appearance of improper conduct; (9) avoiding and opposing all forms of discrimination and harassment; and (10) sharing credit for work and achievements. These elements are surely not exhaustive, and the codes of ethics in specific fields add additional standards or norms. It is remarkable that codes of ethics in very different fields, such as financial services and engineering, often contain similar points.

Consider how these standards add usefully to one's professional commitment. The above example of being a mentor to disadvantaged and underprivileged young men is usefully supplemented by the writer's adding that activities should be informed by current research and standards for mentoring programs and will be developed with advice from those who do research on them and discussed in professional societies. The activity could even aim to develop ethical guidelines for mentors, so as to be clear about the purpose of the program. The program itself is seen as a way for the city to show its compassion and benevolence to its citizens, including those in more difficult circumstances, and such a program can be seen as right, proper, and cost-effective for cities to have. In this way, elements of ethics and professional standards are usefully brought into one's professional commitment, providing grounding of one's purposes.

> ## Professional standards and norms are an obvious way of elaborating on one's commitment.

Using concepts of ethics and professional norms in this way is a bit novel but increasingly welcomed by others all the same. Indeed, the argument can be made that as role-based identification is receding and becoming less prominent, paradoxically the need increases for stronger awareness and integration of ethical and professional awareness into one's actions and commitments. No longer are these influences always strongly present, but there is no doubt that these are still much needed and valued. Who wants to deal with the unethical and unprofessional conduct of others? People want to know what they can expect from others. A lack of professional and ethical awareness is the complaint of the day. While American society and education is presently in a void or transition about this, and schools do not want or know how to teach these matters, it is not very difficult to elaborate on one's commitment with a sense of professional norms and ethics. People want to deal with others who will do the right thing and not cause trouble. People who verbalize their attention to ethics and professional norms make at least a step in that direction. It is well worth the consideration for getting along with others. Professional standards and norms are an obvious way of elaborating on one's commitment. (Ethics are discussed further in Chapter 11.)

People often experience some challenges in developing their commitments and expressions of them. Cynicism and nonprofessional attitudes are a fundamental challenge that downplay the psychological and material benefits of commitment. There is value in constructing commitments that bring fulfillment in different ways, but saying, "I'm just a schoolteacher" is to cynically diminish the rewards of teaching. In our experience, people in business schools are especially prone to being cynical of career choice and satisfaction. There are things that money can't buy. Some experiences are inherently rewarding, and psychological and material rewards emanate from putting commitment in service of others. There is value in constructing commitments that bring fulfillment in different ways. Past generations and philosophers have long agreed that having a purpose often brings happiness; commitments help give meaning to one's life and put people on a path that provides a multitude of enjoyable and necessary experiences. People do make their destiny, often by chance:

> As a way to keep their costs down while holding on to promising associates, many (big law firms) offered the graduates the chance to take up to a year off before starting as associates, complete with a stipend of $60,000 to $75,000. When Latham & Watkins asked Mr. Richardson to defer his start date, he took his interest (to) a nonprofit policy group based in Washington. ... Now, (he) has decided to say "no" to Latham and stay with public interest law, even though it pays far less. "This is an amazing work environment," said Mr. Richardson, who graduated from the University of Chicago Law School. "I'm working with a lot of really smart people and getting published. I'm not sure if there's anywhere else I could do this." With the deferral year ending, some newly minted lawyers are surprised to find themselves reconsidering their career goals.[12]

Explaining one's commitment also requires a little creativity and imagination. Past experiences and skills are connected with those sought for the future. Someone who wants to develop his or her commitment to fund-raising for hospices might find that past or present skills in marketing or event management are relevant or transferable for fund-raising. Volunteering, taking courses, and giving family care are all examples of experiences that are relevant to showing a pattern of commitment to aspects related to hospice care. Reasons for having done something in the past may be relevant to explaining how one's past is related to one's future. Commitments often reflect interests that have been present for a longer time, even as the present focus is clearly different from that in the past. Looking at one's past is often about finding new threads. Such creativity is especially needed when commitments are designed in new fields or require new skills; it is part of the age-old problem of breaking into new fields and jobs. Box 8.1 reflects on the use of recent scholarship to strengthen one's professional commitment statement.

BOX 8.1   PUBLIC SERVICE MOTIVATION

A few years ago, Jim Perry gave renewed impetus to the study of public service motivation (PSM). PSM is defined as an individual's predisposition to respond to motives grounded in public institutions (or, alternatively, concern for issues in the public sphere generally). PSM can be measured, and it is often measured according to six dimensions: a person's attraction to public policy making, commitment to the public interest, civic duty, sense of social justice, sense of compassion for others, and willingness to make self-sacrifice.[14]

Studies show that people in the public sector are significantly motivated by these elements. PSM is positively associated with participation in professional organizations and levels of education, but it is also shaped by working experiences; experiencing a lot of red tape decreases one's motivation, of course, but having a sense of structure and efficacy for increasing contributions increases PSM too.

These studies provide some useful concepts that carry one's thoughts and professional commitment statement further. "Attraction to policy making" is a good concept to explain ongoing interests in an area. "Efficacy" can be useful to describe the kind of setting that one is looking for or the kind of person that one is. "Self-sacrifice" can describe one's current commitment to making a larger contribution in the future. Sometimes academic research contains new concepts that can be put to good use.

Articulating one's commitment usually takes a few tries and iterations. Initial efforts often see commitments that are too broad, too narrow, or too far-fetched. When people cast themselves too narrowly, they may lose out on opportunities that also might be interesting to them. When people cast their commitment too broadly, others may feel that they lack adequate commitment to any specific area or professional endeavor.[13] Their commitment is too broad to be taken seriously. This is also a problem with far-flung commitments that are inadequately prepared. People are apt to question one's sense of realism when the desire to become a sheriff is not accompanied by twenty years of law enforcement experience; the appropriate focus for the future is the immediate next job. These problems reflect an insufficiently reflected mind.

Commitment is about not only what we want to do but also our roles in relation to others. A successful commitment is one that others welcome and accept. The articulation and expression of one's commitment often take practice and a bit of perfection through others. This is akin to an actor who not only practices a role one hundred times before going on stage but also perfects the role in subsequent performances. Getting feedback from others leads to ongoing refinement and improved articulation that improve acceptance as well as the commitment itself. Practice makes perfect, and there is much satisfaction to be had when others show their welcoming and appreciative support.

Finally, people sometimes introduce concerns about money a bit too soon in the development of their commitment. People need money, and they want to do well financially, but an obsessive focus on well-paying jobs can lead them astray, as the above quote may suggest. In our anecdotal experience, making money as a vocation is attractive and fits the talent of only a small minority of people. People need to excel in their work, because money usually is the result of other people wanting our service or product; the exceptions to this are very few.[15] People are unlikely to do well in any job that is inconsistent with their strengths and talents. Of course, some jobs do pay more, and it worthwhile for people to consider the financial and nonfinancial consequences of their job search options *after* they are clear of their strengths, their commitment, and the specific matters such as the number of hours, job security, off-site travel, and so on. The accompanying note provides detailed information on the public sector and useful Web links.[16]

Inevitably, commitments are personal, and the development of them is personal as well. Appendix C includes detailed and annotated examples. People have their own journey to take. Finally, whereas the above sections focus on commitment in the larger sense, it is obvious that people also need a commitment to their employer and others with whom they work. Commitments are surely needed to look after the interests of employers, and if we want support from others, we will do well to get along with and support them too. Many of these matters are discussed in Part 2, and there is no need to repeat specific social skills matters here. But it surely helps to add consideration for one's employer and colleagues as part of one's commitment.

Our commitments and contributions are an essential part of how others know us at work. Commitments are as varied as the people making them and are seen as an act of self-expression and self-leadership. Professional commitment statements are not about a specific job but rather about activities that include a range of possible jobs. Elements of a professional commitment statement include the following:

- an area (or line of business) in which people want to work;
- a range of activities or skills that people want to apply in this area, giving shape to a range of specific contributions that people would like to make;
- a pattern of prior experiences that shows development of these skills or commitment to this type of contribution;
- current job or other experiences that currently apply or further develop these skills;
- an indication of near-future involvements showing growth consistent with expected experiences, skill, and qualifications;

- standards or evaluation criteria pertaining to one's commitments and achievements; and
- ethics and professional norms or roles by which people are guided in their work activities.

Developing a professional commitment statement does not always come easy. It reflects what people like to do and are good at. Often people do well to talk with people in organizations about specific expectations and requirements that are needed for jobs or career paths in which one is interested. After developing and articulating a professional commitment statement, one can usefully further develop it by infusing it with a sense of professional standards and ethics. The fully developed professional commitment statement is useful in networking and developing one's career, which is the subject of the following chapters.

9

Interviewing and Networks

Nothing succeeds like the appearance of success.

—George S. Patton (1885–1945)

Interviewing and networking are essential to professional success. People in the same area of interest meet each other and exchange what they are interested in, what they are committed to, and what they are working on. Expressing one's professional interests and commitments is an important part of connecting with others and being invited for job interviews. People need to find appreciation for each other's commitments, and if they are to work together, they should be on common ground regarding their mutual interests and purposes. In addition, interviewing and networking also put a high premium on people skills. People need to demonstrate their ability to play a professional role well and do so with very good social skills.

This chapter focuses on interviewing but with a concern for networking too. In today's world, success in one leads to success in the other. The expression "It is not what you know but who you know" is commonly used to explain how people's networks help them get invited for a job interview and then to also be selected for the job. Interviewing and networking often go hand in hand; people in networks share news about opening opportunities and also help each other succeed. It is thought that when people are invited for an interview based solely on the strength of their résumé, they may have only a 20 to 30 percent chance of success of getting the job, but when people are known and supported by others, their chance increases to 60 to 90 percent. These experiences drive home the point that professional endeavors are not undertaken in isolation but also require collaboration, support, and acceptance from others.

Interviewing and networking share a strong common focus on connecting. Indeed, they are quintessential applications of getting along (Chapter 4) and connecting (Chapter 5), as well as the application of the professional commitment statements mentioned in the previous chapter. Commonality is found in what people can do and contribute to others, but these professional interests also need to be transformed into a relationship or at least the beginnings thereof. But interviewing and networking are also more than applications of these earlier concepts. The context of interviewing and network also invites additional concerns that extend these concepts.

For example, both interviewing and networking also focus on uncertainty and risk reduction. There is uncertainty in interviewing and networking about what people are saying (e.g., "Are they really as good as that? What exactly is their experience? Do they really know that person? How well?"). In interviewing, there also is uncertainty about how people will fit in with others once they are hired and how they will adapt to situations. For the interviewee, there is uncertainty about whether the organization will live up to its implied promises and image (e.g., "Are the people here really that friendly with each other all the time? Will they still support conference travel once I get hired?"). The consequences of making bad decisions can be very large (organizations have to live with people for many years and vice versa, and many employees have additional concerns for their family members), and thus a good part of the interviewing process is structured around reducing risk. Networks are central to that as well.

The experience of interviewing and networking also suggests that things other than professional qualities may matter. Sometimes people are looking only for a person who will get along and do the job without much fuss; they may not be looking for an outstanding person or one with career orientation. Very top positions often involve sensitive interests, and organizations may want someone who is controllable and dependable and who does not show much leadership initiative. Organizations may feel a need to give priority to balancing diversity and thus prefer a female or minority candidate (though in a few professions, such as nursing, that is a male). Some supervisors and coworkers are intimidated by excellence and do not want that. Interviewing and networking bring attention to a broader range of interests that come into play.

Competence is always important, but excellence may not be. People skills also matter in interviewing and networking. The formula is "competence plus," and the usual scenario is that people need to play up their flexibility, dependability, adaptability, pleasant personality, and support for diversity. Indeed, even highly talented people do well to have these qualities too.

Interviewing makes most people nervous. People often are uncertain about what will be asked and how to answer tricky and difficult questions. Almost everyone feels nervous before, during, or after interviews. A focal concern deals with questions that may be asked, and people want to put their best foot forward. Interviewees may be seeking a good or best answer that will make them be more accepted, or they may be concerned about having the "right goods." There seems to be much at stake and so much out of one's control. There is a good deal to get nervous about.

Let's examine some of these interview questions:

- "Tell me about yourself."
- "Why do you want to work here?"
- "Where do you see yourself in five years?"
- "What is your greatest weakness?"
- "Why did you leave your last job?"
- "What did you dislike about your last boss?"
- "You seem to have changed your goals a bit often."
- "Can I call your current boss?"
- "Are you married?"

- "Do you work on the weekend?"
- "How much money do you want?"

These might seem like simple questions, but it doesn't take much to appreciate why these make people nervous. Almost any answer leaves a person open to the criticism of others. For example, if people express a desire to go far in five years, they might be seen as too aggressive (and may be an inconsiderate or poor team player), but if they are not very aspiring, then they might be seen as not motivated or assertive enough. How is one to find the right "sweet spot"? Can that even be done?

Fortunately, recasting or positioning these questions in the context of one's professional commitment does much to take the edge off these questions and make them doable. Some can even be a breeze. The starting point is to put these questions in the context of one's professional commitment. That is often the basis for answering these questions. In the spirit that an example often clarifies the concept better than a long exposé, we provide the following, based on the example in Chapter 8 of the professional commitment statement for developing a mentoring program for disadvantaged and underprivileged young men. This is now used as a basis for answering the above questions:

"Tell me about yourself."
"I am very interested in serving disadvantaged and underprivileged young men."
"Why is that?"
"When I was a teenager, my mom raised me alone, and I was in a neighborhood where there were many disadvantaged and underprivileged children. Those who lacked support from their family, to help focus on the future, often did less well and sometimes ended up quite badly. I was lucky; my mother really helped."
"So how did you come to mentoring?"
"I came to the idea that guidance could or sometimes needs to be provided by others too. About five years ago, I got involved in a community support program and focused on giving guidance. In just a few months, we had some success cases. For example .... Do you want to hear more?"

"Why do you want to work here?"

"I think this organization can help me to further my experience and goals. I want more field experiences, for sure. And I also want to learn how to develop a program, or work in program management, and to bring resources to the community. I'd like to leverage my knowledge by getting others involved too. Beyond this, I think your organization has other activities going on, and I would like to explore whether any of my skills are helpful in those areas too."

"Where do you see yourself in five years?"

"I hope to develop my program skills and abilities further. In time, when appropriate, I'd like to do more. I'd like to, one day, be responsible for a program. That is my dream, but I don't know if that will be in exactly five years."

> Being clear about one's professional commitment makes these questions much easier to deal with.

"What is your greatest weakness?"

"I get very involved in what I do. People need to know what motivates them for public service, and this motivates me. I really want to succeed at this."

"Yes, but that sounds like a strength. What is really one of your weaknesses? You can tell me, we really want to know."

"Well, I get very involved, and sometimes I need to dial back. But I listen to others. I am also very mindful that others have motivations to do other things that lie in other areas and that these are also much needed."

"Why did you leave your last job?"

"It wasn't so suited for my career goals. I want to serve the disadvantaged and underprivileged or, more broadly, in community development activities. I also wanted program management skills."

"So, why did you take it?"

"It was very valuable for me. It taught me about … ."

"What did you dislike about your last boss?"

"My last boss was very helpful, and there is a lot I like about her. I would work for her again. I think it is important to note that we all have weaknesses and our own style of doing things. What makes for a good colleague is someone who knows what these are and who is able to deal with differences without these getting in the way. We all need to adjust a little. My last boss had a style of closing her door, so we addressed the need for people to access her too. So we agreed that between 3:00 and 5:00 her door would be open, and that solved the problem for everyone."

"You seem to have changed your goals a bit often."

"About seven years ago I thought I wanted to go into computers and ITC, but I realized that was not my strength. As it happens, there are now quite some applications and use of ITC in what I want to do. For example … . I also learned about dealing with deadlines. I now consider IT as secondary assets that I have, and it is very beneficial and valuable. For example … ."

"Can I call your current boss?"

"I'd rather not at this time, until you are ready to make an offer. Loyalty is very important, and this could be wrongly interpreted. I am quite happy in my current job, and I want to keep it that way, of course. But I did give you some other references. When and if all is done, you can surely call my boss, but I want to know first, and the timing is important. I am sure you can imagine."

"Are you married?"

"Marriage is important, especially for raising children. I am not currently married, but perhaps one day. I also think that diversity is very important, and people are free to make up their own mind, of course. Warren Buffet once said, 'It's very important to live your life by an internal yardstick.' Well, people have their own views on personal matters, and in any event these views must not interfere with one's work. Tolerance and professionalism are important values for me, and I hope for others here too."

"Do you work on the weekend?"

"Sometimes, when needed. People need a balanced life, but sometimes things happen. We need to be available for emergencies, of course."

"What if there was a need almost every weekend?"

"It is important to be flexible. Well, perhaps I could take off some other day then. We all have errands to run, for example. As I said before, I am very committed in my work and get involved in what I do, but no one works seven days a week, every week, of course. *Does that happen often around here?"* "No, seldom in fact. We just wanted to see how you would answer this question or deal with such a situation."

"How much money do you want?"

"I want the going rate. Of course, no one takes a job for less money, and my current salary is … with additional benefits that are important to me. I think it is too soon to talk about money, but I imagine that any job would offer a raise from my current salary and be competitive, of course. Do you yet know how much you have in mind to offer? Thanks for telling me that. Well, it is too soon to talk about such things now, but I am willing to talk about money when appropriate, of course."

This dialog is a complete example of how to address the above questions. Being clear about one's professional commitment makes these questions much easier to deal with; it is the basis. Yet the above shows that one should pay attention to the context of the situation, play up flexibility and reasonableness in the process, and emphasize answers that show one's propensity to get along and use a bit of diplomacy where needed. The formula is "professional commitment statement plus."

The above dialog also shows a few different matters. People vary in their commitment and experiences, of course, but knowing how one's past leads up to the present and the future is key. Though the substance varies, the application is the same. Someone who applies for a job as a senior budget analyst will find it similarly easy to apply his or her professional commitment in the same way. For example,

> *"Tell me about yourself."*
>> "I am very interested in budgeting, budget analysis, and help-ing organizations make and implement good decisions."
> *"Why?"*
>> "I have a knack for numbers, and I strongly believe in public service and its purpose, so doing this in the public sec-tor makes so much sense to me. So about ten years ago, I took a job as a junior budget analyst and really enjoyed it. For example … ."

These examples also show how personal experiences and values are readily integrated and added to strengthen one's answers. These do not detract from one's being professional or are not inappropri-ate, but the task is to show how they are related to one's professional commitment. Thus the budget analyst will undoubtedly add at some appropriate point that he or she strongly believes in accountabil-ity and transparency. Personal experiences are relevant, providing insight into the motivation for professional decisions that provide depth and continuity. They give the reasons for why people are inter-ested in what they are, as well as insight into the strength of their purpose. It helps explain why a person is likely to stay committed to that which they express.

Some readers may be concerned about our having included the question about being married. This is clearly a personal matter that is not job related and that (99 percent of the time) in the United States would be considered inappropriate and illegal. All human resources management textbooks, our own textbook included, instruct inter-viewers to not ask questions about race, religion, personal situations, and gender; all questions should be job-related. However, as a practi-cal matter, the questionable illegality of such questions does not stop people from asking them. How we deal with these questions and situations is key and a good opportunity for practicing diplomacy (Chapter 4). There is no need for professing indignation or getting hostile when asked whether we are married or single. These questions, by design or accident, test one's ability for being skilled in dealing with difficult and awkward situations—the workplace brings up ample situations that are even more unpleasant. Answers that are factual, non-defensive and which bring the discussion to a work-related aspect are usually appropriate and acceptable. Later, you can decide whether you still want to work there. We do not recommend asking illegal questions. The above example relates the question back to diversity in general, and it shows "getting along" by avoiding hot button topics. Most people in the U.S. find marriage an important institution, and the job interview is not the setting to take issue with that.

Interview questions may also include situational questions through which interviewees demonstrate their thinking processes and judgment. A typical question is "Say a coworker tells you that he submitted phony expense account receipts. Do you tell your boss?" Answering such a question requires people to have the ability to relate the question back to work-related processes. People often handle such questions by giving both content and process parts. Even if the answer does not fully come together (there are 1,001 variations on this question, and no one can be prepared for all), at least some general true position can be given. An answer is sure to include that it is wrong to break the law or policy and also wrong to take the law into one's own hand. It is also important to be sure of the facts first ("Did this really happen? What exactly happened?"). One might also assume that the organization has a way of dealing with such situations (it might have happened before). It is important to hear from the person first, and many organizations might give the person an opportunity to correct such issues on his or her own accord first.

It is well-known that quite some people exaggerate and inflate their résumé a bit. People also do that in job interviews. Interviews involve résumés, which should be short but complete, be very professional looking, and have easy to find information.[1] Well, people want to put their best foot forward, of course, and the quote at the start of this chapter talks about the appearance of success. Are we really as pleasant, nice, professional, and flexible as we portray in interviews? The saying "When you go in for a job interview, I think a good thing to ask is if they ever press charges,"[2] gets to the point of exaggerations and omissions being made in interviews. There is always doubt, and the purpose of background references is to get confirmation. But lying crosses the mark. Claims to accomplishments that were not done might sound too good to be true, cast doubt and uncertainty, and not be supported by background references or adequate detail in interviews. People have been terminated because they lied on their résumé or in interviews.

In our experience, there is no substitute for the real deal of having qualifications, a record of relevant experience, and good commitment (Chapter 8) as the basis for addressing interview questions. Those who meet these qualifications do not need to exaggerate their résumé or make omissions. Indeed, having a professional commitment plus the substance and a sense of diplomacy makes dealing with interview questions much easier.[3]

To continue a bit further, interviewing success requires more than answering questions. There is a role to be played too. A job interview puts candidates in a situation in which they are expected to show how they would act or reason if they were hired. People are asked to step into the role, and they are assessed by others for their ability to play such roles. Seeing is believing. Thus, professors are asked to teach, and budget analysts are asked to show their budgeting skills, for example. Résumés and background references are not enough. If people can't act the role during the interview, then when will they? Uncertainty and risk reduction are everywhere in the interviewing process.

Why do people get dressed up for job interviews?

Everyone knows that grooming matters, and conservative and appropriate grooming is a starting point in interviews. What is exactly appropriate depends on the setting, and some settings are far more casual than others these days. Still there are limits and expectations. Men should wear ties, and women should wear nonrevealing clothes. Both should go to the hairdresser or barber. Men do well to buy a new shirt that looks crisp and to polish their shoes. Details matter in every business, and this is just one way of showing that. If you can't afford to look the part, well, others will and are thus more likely to be selected. But this point is not always fully appreciated. Consider this:

> Why should I take out my earring below my lip? It is part of who I am. I should be judged on my abilities, not appearance. I am German, and all German political parties have diversity and tolerance in their platform. I am applying for a job with the German Ministry of Foreign Affairs. I don't think people in Europe are as conservative as those in the U.S. The earring is part of who I am.[4]

There may be times when in the German Ministry of Foreign Affairs it is probably fine to wear an earring below one's lip, but there are likely also events when doing so is not OK, causing a poor perception of decorum among German civil service staff. Risk aversion is everywhere. It is hard to know what makes a poor first impression in the mind of others, and so avoiding risk is the first course of action. People need to show that they understand the role and are willing and able to play it. It would also be expected on the job too. (The earring goes out.)[5]

The Internet is full of stories of poor interview conduct that was used as reasons for not offering someone a job:[6]

"He asked me to speed up the interview because he had another meeting."
"She kept telling me about her personal problems."
"The candidate kept looking around the room."
"The woman answered her cell phone twice during the interview."
"One guy ate a sandwich."
"The candidate used profanity when describing something negative about a previous boss."
"A woman came in with open-toe shoes and a slit on her dress up to her backside."

"He showed up in jeans and a T-shirt."

"He had dirty fingernails."

These behaviors are inconsistent with professionalism, social etiquette (Chapter 2), and risk-averse conduct. In addition, other problems are mentioned, such as not providing evidence of the degrees or skills listed on one's résumé. Though the above cases most likely involve entry-level positions, those in senior positions show other problems that similarly reflect poorly on their ability to play the role:

- "She had not attended any professional conferences in over three years."
- "He seemed offended when we asked him to show his skills."
- "The council person thought he made a joke in poor taste."
- "One of the references, who is very well-known the field, couldn't remember much about her."
- "During lunch, he had three glasses of wine."
- "It was a quite a résumé, but many people felt awkward around him. Some said he was creepy."
- "The candidate wasn't aware of basic changes in law."
- "I have seldom heard someone so eloquent, but after two hours I still didn't have the answers I needed."
- "The candidate made a comment about race. We have a zero-tolerance policy for that here."
- "The candidate asked how much we were paying before we were ready to offer the job."

It is essential to play a professional role.

The point is clear. We need to play the part in a professional and very risk-averse way. People are often willing to put up with some less than stellar role-playing from a candidate that they want to hire, but it is essential to be professional and to be able to play that role.[7]

While the text above deals with some frequent "no-nos," the previously mentioned tips in Chapters 4 and 5 apply here as well for getting along and connecting with others. Getting along requires that people give information that helps others make a decision. They should have a pleasant personality, not bring trouble, avoid hot button topics ("Let's avoid talking about politics."), deal with difficult questions and situations with grace and tact, and go lightly with excellence (remember, most people want only competence). The list of items in Chapter 4 seems perhaps long, but it surely deals with such issues as the following:

- Practicing active listening skills
- Letting others sit down first
- Remembering to smile
- Not interrupting others
- Making the interview a pleasurable experience for all
- Being sure to give others the information they are seeking
- Not asking or probing into sensitive matters
- Not talking about money or reimbursement unless asked to do so
- Being self-assured but not overassertive (or "cocky")
- Being competent but not a "show off"

These are useful pointers to remember, because every interaction has potential for raising difficult matters. There is danger around every corner, in every interaction. They are some "fine line" issues, such as the latter two points. We can give hints of what else we can do and how we can help, but if others don't seem interested, then there is little need to go there. Interviewees should help make the interview a pleasurable event for all, but this is not a time to tell jokes. There is much to be enjoyed in sharing one's commitment and exploring and identifying common interests and common passions. We need to show that we can be pleasant, competent, and get along. People with little experience in interviewing or their industry do well to ask those with more experience what is expected. It helps to have a chance to role-play a bit. Practice makes perfect.

Connecting is the ultimate purpose. It is likely that during an interview, people find common interests and perhaps even comparable past experiences. People can show that they understand and support others in their interests and be quite specific about how they would support or work with others if the opportunity presented itself. People may even find common hobbies ("What do you do for fun?") and similar pasts and commitments. Some people may already know these things about you, but not all people do. Hence, to the above we add the following:

- Find common professional interests and commitments
- Demonstrate competence and professional values
- Support and appreciate others' interests
- Find common personal interests

These final points may be the keys to getting the job offer. The previous points are all about risk reduction, but getting the job requires that people find commonality, value, and support too.[8]

There is much to be gained from understanding that the interviewing process is an impossible job for which interviewers, too, are inadequately prepared. Doing so provides a few additional ways for one to exhibit good people skills. These days, most managers must do their own hiring with little support from the HR office. Interviewing managers and staff may have only a handful of past experiences in hiring others. Interviewers seldom receive training in hiring; organizational training is usually about completing forms and avoiding complications that come from treating people unfairly. Some people do try to be systematic in their interviewing efforts (e.g., asking all candidates the same questions to facilitate comparison later), but there is a lot that often is haphazard. Beyond this, many managers and employees are very busy. For them, this is yet another task or chore they need to do, and it is one that takes a good deal of time away from immediate priorities. Interviewers know that interviewing is important, but those being interviewed do well not to assume a greater level of skill and thoughtfulness in interviewing than may exist.

A very large gap exists between what is readily known and verified of others (such as degrees, years of experience, and some achievements) and that which people ideally would like to know before hiring someone:

- whether the person has the qualifications and basic (technical, people, other) skills and knowledge for the job (How do you know?);
- whether the person has the ability to quickly pick up the new skills and knowledge that are needed (How do you know?);
- whether the person deals well with new or difficult situations in a professional and collegial way (How do you know?);
- whether the person is honest and knows right from wrong (How do you know?);
- whether the person has a pleasant, easygoing personality and is well liked by others (How do you know?);
- whether the person works well with others, and if the job involves supervising others, whether the person is good at motivating others as well as dealing with discipline (How do you know?); and
- whether the person has self-leadership and is well organized (How do you know?).

Interviews can go only so far. Whatever a candidate says or shows, the interview cannot hope to satisfactorily answer the important question of whether the excellent answers and skills shown during a job interview are anything more than a well-orchestrated act. People have had the experience of finding smooth-talking people being stubborn and inflexible once hired. Part 4 deals in great detail with personality problems that explain the fundamental unreliability or insufficiency of interviewing. (Then why interview? Well, interviewing does give more information about candidates, especially their ability to fail in the before-mentioned ways. This is why interviews often involve more than one person; we need an interviewee who does not fail. Interviewing also brings new people to the organization.)

It is difficult to hire someone without satisfactorily addressing the above questions as well. Interviewing may be necessary, but it is insufficient. Answers must come from others who know us well, especially those who interacted with us in previous jobs involving these matters. Reference interviews are one of the most poorly executed arts of interviewing.[9] Interviewers sometimes get enamored with a candidate and then don't want to hear anything that is negative—they want to confirm only. This is even more so when other interviewers also feel this way. People often already have made up their mind about whom they want to hire, and they are loath to detect negative information about them. People also wrongly believe that interviews with references are futile, because they are hesitant to say negative things or give only short answers. That need not be the case. Answers are a function of the questions asked, and people do well to pose questions in ways that invite more than a "yes" or "no" response. Consider the following question and response from Steve Ballmer, CEO of Microsoft:[10]

Q. How do you assess job candidates?

A. If they come from inside the business, the best predictor of future success is past success. It's not 100 percent, but it's a reasonable predictor. For an external candidate, what I've found is that reference checks are super-important. I didn't used to believe so much in reference checks. You can always get somebody to say something nice about you. But the truth is, if you ask enough questions and you ask around, you can really get a profile of who's accomplished various things and who hasn't.[11]

A complete discussion of human resources management interviewing techniques is beyond the scope of this book, but we can give some examples. For example, instead of asking, "Did he or she get along well with coworkers?"[12] we might ask, "On a scale of one to ten, how well did he or she get along with coworkers?" Then, "Can you give some examples of why you give only a six and not an eight or nine? Was it a behavior or personality matter? Or a competency or job performance issue? What did others often say?" and in this way get more specific information. Another question is "The job for which the candidate is applying requires judgment about ... . Would you have trusted the candidate doing so?" and then get into a discussion with examples about the strengths and weaknesses of the candidate. Or, "Can the person be trusted to pick up or entertain an important client or elected official?" A question to close a reference interview is "Would you hire this person again?" and then "Why or why not?" Reference interviews are an essential ingredient of the interview process indeed.[13]

The need to talk with those who have worked with someone is demonstrated by the extreme case of Major Hasan, an army psychiatrist, who after facing deployment to one of America's war zones killed thirteen people and wounded thirty others in 2009 in a shooting rampage at Fort Hood, Texas. Previous coworkers and even some supervisors had long raised questions and flags about Major Hasan's e-mail, behavior, criticism of the military, loyalty to Muslim fundamentalism, and state of mind under stress. Yet the system failed, and U.S. Defense Secretary Gates noted "that troubling information about individuals is often withheld or filed discreetly away instead of being shared." Successive supervisors kicked the problem of Major Hasan to the next command for reasons of expediency. The postincident review committee recommended that several officers be referred for possible punishment for not properly supervising Major Hasan.[14] The morale is that it pays to double check and not rely on formal assessments and résumés. People who had worked with Hasan had long made their assessment of him, and they could have been spoken with.[15] The case of Hasan is extreme only for its consequences, not about the need for reference interviewing.

Yet even with background interviews and reference checks, residual doubts are apt to remain. It is at this point that internal support becomes even more important. it is thought that when people are invited for an interview based solely on the strength of their résumé, they may have only a 20 to 30 percent chance of success, but when people are known and supported by others, their chance increases to 60 to 90 percent. It is essential that at some point someone inside the organization be willing to support or even vouch for the candidate: "Yes, I know Mary, and so do others in the field. Everyone says that Mary is an excellent professional who gets along well with others. The interviewing confirms that she has the skills that we need." The network of one's acquaintances, including past coworkers and bosses, is essential for putting to rest doubt about someone who is unknown. It allows others to be an advocate for the candidate and thereby put his or her credibility on the line. That credibility through others is not enough to get a job, but it often is the necessary and missing ingredient. (Beyond this, another way of dealing with uncertainty is through probationary and short-term contracts. These allow employers to mitigate employees who do not work out. This is discussed in the next chapter.)

Being aware of these limitations and processes provides an opportunity for job seekers. First, interviewees can volunteer information that may help them deal with some of the above questions. It may not be enough to just answer questions, because what was not asked can be a barrier to decision making later. Second, they can ask at the end of interviews whether interviewers have gotten all the information that they sought or that is on their mental checklist and offer to be available if something comes to mind later. Third, job seekers can be helpful by ensuring that references are easy to reach. Instead of giving just three names, they can give six, and they can give permission for people to call their past employers and coworkers. When possible, they should be sure to include names of people who are known or respected by those doing the interview.

Interviewing is a difficult, nearly impossible, and time-consuming job. Candidates do well to help interviewers do their job by ensuring they get the information and credibility for the candidates that are needed.

Networking is about getting to know people in the same area or line of work. Networks include people in the same skill area (e.g., information technology, budgeting, or environmental law professionals), industry (e.g., hospitals, local government, or social service agencies), or geographic area (e.g., local chapters and statewide or national associations). People in these areas often help each other, such as by keeping each other abreast of latest developments and professional opportunities. Though associations often have electronic newsletters, people who are active often meet each other face-to-face and find ways to exchange more and connect with them, in ways discussed above. As the quote at the beginning of Chapter 8 reminds, 80 percent of success is showing up. People make friends.

It is thought that seasoned professionals with seven years or more of experience belong to a few different associations and often know two hundred or three hundred people in this way. Some people are known very well, and others are known well enough to send an e-mail or make a call when needed. People cultivate these networks by going to meetings. The first time people go to meetings of professional associations, they may know no one, but those who show up five times know half the crowd. People also send e-mail to others from time to time, sharing news or reports about what their office did and what may be relevant. They also send out vacancy announcements. Being part of professional networks increases security and information. Commitment and persistence pay off.

Not all professional contacts and networks are equal. Some people are in a position to be more helpful than others, and some people are more helpful. The concept of a winning network is one that includes people who are willing and able to support others in their professional development and advancement. People are lucky to have one or two senior professionals in their corner. People cultivate these relations over a few years, such as by working on their projects and supporting them in other ways. Professional associations often include committees on which people volunteer and that lead to interactions with a small but motivated set of people. Many professional association committees are understaffed, and so any motivated person is much appreciated. Those who do good work are often noticed by others in the organization, such as chapter or national association presidents and officers. Those who know others in this way are often willing to say nice things about them. They make excellent references, and some have very impressive titles and connections indeed. (For interviewers, candidates who know such people show clear commitment and sustained purpose.)

Winning networks also include former classmates, from high school, college, and graduate school. You never know where people end up, and having a longtime association with others can be a source of both pleasure and valuable introductions. These people need not be in the same field as oneself, but they may have valuable contacts who can make a difference. Someone might have become an engineer who has contacts with the local government building department director, who happens to be looking for an urban planner; likewise, those in professional associations who at first may not seem relevant to one's interests may yet be so one day. Most people have had the experience of getting jobs in quite unexpected ways.

A supportive network is a valuable asset. These days, many people spend a good deal of their own money to attend conferences, and it is therefore especially valuable to get as much benefit as possible from conference attendance. "To dos" include the following:

- Learning from presentations and participation in ways that benefit one's job
- Exchanging business cards for later use
- Sharing personal experiences and interests that may create commonalties
- Helping on association committees as a way to interact with others
- Following up on and soliciting e-mail exchanges between meetings
- Asking for help or introductions when needed

Sometimes new people are a bit too shy to introduce themselves. It is not enough to only go to the meeting and listen to presentations. Being shy is a handicap that must be overcome. If others don't know us, then insufficient benefit has been realized. It is important to step forward and introduce oneself. Sometimes people attend from the same organization, but sticking together in such a way also reduces opportunities to meet new people. Sometimes it is best to split up and reconnect later.

After meetings, it is important to follow up and keep the contact going. People send others news of their organization, such as reports, articles, or notices of relevant upcoming events. These can be sent through a LISTSERV of associations and to people with whom business cards were exchanged. By participating in electronic networks in this way, people often make valuable connections in the course of the year.

In our work with professional-degree students, we help them build and expand their network. Many want a boost to their career but are unclear about what is needed to get the next job. As is typical, no material exists about their specific next job; rather, they must ask either those who are in such jobs or those who hire those people. These people are identified through their current acquaintances or friends or simply through cold calls.[16] Students identify four people for conducting exploratory interviews. The following questions are used: What kinds of jobs are available? What are the ideal qualifications and experiences for the job? What specific skills are desired? What experiences are valued? How can you best get those jobs? What advice does the interviewee offer for someone like yourself who is pursuing your career? These are general questions, and students often add additional questions that are specific to their field or interest. These are only for starting conversations; short responses are to be avoided. Prior to this, students develop a professional commitment statement that has been refined over a four- to six-week period.

The experience is typically extremely positive, leading to specific information about what others are looking for in their ideal candidates. Interviewees often ask how students came to their interests, and answers often lead to finding common interests or backgrounds. Students also get leads to others to interview. The exercise has been done in the United States and in some Asian countries. The following is a rather typical assessment of this exercise:

> I probably should have begun networking like this several months ago. Making these contacts forced me out of my "comfort zone" and make valuable contacts. On the whole, I was very surprised at how receptive everyone was and how they all seemed quite willing to offer advice, assistance, and career guidance. Scheduling the interviews was surprisingly easy, as everyone was willing to meet with me only one or two days after I first contacted them. During the interviews themselves, everyone spent an incredibly generous amount of time with me, ranging from forty-five minutes to over an hour and a half. Doing this assignment has tremendously decreased my anxiety and given me greater overall confidence about my career goals.

Many people state that they gain access to senior people they did not expect to meet. "I met a VP of development here in town, and she told me how she got into that position. I also learned about how important the professional association had been to her advancement and learning of the field." The interview is used as a conversation. Usually connections are made, but it is common to have an interview that does not result in this. In addition, although the interviews are only about the above questions about professional development, about 15 to 20 percent of students report getting a new job or internship offered within four months of these interviews. The person whom they interviewed works in an office that happened to have an opening, and in a few cases jobs are created for the people who interviewed. It is rare, but very positive, to have others call them in this way, and this is remembered. Imagine if people conducted ten such interviews.

Networking works.

Interviewing and networking are part of the professional experience and quintessential applications of expressing one's professional commitment, as well as applying the information from the previous chapters on getting along and connecting to these situations. Though interviewing makes most people nervous, the examples show how being clear about one's professional commitment helps position the questions as an opportunity for expressing it, while also showing consideration for other aspects that interviewers are likely interested in. These aspects include being flexible, pleasant, and understanding; supporting the interests of others; being competent; and supporting diversity. This chapter also shows that interviewing is quite difficult and that interviewees do well to ensure that interviewers get the information they likely need to make a decision. Networking matters and is usually key to improving the odds of getting a job offer. People increase their networks by joining professional associations and participating in them, and doing so increases access to people who help and support them. Networking and interviewing often go together, and those who network will find the missing link to getting good jobs.

10

Expectations

We make a living by what we get, we make a life by what we give.

—Winston Churchill[1]

Navigating the first few months on the job is often a journey about moving from initial hopes to the reality and understanding of real possibilities and constraints. It is a time of getting to know others and how the office works. It is about getting to know others' expectations of themselves and their work and discussing how their expectations may affect us; it is also a time for articulating our expectations and professional commitments to others and discussing them. It is a time of aligning oneself with the working styles of others and of dealing with expectations for fitting in. Indeed there is much to discuss with others in the first few months.

Yet the need for communication about expectations continues well beyond these first few months. Circumstances change, and people want to discuss how these changes affect them. New opportunities come up. As one set of goals is reached, new ones are articulated. People come and go, and new people have different ways of working. The job situation requires that people communicate what is working, what is not working, and whether the current situation is consistent with what they would like to achieve. Communication cannot solve all problems, but professionals recognize the need for it. We cannot assume that others know our interests, and we do well to assume that we do not fully know the needs and expectations of others too. The days of managing by biannual feedback are over.

This chapter discusses practical approaches to shaping and managing expectations at work. It provides both a general approach and a specific model to further performance and realize one's professional goals. A psychological contract is defined, generally, as an understanding between an employee and his or her immediate superior with the purpose of increasing role clarity and commitment.[2] Despite the name, this is not a written contract but an informal mutual understanding that many people find intuitive and easy to use. Informal understandings have always been part of how people deal with the above matters. Formal contracts and policies seldom stipulate in detail what work is to be done, how that work is to be done, and how that will likely further one's professional commitments and career. In our experience, people report very good success using the approaches described here, and other approaches to communication are also noted.

A long and distinguished history exists of calls for increased workplace communication in the management literature. In the 1930s, people like Mary Parker Follett noted that respect and communication are essential to how we interact with each other at work. In the 1950s, "Theory Y" suggested that people have a need for realization and that many people are not content with just following orders. In the 1970s, management thinkers noted the need for making the undiscussable discussable, so that people can better deal with what comes up at work. In the 1990s, empowerment requires that people do more and make more decisions, hence requiring increased communication. Today, during the 2010s, young people want to feel good at work and have work that furthers their career, hence requiring communication about expectations. The call for more communication is a persistent one.

Yet not everyone welcomes increased communication, and some people do not see the need for it. In dealing with communication and these challenges, this chapter extends previous chapters on social skills. Getting alignment about one's professional goals requires mutual understanding that is a two-way street; to get one's point across requires good listening too. Getting support requires giving support and hence being attuned to the interests and concerns of oth-

> **A psychological contract is defined as an understanding between an employee and his or her superior.**

ers. Those who want support and change will often find it necessary to also give support and deal effectively with some common communication barriers.

People have all kinds of things that they may wish to talk about concerning their expectations and work experience. Some people want to talk about work processes, quality standards, workloads, interactions with others, work schedules, and responsibilities. Some want to talk about communication and work styles, as well as interpersonal relations among people. People often get conflicting messages and want some clarity. Others have a need for clarifying expectations regarding performance, performance evaluation, career development, and possible rewards. Some may also have expectations about training, conference attendance, desirable assignments, challenging growth opportunities, and so on, all of which are related to career development as well. The things that may be on people's minds can cover a broad territory indeed and occur during the first few months of any new job and continue thereafter.

Communication processes need to be open to people's bringing up these matters, and communication processes that do so can bring many benefits for workers and their organizations. Getting along requires that people do their job well, timely, and reliably, and many of the above elements are related to increased performance. Communication about mutual expectations can also help parties appreciate each other's constraints and reduce expectations in areas where they are unlikely to be satisfied. Understanding what workers want from their jobs also helps; though not all desires can be met, managers may have other opportunities, often unbeknownst to employees, that provide workers with opportunities for having interesting work experiences that further their professional commitments and job skills. Some meaningful things for workers are of little consequence for organizations and easy for them to give. Communication that is focused on clarification and opportunity can lead to many benefits and win-win situations.

People have their own interests and commitments, of course, and effective communication about expectations requires thinking from the perspective of others. The purpose of such communication is to increase alignment between oneself and the organization and others. Arguments are to be made that are persuasive to the interests of others, going beyond one's own interest. Benefits to others and the organization are to be highlighted and emphasized. Costs to others of inaction are also relevant. Yet people do well not to assume knowing what others' interests are. The duties of the office do not always drive the needs or interests of others. Others may have a different priority regarding professional goals or ethics. People have their own commitments, and communication requires a two-way process that includes exploration and definition of others' interests and goals.

As defined previously, a psychological contract is defined, generally, as an understanding between an employee and his or her immediate superior. Figure 10.1 makes a schematic depiction and expresses the notion of balance. There is a giving and a getting by two people, and the process is of two people discussing and agreeing on what each is to give and get. Psychological contract processes are

Psychological Contract		
	Expect to Get	**Expect to Give**
Worker		
Supervisor/Others		

Figure 10.1 Psychological contract. Adapted from Osland, J., Kolb, D., and Rubin, I., *Organizational Behavior: An Experiential Approach*, 8th ed. (New York: Prentice Hall, 2006).

probably easiest to initiate by workers within the first few weeks or months on the job, when things are still new, though they also can be used later.

This simple notion includes a few tactics that help people reach alignment and agreement. First, parties are not obliged to accept on face value what others would like to get or what they are complaining about. People may want all kinds of things, but others are not obliged to entertain unreasonable propositions or requests. Someone who wants to come to work when he or she wants to does not have a reasonable expectation, and the job of the manager is to explain that. Someone who wants a promotion but whose performance does not merit it is not asking for something that can be entertained. In organizational life, it often is quite useful and necessary to have these conversations about what is reasonable. Evaluating what people articulate is itself a major element of the psychological contract and an opportunity to articulate professional interests and norms.

Second, people may offer substitutes for what people ask or bring up. Managers do not need to support what cannot be given. Travel support for conference attendance may not be available, but there may be other ways of helping acquire knowledge such as tuition reimbursement. Promotions may not be available, but opportunities to be more competitive are. Beyond this, alternatives can include reciprocal requests. Someone who wants flextime might be asked to pitch in during extremely busy times in the office—flextime can cut both ways. Those who want others to address them in a friendlier manner might be asked by others to clean up their work space more often. These two activities have little in common, other than that they improve outcomes for other people. Being helpful and going beyond curt answers allow people to show an earnest commitment to others and their contributions.

Third, the understanding is not a legal contract, which, for some people, raises questions of enforceability and purpose. Why bother with something that others can simply ignore later? Accountability is what it has always been, namely, something that is sometimes of an informal nature. People who fail to support others are themselves, in turn, not supported. People who fail to deliver eventually suffer the consequences of being passed over for promotion, getting fewer desirable assignments, and so on. Managers who do not take good care of their workers will find their best workers searching for other opportunities. There have always been decidedly real consequences to soft skills. Work life is more than a legal contract.

Consider for example the employee with the professional commitment to work with disadvantaged and underprivileged youths. The situation may arise that after being hired he is asked to help others on a variety of community-related projects, none of which deal with the motivation of the professional commitment articulated in the job interview. It happens. After a few weeks, the new employee is concerned about where this is going to go.

The worker goes to his supervisor's secretary and schedules thirty minutes to evaluate progress thus far. The new employee expresses to the supervisor how happy he is to have been hired and he really looks forward to the future. However, the work thus far does not seem to have much direct relationship to his interest. The supervisor, a bit surprised, explains that it was not his intention to cause this concern for the new employee. There are some important projects occurring in these weeks, and the office thought it would be useful for the employee to get some general exposure to people and projects. Also, there are plans to increase outreach efforts to disadvantaged and underprivileged youths in about two months. The supervisor acknowledges that these plans have not yet been fully thought through or discussed with the new employee.

The new employee is happy with this news but also puzzled why the supervisor did not communicate any of this before. Will this be the communication pattern? The employee expresses that he would much like to be involved in any planning. Following up, the new employee and supervisor discuss communication patterns and how the new employee will know what is going on in the future. The supervisor agrees to do a better job keeping the new employee informed. To show this, the supervisor invites the employee to a staff meeting about this in about ten days. The lesson is ask, and you just might get something.

This example shows the merit of not letting things go or pass on without comment. For example, the new employee could have decided to say nothing, thus avoiding making waves (and thus better fitting in). Yet doing so would have left an impression on others that the person might not be someone who takes initiative or someone who is as fully committed to the professional pursuits mentioned in the job interview.

A few months later, the supervisor goes to the employee and notes that it has been some time since they last spoke about the employee's performance and general satisfaction and where some room might be for improvement or adjustment. When meeting, the employee states to be generally happy but a bit disappointed that the outreach efforts to disadvantaged and underprivileged populations did not target youth as much as he had hoped. There was little funding and support for doing this kind of project. Beyond this, there are also some conferences that the new employee would like to attend, and he would like to ask to be more involved in program management in order to continue making progress on their professional commitment.

The manager acknowledges this situation. Funding is very tight this budget year, and resources are not much available. However, the supervisor notes that the new employee has made many important contributions, which he lists. Recognizing the new employee's professional interest, the manager inquires whether the employee would like to be part of the new grant-writing efforts, which would help the employee with program management skills. The experience could also be used for getting grant money for working with disadvantaged and underprivileged youths, including networking with relevant funding agencies. However, the supervisor makes the new employees acknowledge that this is no promise of success here.

In addition, while the manager is happy to help out, he lets the new employee know that some people in the community were taken aback by some comments he made. There is a need to be a bit more diplomatic. Things that can be said in the office cannot always be said in the same way in public. The matter came to the attention of the city manager by a council person. Hence, for the next month, the employee is asked to keep quiet and a very low profile in the community, and any comments that are made should first be run by the supervisor. The new employee is visibly upset—it was not what he

3

had expected to hear. The supervisor also asks the new employee to help out with another program that is unrelated to disadvantaged youth. Work life is a mixed bag, but the process of communication allowed both parties to get more of what they want and thus improve their situations. It is a win-win improvement over the status quo.

As a second example, we show how the psychological model is used in class settings, showing a group process application. On the first day of class, after reading the syllabus and addressing general questions, the professor asks the students what they would like to get from the class. A column titled "Expect to Get" is put on the board. Some typical answers are "getting an A," "learning practical applications," "having interesting discussions," and "no surprises on exams," for example. These requests help the professor understand class interests, as well as clarify to students what is possible given the nature of the class. For example, "getting an A" is possible, and the professor clarifies what students will likely need to do to get that. "Having interesting discussions" will also happen, but the class is not only about talking—there is serious lecturing to be done too, which is efficient for learning the subject. Thus, matters are clarified and professional norms and purposes are articulated, only that which is acceptable is put on the board.[3]

Next, the professor asks the group, "What is needed for you to get what you want?" A column titled "Expect to Give" is put on the board. Typical answers are "doing homework," "coming to class," "studying for exams," "sharing experiences," and so on. The professor also quantifies how many hours students should expect to study every week. The entire group discussion takes about twenty-five minutes, plus about twenty minutes for going over the syllabus (which precedes this discussion). Beyond this, the two columns are copied and distributed to each of the students. About three to four weeks later, the professor follows up and asks how he is doing according to the psychological contracts and whether any changes are needed. Needless to say, the group psychological contract strongly contributes to high class motivation.

The latter example also shows the importance of follow-up. Trust is earned through actions, and people do well to follow up a few days or weeks later, reiterating key points. Perhaps the other person had some additional thoughts to add. A psychological contract is continually used and updated, usually over a three- to twelve-month period. During this period, people periodically return to the contract to discuss changed conditions or unforeseen barriers. All of this provides opportunity for rearticulating one's professional commitment. Contracts are usually redone once circumstances have changed to such an extent as to require the development of a new psychological understanding. Appendix D shows a sample psychological contract that is quite detailed.

The psychological contract is consistent with many theories of motivation. Path–goal theory, for example, states that people are motivated to pursue goals that they value, understand the path for achieving the goals they perceive as feasible, believe that they have adequate resources and means for doing so, and perceive the costs and risks of pursuing their goals as consistent with the anticipated benefits and payoffs. Psychological contracts further such motivation by clarifying the goals and resources, substituting infeasible goals for more feasible or desirable ones, and providing opportunity for addressing whatever barriers employees may perceive.

These ideas are not new, but they surely are not always well executed at work. Odiorne discusses the backbone of Management by Objectives (MBO) in state government.[4] He identifies five main tenets:

1. "Tell Me What's Expected of Me in Advance."
2. "Give Me the Resources to Do the Job."
3. "Leave Me Alone as Much as Possible to Do My Job."
4. "Let Me Know How Well I Am Doing in My Work."
5. "Reward My Accomplishments."

Few people would disagree with these principles. MBO can be regarded as a forerunner that has found expression in psychological contracts and other modern management practices. Interesting, the article was written a long time ago, in 1976. It still sounds relevant and fresh. Psychological contracts still provide a process for workers to articulate these matters, reduce uncertainty, and find accommodation with their superiors and organizations. Everyone needs to know with some certainty what is expected of them, and many professionals want to ensure that these expectations are aligned with their professional interests and goals. The psychological contract provides a process for doing so. It also provides for a discussion about overcoming barriers and for dealing with them when they arise. Conversations are also needed about rewards. As we write this, U.S. economic conditions are weak, and many public employees are being furloughed. Expectations of rewards cannot be what they once were and are just as likely to include matters of job security and competitive skills development. We need a process for managing expectations, indeed.

Though the notion of developing informal understanding is widely accepted, the term *psychological contract* is of more recent vintage, dating to the early 1990s. Prior to that, the term was largely used with philosophical meaning, as an understanding between broad groups in society (e.g., the psychological contract between labor and government). The above use is that of a management or people skills tool. Today, the term is a bit more common, though sometimes still in a broader sense (e.g., the relation between companies and their employees) instead of a specific understanding between two parties.

In 2002, a survey of senior local government managers found that 57.3 percent of respondents report that in their jurisdiction most supervisors establish informal understandings or mutual agreements with employees.[5] Very few managers call them psychological contracts, and only a third, 20.7 percent, report that the agreements included processes described above. The study also reports that understandings cover a broad range of topics: workloads (mentioned by 87 percent of respondents as being part of understandings with employees), working relationship with immediate superior (79 percent), work schedules (75 percent), job security (70 percent), rewards (59 percent), promotion (58 percent), responsibility or authority (56 percent), how and when feedback is given (53 percent), interpersonal relations (45 percent), career development

(44 percent), influence over what happens to them (41 percent), training (40 percent), specific behaviors or conduct of managers or employees (36 percent), performance objectives (34 percent), individually preferred working styles (29 percent), individually preferred communication styles (28 percent), loyalty (28 percent), and following orders (24 percent). Thus, topics are broad reaching indeed.

In an open-ended question, respondents were asked about the greatest benefits of having psychological contracts. Respondents overwhelmingly reported benefits of (1) improved understanding and agreement on employees' and managers' responsibilities (40.7 percent of responses) and (2) increased communication and improved relationship (32.1 percent). Some other comments also include improved productivity (11.1 percent) and increased trust and peace of mind ("one less thing to worry about"). Statistically, the study also finds significant associations between the use of psychological contracts and performance management strategies and perceptions of employee trust in management. Though studies are lacking, one may surmise that the use of psychological contracts has since increased and is becoming increasingly common.[6]

Psychological contracts are also associated with increased leadership and innovation. A study of very senior public managers (executives) in Taiwan finds that about 55 percent of such very senior public managers have informal agreements (psychological contracts) with political appointees (who are deputy ministers or ministers) that concern understandings about which policies and programs executives will take initiative for and how appointees will provide legitimation and oversight of those executive initiatives. Among executives with such psychological contracts, 76 percent agree or strongly agree that their agency frequently develops innovative programs, compared to 46 percent of those who do not have such agreements with political appointees. Likewise, among those with psychological contracts, 83 percent agree or strongly agree that they are able to make policy decisions in their area of work, compared to only 51 percent of those do not have such agreements. One should not be surprised that having agreements about taking initiative increases initiative taking, too.[7]

People may find many opportunities to have such conversations, such as over lunch or in a private coffee break. However, people generally agree that the performance appraisal itself is not an appropriate moment for such a discussion, as it is fraught with legal implications. The beginning of a performance appraisal period is thought to be an appropriate time for discussing expected performance levels (as just noted, people do want to know in advance what is expected of them). Such a discussion allows workers to clarify expectations and discuss resources, conditions, and feedback. It can include a conversation about desirable improvements from the previous period and opportunities and barriers for realizing these. However, even the beginning of the performance appraisal period can be constrained in nature and not necessarily include discussing employee career development objectives.[8] The context of future appraisal may make some people defensive and risk averse. Most people suggest separating the psychological contract entirely from the performance appraisal.

Initiating an open dialog is sometimes problematic. Not everyone welcomes increased communication, and not everyone is experienced in having such conversations. People increasingly take initiative for such conversations, but it is important to anticipate and effectively address some challenges. First, some people may be unfamiliar with people articulating their expectations or having a discussion about them. Many managers may not reach out to subordinates because they fear having extra problems that they don't want to deal with. Thus, subordinates may need to go to their superiors and suggest making time for such a discussion. Asking someone how you can do more for them is apt to be welcomed, and the discussion about contributing to others is a good time to articulate what others can then do for you: "That's a good idea, but I also want to get involved in contract management too, as it gives me skills I am looking for." Among those who are unfamiliar with the process, it often is necessary to explain that the conversation does not involve guarantees about the future.

Second, some people have a noncommunicative style. Such statements as "This is how we do things around here" and "Don't worry, I will take care of that later" are heard as conversation stoppers. People vary in their reasons for not wanting to have such conversations. They may believe that some things should not be discussed. They may believe it is their duty to decide what is good for others or that others should wait their turn. People may have come up through these

> People increasingly take initiative for such conversations.

approaches, and they expect others to play by these rules now too. Some people have a single mode of dealing with others. These outdated ideas are still in existence, however, and in some cultures they are very widespread. Ultimately, these noncommunicative processes are designed to ensure control over others, which is seldom in their interest. Confronted by such patterns, others can force a conversation, but receptivity or follow-through may be disappointing when others really do not care about the professional goals of others or believe in noncommunication at the office. Open communication cannot solve all problems, but it can bring them to light. See also the Box 10.1.

Third, some people, and some cultures, still expect to largely follow others' orders at work. Communication, when used, is then used for communicating and acknowledging orders. People are concerned about getting on the wrong side of others by articulating demands or expectations. Such orientations are often found in hierarchical and traditional cultures, and members of these cultures seem to have especially low expression and self-initiative. Communication is also used for justification ("I just followed your orders."). These patterns are problematic for superiors trying to get subordinates to express their goals and needs. Persistence, encouragement and some examples or modeling are sometimes needed. Fourth, while many young people are quick to agree about the need for communication, some may not know how to be effective in discussing matters with others at work or know even what to talk about. Nonprofessional attitudes often lead to a lot of nonprofessional talk and judgments. Some young people have unrealistic expectations, thus requiring patience from managers who need to explain to them how things work. But some younger people are not open to the message and may decide to leave the organization in the hope of greener pastures elsewhere. Others may complain in nonprofessional ways, such as putting their gripes on company or public bulletin boards, and talk to managers in nonprofessional

BOX 10.1 SILENCE

Well, there are situations when one's boss is not available to discuss expectations or much of anything else. There are those who are not given to open discussions. There are bosses whose idea of getting along is having subordinates who do what they are asked to do and being a good boss is not asking them to do anything that is too much. Some bosses even ask surprisingly little and find opportunities to reward subordinates for their loyalty and limited but focused contributions with salary raises and promotions when these are available. It is a tried-and-true formula.

People may be comfortable with silent understandings, but they come at a price. Silence does little to address inadequate and mediocre performance, deal with unethical behavior of some employees, or promote new activities that keep the organization vibrant. Indeed, units with managers who avoid communication tend to have these problems, and anecdotally their achievements often are modest. The situation gets even worse when silence is accompanied with harsh, unreasonable, and stressful expectations.

Communication is a necessity in the modern world. Employees do well to seek out and have dialog with their bosses about their expectations and goals. As Wall writes, "Nothing kills relationships more surely than issues left unspoken."[9] Well, psychological contracts may not always be fully possible with some people—some people are unable to talk about or settle anything. Employees do well to reach informal understandings as often as possible about things that matter to them. Silence has a price. Modern companies and management try to increase communication, but not every manager follows suit.

ways, in the same ways as they might talk to their friends or parents. As discussed in Part 2, such patterns are not appropriate, but managers will surely want to take the time to help good employees understand how to communicate their concerns.

Finally, managing expectations is also used in a somewhat different context, as a bureaucratic strategy to reduce efforts or increase benefits. Workers manage their bosses' expectations by talking up how difficult things are. If efforts are to be undertaken, then more resources are needed and rewards should be higher. These processes are readily understood in the context of Figure 10.1 as affecting the valuation of what people are being asked to give or what they want to get. As in all human efforts, there is gaming that sometimes occurs. As mentioned before, people need not accept claims on face value, and part of the psychological process is the evaluation of propositions. Buyer beware. Facts, claims, and assumptions are surely contestable. The management of outcomes is discussed in the next chapter.

Employees who join organizations will surely want to articulate their professional commitments to make progress toward realizing them. They will want to communicate and discuss other matters and expectations too, such as those regarding work processes, interpersonal relations, job performance expectations, and rewards. This chapter discussed a model of open communication called the psychological contract. A psychological contract is defined, generally, as an understanding between an employee and his or her immediate superior with the purpose of increasing role clarity, commitment, and expectation. It complements formal policies and contracts, providing information and alignment that help people get along and realize their goals. Though informal, it is based on mutual agreements that are implemented through accountability of collaboration and support. Psychological contracts can deal with a very broad range of issues, are usually established at the beginning of employment, and are periodically updated. Psychological contracts are associated with increased job commitment and innovation; ask, and you might get.

11
Ethics

A man without ethics is a wild beast loosed upon this world.

—**Albert Camus**[1]

The workplace is filled with scandals, for sure. There is no shortage of misbehavior or lies that comes to light and causes temporary uproars, large and small. People are sometimes asked to find other jobs when their behavior is seen as indefensible or intolerable. There are those who treat others in unprofessional ways, sometimes making prejudiced and near-slanderous statements. There are those who embarrass the organization through their work or conduct. There are people who exaggerate or lie on their résumés. There are those who shamelessly use other's work for self-promotion. There are people who use sexual relations, intimidation, and blackmail to get ahead. There are some who misrepresent their expenses on their invoices. People promote themselves in all kinds of ways, and scandals ensue when these acts of dishonest or improper conduct come to light. Becoming embroiled in these matters is very bad for one's reputation and, at times, even career ending.

Ethics is about more than scandals, but these do bring a focus to the need for ethics. Ethics is generally defined as "the values and principles that guide right and wrong behavior."[2] The concept of values and principles points to guidelines that people can use in their daily work. The workplace brings up many difficult situations, and it is not always very clear what should be done, and some guidance is often useful. Many of these guidelines and boundaries are based on legal, moral, and professional rules, such as not stealing or lying, promoting the public good, being loyal, being honest and account-able, and so on. While most people support these principles in the abstract, applying them in specific instances is not always easy. Yet the professional self, and the execution of one's commitment, requires attention to ethics.

People skills surely affect the application of ethics. It is necessary to read the situation and intention of others. People need to pick up on subtle clues and cues that something might not be altogether right or even be dangerous. We need to be attuned to our motives and purposes and not be the wild beast (or vixen) in the above quote. Diplomacy goes a long way in dealing with ethically difficult situa-tions and such persons. We must act in ways that still get us along with others, and those with good people skills may find more options for acting in ethical ways. But people skills are surely a double-edged sword, as they are also used by others to deceive people and lead them down wrongful and compromising paths. Indeed, even those with good intentions will sometimes want to lead others down a path. Thus, naïveté with regard to others is not a viable option at work—one is reminded of the case of Madoff who famously oper-ated the largest Ponzi scheme in history.[2a] Some skillful mastery of people skills is needed to stay out of trouble and even promote a few good causes.

It is customary and useful to distinguish between a low road and a high road of ethics. The low road of ethics focuses on legal compli-ance and staying out of trouble. Ethics and law share in common a concern for norming and regulating behavior, and there is certainly a good deal of overlap; laws often reflect a prohibition of unethical action. The law includes rules and definitions about the nature of harm to others and how to address that, the need for disclosure and honesty and penalties for violation of them, and various rules about workplace harassment, privacy expectations and freedom of speech rights in the workplace, and many more. It is wise to know the letter and the spirit of the law and to avoid risk in these matters. While not every illegal act is caught or punished, a career is long enough for illegal acts to catch up with a person. It is wise not to roll the dice too often in matters of law.

The high road of ethics seeks to apply ethics to defining one's scope of duties and to performing those duties. This is an aspirational use that recognizes that people have discretion in how they go about their work. One can choose how much of the public good to serve and whether to take on work that does so. One can choose to instill a high sense of commitment and purpose in one's actions, or something less. Ethics can be an aspirational affair, one that inspires people to go beyond mere compliance with legal rules. Indeed, the high road of ethics inspires people to action and colors the way in which people approach their job and psychological contracts. The high road of ethics goes beyond the legal minimum; it is about shaping the character and purpose of one's actions. Ethics affects how people give substance and meaning to their commitment.

Ethics involves both the low road and the high road—we need to conform to and be guided by the law, but the people we deal with also expect us to go beyond this and have sincere enthusiasm for the mission and work to be done. Albert Schweitzer once said, "The first step in the evolution of ethics is a sense of solidarity with other human beings."³ Ethics and people skills reflect this. Ethics is not about adopting "holier than thou" attitudes or preaching to others about what to do. They also are not about avoiding compromising or wrongful thoughts—those will arise anyway. Rather, the questions are what to do with them when they arise, how to act, and what to say. Ethics is seen as a practical and applied effort, as the application of people skills to ways that reflect appropriate and higher purposes in dealing with people. It is not about philosophizing, moralizing, or debating when there is nothing at stake; it is about knowing how to act toward others when there is something at stake. Ethics at work is a contact sport.

The challenge of ethics is not a new one; concern with ethics goes back to biblical times. The Greeks and Romans were also concerned with morality. Ethics is a human issue that each person must deal with, in every setting. Here we apply it to the workplace, in our times. This chapter extends the previous chapter by adding a focus on value and ethics to psychological contracts. Our sense of ethics deepens the psychological contract by adding a sense of trust and predictability about us. The following section discusses some cases and shows the challenge of applying some broad guidelines.

Consider the following:

1. You just promised your boss to take responsibility for a project that will last nine months, and now you are approached by another employer about a job opening there.
2. Your boss encourages you to make a request for an extra computer and some temporary staff, even though you don't really need them.
3. Time pressure is high, and you decide to do a little less than your best on some minor aspect of your project to stay on track and maintain progress on the larger objectives.
4. Bob, your assistant, has helped you on numerous occasions, even with some minor personal matters, but his work quality has become borderline in recent months. At what point is an unsatisfactory appraisal in order?
5. You exaggerate your performance just a little when applying for a performance reward.
6. Jill and Bob stay alone in the office to finish a project. Jill thanks Bob for his help, and she gives him a kiss that is a bit too much.
7. Through your work you learn of a great deal in your line of business that can bring you great personal benefit, and you or your family takes advantage of it.
8. You want to position yourself for future promotion by taking on work that you really don't know how to do yourself, but you plan to lean on others to help do it for you. They have helped you in the past and will do so again.

9. You add a few extra charges to your travel invoices. They aren't really for business purposes, but you also lack some invoices for those that are, and it all balances out.
10. A contractor lets you know that he wants to make a donation to a community nonprofit organization of your choice.
11. A subordinate gives you two tickets to a football game. He can't go and thinks you might enjoy it.

These situations are all quite common. They are shown here in relatively modest or minor degrees rather than in larger degrees that would make responses more obvious. Yet the path to perdition often is paved with smaller steps, some of which are not even recognized as such or necessarily wrong. A lot depends on how these situations are handled, and the above list points to critical tensions that exist or may exist. According to one survey, six of every ten local government employees say that they have witnessed misconduct at work over the past twelve months.[4]

Ethics issues often pit self-interest and personal pleasure against the greater good or proper conduct. The nature of personal interest is not only *financial* (which goes to corruption and graft) but also *career* advancement (notably, getting promotions or favorable assignments) and *pleasure* (which may involve flirting, good food and travel, recognition, and flattery). People do want and enjoy these things. While strong efforts to pursue these matters are often held in check by the reality of organizational processes and law, the limits of one's behavior become problematic when the greater good or legal standards are not entirely clear. At what point does a football ticket, a donation, a personal favor, or a sexually tinted wink cross the line?

The short answer is that while people need to be familiar with the letter and spirit of the law, laws and institutional rules cannot possibly be expected to define and address every human situation that can come up. People will often need to decide and declare to others what crosses the line for them. Expressing this often requires having good diplomatic skills, such as, "I don't think it is in our interests to do or accept this" or "I appreciate the offer, but I can't accept such gifts; it is too large," while in other ways, and at the same time,

> # No is a powerful and necessary word.

showing support for the professional relationship. Usually, a valuable purpose of stating such lines is to maintain one's freedom to commit oneself to organizational and public purposes and to not be compromised by the actions of others. *No* is a powerful and necessary word.

This also points to the second common scenario that pits *individual action against group loyalty*. Groups are a fact of life, and group acceptance is required for getting ahead and providing a bit of a safety net against uncertainty. There is a need to fit in and get along to get ahead. Yet adopting or pursuing standards that are different from those of others can cast one as a bit unreliable or on the sidelines. Group members are expected to support each other; a bit of compromise and adaptability is in order. It is not always easy to say no to one's group members, as the personal cost can be high. There is a bit of fear in the air here.

Kohlberg's well-known theory of moral development also points to this.[5] He notes three levels. The lowest level (called preconventional) is based on promotion of self-interests subject to avoiding punishment from law and rules. It positions people *apart* (or outside) any groups; the phrase "we're all in this for ourselves" comes to mind in describing this approach. The second level (called conventional) is based on compliance with group norms and positions people *within* groups—one does what is needed to get along and strengthen relations with others. This is the realm of the "good ol' boy" and "be a nice gal" networks. The third level (called postconventional) recognizes that people develop their own sense of right and wrong; it positions people *above* groups, requiring people to negotiate with other group members about what is right and wrong. Group norms are subject to discussion and agreement.

The tension between being part of the group (Stage 2) and being apart from the group (Stage 3) is a real one. Pressure and expectations are often subtly and forcefully applied: "You really should help Bob with his project," "It would be nice if you could help Janet on Saturday," "Don't worry, we all do this around here." There is fear of being cast out of favor and derailing or impeding one's career: "You would do this for me too, wouldn't you?"

Diplomacy and the art of getting along are needed to tactfully address these pressures. In this day and age, being seen as someone who wants to avoid bringing problems to a group can be useful and beneficial ("I want to avoid doing something that could bring problems later.") as can showing loyalty and commitment in others ways ("I don't want the extra pay, and I will do this for free. It is important that Janet is helped on this, as it helps everyone."). We do not need to sign off on another's work that we know is inadequate or even fraudulent in some way. Rather we can ask the person to correct the deficiency or work or bring the matter up with others in the organization in a way that provides a collective resolution ("Let's ask Jill's boss about this matter before moving forward."). We can diplomatically ask for slight delays that give extra time to get things right. Hence, some useful phrases for dealing with ethical matters are as follows:

- "I think the purpose is good, but doing it in this way could cause us trouble."
- "I'd like to check with others before doing this."
- "I can't accept this."
- "Let's find another way of doing this that doesn't carry so much risk."

Work situations force people to articulate how far they are willing to go. People will need to articulate areas of concern and specify possible negative consequences. We cannot agree to everything that comes our way. Lines need to be drawn and done in ways that still show our commitment to the broader purposes of others and the organization, and we also need to work with others to find better ways forward.

Various general guidelines and standards of ethics have been proposed, but general guidelines are often inadequate for that. The problem is akin to that presented in Chapter 1, in which the limitations of adages are discussed. For example, some common moral principles are "do not harm," "be honest," "speak the truth," "honor agreements," "be accountable for one's actions," "act with integrity," and "consider the consequences for others and future generations." Such guidelines are deficient as a guideline to action. Moral guidelines often are ill specified (e.g., what is dishonesty in a specific setting?), are sometimes in conflict (e.g., speaking the truth and considering consequences—where does spying fit in?), do not deal with the reality of specific situations that bring up additional concerns (e.g., self-sacrifice versus obligation to take care of one's family), and do not always sensitize oneself to situations that have ethical pitfalls (e.g., one can be deceived by others who claim to act in one's best interest).

Being aware of one's moral principles is not always enough to be effective at work. Some authors also pose questions that moral principles inspire, such as the following:

- What course of action brings the greatest good for the greatest number of people (utilitarian ethic), or what course of action brings the greatest public benefit?
- Would this action be undertaken by someone of exemplary or virtuous character (virtuous character ethic)?
- Will this action deprive others of their rights (rights ethic)?
- Do I feel comfortable explaining my action to the public and my close friends (disclosure ethic)?
- If I were in the position of another person affected by my actions, how would I feel (Golden Rule ethic)?
- Do the benefits of this action sufficiently outweigh the negatives (proportionality ethic)?

Surely, these questions do sensitize one to possible issues, such as conflicts between personal interests or benefits and greater, public or organizational, purposes. They may also begin to suggest solutions in dealing with problems. The disclosure ethic (also called the "TV rule") most assuredly puts a lid on actions or justifications that push the envelope of propriety. What is possible in theory may not be sound in practice. They seem to push people to go beyond the legal minimum to something more that is more desirable. However, it seems unlikely that people have

> The TV rule assuredly puts a lid on actions or justifications that push the envelope of propriety.

the time to consider these questions in the heat of the moment, when an instant reaction is needed. Ethics often requires snap judgments. Though the TV rule might be helpful to give one a brief pause ("Let me think about that a little …"), some of these questions seem more useful as justifications after the fact.

In a broader context, organizations have increasingly recognized the need to draw the line on ethical conduct and to do so through specific examples. As Thomas Jefferson once said, "I consider ethics, as well as religion, as supplements to law in the government of man." It is not enough to merely set broad codes or principles; people need specific guidance for how they should act in specific instances. Codes are broad statements of ethical principles, but it is the specific actions that are associated with improved conduct and performance. Examples include making ethics and ethical judgment criteria in promotion, appointing managers who uphold ethical principles, encouraging reporting or ethical wrongdoing, and offering ethics training that addresses the specific issues that come up in their lines of work.

Indeed, ethics training is increasingly common at work. People need to be told how they should handle a broad range of specific situations. As regarding the previously mentioned numbered items,

1. Considering another job surely does bring up qualms about keeping promises, but people have a responsibility to know their market value (and look after their family). One way of dealing with this is to ensure that one's boss does not suffer harm, perhaps by finding a replacement person for the project or not accepting a possible offer until the project is completed.
2. If a computer and temporary staff are not needed, perhaps a request could be made for something else that is needed.

3. As long as one is not cutting corners or preparing deficient work, doing so may be appropriate. It is a good idea to check with one's supervisor.
4. Help and friendship do need to be kept separate from workplace performance. People are always given extra help, but at some point performance standards do need to be set. The problem is the compromised boss, and some underperforming subordinates do use compromising tactics.
5. Highlighting achievements is one thing, putting down falsehoods is quite another.
6. Sex is a classic workplace technique that is used to control and compromise others. It is time for Bob to place firm limits on Jill's behavior.
7. The appearance of a conflict of interest often needs to be avoided, especially in the public sector. What is legally allowed may not be tolerable for organizations. This is a classic case in the tax assessor office, and the response should be no.
8. This is really a borderline case. The problem is really with the organization or supervisor that would give such work to someone who they know is not very good.
9. People are very strict about money—any aspect of falsified invoices is a crime. This cannot be done.
10. This too looks like an appearance of a conflict situation. You can thank the contractor for his or her consideration, but the decision should be made by the contractor and be independent of any business with the contractor. Consult the agency's legal staff.
11. It's a nice consideration, but we would pass it up. It could compromise future judgment and even become the source of office gossip. Buy your own tickets.

Many professions also have their own specific issues. Law enforcement deals with myriad sensitive and corrupting issues. Those in custody deserve to be treated with respect and dignity, and standards need to be set for how this is shown in practice. Law enforcement officials operate in an environment of wrongdoing, and prolonged exposure can have a corrupting effect. Likewise, accountants face their own pressures and judgments for keeping track of debts and liabilities. These matters are not always fully regulated but affect bond ratings and budget decisions that impact many. Nurses also face very different situations that involve making full and timely disclosure of diagnoses, providing options for second opinions, and so on. There are specific issues that come up.

Paying attention to ethics training and giving instruction on how to handle such matters is seen as a top management responsibility. There is broad agreement that exemplary moral leadership matters and that top managers set the tone for ethics by ensuring that such training, discussion, and enforcement happens. "A fish rots from the head down" is a graphic but accurate depiction of the need for leadership from the top and the pervasiveness of ethical problems in organizations when this is lacking. People often think that their sense of morality is stronger than that of their environment, but it is difficult not to be affected by shady ethics when these are widely present. Willy-nilly, people find themselves eventually making compromises to get along—it routinely happens. Even with a large umbrella, people still get wet in the rain. Organizations and their leaders increasingly recognize this. They do not want the distractions that are caused by unethical actions. Thus, directed from the top, many managers are taking an increasingly firm line on unethical matters. It is necessary. Still, research is also showing that some level amount of unethical behavior is likely unavoidable (see Box 11.1).

Beyond this, the benefits of the high aspirational road of ethics are increasingly apparent to many organizations and individuals, though surely not all. Some studies find that adherence to ethics is also associated with a higher level of performance, though the evidence is mixed. At issue is not only minimization of distractions but also reinforcement of mission and professional relations and expectations among organizational members. Ethics, broadly or aspirationally defined, is a way to get departments to ask what is in the best interest of the organization and its stakeholders. One can imagine organizations that ask departments to develop new efforts in this way on an annual or semiannual basis. Likewise, individuals can articulate ethics in their commitment and actions. Chapter 8, on professional

BOX 11.1   ATTRACTION?

The approach presented here is one of individual decision making. Ethics is often discussed in this manner, but a growing body of evidence shows that this is not always so. People may episodically or continually experience overwhelmingly powerful cravings for money, power, and sex that overwhelm their rational decision making, even at the expense of their career and reputation. Harvard researcher Hans Breiter and his colleagues found that the craving for money activates the same regions of the brain as the craving for cocaine, sex, or any other instant and intense pleasure.[6] Such urges are associated with dopamine, the neurochemical that also causes obsessive and overpowering cravings.

Many people have experienced exceptionally strong cravings for money, power, career success, and sex at some time that overwhelmed their sense and better judgment. Some people also have an exceptionally strong attraction to living on the edge. These experiences are similar to falling in love. Of course, not everyone who experiences such strong cravings acts on these at work, but work is a significant focus in many people's lives, and a good amount of time is spent at work. So the cravings sometimes do come out at work. Science is just now beginning to catch up with this phenomenon, and we think that a lot more about this will be written in the coming decade.

Good estimates are lacking, but it seems fairly common to have someone with compulsive unethical conduct in one's work group—our experience suggests about a 1-in-3 chance assuming an average workgroup of 10-12 people. Such behavior by one affects the lives of many at work, and saying "no" and exercising better judgment is a frequent practical reality for many people at work.

commitments, shows how professional standards and ethical norms can usefully elaborate one's commitment. Ethics prompts not only having concerns for undertaking actions that help others but also doing so in ways that inspire trust through openness, integrity, fairness, and accountability. There are clearly things that can be done to emphasize the trustworthiness and integrity of one's actions.

Northouse proposes five principles of individual, ethical leadership: having respect for others, providing service to others, building community, manifesting honesty, and showing justice.[7] Dobel adds to this the need for prudence or foresight; good intentions are not enough.[8] To be trusted, people must also show efficacy by achieving outcomes, getting the support from others, and avoiding pitfalls and problems that cause current or future problems. These are proper pointers, but, as always, specific pointers and action are needed. People need to decide for themselves how much emphasis they want to put on these matters, though in most settings people would surely be expected to show commitment to these matters.

Ethical risk lies around every corner. No one is perfect, and missteps happen. People's better judgment does get away from them at times. For example, attention recently has been drawn to young people posting things on Facebook and other social media networking sites that may involve their colleagues or even their boss in unflattering ways. Whether this is an ethical or other lack of judgment is questionable (does the Golden Rule apply here?), but provided that laws have not been broken, people are usually given a warning and opportunity to improve. A distinction exists between someone who sometimes does something that was not the best and someone who repeatedly and in multiple ways is at the forefront of trouble. One suspects that ethical punishments are seldom a first-time event and that people have an antecedent history that leads up to such events. Developing a sensitivity to one's own inclinations that may be ethical shortcomings is surely a first step toward avoiding ethical trouble.

Finally, we'd like to raise a somewhat provocative question: is professionalism possible in organizations? While answering such a question could take up a whole book, the preceding chapters suggest some thoughts. If professionalism means a single-minded and faultless commitment to ethics and excellence, then the answer is likely no in most settings. Earlier, in Chapter 4, we warned of the danger of an overzealous pursuit of excellence. Here we note that people have ethical lapses and that plenty of people follow the low road of ethics as simply not running afoul of the law. Later chapters on mental health also dispel the possibility that organizations could have a single-minded and faultless commitment to ethics and excellence. We might note that being ethically and professionally excellent are also seldom criteria for high office; we invite readers to determine for themselves the number of people who meet such standards.

Rather professionalism in the current culture has come to mean something far less: a common commitment to language and behavior that avoids the baser and idiosyncratic elements of human conduct. For example, people should not shout at each other and not make personal accusations. They should conduct themselves in some minimally acceptable way, perform in decent ways (however defined), and avoid illegal conduct or unethical conduct that harms the organization in some way. This is a most valuable and necessary standard too. At this lower level of professionalism, organizations try to avoid occasional slips and encourage some upward spikes, and a mix of professionalism and personal agreeableness seems needed for one to get ahead and to be successful. While there is good reason for setting a higher standard and striving for more, some organizations anecdotally find even this standard quite the challenge. Surely, professionalism is possible, but it depends on one's definition of it. Of course, more would be better.

Ethics is about conduct in specific situations, involving both a low road of compliance (and punishment avoidance) and a high road of aspirational goals and conduct. Though standards and norms are often discussed (honesty, integrity, purpose, accountability, openness, social justice, etc.), these are not always easy to apply in specific situations. Rather the focus here is on addressing specific situations that often come up. To be ethically competent at work is to recognize these situations and know how to deal with them. Many of these involve trade-offs between personal interests and those of the organization or society or trade-offs between individual action versus group membership. This chapter suggests that people will often need to define and articulate their own standards and that doing so requires a use of diplomacy with others, recognizing that others may set standards a bit differently for themselves. Dealing with ethical issues often involves:

- identifying an aspect of concern and articulating its possible negative consequences,
- discussing it with others in ways that promote a joint response to the situation, and
- adopting a high road of ethics for oneself while recognizing that others are likely to adopt other standards.

12
Leading

He had a knack for getting things out of people that others never got out of them.

—Don Hewitt (producer of *60 Minutes*)[1]

People who have professional objectives will surely want to undertake new activities or shape existing efforts along these lines. One aspect of reality is the need to get cooperation and support from others for whatever we want to do. We need to get others to agree which activities are desirable, feasible, and necessary. We need to get them to agree that certain standards should be met, whether they are about program performance or about doing the right thing by stakeholders. We also need to get them to agree to provide mutual support to help realize certain tasks, such as taking turns attending meetings or answering phone calls. Collaborating with others and getting them to get other people to do things are essential people skills. Getting others to work with us and do certain things well greatly affects the performance of our own goals as well as those of our organizations.

Getting others to do certain things involves both social skills and professional knowledge and judgment. Social skills are involved in making our requests to others in respectful and polite ways. Professional standards and judgment are involved in deciding what to ask of others and at which standards they should perform.

Social skills are involved in dealing with others' responses, including their concerns, resistance, and performance level. Professional judgment is needed to decide whether and to what extent to make performance an issue in light of other priorities and performance of a department. Social skills and professional knowledge are needed in pursuit of one's development objectives, and they are greatly and inseparably intertwined.

In an older time, this chapter's topic would have been called "directing," but that word has fallen out of favor as being too autocratic for our times. Students of public administration are well familiar with the acronym PODSCORB, which describes the seven tasks of leadership: planning, organizing, directing, staffing, coordinating, reporting, and budgeting. These tasks, first stated in 1937,[2] remain relevant today. Directing has since become parts of supervision and communication and, most recently, cooperation and collaboration. Leadership is now also broadly expected. Everyone is expected to take initiative for doing their work well and overcoming barriers and obstacles, not only those in high positions. Just doing one's job well is no longer enough for getting promotions in most organizations; people want to see some leadership, initiative, and the ability to work and get along with others.[3]

Leadership has become a huge topic, filling libraries galore. Some studies focus on the roles of agencies in society and of the need for agency leadership. Other studies focus on the role and task of leaders. The point here is not to review the leadership literature but to focus on only a few aspects that relate directly to people skills. Leadership theorists are also quick to say that no one leadership style is effective in every situation, and that is certainly the case in getting cooperation from people.

A repertoire of approaches is needed, and the need for having both social skills and professional knowledge and judgment is evident in such leadership. Some people have solid or excellent professional skills; they are masters of their domain. Yet their careers are stunted when they get inadequate support and cooperation from others. They find themselves operating as islands at work, sometimes shunned by others. Other people have good social skills but lack professional knowledge or judgment. Many are great colleagues and quite loyal to their organization; these qualities often get them promoted to supervisory levels where their social skills are valued. But they lack professional vision and judgment to lead their units further. Others know this, so their career growth is stunted. There is much to learn from both of these types of people. Both social skills and professional knowledge and judgment are needed in the exercise of leadership.

Leadership theorists argue that people need a range of different strategies that are appropriate for the situation, but the context of society and times point toward some broad parameters within which most leadership behavior is expected to fall. Supervisors have formal power and the authority to issue commands, but they are to be used as a last resort. Western culture has a very uneasy relationship with following orders; people like their freedom and sense of control, and being at the whim of others' fancy produces strong negative emotions of resentment and anger. Requests need to make organizational and professional sense. Moreover, professionals join organizations in fulfillment of professional, societal, and personal pursuits. Adding to this is that employees are expected to take leadership and self-initiative in a number of work-related realms and to do so with professional and organizational purposes in mind. Leaders and others who seek cooperation from others have some explaining to do. Leaders who speak in authoritarian or directing ways soon create resentment and strong resistance. Though some people may be more willing to interpret orders in more positive ways, most are not. Those who make requests or orders without reaching (some) agreement about their purposes are often seen by others as having very undesirable autocratic, paternalistic, and abrasive leadership styles. Only in very exceptional circumstances, such as in crises, are dictatorial orders thought to be acceptable, and even then they are often subject to later review.[4]

The focus on giving reasons rather than orders creates a framework within which different styles and roles can exist. For people in supervisory positions, the coaching role has come to fore, which includes a range of different styles. Coaches articulate group goals and work with workers to gain agreement on individual performance standards (in line with that described about psychological contracts), and supervisors help people achieve these during the year. Leadership is about setting goals and standards, helping people achieve them, and holding them accountable for their performance. Coaches, then, are in turn held responsible for the results of their groups. As in sports, the ultimate sanction (or big stick) is being sidelined (or fired) such that a person is no longer eligible for desirable assignments that produce rewards (Chapter 6 discussed progressive discipline as a means to that). Numerous leadership quotes articulate different aspects of the coaching style:

- "The boss drives people; the leader coaches them" (H. Gordon Selfridge).[5]
- "True leadership lies in guiding others to success" (Bill Owens).[6]
- "A leader is a dealer in hope" (Napoleon Bonaparte).[7]
- "Perhaps the most central characteristic of authentic leadership is the relinquishing of the impulse to dominate others" (David Cooper).[8]
- "If anything goes bad, I did it. If anything goes semi-good, we did it. If anything goes real good, then you did it" (Coach Paul "Bear" Bryant).[9]
- "A leader offers support and help. You can count on them to back you up when you need them" (David Rye).[10]
- "Speak softly and carry a big stick" (Theodore Roosevelt).

Coaches vary in their styles of course, some being more hands-off than others, others having more organization and vision, and so on. As a further example of the coaching style, a university administrator states, in addition to setting goals,

> The contribution I can make from my office—and for the record, there is one—is in setting the processes, background conditions, and climate in which people can do their best work without getting embroiled in unproductive conflict or drama. When this works, it

looks like I'm not doing much of anything at all. As with editing, doing it well usually means going unnoticed. But take it away or get it wrong, and you see the difference immediately.[11]

That style might not work in every circumstance—in some cases more control and goal-directed actions are surely needed. Indeed, leaders are also expected to set goals and standards, which the above quote does not address so well. One size does not fit all, and coaching does come in different flavors, but the purposes and goals are the same.

> The coaching role has come to fore.

The above also creates a basic framework for coworkers. They are to contribute to group goals by doing their own job well and by doing it in ways that do not interfere with others doing their job, which also contributes to group goals. They may also be expected to contribute to group goals by reciprocally helping each other, and those with unique or critical skills may be asked to do that even more (e.g., language or computer skills). For fulfilling these roles, we refer to Chapter 4 ("Getting Along") for specific ways, such as doing one's job, being pleasant, and not causing trouble, and to which professional content and purposes are readily added; we have little more to say here. The literature also includes overuse of the term *teamwork*. Few employees experience their setting as exemplifying teamwork, no matter how often the phrase is used. Few work groups require the same high levels and frequency of interdependency and tacit interaction as, say, an NFL team. While some work settings are characterized by strong teamwork, many settings don't require that. All metaphors have limits.

There are other styles to be identified too. The coaching style has become increasingly important to accommodate the increasing workloads of units. In most departments today, it is inconceivable that any supervisor could make all or most decisions. An increasing amount of cooperation and coordination is to be achieved in modern offices. Communicating and getting cooperation from others are increasingly important to managers dealing with their employees and also for employees dealing with their coworkers. Everyone it seems needs to be skilled in making the right argument to get cooperation from others. Whatever leadership style is used, these realities cannot be ignored.[12]

Getting cooperation and support is necessarily a two-way process. Requests for cooperation come in many different forms, but most, however well intentioned, include aspects that can be bothersome. Some requests are added to one's normal scope of duties and, however easy or modest, cause stress by adding to what people already need to do, and many people are already overburdened. Requests to handle work that is a bit different in scope or requirement can be quite troublesome, requiring one to look into new standards, giving additional attention and even getting approval from superiors and other offices. Suggestions for doing things in better or new ways can be almost beyond the pale for some people—they upset routines, cause many meetings, and add enormously to current workloads. Whatever someone proposes is likely to annoy and involve an effort by others.

Getting people on the same page involves, in the language of Chapter 10, alignment between what we want to get and what they want to give. People need to be listened to, and the process cannot be short-circuited. Being acknowledged, being heard, and being responded to are essential processes of listening and finding mutual agreement.[13] We cannot be so arrogant as to know what is good for others and substitute our judgment for them. We cannot fully know what concerns other people have or assume that others will align themselves with what others believe is for the good for the organization. For people wanting to make a request for cooperation from others, consideration and thoughtfulness are shown by anticipating and addressing their likely concerns, yet respect is shown by not presuming to know what these fully are and by engaging others in a discussion about them. We need to listen to what is said and to hear what is not being said. Getting buy in takes time.[14]

Dialog about requests for cooperation are as unique as the people and subject matter at hand. Though varied, many concerns and arguments will have common features. What people talk about can cover any or all of the following topics, subject only to people raising these issues. People do well to have answers to the following:

- Why do we need to do this? (Identify the driving forces and reason for the request.)
- How does this further the office or mission? (How might it also possibly further the professional commitments and career interests of the people involved?)
- Is the request legitimate, legal, and ethical? Does it also have support from others in the organization, including leaders?
- What exactly is to be accomplished and by when? What are the targets?
- Who is responsible for and involved in executing the request, and what are the reporting relationships among these people? What is the role of the requestor in ensuring progress?
- Are resources adequate?
- Are people able to achieve the desired result?
- What are likely obstacles or challenges in accomplishing the request, and how are they to be overcome?
- What are some examples or models of how the request is to be successfully done?
- What are the consequences of success? (Are they rewards that are part of normal duty or something else?) What are the consequences of failure? (Does it have to be done again, or something else?)

The above questions obviously also address the feasibility of what is proposed. By example, consider the previous example of the young professional seeking to develop mentoring programs for disadvantaged and underprivileged young men (Chapter 8). The above questions prompt some very specific reflection. What is the need for such a program? Is it to reduce neighborhood crime? Increase the local tax base? Reduce pressure on local social services? Pursue social justice? Improve attitudes toward local government? Which arguments are most relevant to whom? What is the evidence of each of these claims? Considering these arguments in dialog with those concerned is likely to begin tailoring program goals and services in certain ways. A mentoring program that responds to a high crime situation is likely to be one that is very different from one that seeks to increase the tax base by training youth in developing and running their own businesses. Other questions also tailor the program, such as tie-in with department missions, perception of local government roles in relation to neighborhood organizations, the availability of people with similar interests or expertise, the goals of funding agencies, and so on. It is clear that attending to these questions indeed strengthens the design and development of programs. It often takes a few meetings to raise these questions and a few more to begin answering them.

Having two-way communication and reasons does not mean that everyone will be persuaded to accept one's idea, of course. As management scholar Kotter states, "One of the most common ways to overcome resistance to change is to educate people about it beforehand. Communication of ideas helps people see the need for and the logic of a change."[15] Getting buy in takes time and repetition of argument. *Berman's Rule of Three* states that people hear only things that have been said three times: "So much gets said in organizations that is not followed up on, that it is rational to take what is said the first time with a little grain of salt. If it is important, the speaker will surely follow up on it. If it is not, why get worked up over it now?"[16] People who have a request for cooperation will usually need to repeat it several times, and answers to the above questions will need to be given several times too.

> **Berman's Rule of Three: people hear only things that have been said three times.**

People have different motivations for giving, and the normal response to a request for cooperation is varied motivation. Whereas some see the request as a great opportunity to contribute to or advance their or the organization's goals, others may be only modestly interested or compliant, and still others may resist any involvement. A helpful heuristic is the 25-50-25 rule,[17] which states that when people suggest a new idea, about 25 percent of the audience will embrace it, 50 percent will be indifferent, and 25 percent of people will reject it. This rule has not been rigorously validated by scientific research, but many man-

> A helpful heuristic is the 25-50-25 rule.

agers feel that it more or less accurately represents their experience. Our anecdotal experience suggests that it is pretty accurate, indeed.

One implication is that people who propose new things should not necessarily expect great support for their ideas. Change often starts with a small group of people who support a new proposal. Surely, not everyone needs or should get involved all at once, and the reality of pilot learning and experiments is that a small group of leaders do much good "biting off" the initial problems and finding solutions for getting things working. The vast majority of people are fence-sitters who will likely come along in time, if and when the new effort works and is beneficial in some way. For now, they have their own priorities and agenda, and the new proposal is neutral toward their interests. One reason for giving people a broad voice is that it helps to identify problems or pitfalls not initially foreseen. Many initial concerns and negative responses may contain very valuable insights that help avoid problems and lead to rapid improvement. Managers may well wonder why they and others did not think of these problems themselves.

For employees who wish to propose a new idea to their superior or one or more coworkers, the above rule can be taken to suggest that workers have no more than a 25 percent chance of getting an enthusiastic, favorable reaction. Most likely, people who propose something will need to repeat it at least three times and each time provide more and more answers to the above questions. As enthusiastic supporters of the idea, employees may also show that the proposed idea actually works. In this way, over time, support for their idea can be built. Getting sufficient support from others often takes time, good reasons, and patient persuasion.

It is paramount to consider that (1) not everyone will support an idea and (2) everyone's support is usually not needed. Resistance is to be minimized, but that does not mean that it is usually eliminated. Yet some people are ideologically opposed to what is being proposed, are not open to reason, or may find any reason insufficient.

The extent to which these people need to be dealt with varies, probably depending on their likely influence on the proposed idea. Some people have a reputation for being contrary, and there is nothing gained or lost by letting them have their say. Sometimes, there is even benefit to letting them go on.

> I had a situation where a small group of people, about four or five, opposed a plan accepted by almost everyone else on the committee. The plan definitely was for the greater good of the organization and several departments, and our authority to make the plan and the specific changes to policy was unquestionable. As it turned out, letting these few people talk at meetings was the best strategy. In time, people had heard all their positions over and over and became tired of their arguments. The more these people talked, the more that others wanted to eventually vote and move on. In an odd way, these persistent opponents made my life easier.

Additional insights exist from considering the development of new ideas and projects over time, as well as the matter of residual resistance. Getting cooperation is not a one-time event but ongoing throughout the life of the project or development of the idea. One may hope that as the project is more successful, the initial 25-50-25 support becomes 60-30-10 or such. It is worth repeating that not all objections and concerns that people raise need to be taken on face value. Reasons for not entertaining some objections may need to be repeated too.

Some important key points or people challenges are often experienced:

1. Getting initial support and motivation,
2. Maintaining initial motivation and support through first results,
3. Bringing new team members on with needed skills and replacing those who fail to perform as processes become more fully known and developed and results more frequent, and
4. Dealing with active resisters and final holdouts.

This is not a book on project management, but proposing and implementing a new idea is surely consistent with that; it can be seen as a project in its own right. The first people challenge, "getting initial support and motivation," is described in the above section. The persuasive argumentation can also be viewed as developing a psychological contract with one's supervisor or coworkers. In such a process these very issues are likely to be raised, as well as additional matters about the needs of those who are to be involved. We might as well know what others expect to get from giving us support and cooperation and then work with them to address these questions too.

By example, imagine the young professional with interest in the before-mentioned mentoring program going to a senior colleague. The young professional wants the senior person's support. Good colleagues support each other, while avoiding asking too much. The young professional asks the senior colleague whether she will support the effort in an upcoming staff meeting, at least to explore the possibilities. The senior person, looking ahead, states that she will gladly do so, but she has limits as to how she can get involved. She can't lead in it or assist in raising money. But she may know a few people in the community who can likely help. In return, might the young professional help out with some data input and analysis for an upcoming presentation that the senior colleague needs to make next month? The young professional is glad to do so. Indeed, he will work this weekend on that effort.

The second people challenge, "maintaining initial motivation and support," is often a significant challenge. If the assessment of others has been wrong or problems occur that far exceed those expected, the momentum and enthusiasm can grind to a halt. People may want to leave the effort, and some may transfer or resign if the stress has been too much. A popular expression is "people don't plan to fail, they fail to plan." People often think of planning as the arrangement of known tasks and resources, but many activities are more akin to asking people to take a journey that has some unknowns. Unexpected setbacks will occur, and the ultimate planning question is how these will be dealt with in ways that both are timely and lead to successful outcomes. Philosophically, we think that *Murphy's Law* (what can go wrong will go wrong) is a bit too dark on this matter, and so we hereby state *Berman's Law*: no one is unlucky all the time. For example, people who chose to stand on the sidelines pitch in when needed. Since the unexpected is to be expected, it can and should be planned for. In short, those who undertake new initiatives do well to budget for 20 to 30 percent more time, people, and resources than might be needed. Delays happen, and the additional time, people, and resources are required to then stay on track and avoid burnout among team members. The *Rule of Seven* states that "people become masters of new skills only after they have applied it seven times," suggesting the need for allowing extra time too. Those who lead often try to keep things lighthearted.

The third people challenge is "bringing new team members on with needed skills and replacing those who fail to perform." Some people will likely experience a change of heart. People's interests change, other opportunities may have surfaced, and, despite the above, it was more difficult than expected. For a variety of reasons, some people will leave or want to leave. Also, a need for new people arises as unexpected challenges come up that now require new people, often with specific skills to meet these challenges. The coach will likely also want to make some team changes—some people may not have performed at levels that are needed. Thus, some turnover is normal, and with that comes office drama. The job of those with leadership is to keep their eyes on the ball and on what needs to be accomplished.

> Some turnover is normal, and with that comes office drama. Those with leadership need to keep their eyes on the ball.

People who leave or are asked to leave should be thanked for their efforts—there is no good reason to spoil the well of cooperation from them and others in the future. New people are brought in, and a psychological contract is established with them. Typically, as processes become more routinized, team stability increases, and among team members, people are found to help routinize the process further.

For employees, the above has implications. Others' changes are an opportunity to contribute and distinguish oneself, but some efforts may not have been well thought out or involve people with whom we rather not deal. From the organization's perspective, not everyone may need to lead or even participate in what is new; it may be sufficient to show leadership for something else, perhaps that which is more aligned with one's professional development. If and when the effort continues, people can decide to join later. That opportunity will then come.

The fourth people challenge concerns dealing with active resisters and final holdouts. Most commonly, active resisters are a problem in the initial phases of implementation, including those who are resentful of having been outvoted or overruled. Managers and others typically try to reach accommodation with them, such as allowing them to temporarily do their own thing in the expectation that they will not remain an obstacle. If resistance is active, being counseled by senior managers may be undertaken, including the possibility of progressive discipline through documentation of nonperformance (see Chapter 6). There are limits as to what can be tolerated. People do need to be told what the limits are (some managers fail to do that but instead let things go on and then one day blow up). Managers do show that they are committed to change, progress, and improvement. In most cases, final resisters eventually come to accept the inevitability of change as 25-50-25 becomes 60-30-10; the number of people in the latter group is exceedingly small. Thus, eventually, resistance fades in the face of successful new efforts, and such persons may move on to other groups or find new targets of resistance.

Getting cooperation is a process. Some people are quick to propose what others should do, but the above section shows a process that requires considerable effort and commitment. Leadership is about setting goals and standards, helping people to achieve them, and providing feedback and assessment. A coaching style is increasingly expected. The 25-50-25 rule is a useful heuristic for anticipating the range of cooperation that one expects, and leaders will need to articulate reasons and responses that persuade others to help efforts move forward. Leaders will need to deal with moderate support and even some level of resistance.

In any time period, only a limited number of new initiatives can be undertaken. Leaders do well to choose these well, and workers do well to understand that not all improvement opportunities are likely to be undertaken. People have roles to play, and one role is to deal in a detailed way with the various concerns and problems that are likely to be raised. Getting cooperation is seen as a two-way process of dialog that takes times and persistence. Berman's Rule of Three suggests that leaders will need to repeat these at least three times. Leaders who articulate standards and new ways will not always be liked, and getting others to agree to new efforts is never easy. Workers show leadership and dedication to their professional commitments by proposing improvements related to them and, often, by contributing to other efforts that are being undertaken.

13

Mentoring and Development

Mentor: Someone whose hindsight can become your foresight.

—Unknown[1]

"Get a mentor" is one of the most common pieces of advice that is given these days for advancing one's career. Mentoring involves a relationship between a junior person and a senior person, whereby the mentor provides support, advice, and direction and may occasionally also open up doors or make valuable introductions or connections for the junior person. "Mentors can be game changers," writes Del Jones in *USA Today*.[2] Mentoring is an essential developmental activity. However, finding a mentor is easier said than done.[3] Almost all people who have done well in their career have had people who opened some doors for them; having a powerful mentor is one of several significant avenues to success.

Mentoring is neither a new activity nor even a recent one. In Greek mythology, when Odysseus left for the Trojan War (ca. 1194–1184 BC) he placed Mentor, a wise man, in charge of his son, Telemachus, and his palace. Mentor guided the young (and myopic) Telemachus in search of his lost father. Such pairing of young, talented men with older masters has a long tradition and existed through the medieval ages, where master craftsmen in guilds would train promising apprentices in all aspects of their craft. Mentoring is also common in traditional female homemaking roles (older women teaching younger women how to look after their children, family, etc.). In trade and business, successful businessmen have long taken young, promising people under their tutelage. Donald Trump, in the TV show *The Apprentice*, doesn't quite play the role, but the title indicates the continuing acceptance of the term. In science, PhD and postdoctoral programs are designed to have a long apprenticeship period, and those who are fortunate to serve under known scholars usually have more promising careers themselves.

Some of one's efforts are future focused. People do well to invest a part of today's efforts in creating a brighter tomorrow. Doing well today helps, but it may not be enough. This chapter examines three future-oriented activities to further career development: mentoring, development networks, and professional associations and conferences. These activities have gained traction in recent years. Mentoring helps ensure longer-term developmental needs. Networks are people who, in companies or geographic regions, share experiences and provide mutual self-help. Professional associations and their conferences provide important settings in which to meet potential mentors and network members. A broad range of people is needed to launch a future, and people build a network to help with this. For example, it is not clear that a single individual must fulfill or is capable of fulfilling all of the functions (of a mentor).[4]

A common thread that connects these developmental efforts is the reduction of career uncertainty. People do not know how their careers are going to unfold, they do not know what skills will be needed, and they don't even know with certainty that they will have jobs or jobs with sufficient growth potential. Development efforts expand a person's skills, experience, perspectives, and network, all of which increases the chances of being the right person for the right job at the right time when such opportunities arise. As a Chinese expression has it, luck is opportunity meeting preparation, and developmental activity is about preparation. Developmental activity is a way of reducing risk and uncertainty and thereby producing better returns and outcomes.

Table 13.1 Developmental Activities

On-the-Job Practices (with Developmental Uses)	Targeted Developmental Efforts
Professional commitments	Mentoring
Psychological contracts	Coaching
Taking on new activities	Networking
Deepening work relations	Professional associations
Practicing social skills	Conference attendance

For example, at early stages of one's career development, young professionals experience numerous uncertainties about what sets of skills to focus on and how to deal with people. Mentoring provides clarification, feedback, and reflection, providing for valuable insights that address these hurdles. But mentoring also reduces uncertainty for third parties about their protégé; mentors introduce one to others and thereby put their credibility on the line. Mentors make connections and introductions for others, and the extension of one's network is itself a risk-reduction effort that increases access to jobs that may be better. Not surprisingly, research supports the ideas that those who have more "work motivation" are more likely to have mentors and that those who have mentors are more likely to be satisfied with their career progression.[5]

Developmental activities complement the activities mentioned before. For example, a psychological contract not only addresses current activities but also addresses efforts to help a person better prepare for the future. It seems likely that employees will surely be concerned about such matters in their psychological contract. Practicing social manners and skills helps cement relations at work and may lead to valuable connections and introductions in the future. The activities discussed here expand these future-oriented practices and often provide people with decisive advantages in getting ahead (see Table 13.1).

Though mentoring never totally disappeared, it was not much advocated in traditional management systems until the 1970s. Since then, mentoring has made a comeback and is routinely mentioned, first as a training approach (consistent with the craft model) and more recently as a development approach. Mentoring has also gained broader social acceptance as a strategy for dealing with youth of various backgrounds. Edgar Schein has written much about career development and discussed the potential of mentoring.[6] Two of his students examined some of the roles of mentoring: cheerleader, coach, confidant, counselor, developer of talent, "griot" (oral historian for the organization or profession), guardian, guru, inspiration, master, "opener of doors," patron, role model, pioneer, successful leader, and teacher.[7] It is clear that mentors play a broad range of roles. In recent years, mentoring has also been used in "on-boarding" processes, helping newcomers settle in and become socialized into the organization's customs and values.

Some specific roles include the following:

- *inspirer:* catalyzing and shaping the mentee by explaining the possibilities of a task or position for development,
- *teacher:* helping with practical problems relating to career development and getting along,
- *sounding board:* providing feedback and reflection for the mentee when dealing with challenging situations,
- *resourcer:* bringing key resources and events to the mentee,
- *networker:* introducing the mentee to others, and
- *supporter:* being there to share in difficult and celebratory moments.

Research generally shows that mentoring is effective, at least based on subjective accounts of the people involved. Internal mentors (those within an organization) are more effective in bringing benefits such as social capital and job advancement to the mentee than are external ones. Mentees with internal mentors are also more likely to have external mentors. A survey of executives shows that over 75 percent have had at least one mentor during their career and "research has consistently indicated that mentoring is related to ... positive work outcomes, including higher career and organizational commitment recognition, satisfaction, career mobility and compensation."[8] Mentoring improves learning.[9] Programs of on-boarding often report that pairing new hires with more established employees reduces turnover, sometimes by a factor of two. There is some evidence that salespeople who are in a formal one-to-one developmental relationship with a more experienced colleague or manager outperform those without such support by 20 percent in their first year and are 13.5 percent more likely to survive the first year.[10] Hunt and Weintraub quote the Isaac Stern, the world-famous violinist, who commented on his mentor, "He taught me to teach myself, which is the greatest thing a teacher can do."[11]

Anecdotal accounts suggest some characteristics of successful mentoring relations. First, both the mentor and mentee need a certain credibility. For example,

> The knowledgeable manager cannot know only from books. He must have been through it. Then he has the practical wisdom plus the current state of expert knowledge that is needed. And then he is able to mentor his people. This is the best way to become knowledgeable. The other way is to listen to his people. Listening is hard. It takes time. Sometimes it is 6 months of listening, sometimes a year before it dawns to the manager, where the real problem lies.[12]

The capabilities and performance of the mentor are critical to the success of mentees.[13] Likewise, the mentee must show a serious commitment to his or her job, to wanting to succeed, and to having the talent and perseverance to do so. If it is not credible for the mentee to put his or her trust in a mentor who is less than capable or has poor listening skills, then it is likely not credible to ask mentors to put their efforts in mentees who do not distinguish themselves or who seem unlikely to succeed. Indeed, the success of on-boarding programs are to some extent based on diminished expectations—as a short-term program that requires only modest expertise of the mentor (whose primary asset may be simply being at the organization and knowing its cultures and ways) and modest ability of the mentee (to get through the first year).[14]

Second, mentoring is an active process requiring commitment and engagement: "Mentoring can easily fall apart if we don't actively encourage it along. Whether you're a mentor or a mentee, the answer is simple. Follow up, follow up, follow up."[15] Many anecdotal Internet accounts suggest that mentees need to bring their progress or issues to the mentor. In our experience, mentors and mentees engage in joint projects or activity, as is common in science and business. Third, we see some anecdotal evidence that mentors and mentees develop a psychological contract with each other, as a statement of what each expects to give and get from the relationship. Mentees may have expectations about joining a mentor's network, getting help in developing their own, and being given feedback on important issues. Mentors may have expectations about being given new insights into new developments, getting contributions from the mentee, and being able to make a difference in the mentee's career. These things are surely not always explicit at the beginning, but they do appear to become clearer as mentor–mentee relations develop.

The literature also notes supervisors stepping into mentoring roles. Indeed, some studies suggest that supervisors who fulfill mentoring roles may be especially effective.[16] Supervisors often are key to the development of young professionals, and many successful professors report having been lucky, having had a supportive first or second supervisor who provided essential support and instructions on getting along and advancing their career. What matters is the mentoring function, rather than the mentor, and some of the above studies also note that some people without mentors may find other ways of getting important information and network connections.

Being mentored is associated with numerous advantages, but finding a mentor can also be difficult. Relationships need to be built up over time. It seems unlikely a person would be successful asking a stranger, "Will you be my mentor?" People meet potential mentors at meetings and professional conferences, and the above circumstances imply mentees will need to show themselves as committed and likely to succeed by showing commitment to other matters first. In short, mentoring is about having someone (1) who knows the ropes, (2) who can provide sound advice, and (3) who can open up a few doors. People do well to find such a person or network of persons who can help with these matters and thus help shape a better future. Finding a good mentor is a matter of luck but also of chance meeting preparation.

However, there is much that is not known. We do not know to what extent mentoring relations in on-boarding programs continue after the on-boarding period. Same-gender or same-race mentoring programs have often been suggested for women and minorities to better address their unique concerns, but there is little aggregate data showing that gender or race is a determinant of mentoring satisfaction or success. One of the major concerns about some mentoring efforts is that mentors have been ineffective or insufficiently well positioned to secure or provide relevant introductions or advantages for their mentees. Some anecdotal accounts show that women and minorities have benefited greatly from having a powerful white male mentor who knows the ropes and has inside connections. Some anecdotes also show abusive mentors who "require the mentee to do work that the mentor should be doing or withholding assignments that are coveted by the mentee and that would promote the mentee's growth and development."[17] We do not know how often these problems occur, but it seems likely that these involve a mentor with considerable power over the mentee. As mentioned in prior chapters, making psychological contracts and setting boundaries may be needed in these relations as well.

Finally, in recent years coaching has also been mentioned.[18] Coaching is consistent with modern leadership. Coaching focuses on immediate performance improvement and as such is consistent with supervisors taking an active, hands-on interest in a person's performance. The coaching supervisor helps subordinates articulate goals and works with them to achieve them. One model involves weekly or bimonthly sessions in which the supervisor and subordinate work through different problems that came up and lay out

> Mentoring is about having someone who knows the ropes, who provides sound advice, and who opens up a few doors. People do well to find such a person.

concrete steps for further improvement. Coaching is quite common between supervisors and young professionals. Coaching extends supervision and can lead to mentoring.

Beyond mentoring, many professionals also have developmental networks of people. These networks include a diverse range of people, each person contributing something useful. Some are part of the same organization; others are outside the organization. Some are in the same industry; others are in a similar function in other industries. Some are of the same gender or race; others are of a different gender or race but may provide a different perspective on matters. Some are of the same age; some are quite a bit older with more mature experiences and networks. Not everyone has a mentor or coaching-oriented person, and such a person can do much to substitute for this and find individuals who also provide additional resources and feedback, adding to one's network.

Developmental networks vary greatly. Some function as networks, but oftentimes one's network is just a loose collection of individuals. Female and minority networks exist in most industries, which serve as self-help and a sounding board for many problems and issues that women and minorities experience. Examples of problems include hitting glass ceilings, overcoming isolation, dealing with family–work matters, and finding ways of getting along and fitting in with one's environment. Some groups are within the same industry, such as those in information technology, accounting, or human resources management, and these provide additional networking and technical assistance too. Developmental networks can often give a boost to professional career development:

> I met Karen last year at one of our meetings. We have had lunch a few times together and talk about our family and other women matters. Last week, we had a new job opening, and I called her to ask if she had someone. She gave us some names of people who recently interviewed for them, and a few are just outstanding. I asked our secretary to call, and as a result we interviewed two and made an

offer to one of them. Karen and I also talk about problems that come up in each other's work. We really help each other a lot, dealing with different situations.[19]

Developmental networks can include more senior people too. People often know a few senior people who can be called for advice or opinions. Such persons may have been met at meetings in the past, and it is not uncommon to call such persons and meet with them in their office or have lunch with them. Such persons may offer valuable suggestions on career development or opportunities and thus reduce risk and uncertainty as they make important decisions. Even in the organization's cafeteria there are opportunities to connect with interesting people.

Professional associations are a key source of meeting other people with similar interests. Professional associations involve people with similar commitments. Though professional associations often have newsletters and useful Web sites, the full benefit of joining a professional association comes from developing relations with those there. Conference attendance is usually key to meeting people and forging connections. As mentioned in Chapter 9, "The first time people go to meetings of professional associations, they may know no one, but those who show up five times know half the crowd." Many associations have sections and chapters that help people with similar professional interests or geographic locations to connect with each other. People who are part of professional networks and associations benefit from receiving the following:

- up-to-date knowledge in one's field,
- information about upcoming events and conferences,
- access to people who can provide practical assistance with problems,
- opportunities for volunteering and service that lead to new relationships,
- referral to others who can help or expand one's network, and
- source of job leads, referrals, and recommendations.

Professional networks are formed and maintained at conferences. You never know whom you will meet and how someone can help you, such as through subsequent recommendations, advice, and so on. People in professional networks are part of a communication network in which information is shared and mutual assistance is provided.

A common mistake is to attend professional conferences with an overemphasis on attending panels and discussions. The content matters, for sure, and there is much to learn that can improve one's activities and performance. However, the people who attend professional conferences represent a fountain of connections and knowledge of opportunities. Networking matters. Associating oneself with new people is key—people need to step up and introduce themselves, regardless of any shyness or English-language issues. It is a great time to practice one's professional commitment statement:

Where are you from?
  ○ From Atlanta.
  → From Atlanta. I work for the Public Service Development Institute, where we train state officials. I am especially interested in ...

Is this your first time here?
  ○ Yes.
  → Yes. I especially liked the presentations on ... which is my main interest. What is your own interest? Do you know anyone who is especially good in my area of interest?

Did you like the presentation?
  ○ Yes.
  → Yes. I especially liked the presentation about ... . This is my first time here, and I am meeting some great people. I think my office should get more involved, perhaps by making a presentation next time. How is that done? Is there anyone on the program committee whom I should talk with?

How did you like the tour?
  ○ The field trip was great. I did not know about the caves.
  → The trip was interesting. In fact, the entire conference has been very useful. This is my second time, and I think

> I should get more involved. What opportunities exist for volunteering and getting more involved? Whom should I talk with?

The point is clear. Meeting others in a professional context is a great opportunity to further one's professional interests, of course. Professionals tend to be understated, and mutual introductions are often a relaxed and laid-back affair. People who know what they are looking for will find professional meetings a valuable source of connections and engage in follow-up to cement new relations. People indeed send reports, announcements, e-mail, and so on after meeting in the course of the year. Not all contacts develop into relations, of course, but it takes only a few good relations (along with good performance) to significantly further one's career. Ask, and eventually you just might get what you want.

Finally, development is also associated with continuing education. Going back to school often is associated with the demonstrated desire to get ahead by investing in one's skills. As one public manager states, "We have a very liberal tuition reimbursement policy. We don't require people to pursue continuing education, but we surely know who is and strongly consider that in our personnel decisions." Thus, education is not only about getting more skills but also a signal to management about one's commitment. And besides, connecting with others in class has helped more than just a few people get a next job. You never know whom you will meet and how that person may help.

Development activities have become increasingly popular in recent years, supplementing those that are already part of the on-the-job repertoire. Mentoring has been often mentioned, though it is sometimes difficult to find a good mentor, and not every mentee is a worthwhile prospect for potential mentors. Coaching styles of supervising can also help improve performance and skills, and these can surely be discussed as part of one's psychological contract. Many people develop a network of people who can provide support and thus reduce career uncertainty. Some are of similar circumstances, whereas others are in quite different ones, offering different skills and insights. People often meet others by participating in professional conferences that, hence, are among the most important developmental activities that people can undertake. You never know how someone else can help you.

Section

Four

The Human Condition Explored

14

Getting to Know Us

You have to row with the oars you have.

—**Popular Dutch expression**[1]

The topics of the previous chapters have a way of coming back to us. A little self-knowledge is essential and goes a long way toward our making better decisions and working with and through others. What people choose as their professional commitment statement is tied up with their perception of how they see themselves in the world, what they enjoy doing, and what their assessment is of what they are good at; not everyone has the talent to be a pop star or scientist, for example. How we communicate with others is also related to our social skills and our ability to manage ourselves in the presence of others. We need to know when, for example, we are about to lose patience with others and how to handle that. Our willingness to draw lines and confront others over their performance and behavior is affected by our experience of others doing the same with us in the past. People skills and self-knowledge are connected.

But what is it that we need to know, and how is this knowledge to be used? Work life experiences change throughout one's life. Life has its phases and passages, as does work life.[2] Different phases of work life offer different key challenges, shown in Table 14.1.[3] It matters that these challenges are handled well. There is little doubt that

Table 14.1 Work Life Phases

Phase	Key Career Challenge	Key Life Challenge
Early twenties	*Career choice:* Knowing one's strengths, choosing a field or career	Intimate relationships and partner selection
Late twenties	*Fitting in:* Getting initial job experiences, making alliances, developing skills for the job	
Thirties	*Building out:* Advancing one's strengths and relationships, carving out a valued area and sector	Parenting and increased responsibility
Mid-forties to early fifties	*Reassessment:* Acknowledging what did not work, finding renewed meaning in work, making a plan for the second half of one's career, actively starting retirement planning	Midlife assessment
Fifties	*Staying productive:* Staying on top of one's game, adding value to the organization, taking on additional leadership roles	Financial success
Sixties	*Preparing for retirement:* Being productive but also passing the baton, mentoring, and preparing for life after career	Staying healthy
Seventies	*Postretirement life:* A little working or consulting for pleasure	Postretirement lifestyle

Source: "Life Challenge" adapted from Levinson, D., *The Seasons of a Man's Life*, Knopf, New York, 1978. See also Levinson, D., *The Seasons of a Woman's Life*, Knopf, New York, 1996.

these key challenges define one's moment and affect one's career. When people are in their twenties, key challenges are to figure out what career they will pursue and deal with fitting in and launching their career. When people are in their thirties, the key challenges are to fit in, establish alliances, and get a first promotion. The key challenges of people in their mid-forties and beyond are recharging, finding new meaning in work, and planning for the second part of their career, while building out leadership skills. This chapter discusses the key challenges of those in their twenties and thirties. Table 14.1 also shows the challenges of people in the later phases of their career, which are discussed in Chapter 15.

The work challenge for people in their twenties and thirties can be characterized as creating or finding a space in society for themselves. People need their authenticity and independence for doing things that give them pleasure, yet they may find an uncomfortable fit with jobs and expectations provided by their parents' generation. Young people's values and aspirations often differ from those of the older generation. People often struggle to express themselves, learn about themselves, and address the constraints of social structure and personal limits such as relating to their talents and mental proclivities. People need to find their own career track.[4] For some people this effort is very large, though others fit easily within the established order of things. But almost all young people experience the need for making adaptations and decisions of some kind, often in the face of having little information about the world in which they will need to fit. Autonomy versus adaptation is a theme throughout most people's lives, but it is especially vivid in this period.

Having self-knowledge is basic to managing these key challenges. We are not all the same. In a competitive world, it is good to take advantage of any special skill. We need to find out what these are but, at the same time, also know and manage our weaknesses. For example, not everyone is good with numbers or likes to work with people. People who are given to migraines and those who deal poorly with stress do well to avoid situations that minimize these. These are often lifelong matters, or affecting a major part of one's life, and cut across all phases and passages of work life. In short, we need to know the "machine" that are, but sometimes it is hard to find the user manual that is right for us. We need to know who we are and how we work.

The following shows how knowing oneself and taking a little action can often make a big difference in dealing with career challenges. Organizations do not always help people to explore themselves; people evidently need to take their own responsibility for getting to know themselves. Sometimes people have a wrong idea about themselves or what they want to pursue, and feedback then often shows up as a series of disappointments. A little self knowledge and career research can make a big difference in developing a good career for us.

As a caveat, we note that not everyone goes through all passages shown in Table 14.1 in the age categories as shown. Some may experience a midlife career re-assessment earlier or later, or never experience many concerns about staying productive. There may also be 'second chances' and some people may experience a stage twice. Culture and economic growth factors may also affect specific stages in ways that are at present insufficiently researched. All stage models are subject to empirically-based concerns of validation and variation, even though they do seems to point o common issues that are ore often mention and fit anecdotally well with the experiences of many people.

A variety of career choice tests are available that help identify fundamental orientations and strengths of people which informs major decisions, such as what to study or what career to pursue. People tend to enjoy and excel what comes natural to them, and the Professional Commitment Statement, discussed in Chapter 8, assumes that a person has good insight into their basic strengths and orientations, and that they are able to discuss a pattern of experiences that is evidence of one's fundamental orientations and features. Self-knowledge comes from many different sources, notably prior job experience (where one's attributes are strongly revealed) and education, but a variety of career choice tests also provide insight into one's basic orientations, proclivities and strengths. It is useful to consider these as relevant information about oneself, too.

Some tests link general personality to occupations, and chief among these is the *Please Understand Me*, the adaptation and popularization of the *Myers-Briggs Type Indicator* provided by David Keirsey.[5] The self-test consists of seventy items that result in sixteen personality types that are each associated with different occupations or activities, such as architect, seller, journalist, entertainer, artist, scientist, teacher, inventor, promoter or entrepreneur, administrator, planner, and so on. Some personality types point to several different occupations. The attractiveness of this instrument is that it is grounded in very fundamental features and characteristics of people that are often set at a very early age and remain stable over their lifetime; it makes very clear why people who are good at, for example, selling not often also have personality features that make them good at science. These two seldom go together. Arnold states, "Our attitudes, that is, the things we like and dislike may be more changeable, particularly in early adulthood, but our preferred personal style remains pretty constant."[6] Different people will find strengths in different pursuits, and people do well to know and embrace their own. People surely learn new skills and to adapt, but underlying personality characteristics and strengths remain very constant. In addition, personality configurations vary in prevalence. For example, some temperaments (broad groups of personalities) are well suited for observance of others' rules and leadership; these temperaments are very common, and people with these temperaments have a lot of company from other like-minded people. Such people tend to feel naturally at home in organizations and at school.[7] But personalities that emphasize creativity, empathetic compassion, and inquisitiveness are far less common in society; the journey of such persons is often characterized by their searching for their place in society and trying to follow rules and orientations that do not come naturally to them. They often feel a bit out of place in society. Personality is a major factor that shapes the journey of people at work, and tests can help clarify this.

The details and description of various temperaments and personality types are too much for discussion here or in any other book; the sixteen personality profiles are all rich in detail and implications. The *Myers-Briggs* test has become a staple of delivered Western cultural inheritance, and the significance of the test means that it should be taken. Predictably, different personality types tend to respond very differently to this test and its results, and the only way of discerning its relevance is for people to take the test and

> **Personality is a major factor that shapes the journey of people at work.**

use the information that it provides for one's career development. Another compelling aspect of taking a broader view is that test results are also related to mate selection preferences, which, too, is a key challenge for people in their twenties and early thirties.[8] At this time of writing, this test can be found free online.[9]

A second type of career test focuses on specific preferences for work tasks, relationships, and conditions. Chief among these is

Edgar Schein's popular *Career Anchors*.[10] This test consists of forty self-scored items about work (rather than basic personality features). The test results are eight career anchors, features that weigh strongly in a person's preference: technical expertise, general management, autonomy, security, entrepreneurship, service (dedication to a cause), high challenge, and balance with personal and family life. The discussion of these career anchors includes specific jobs and occupations. For example, those with high preference for autonomy might consider being freelance consultants, professors, small businessmen, field salespersons, and so forth. People can score high on multiple anchors, which thus suggests more specific career choices for consideration. A variety of other career-interest tests also exist, such as the *Strong Interest Inventory* test, with about 291 questions.[11] Some career-interest tests link back to the *Myers-Briggs* test.

A third career type of test focuses on specific job skills. Chief among these is the U.S. Department of Labor *O*NET*.[12] This test assesses aptitudes in basic skills, complex problem-solving skills, resource management skills, social skills, and system skills. There are thirty-five items, and the result is a listing of specific jobs that match with these skills. The online features allow people to readily access specific tasks and outlooks for these jobs, which include attention to specific work interests (practical, procedure oriented, investigative), personal working styles (detail, innovative, stress tolerance, etc.), and values (working conditions, independence, achievement orientation). The specific job can also be linked to salary surveys of the U.S. Bureau of Labor Statistics, Employment and Wage estimates.[13]

In practice, these tests are to be used in triangulation. We strongly recommend those discussed above. Though the specificity of the latter databases is appealing, the lack of broader integration with personality and work styles is a significant limitation; the point is to make a career choice that is consistent with oneself, of course. There are also additional tests that assess certain aspects or traits that may be associated with specific careers or business success. For example, the "Big Five personality traits" are found to be empirically associated with success in organizations and career development.[14] These five traits are openness (to new experiences and ideas), conscientiousness (efficiency, self-discipline, etc.), extraversion (outgoing and social interaction), agreeableness, and neuroticism (emotional stability and confidence). Assessing these features points to areas on which a person may want to work a bit; few people have personalities that are naturally strong in each of these areas.

A career choice is not an armchair decision, and the above tests will still require additional self-research to determine specific features and conditions that are part of any final choice. Experience at work validates what one likes and dislikes, and often brings up new opportunities that one did not know about. The interviewing of job holders (Chapter 8) enlightens about actual working conditions and requirements for success.[14] Career choices often require both a broad and narrow decision; first about the kinds of activities one might do (e.g., "something with numbers" such as accounting or engineering), and then, second, about the specific details that make it consistent with one's strengths, future outlook, contributions that a person wants to make, as well as have appealing work activity and being consistent with personal preferences such as geographic limitations (e.g. being close to one's family), family planning, lifestyle choices, and decisions about how much money a person is looking to make, now and later. Career choice tests deal more with broad decisions, but we need to first know who we are because we can embark on the details of narrow choices.

Further action is needed to address the narrow and specific decisions, and we refer to Chapter 8. People will inevitably need to get more information about specific careers such as opportunities, the nature of work, compensation, etc., than can be found on-line. If you want to learn about careers in accounting, one should talk to a few accountants. The exercise of interviewing existing jobholders usually provides important, additional information. The accounting work in large and small firms may differ substantially. Some accounting may focus on international firms, or on forensic accounting in connection with court cases. People in the industry can best describe what specific work really involves, as well as training, qualifications and other factors on which success rests. Only after one becomes clear about this, people can better evaluate how a specific career path fits with their strengths, interests as well as personal preferences such as for location, working conditions, job security and compensation.

As regarding compensation, it is worth reminding that aspiring to a high paying job in which one has little inclination is unlikely to be very successful. In high paying careers, only good performers tend to get top level pay. Also, as it turns out, with exception of some rather low paying professions (e.g., education) or high paying entry jobs (finance), most entry and mid-level jobs pay within a rather similar band. Jobs that require technical skills do tend to pay more. Public sector jobs are roughly on par with private sector jobs. The private sector advantage is usually at the end of the pay scale for high level executive jobs. Though some choices can surely be made with compensation in mind, it is also important to find a career that suits one's talents and other needs; money is but one of several considerations. Not everybody in finance lands a job on Wall Street.

In some cultures, parents play a major role driving the career choices of their children. Boys, in particular, are often encouraged to study business or other well paying professions, while girls are sometimes discouraged from pursuing certain careers. Even when parental influence is not overt, many people still feel a need, in their own mind, to choose in ways that will make their parents or society proud of them. The desire to satisfy one's parents (or family) often is strong; children of deceased parents sometimes ask what their parents would have liked to see them become, which is seen as a way of honoring their memory. While this may be unproblematic when parental and a person's career choices coincide, the matter of career choice sometimes pits children against their families in a bid for greater independence, adding an additional personal dimension to this matter.

Finally, some people just can't seem to make a decision what they want to do. One sometimes comes across people in their 30's who have yet to figure out what they want to do. This has different causes, such as inadequate experience with specific jobs, an over-abundance of capabilities, a lack of specific capabilities or academic interests, or talents that do not translate into specific careers ("I like dealing with people, but I have no specific interests"). It often also points to personal factors, such as a lack of confidence, fear of decision-making, personal constraints that limit choices (young children, aging parents, not driving, and lack of money for studying).[15] Underlying these can be mental health conditions such as significant depression (see chapter 17). Some people learn that they have these conditions as a result of confronting career choice decisions. Life is what you make of it, and counseling and treatment often are good and necessary. Sometimes, when people are undecided, they need to give themselves a few months for researching two or three likely options by interviewing and talking with people. This often results in additional information that leads to a final decision.[16]

Fitting in is also often a key challenge for people in their late twenties. After deciding what career to invest in, one or more initial jobs in these lines of work will result. Abstract or academic discussion about being courteous, not pushing hot buttons, and so on is one thing and about which few will disagree, but getting these things right in practice is quite another. Many people will have worked minor jobs during college that provide valuable and necessary lessons on fitting in and getting along with others. The main conclusions of the chapters about getting along and fitting in are summarized in Table 14.2. Almost everyone experiences difficulties of some sort that require adaptation. Fitting in and getting along are obviously important to

Table 14.2 Basic Values and Behaviors for Fitting In and Getting Along

Social Manners	Getting Along	Other
Courtesy	Doing your job well and reliably	Communicating with redundancy (Chapter 3)
Respect	Being pleasant	Finding common bonds and ties (Chapter 5)
Welcoming	Supporting others	Setting boundaries (Chapters 6, 12)
Effective	Avoiding hot buttons	
Able to connect	Going gently with excellence	
	Handling difficult situations with little fuss	

one's career, as being accepted and getting promotions are critically needed. When the challenge of fitting in is not well addressed in this period, problems usually continue throughout later jobs, sometimes with very bad consequences.

To be sure, at issue is not always a personal deficiency. In a global world, people are socialized into different cultures, and according to Hofstede, one of the ways in which cultures vary is their emphasis on individualism versus collectivity.[17] People in individualist cultures (e.g., the United States and United Kingdom) tend to be more assertive and direct than those from collective cultures who are more concerned with group harmony and have learned to be concerned about negative consequences of direct behavior. Similarly, the cultures or practices that one has learned from one's family and peers may differ from those of any specific workplace. In some families, children are encouraged to speak their mind and give their opinions, and some public schools in the United States reinforce this. These conditions are unlikely to occur in the workplace. The ways in which one is to be pleasant vary according to the culture and customs where one is. There are good reasons why social adaptation is a constant in new jobs.

In addition, the challenge is not always about adopting certain behaviors. Sometimes people do not recognize their actions as being deficient; if they knew that what they were doing is giving them trouble, some might stop doing it, of course. Another problem is that people may be unable to sufficiently stop the behavior that is causing problems. Some people cling to their beliefs for a very long time, even when they bring problems. Another issue is also that people may be insufficiently clear of what is expected of them. Telling them to act differently or in a certain way does not mean that they will know from experience how to do so.

The good news is that workplace behavior is not a single target but a range of acceptable behavior within which people should fall. Figure 14.1 suggests that the challenge is to avoid behavior that is seen as too extreme. Typically, people will give hints when something needs change, and it is wise to ask after a few weeks and months

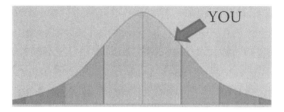

Figure 14.1 A range of acceptable behavior.

whether there is anything they would like to see changed. A psychological contract, discussed in Chapter 10, could surely be used for this purpose. Below are some common problems of fitting in that can be observed, along with some suggestions.

Overassertiveness. Some people come from cultures that are highly assertive and individualist. In some of these cultures, dialog and debate are prized as ways of arriving at the truth. In others, people are expected to take action first and justify their choices later. In still others, people are expected to tout their achievements or associations. A person might have good reasons and benefits for being assertive, but these manners also often rub those from other more conventional and group-oriented cultures the wrong way; they may see it as boorish, rude, or loud. Overassertiveness also often ignores subtle signals of disapproval that are given.

The essential lesson is that one's values are seldom the only or even the best ones; there is a trade-off between being right and getting along. Some people have the belief that one's values are right and proper, such as a search for truth, action, or achievement, yet others may hold these values as less important than their values of, for example, getting along, knowing one's place, making group decisions, or taking turns at being recognized. Another problem often is that people from such cultures may not know how to act in ways that others expect. They have less experience in group-oriented action. It is difficult to change one's way when there is no alternative behavior to fall back on. Then, toning things down is more than just about doing something less; it is also learning a new way of being. Not surprisingly, people may have a few difficult episodes before the new ways are learned and adapted as part of their new repertoire.[18]

Lack of reliability. Some people are just too unreliable—they don't show up on time, and their work is late and sometimes below quality. The older generation calls this a lack of commitment and enthusiasm, and keeping such persons around may breed resentment from those who do more. These people need to step up their game, but when they are asked to do so, some acquiesce but quickly fall back into bad habits. This can have several causes, including a genuine lack of commitment to the job or organization ("I am here only until I get something better."), a lack of professional norms ("I don't understand what these people get so worked up over. Why does everything need to be so perfect?"), or a lack of energy ("I just can't get up on time." "I can't find the enthusiasm that others have."). These matters really do point to matters deeper than just behavior or doing one's job. The latter may also be pointing to physical or mental health problems.

For some, a lack of reliability may reflect a lack of self-discipline. This is a common human approach to reduce pain or unpleasant experience, by putting off that which one does not want to do. Procrastination often reflects deeply ingrained habits and beliefs that may be hard to change. One person states it as this:

> The problem isn't whether the advice is based on science or not. The problem is that you need to find self-discipline in order to execute the strategies in the first place. ... That's the part I need to read three hundred pages about. If we each had the self-discipline to accomplish whatever we set out to accomplish, the world would be a very different place. But what we have instead is a world divided into the people who have self-discipline (those with good careers, good bodies, and good mates) and people who don't.[19]

Whatever the cause, people do need reliability and performance from people at work. Overcoming procrastination is a formidable challenge for some people that is brought to the fore by work.

Just too different or weird for us. All people have their own talent and style, but the limits are reached when others begin to comment that they feel uncomfortable in the presence of someone or that they would be embarrassed or concerned about introducing a person to a client or senior official. They also need to feel safe in the presence of others. The problem comes in several different ways: dressing inappropriately, having unusual nonverbal behavior, saying the wrong thing at the wrong time, or being insufficiently deferential. Dress codes for both men and women need to fit in with what others are following. Being too flirtatious is a problem that creates resentment. Personal hygiene needs to be appropriate; people who don't take showers or change their clothes create problems. Some people stare at others or look at them in ways that make them uncomfortable; even unintentionally, this is a problem. Some people say things at meetings or to key stakeholders that are just off and make others cringe. No matter what one's performance and degree are, there is a point that these problems will not be overlooked. When these matters are said about someone, especially when they are shared by others, it is a sure sign of that person not fitting in enough.

One would think that these are minor matters to be corrected, but while supervisors often ask for specific changes, some people are unable to follow through. Some of it is learned behavior that is difficult to unlearn. A woman may have learned to use provocative clothing, and she might feel uncomfortable with anything else. Not washing one's clothes may be an eco-friendly policy ("for whom?" the office colleague is apt to ask). Looking at people in an odd way may have been what one has always done ("I learned this from my uncle."), and, as in the above section, a person may not know how to change this. Not being able to control one's tongue can reflect impulsiveness that may be difficult to change; just counting to ten sometimes may not be enough. When simple approaches to these problems do not work, then deeper problems may be indicated.

Lack of street smarts. People need to pick up new skills, new techniques, and new ways of valuing people or circumstances on the job. Really, school is just about the basics. No matter how well one performed in school, on-the-job learning is a reality. We sometimes say that a master's degree takes four years—two years in school and another two years in the job. People pay attention to how well others pick up new skills and whether they are able to eventually contribute their salary's worth. Just following orders and being nice are not enough in many jobs.

Some people do better in the classroom than on the job. Some people are just unable to pick up what needs to be done and do it well. This can have many causes, such as having made a wrong career choice that requires skills that one just doesn't have. Some people just lack the ability to pick up and process new information quickly and accurately—arguably, they should not have been hired in the first place. Another problem is a lack of street smarts or practical common sense, whether from a lack of experience or from a lack of ability. This is a difficult learning issue to address, and it may require a person taking more time (another job?) to learn what is needed or taking a lower-level job where the lack of judgment can do less harm. We see people with a lack of practical street smarts in all areas, including science, where a lack of practical ability hinders scientific progress.

Lack of fit. Sometimes people are hired with excellent qualifications and recommendations but are later let go for lack of fit. What's up? Problems may have been their inability to learn new skills or the organization's changing its need for skills. Another problem is the inability of the person to fill a critical need or role and to be valued for that. Those who are critically needed are more likely to be kept around or even promoted. People have to be seen as essential in some way. Another problem may also be a lack of connecting or bonding with people, as discussed in Chapter 5. We need to make a few friends at work, however superficial these friendships may be. People like to feel a commonality with others, such as a common past (location, education) or common interests (hobbies, likes). Bonding alone is not enough, but a lack of connection when there is also additional evidence of people skill problems can often be the difference between keeping people and letting them go. Then the problem might be summed up as just "not the best fit with us." It happens.

The above lists several challenges that people may experience, and many people experience one or several that are their particular issue to deal with. A key challenge often is being unclear how to address what others see as deficiencies ("I hear what you don't like, but how

BOX 14.1   EMOTIONAL INTELLIGENCE

The term *emotional intelligence* was popularized in 1995 by Daniel Goleman, a *New York Times* journalist, in his best-selling book *Emotional Intelligence: Why It Can Matter More than IQ.*[21] Life is not only an academic test, and getting along with people matters. Emotional intelligence (EI) is defined as the ability to recognize emotions in oneself and others and to use this knowledge for improved self-management and relationships with others.[22] EI consists of four domains: self-awareness, self-management, social awareness, and relationship management.[23] In work, people do well to be aware of what they and others are experiencing. "At the heart of EI is a process of recognizing and bringing into awareness (consciousness) emotions that are experienced by oneself and others and then using this awareness (information) skillfully (indeed, intelligently) in subsequent decision making and action," write Berman and West.[24]

Emotional Quotient (EQ) tests usually assess about twenty to forty different aspects of these domains activities, involving fifty to three hundred test items.[25] EQ tests are a broad assessment of one's emotional skills. A variety of EQ tests can be found online.[26] EQ is not limited to workplace uses and is basic to getting along; it seems plausible that those with low EQ test scores will experience many of the problems described in the text. EQ is also finding its way into job interviews. For example, people may be asked about a specific time that they positively influenced a worker, were surprised by something they said that had negative impacts on others, or made an effort to tone down their behavior or about how they deal with jealousy, how they react to deadlines, how often they believe they should express appreciation to others, how they respond to let downs and let downs experienced by others, and so on.[27]

> The term *emotional intelligence* has made it into the popular lexicon, and at present efforts are being undertaken to make it part of workplace behavior, in specific areas. The topics and content of this book are consistent with the deepening in understanding about human relations and interactions that is increasingly present. It is worth it for people to take a broad assessment EQ test.

do you want me to act in such situation?"). Thus, people often seek counsel from books and friends, but straight-forward and simple advices do not always work. Deeper knowledge about oneself may then be needed (as an example, see Box 11.1). People sometimes are in denial or unwilling to address feedback which makes them uncomfortable or which contradicts other strongly held values, but knowing which problem one has is also part of essential self-knowledge, as well as strategies that work. It is self-evident that overcoming one's challenges fortifies self-confidence and furthers one success.

Beyond making career choices and fitting in, the beginning of one's career in one's twenties includes making efforts to sustain and build out one's role in organizations. The above issues of fitting in and getting along remain important foci of one's professional development—the experience of the workplace usually forces people to do some important learning. Practice makes perfect in finding out what the system wants from us and how we can give. We learn how to avoid creating enemies. People who survive the first two years of an organization often get opportunities to grow further in it. Yet, in addition to the above, two new areas of people skills often surface: professional networking and ethics. Though these matters have already been mentioned in Part 3 of this book, it is worth highlighting these in the context of initial career development.

First, once a career path is chosen, the need for industry networking becomes more apparent. Professional associations are now seen as exciting and important sources of networking, new knowledge, and upward mobility. The benefits and tactics discussed in Chapters 9 and 13 are now taken seriously—people are apt to read journals and go to conferences and perhaps serve on committees. Knowledge develops quickly, and we prove our worth by staying on top of things. Being five or ten years out of school, we don't want to fall behind. Many people make it a point to go to at least two professional conferences a year. People in their thirties often need to make choices about specific industry niches and organizations in which they can best further their career, and access to a network of professionals obviously helps.

There is also the lesson that developing professional relations and friendships requires time and money. Going to conferences costs money, and a substantial part often is not reimbursed (though it may be an income tax deduction). People will go out with others and pick up the tab. Parties will be hosted at home. Writing e-mail and giving someone a call take time. Following up with those we like or want to stay in touch with takes time and sometime a bit of money too. People show through their actions where their commitments lie toward others.

Second, any multiyear journey has its bumps. Ethics often come up in some fashion. It is easy to make a misstep in some way. Greed and pleasure do get the better of us. Perhaps we signed an affidavit that we should not have or had an office romance that we now regret. We do not always keep our promises, or we engage in image management with little substance and intention to deliver. Making excuses is easy, and some people live in a world of excuses. Yet something usually happens to signal that one needs to deeply examine one's sense of ethics. Ethics goes from being an academic or tabloid discussion to something with real career consequences for oneself. It is said that life has a way of first throwing pebbles one's way, then small rocks, then larger ones, and finally crushing boulders that are career ending if not heeded. Most people heed the call to get their act in order, but not all people are able to resist whatever it is that is calling them.[28] People come face-to-face with other personal behaviors and orientations that become problematic for themselves or others. Some of these are discussed in further chapters, but they do include late-night partying, attention seeking, lying, substance use, and so on. There often is truth to the saying "We have seen the enemy, and it is us." Not everyone will have issues, of course, but more people seem to have such matters than there are those willing to talk about them.

The thirties are often a time when ethics and personal issues are dealt with. Those who end their thirties with an untarnished record, as well as with professional accomplishments and a supporting network and well-learned lessons in self-management and getting along, will surely have a leg up in getting ahead. Knowing a lot of people helps one to find new job opportunities. Being known as someone who gets the job done, who stays out of trouble, and who is pleasant to get along with is often a necessary qualification for being selected. Together, these aspects do help build out one's career path and land opportunities. The efforts that people undertake in regard to these matters further define who they are. Of course, other things also happen when people are in their thirties, such as family planning and personal and professional crises (e.g., reorganizations and downsizing), that affect one's plans. These are discussed in subsequent chapters.

Launching a career often involves challenges that benefit from the development of self-knowledge. Both broad and narrow career decisions are needed and require substantial insight into one's strengths and abilities; while career tests help, personal research in the form of interviews and internships often firm up these decisions. Launching a career also involves matters of adapting oneself to the challenge of fitting in. People experience different challenges such as dealing with over- or underassertiveness, reliability, performance, individuality, practical ability and learning, and connecting, all of which can affect their ability to fit in and get along at work. Beyond this, many people experience one or two issues that come up for them and that provide further self-knowledge. We also bring attention to increased networking and ethical conduct people encounter in their thirties.

15

A Gesture of Balance

The unexamined life is not worth living.

—**Plato**

The launching of one's career brings up a host of challenges, many of which have been previously discussed in connection with people at work and career development. Yet career development also brings up other issues concerning the integration of work with other aspects of one's life. In both East and West, work has become an increasingly time-consuming and demanding affair. How people deal with the stress of work affects their personal life, and how well they manage the many tasks of their personal life affects their ability to take on work challenges. People often try to keep their personal life separate from their interactions with others at work, but they cannot keep it separate within themselves. The interface between work and other aspects of one's life brings up psychological and other issues that will not be denied; they must be dealt with.

Whereas the previous chapter focused on the very early stages of work experiences, this chapter discusses several integration challenges that are part of the human condition in later stages. One issue is stress and stress management. It is inevitable and part of the modern condition that people have many responsibilities and new challenges in both their work life and their personal life. The integration between work and nonwork activities for many people presents far more activities than can reasonably be taken on. The result often is stress, and this chapter discusses practical strategies for reducing and managing stress. The ability to manage one's work and nonwork activities not only adds to personal well-being but also affects work performance; it affects how much work is done and how well that work is done.

Second, we examine some existential matters. People are learning animals, and a need for periodical rebalancing exists as people acquire new lessons and insight into themselves and others. In midlife, people get to deal with some more true facts. Some career objectives have not been achieved and are unlikely to be achieved. Lessons in dealing with people may leave one wary. Half of one's career life is over. A key task at midlife is to find renewed energy and meaning, often of a different kind, for the work that is to be done. A need exists to replace the youthful dream of the past with more mature objectives and goals that are appropriate for one's current position and goals for the remaining future. Existential questions are of course not limited to midlife and often come up earlier too. Finally, this chapter concludes with thoughts for the later years of one's career.

Seen in the light of the above passages, it is fair to characterize the human condition at work as also including an unending search and effort to maintain balance. Broader still, there is balance to be had that involves one's work activities and different roles in life, a peaceful mind versus an agitated and restless mind, a healthy body versus an overstressed and underexercised body, and professional and personal realization versus mere fulfillment and compliance with the desires of others. Though perfect balance is seldom attainable or even definable, people recognize a need for not letting things get too far out of whack. When cracks appear, they demand our attention. This chapter provides some basic frameworks and refers to material of the previous chapters that highlights application.

It should be noted that employers increasingly offer a broad range of programs that benefit employees' well-being.[1] Regardless of these programs and employers' reasons for offering them, it inevitably remains the employees' own responsibility to integrate work with broader aspects of their life in a harmonious and balanced way. Some employer well-being programs are mandated by law (e.g., health insurance), whereas others help employers attract and retain talent (e.g., on-site day care center, flextime, tuition reimbursement). Here our focus is not on the effectiveness of these programs for employers but rather on the challenges that face employees. While many of these employer-sponsored programs are helpful to some extent, surely not all are relevant to the matters discussed here.

Also, not everyone experiences the matters discussed here in equal ways; people and cultures vary. The above tasks tend to come up for people at different times in their careers, but they could come up at any time or not come up at all for any individual. Not everybody chooses to make families, but those who do experience increased pressures from these roles and obligations—one study reports that parent are the most stressed of all demographic groups.[2] Fertility rates in Taiwan and South Korea are, respectively, a paltry 0.94 and 1.15, for example, far below the normal replenishment level of about 2.1[3] —job stress and the cost raising children are commonly reported reasons for this. Likewise, not everyone experiences a midlife career reassessment; for some people, the career opportunities just keep popping up, offering little time for reflection until people retire. People surely vary in what they prioritize and experience.

People in their thirties are often characterized as taking on increased challenges and responsibilities. People are apt to search and explore new career challenges and opportunities, embarking on new and uncertain territories with new and unfamiliar challenges. A lot of investment is made in the beginning of one's career, including in new interpersonal roles associated with marriage, civil unions, or other partnerships with significant others, as well as, often, parenting roles associated with family development. In addition, many people take on substantial financial challenges and obligations involved with these activities (new babies, home mortgages, and sometimes business loans) while also dealing with other challenges of personal growth and development.

Table 15.1 Stressors in Life and Work

Top Ten Stressful Events in Life[1]	Top Ten Stressful Events in Work[1]	Job Stressors Mentioned Elsewhere (Unranked)[2]
1. Death of a spouse (100)	8. Fired at work (47)	Workload
2. Divorce (73)	15. Business readjustment (39)	Lack of control over work, random interruptions
3. Marriage separation (65)	16. Change in financial condition (38)	Feeling undervalued, lack of support
4. Jail term (63)	18. Change to a different line of work (36)	Having to take on others' work
5. Death of a close relative (63)	22. Change in work responsibilities (29)	Getting a new boss
6. Injury or illness (53)	28. Outstanding achievement (28)	Mistrust and unfairness
7. Marriage (50)	30. Trouble with boss (23)	Pressure from managers
8. Fired at work (47)	31. Change in work hours or conditions (20)	Unclear policies or direction, managers changing their mind
9. Marriage reconciliation (45)	41. Vacation (13)	Career and job uncertainty
10. Retirement (45)		

Source: (1) *Holmes-Rahe Life Stress Inventory* (rank order of stress shown; life change units shown in parentheses). For the survey, see http://www.harvestenterprises-sra.com/ The%20Holmes-Rahe%20Scale.htm. (2) Various. See also Health Central, "Top Ten Stressful Life Events as Predictors of Mental and Physical Illness," June 29, 2010, http://www.healthcentral.com/anxiety/c/157571/115211/life-predictors; Skillsoft, *Research into UK Workers Stress Levels*, Compass House, Camberley, UK, 2008. http://www.skillsoft.com/infocenter/whitepapers/documents/research-into-uk-workers-stress-levels.pdf.

It has become common to discuss these challenges in the context of stress. Stress is commonly understood in psychology as a state of bodily and mental tension that results from a change or impetus to which a person is seeking to respond and adapt.[4] Table 15.1 shows a variety of job stresses. Among the most widely cited stress scales is the *Holmes-Rahe Life Stress Inventory*, which includes various job stressors, though it focuses on event changes rather than constant stresses such as having trouble with a boss or a hostile coworker.[5] Though Table 15.1 shows that some life events are more stressful than job events, clearly work is a source of stress. Surveys regularly report that work life is stressful all or most of the time for many people. According to one survey, "80% of workers feel stress on the job, nearly half say they need help in learning how to manage stress and 42% say their coworkers need such help."[6] The right-hand column in Table 15.1 shows additional sources of job stress.

Stress is a subjective matter, referring to the ability of people to handle and address different stressors, including stress itself. Some people develop strong negative sensations from even modest activity, whereas others can tolerate a higher level of activity. People vary in their ability to handle conflict, ambiguity, disappointment, and multiple deadlines, for example, and they also vary in their reactions to stress. Some people develop only minor symptoms from stress, whereas others experience modest to high levels of body aches (e.g., head, shoulder, back, digestion, etc.), sleeplessness, and other symptoms. Stress increases the flow of adrenaline and cortisol, which increases the heart rate. People need to know how well they are able to respond to the situations in Table 15.1 and the resulting stress.

The *Holmes-Rahe Life Stress Inventory* includes mean life change units (LCUs) shown in brackets. As an average and rough guide, scores over 150 suggest a life crisis. The point is people often experience multiple stressors. A major change in work duties could involve Items 15, 18, 22, and 31, adding up to 124 LCUs, which, with a few other personal or other work-related issues, would quickly put someone over 150. (Comparing the right-hand items with those in the middle, it seems reasonable to assign each 20 to 30 points, though this is just our opinion.) But many studies show that the cumulative effect of multiple stressors is more than additive, adding 25 percent or more to the total score.[7] The effects of multiple simultaneous stressors is said to be "superadditive." Hence, a few personal issues along with a few work-related problems quickly become a significant source of stress.

It is common in the business literature to note that stress is not always a negative, but the reality of modern life is that most people have too much of it. It is said that some amount of stress is needed to bring activity (without some amount of pressure, people might do very little) and that some level of disagreement and conflict is healthy as well. It is also said that with some activities (e.g., public speaking, parachuting, etc.), some people experience negative emotions and sensations, whereas others experience positive ones. Whatever the merit of these theoretical propositions, the task for people today is to reduce their stress. Moreover, people often underestimate the effect of changes and challenges that they take on, such as starting a new job or moving to another city. People underestimate the impact of family development on their ability to meet work expectations. Thus, people often have more than enough stress in their life.

Managing stress is therefore a major part of the human condition. Prolonged experiences of even moderate levels of stress are to be avoided or reduced as much as possible; though research is not yet definitive, it is increasingly held that stress kills and that it is also associated with a reduction in judgment, performance, and people relations at work. Here we focus on strategies for reducing stress. Total elimination of stress is, of course, seldom possible.

Stress avoidance and activity selection. In the spirit of the saying "an ounce of prevention is better than a pound of cure," there is wisdom in both not taking on too many activities and creating conditions that favor working successfully on new roles and endeavors. For example, we observed that in Orlando, Florida, where we once lived, young people who married with the intention of raising a family often bought a home that was within blocks of their parents or other family members who would assist with child-rearing duties. Even though housing looks like any subdivision in the United States, some have extensive and close-knit social structures that also assisted those without families. The increased support network obviously reduces stress in a multitude of ways. Prioritizing our roles and activities, and creating favorable conditions for their success, is necessary in today's world. Postponing having children until people are financially able to create favorable conditions for raising them is surely a sensible strategy.

There is also value in recognizing that people vary in how much activity they can take on. For example, Type A personalities are sometimes defined as high-achieving people who are ambitious, assertive, businesslike, controlling, competitive (aggressive), impatient, task oriented, and deadline conscious.[8] Type A personalities often work with a high level of stress and are comfortable with it. They take on a lot of work. By contrast Type B personalities are described as easygoing, relaxed, more patient, and often lacking a sense of urgency or time pressure. Of course, not everyone falls into these two categories, but the point is to know what one is comfortable with and can put up with. This includes, in this case, Type B personalities often avoiding interactions with Type A personalities, who are seen as a source of undesirable stress, and Type A personalities avoiding those with extreme Type B behaviors whose lack of urgency causes Type A personalities undue stress. It might be noted that the distinction between Type A and Type B personalities was developed in the 1950s with eye toward predicting heart disease (personality as a risk factor).[9] People do well to choose wisely what they take on and ensure the conditions under which they think they can be successful.

Relationship management. Another approach to reducing stress is to structure working relationships on a more solid footing. Misunderstandings and misalignment are common in all working relationships, but it surely helps to reduce these by establishing clear expectations in advance and having open lines of communication when troubles do result. Surveys show that a lack of control over one's workday is a major source of stress. The strategy of psychological contracts (Chapter 10) is surely helpful to reducing uncertainty and increasing shared understanding in working relations and ways in which work is to occur. People also vary in their need for appreciation, and it is sometimes helpful to make such needs explicit as requests. Psychological contracts can cover a broad range of issues, such as due dates, when and how things are communicated, working conditions, responsibilities and rewards, and many other matters; they may not always result in complete improvement, but they can make matters better.

It seems also quite common that almost everyone has someone with whom they do not see eye to eye at work. The causes of this are myriad, such as allegations of unethical conduct, performance standards that are too high or too low, people with rough interpersonal

> **Managing our relations in ways that avoid stressful encounters is an essential key to workplace happiness.**

skills or lack of social graces, people with ambitions who use their "sharp elbows" in adversarial ways, and so on. Having someone we do not like at work is a source of demotivation and ongoing stress. Almost everyone needs to then draw some lines in the sand, setting boundaries to interactions. There are things that people will not put up with, and it is good to have support from others on these. Managing our relations in ways that avoid stressful encounters is an essential key to workplace happiness.

Beyond these people issues is the need for time management as a way of reducing stress. The simple act of planning one's day and week as a series of targets helps ensure that planned work in fact gets done and that when one is distracted or interrupted, an early warning is given to reschedule and make task completion a main priority.

Physical activity. Almost everyone agrees that physical activity reduces stress. Exercise strengthens the body and immune system and increases endurance. Exercise makes people feel better and more fit. Physical activity stimulates various brain chemicals that leave many people feeling happier and more relaxed than before they worked out.[10] It also reduces the level of cortisol that is associated with heart disease and fat buildup. Exercise releases endorphins that are a natural pain reliever and antidepressant, which give people a natural high and euphoric feeling after working out. Many people also feel that muscle tensions associated with work stress are more relaxed. The benefits of exercise are well-known and associated with improved health; though exercise does not address underlying causes of workplace stress, it can address some of the symptoms. Similarly, some people benefit from taking a hot bath or shower after work or from walking leisurely to calm themselves down.

Resting the mind. One of the more troublesome features of being human is our mind; though it is associated with many positive benefits and obviously needed, the mind is also prone to incessantly producing thoughts that incite and lead to stress symptoms. It is hard to switch off one's mind after work; troublesome and intrusive thoughts about the day's events continue to arise and stop only when they have been replaced by other thoughts. No wonder that people turn up the music in their car in an effort to distract their mind.

A key restorative and stress-eliminating activity is to take one's mind off work. Almost everyone needs a day of going to the park, going out with friends, or going shopping or to a movie that takes their mind off work and has it focus on other things that are associated with pleasure. Willy-nilly, people experience their bodies relaxing and the mind being restored. People know well the value of having had a restorative weekend. Having been able to focus on other things, people often also experience new thoughts when they later, perhaps on Monday, return back to work activity. Meditation is a harder road to take toward relaxing the mind and controlling intrusive and obsessive thoughts. Switching off the mind is one of the hardest human things to do. A first place to start, however, is recognizing the mind as a thought-producing machine that is incessant in its production of thoughts. We do well to sometimes ignore the many thoughts that it produces, especially when these do not serve the need for rest. The next chapter discusses this in greater detail.

Managing our responsibilities by prioritizing, creating favorable conditions, managing relations, and effectively dealing with stress symptoms is part of the modern world. People's need for addressing these matters often emerges strongly in their thirties, though it is not unknown to students in their twenties. Strategies learned in one's twenties for dealing with the stresses of studying, dating, and having part-time jobs form the basis for dealing with increased stress and strain later. Somehow, we need to slow down, reduce the activities that we take on, and be smarter at how we handle them. Only then do we have a chance of finding balance among the different roles that we would like to play. People often use their holidays for deciding what activities they will give up and not do in the next quarter. If we cannot reduce our activities or find smarter ways to do them, then stress is the inevitable result. The above matters often come sharply to the forefront in people's thirties but continue throughout their career in their forties, fifties, and sixties.

Paradoxically, as people focus on these matters for themselves, they come to see that others also share these experiences and concerns; using the people skills discussed in previous chapters, we find opportunities to thicken workplace connections by supporting and assisting others with these matters too. People who work together often find opportunities to help each other in the above matters. Coworkers with children may offer to share babysitters or look after each other's children. Coworkers may decide to exercise together or introduce their coworkers to new sports. Coworkers also share with others new events in town that give people something new to do on the weekend. People surely appreciate that others have improved their weekend and other nonwork activities in some ways. People skills at work are sometimes to connect in this area too.

The mid-forties often is the beginning of a shift in work motivation that is, psychologically, a recalibration with the lessons that have been learned. People in their twenties and thirties at the early stages of their careers are heavily motivated by the need for achieving status, increasing compensation, obtaining societal or parental approval, and achieving a modicum of job security that may come from successive promotion or recognition. These needs drive a succession of career targets that all serve the need for successive promotion and recognition. The beginning of one's career is a period that is often characterized by sustained and increasing acquisition of material and social achievements, including careers, titles, homes, cars, a spouse, and family.[11]

Though acquisition surely continues throughout a person's life, these motivational bases do come under strain as the lessons of experience are considered. After about fifteen or twenty years of work, the following strains may start to show, though for some these come earlier and for others they come later or not at all. Some goals that we set for ourselves have perhaps not been realized and are unlikely to be. Perhaps some goals were misguided or guided by insufficient knowledge of our actual abilities and skills. Although we worked hard, we did not get some of the lucky breaks that others did. We also made unwise career choices that limited our achievements, and we continue to do so. Moreover, with just another fifteen to twenty years left to retirement, a more mature dream for the next phase of our career is needed, including that of acquiring a large enough nest egg for retirement. It seems we do change our dreams a bit.

People are also apt to reassess their relations to others. Inevitably, people experienced the joys as well as the betrayals and limitations of dealing with people. Though people are likely not as bad as the portrayal in some Hollywood Wall Street or corporate espionage movies, we sometimes see them as having their own agendas and a self-centered and less than caring or supportive attitude. We may also begin to wonder whose life we are living. If we have focused a lot on accomplishment, then perhaps we feel that we are missing the pleasure that comes from having a close group of real friends. If we focused on what we thought would please our parents or society, we might not find the satisfaction or recognition that we might have craved. Surely, some measure of goals and sacrifice is required, but has there been too much?

People may also experience several postachievement letdowns. Having worked hard for a deal, a promotion, or another achievement, people might be engulfed by a sense of emptiness. At issue is not only a postadrenaline letdown but also the realization that certain achievements may have been less inherently rewarding or exciting than ever imagined. The desire for having a new car, larger house, or better position may be more motivating and fulfilling than the hassles that come with car and home ownership and one's new job duties. In addition, people may also be a bit disappointed with themselves. We are our ethical failings. Undoubtedly, people have done some things about which they are not very proud.

At one's midlife, the accumulation of these matters begins to impress, and one's youthful goals seem increasingly unrealistic and in need of a makeover. People obviously need to go through their own journey on these matters, and they may or may not experience these matters. They may also have other matters such as divorce, physical limitations, disruption of business, or programs that cause them to question their previous investments of time and effort. The matter involves recalibrating what they thought would bring them fulfillment and happiness and replacing this with mature insight into the nature of things and their own abilities. The psychologist James Hollis stated the challenges succinctly:[12]

> The psychology of the first half of life is driven by the fantasy of acquisition ... but the second half demands the relinquishment of identification with property, roles, status and provisional identities and the embrace of other, inwardly confirmed values.

The essence of midlife is the opportunity and invitation to let go of youthful illusions that were inevitably part of the youthful dream as well as the needs that drove them. The point is not to adopt some list of essential knowledge or wisdom points but rather to identify, examine, and recalibrate one's own assumptions. Midlife is sometimes also called the age of disillusionment. The invitation to debunk old girders and strings can be as deep and profound as people make it to be.

Letting go allows people, paradoxically, to act with even greater power. By giving up the illusion that making even more money will make them happier, people are free to consider and choose pursuits that serve other needs. By giving up the illusion that a life of sacrifice is noble, people are able to more freely choose their sacrifices and for whom they make them and spend more time on their own needs and nourishment. By giving up their trust or distrust of humanity in general ("all people are good or evil"), people are free to assess others on the merit of who they really are and make decisions on a one-on-one basis. By giving up the pursuit of an infinite number of tasks and goals, people are free to also enjoy other pleasures, including the pleasure of dealing with people and nature in the here and now. Midlife includes the possibility for people to advance aspects of themselves that may have been ignored or neglected for many years and provide a renewed sense of purpose, energy, and meaning for the second half.

It is important to emphasize that there is no correct set of knowledge or insights to be had; this is not a knowledge test. What is a letting go of old fantasies about careers for one is for another a rediscovery of the joys of work. What is a toning down of the need for social acceptance by some is a rediscovery of social connections for others. The task at midlife is not about finding new activity but about discovering how and why things are done. One can still be a developer, but instead of focusing on the next new car or expensive hobby, one might focus on giving back or developing new eco-friendly and sustainable buildings. One can still be a public manager, but the focus is no longer on seeking societal approval through increased positions of power but rather on the inherent meaning that the role can give to others and as an opportunity for expressing new aspects of oneself. It is perhaps not surprising that people like Bill Gates at midlife turn from acquiring wealth to shedding it with renewed meaning and purpose.

People vary in their responses to the above invitation. People may experience the above concerns earlier, later, or not at all. There does seem, traditionally, for many people a point, somewhere in their forties or fifties, when the lessons of the past call for a reckoning and midterm course correction. Reflection is not for everyone, and some people are motivated to keep on going, setting new and higher goals for themselves (though, predictably, this may not always result in the level of maturity or insight that is expected). Some people who lack a positive outlook or creativity may fail to find renewed meaning and

> **The essence of midlife is the opportunity to let go of illusions and find renewed purpose and meaning.**

purpose and thus instead become cynical and withdrawn. Others decide to make a grand shift toward emphasizing family instead of business or careers. People respond to the invitation of shedding youthful illusions in different ways.

The above reflections are surely not limited to midlife, and many of the above specific insights make good sense in one's 20s or 30s too. It is interesting to reflect on the implications of the above thoughts for people skills. A deeper reflection and understanding of oneself can certainly lead to greater appreciation for the travails and journeys of others, thus leading to a reappraisal of our connections with others. Workplace communications are increasingly friendly but shallow, and some communications are not even friendly. Our own understanding and reflection can be used to reach out and connect with the journeys of others. We can show and articulate that connection in a deeper and more meaningful way because we know our own experiences. Midlife offers the opportunity for us to recalibrate the way in which we relate to others. Not everyone follows this path, but it exists for all.

We end with a few observations about the tasks of those in their fifties and sixties. It is a period of staying active and competitive and assuming leadership in whatever position one has. At midlife, people become concerned with avoiding obsolescence and ensuring their marketability. There are changes in technology, laws and policy, product and services, fashion and client tastes, and so on. There is balance to be shown between one's current activities and responsibilities and the changes in society and one's profession at large that require sustained investment. Being narrowly focused can cause a lack of marketability.[13] The balance between one's job and the reality of one's organization and the marketplace require ongoing assessment. Staying competitive remains important, which often leads to taking on extra assignments and administrative leadership tasks that add value to one's employer and professional network.

Paradoxically, the generational focus of one's efforts comes full circle. When people are in their twenties and thirties, their long-term investments focus on becoming more attractive and competitive for the older generation that makes hiring decisions. For those in their mid-fifties and older, the focus is on the younger generation that now is the source of energy and effort for success today and its continuation to tomorrow. The workplace has always involved a relationship between the generations. There is benefit to be had from supporting and developing a younger group of people who provide the energy and commitment that move things forward. They are often a source of new contracts and even jobs. They are able to establish their own connections and networks. Mentoring is another way of building up the performance and loyalty of people. There is pride, fulfillment, and balance to be found by being a good mentor to others and by leaving things in the good hands of the next generation.

Finally, the last stage of one's career again requires a major personal reinvention, ten to fifteen years after midlife. People once again need to find balance between their circumstances and their conditions. Retirement requires a new identity, a new lifestyle, new interests, and new friends. People are increasingly conscious of arriving at retirement in good health. Retirement provides increasing options for getting involved and being connected with others; the Internet (Web sites, Facebook, and blogs) has increased access to information and online groups with which to share interests and to meet socially. Some universities offer programs for retirees. Families are only one of several foci for people in retirement; people are increasingly aware of reinventing themselves in postcareer life. As one person states, "I have never seen people happy who retire *from*; people who are happy are those who retire *to*."[14] Today's retirement is about forging a new identity, a new purpose, and a new set of circumstances that are consistent with one's anticipated future conditions. There is a new phase, with many years ahead, to take advantage of. Seen in this way, careers involve a series of personal transformations.

Every career requires attention to the integration of work with other aspects of one's life and well-being. This most obviously involves problems of stress and time management as people deal with balancing different roles and activities in their life. Not every activity can be taken on; choices are to be made. We suggest that people (1) prioritize activities and be cautious in choosing the activities they take on, (2) develop effective coping mechanisms for dealing with situations that are likely to cause them stress so that the amount of experienced stress is reduced, and (3) develop strategies such as exercising and resting the mind for dealing with and reducing stress that they do experience.

But beyond this, people's career life will necessarily also involve that they periodically reassess their needs and integrate their lessons into their worldview and career plan or objectives. One such moment is midlife. The essence of midlife is the opportunity to let go of illusions and find renewed purpose and meaning. Though some people in midlife turn cynical, midlife is an invitation for people to explore and define new aspects of themselves and to integrate these into their work activities. By doing so, people may establish a new sense of balance and purpose between what they do and what they are or would like to become. Not everyone goes through such a reassessment, but many people do experience transition issues. There is a sense of balance to be had. As it turns out, letting go of illusions is also relevant to happiness at work, as discussed in the next chapter.

16

The Search for Happiness and Fulfillment

Whoever is happy will make others happy, too.[1]

—**Mark Twain**

It feels good to be happy, and people are predisposed to seeking happiness. They do so in all aspects of their life, and work is no exception. People seek out careers that they think will make them happy, and they do work in them that they think will make them happy as well. We prefer to work with people who make us happy; other chapters in this book make the point that we like to avoid those who bring out negative emotions in us. People seek out happiness in all kinds of ways. Even the delay of gratification is itself associated with some measure of happiness and satisfaction, and the anticipated future outcomes are presumed to make us happy as well in some way. One way or another, all people try to create happiness for themselves.

This chapter discusses happiness and fulfillment at work. This topic is of interest to almost everyone. Some readers may well have opened up this book to this very page, being interested in and curious about what we might have to say on this topic. Happiness and fulfillment are emotions that, as all emotions, arise from stimuli that include thoughts, behaviors, and physical conditions (see Appendix A). Happiness (or joy) at work usually comes from (1) attaining goals or a set of circumstances, including meeting one's needs, and, to a lesser degree, from (2) enjoying the work one is doing (such as when one is in the flow of things or when work has the right balance of control and challenge).[2] Fulfillment (or contentment) is usually associated with the assessment that all one's (major) desires or needs are being met; fulfillment is associated with a lower level intensity of feeling than happiness. Many emotions are fleeting or short-lived, and happiness and fulfillment are no exception; to be frequently happy requires that stimuli causing it be periodically created and experienced.

Authors obviously vary in how they define and measure happiness, and the literature is also strongly concerned with well-being. Happiness is strongly associated with well-being, and some authors such as Warr define happiness *as* well-being,[3] a contented state in which one feels good (pleased, glad, etc. as opposed to sad, dejected, etc.), has enthusiasm (as opposed to feeling lethargic or depressed), and is comfortable (calm, relaxed, etc. as opposed to anxious or fearful). Happy people often have enthusiasm and feel good and comfortable in the moment. While we regard happiness and well-being as distinct, it is obvious that the two are closely connected and that a key goal of happiness is, of course, well-being. Psychological well-being requires some measure of contentment and the periodic experience of happiness.

Happiness and fulfillment are not only sought after but a bit hard to come by for most people. According to one author, surveys suggest that only 11 to 17 percent of people are "brimming with happiness all the time" while about 60 percent say they are frequently happy, and about 25 percent say they only infrequently experience any happiness.[4] At work, happiness and fulfillment seem to occur intermittently; spells of happiness are intermingled with experiences of negative emotions such as fear or disappointment, as well as emotionally neutral experiences of doing "just work" without happy feelings. As shown in Appendix A, the human condition includes a wide range of negative emotions (such as fear, sadness, contempt, anger), and work provides many occasions for bringing them up. The Latin origin of the word *emotion* is *emovere*, which means to move, and emotions certainly move us. Whereas many positive emotions involve the thinking processes in the prefrontal cerebral cortex, many negative emotions arise or involve the limbic system at the base of the brain stem, which is easily aroused and effectively refocuses one's thoughts on threats indicated by negative emotions.[5] While all people want to have ongoing experiences of happiness and fulfillment, the human condition at work is pretty much stacked against that.

Some studies suggest that as much as 50 percent of one's happiness is genetically determined,[6] 10 percent is based on life circumstances (e.g., income, marital status, health, socioeconomic status), and the remainder is one's state

> Some studies suggest that half of one's happiness is genetically determined, and much of the remainder is based on one's state of mind.

of mind. Whatever the exact configuration of these factors, general agreement exists that genetic and mind attitudes greatly affect one's happiness. As regarding genetics, the prevailing scientific belief is that one's physiology provides a "set point" or "baseline" of happiness that varies among people. Though the science of happiness is not complete, many hormones and processes are known to increase happiness. Endorphins, produced by the pituitary gland, produce morphine-like effects and are triggered by sex, pain, exercise, certain foods (e.g., red pepper), acupuncture, and thoughts. Dopamine is associated with arousal, desire, and interest, in a positive and pleasurable way (people like to anticipate positive things). Testosterone and serotonin also affect happiness. Thus, people's production and regulation of various substances affect happiness. Low levels of baseline happiness may suggest physiological problems that can be alleviated with medication. In the United States, about 10 percent of women and 4 percent of men take antidepressants. This is discussed in Chapter 17.

As regarding one's state of mind, people can affect their happiness by being aware of circumstances that affect them (and shaping them as possible) and by being keenly aware of their own thoughts that contribute to arising positive and negative emotions. Abraham

Lincoln is quoted as saying, "Most people are as happy as they make up their minds to be."[7] Lincoln suffered from depression and likely would have been on medication if he were alive today,[8] but the point is well taken that people are responsible for knowing those things that make them happy and fulfilled. While workplace conditions usually do not favor people being happy and fulfilled all the time, there is much that can be done to increase one's experience of positive emotions. One's thinking or perception affects one's subjective experience of happiness, and some research also shows how thinking affects activity in regions of the brain that are associated with emotional processes.[9]

Given the above, some authors like Seligman define the formula for happiness as "one's happiness set point + life circumstances + habit patterns to producing happy thoughts and happy activities."[10] Those matters relating to work are the focus on this chapter.

Finally, happiness and fulfillment exemplify the powerful role of emotions in one's life. People are prone to overestimating the role of logic and rationality of their mind. People spend a good deal of effort strategizing and thinking about how they can be happier. When people experience pain (e.g., when a colleague or boss utters unkind words in their direction), their mind quickly jumps into action, often first trying to rationalize that "it was not really meant that way" or undertaking other efforts to make the pain recede. When that doesn't work, the mind tries to develop strategies that might otherwise make the pain go away (e.g., "I will make her go away."). Emotions powerfully drive one's thoughts and actions. This is not to say that emotions are always present or influencing one's thinking, but they are surprisingly more present in and relevant to people's actions than people are commonly aware of.

Happiness at work involves (1) attaining one's goals or set of conditions, (2) enjoying the work that one is doing, and (3) assessing that all one's (major) desires or needs are met. A good deal of research exists on circumstances that affect people's happiness and well-being at work. Warr summarizes this work as involving twelve general categories of concerns:[11]

1. Opportunity for personal control
2. Opportunity for using one's skills
3. Externally generated goals
4. Variety
5. Environmental clarity
6. Contact with others
7. Availability of money
8. Physical security
9. Valued social position
10. Supportive supervision
11. Career outlook, opportunity, and security
12. Equity and fairness in employment

Though there are also other ways of combining the voluminous literature, the obvious point is that the above conditions affect one's ability to experience goal attainment, work satisfaction, and contentment. Some of these facilitate task achievement. Happiness of goal attainment requires self-directed efforts and some measure of control over one's time and needed resources; frequent interruptions by others and mandated changes of direction detract from the pleasure of achievement that one might experience. Clarity concerns the predictability of one's roles and others' expectations,[12] all of which further goal-oriented planning and achievement. Using one's skill also furthers goals and additionally provides creative pleasures associated with personal growth and overcoming challenges; variety of task furthers this too. Externally generated goals concern organizational roles and goals that may be consistent with one's own goals and that provide a focal point for one's efforts; they often include organizational rewards and opportunities for growth and socialization too. Social interaction provides many additional benefits, such as support and new opportunities and a reduction of isolation and loneliness at work.

These conditions associated with happiness also point to other nontask-oriented factors that affect happiness. People also have a need for belonging and acceptance; social interaction also reduces isolation and loneliness at work. People also measure acceptance and success by socioeconomic status, by the social position of their job, and by comparison with others. Money, too, is a ubiquitous measure; it not only is a measure of one's social-economic position but also creates contentment about meetings one's needs by meeting family obligations, securing a postretirement future, and providing a measure of independence. Money alone does not make one happy, but it is necessary for happiness. Other conditions include supportive supervision, a clear career outlook and plan, and a sense of fairness about work treatment and rewards. Willy-nilly, the focus on conditions affecting happiness also turn on knowing one's needs, of course.[13]

There is some question about the exact relationship between these conditions and happiness. Some level of each of these twelve conditions seems needed, but beyond a minimum, the effect may vary. For example, too much task variety quickly becomes very stressful, and too much contact with others is distraction that in turn causes stress when not enough work gets done. Having too little money demotivates, but beyond a point other factors often determine job satisfaction more strongly; one study found that annual income up to $75,000 in the United States increases emotional well-being and happiness, but not thereafter.[14] Thus, being able to get the right amount of the above factors is key.

The above section follows traditional lines of research and posits a view of the degree to which people are able to shape their objective working conditions to meet their needs for goal achievement and enjoyment of work processes. A modern critique of this is that it insufficiently includes consideration for people's subjective perception of their conditions and desires and in this manner to further increase their happiness. At issue is not merely a reassessment of one's goals in light of constraints (which could lead to downgrading one's aspirations) but rather a search for opportunity in one's conditions that goes well beyond task achievement and social comparison. Happiness is associated with optimism, and happiness begets more happiness by focusing on the positive possibilities and enthusiastically working toward them.

One of the most obvious ways to find happiness is to redefine goal achievement, often in some radical ways. Frequent interruptions and redirections from higher-ups are opportunities for closer relations with them. People in higher positions usually are motivated to serve the needs of those in even higher positions in the hope of themselves being promoted by them to better positions. Interruptions are the opportunity to better understand the needs of others and to serve these needs. The achievement of task is replaced by the achievement of alliance with others and the achievement of one's own promotion—a goal of a different kind. To be sure, doing so can make use of the tools of the previous chapters concerning psychological contracts and ethics to further the goals of others and thereby one's own. Doing so may even be a shortcut to being promoted, compared with the long grind of annual performance appraisals of doing one's time. People have to make the best use of the situation that they have.

This is but one example that gets to the importance of taking the effort and time to develop new opportunities in one's situation. Surely, negative thoughts and emotions arise quickly on any situation (fear, despondency, futility, envy), but the point here is to quickly tune these out and focus one's mind on creating a positive opportunity that, in turn, provides positive emotions of anticipation. Positive psychology is the study of positive human functioning in such ways that increase enjoyment, creativity, and fulfillment. Positive psychology builds on previous humanistic orientations in psychology but got renewed emphasis in the late 1990s when Seligman, a past president of the American Psychological Association, suggested this as an alternative to traditional psychology that has emphasized human ailment and psychological disorders.

Studies in positive psychology increasingly emphasize the role of subjective positive interpretation in events and circumstances of people. The ability to keep a positive outlook is a recurring theme and conclusion about that which distinguishes happy people from unhappy people. Associated with this are also specific mind habits and skills such as being proactive (e.g., trying to make the most of every day), rejecting victimization (e.g., emphasizing aspects over which one does have control), using one's own wisdom, and learning from past experiences to produce better results in the future. Baker describes six specific strategies used by people who experience high degrees of happiness and fulfillment:[15]

- expressing appreciation and gratitude for things around us that give us pleasure and satisfaction;
- creating choices that expand our options and give us a sense of freedom rather than constriction or confinement, including seeing happiness where others do not;
- taking responsibility and rejecting victimization, that is, having a sense that "you can handle whatever life dishes out";
- leading with one's strengths (and knowing what these are);
- using positive and powerful stories and language to expand freedom and space; and
- living a multidimensional life that promotes work, relationships, and health.

Positive psychology has been criticized as being incomplete or shallow as it does not explicitly also deal with ailments and problems that work against the above. For example, intrusive negative thoughts and high levels of anxiety are obstacles to the above practices; other approaches such as cognitive psychology, which examines the basis of one's thoughts and behaviors, are necessary too. Subsequent chapters examine some widely prevalent problems, but positive psychology has a point about seeing the glass as half full. People do create their own reality of the moment and in doing so often set the stage for how they approach the future and sometimes reinterpret the past. There is no inherent "one truth" or reality about anything, and one person asks "whether a little self-delusion is necessary for happiness."[16] All situations are open to multiple interpretations; in what is an extreme example, Victor Frankl's book *Man's Search for Meaning* is about finding reason for living in a Nazi prison camp.[17] Setting new goals at work brings forth "new life," as does defining one's activities in positive ways. Consider the following quote from Pattakos:[18]

> Every day, Vita delivers my mail—cheerfully. It's her trademark attitude. One day ... I wanted to know more. "How do you stay so

positive and upbeat about delivering mail every day?," I asked her. "I don't just deliver mail," she said. "I see myself helping to connect people to other people. I help build community. Besides people depend on me and I don't want to let them down."

Happy thoughts bring happy feelings.[19] The attendant positive feeling of contribution is real as anything. Vita could also tell herself that all is in vain, that many pieces of mail will just be thrown away as junk mail. The resulting negative feeling of despondency is also real. There is a point about taking responsibility for the feelings that we feel and for deciding how we choose to view the world. Positive psychology suggests that people take time out to develop thoughts of appreciation, satisfaction, opportunity, caring, consideration, fairness, and other matters that generate positive feelings and empowering thoughts. The point about "a little self-delusion" is emphasizing the positive but not ignoring or creating things that could affect one's productive functioning, of course.[20] Negative thoughts and emotions often come up at work (e.g., fear,

> There is no inherent "one truth" or reality about anything.

anger, blame, injustice, etc.),[21] but these can be acknowledged and put aside. As Voltaire (1694–1778) long noted, "Life is a shipwreck but we must not forget to sing in the lifeboats."[22] Happiness and a positive outlook are also learned skills. Eventually, such positive thoughts will arise more often and naturally, as will positive feelings.

The above is also not about denying unpleasant realities or living in a delusional state. Things do happen that hurt or threaten and that require our attention. The paradox is that the more problems one has, the more one also needs to articulate and find positive opportunities and possibilities. Positive emotions associated with happiness tend to be short-lived and are readily killed off by negative ones, and therefore positive emotions need constant re-creation. The human mind provides ample justification for negative feelings, but happy people do a remarkable job of recognizing and putting these aside. People create their own happiness, even in dire circumstances, by finding new opportunities and things to be grateful about.

Finally, it seems that happiness is, at least in part, a learned behavior that is also reinforced by culture. National cultures sometimes play a role—anecdotally, American culture is an optimistic culture but not one in which people are very happy. By contrast, Brazilian culture may be among the happiest that we know. People smile and see fun in almost everything, bringing positive feelings and levity to the moment at hand. They surely have problems, but a lack of levity is not one of them. In addition, we lived in Miami and New Orleans where a lot of poor people appear much happier than some very rich people—money matters, but so does culture. Organizational culture also plays a role. Some workplaces just have a nice atmosphere, and people work hard to keep it positive. Even doom and gloom gets caught up in giving the benefit of the doubt. Culture has a powerful reinforcing impact on behavior and norms and on the learned behavior of happiness and fulfillment.

An interesting development in globalization has been the introduction and acceptance of Eastern thought into Western consciousness and vice versa. A core tenet of Eastern thought is that the human mind is given to suffering. This occurs not only through the production of negative thoughts but in more fundamental ways as well. Another core tenet is that people can stop the suffering of their mind, too. It has become increasingly common to consider Buddhism as a key philosophy and practice of Eastern thought, and the following draws on widely accepted tenets of that. (To be sure, the religious practices of Buddhism are not a topic of discussion here).[23]

One of the main sources of suffering that people do is to attach their mind to objects of craving (or clinging or grasping). For example, because people want to be happy, they want a better job, which causes them to work hard and compete against others who also want that job, which also causes them to seek a competitive advantage such as by doing favors for those who might influence the boss, which causes them to get angry with those people when they don't get the job, which causes them to say bad things about whoever did get the job, which causes others to hold that against them, and so on and so forth. In Eastern thought, a main source of people's cravings and aversions is their ignorance or incomplete understanding of the nature of things, and cravings, aversions, and ignorance are seen as main causes of people's sufferings. The above example also shows that many of these causes are sometimes related, with one giving rise to another. This is called "dependent arising," and some people's lives are characterized by strings of cravings and aversions.

In Eastern thought, some principal realities are the impermanence and so-called emptiness of things. A source of cravings and aversions occur because people want more permanence and security than exist in the world. People fight to have their projects meet deadlines, even though change and unforeseen events happen and plans need to be revised. People have (some) aversion to getting older, even though it is inevitable. A family of sufferings arises as people try to make their reality more permanent than it is. Another family of sufferings arises when people ascribe meaning and content to things rather than see them as devoid of that (or empty of inherent meaning). People want to be happy all the time and believe this to be good and possible, even though it is impossible. People want specific jobs and believe that they will make them happy, even though job responsibilities are unlikely to make them happy. Some people believe that going to Harvard will make them happy, and they devote their entire life to it. People do not deeply assess their desires and, consequently, suffer the consequences of cravings and aversions, which projects meaning onto things. In this manner, even positive emotions can be a source of suffering when people have a craving for them.

The point of this approach is to tone down one's desire. The "middle way" is an approach that cautions people to avoid extremes. Love, power, and wealth are transient and cause suffering. Eastern philosophy produces more muted expressions of emotion. For example, the above sits uneasy with Western-style consumerism; it sees those cravings as unwise and as a source of suffering. It may also see Western cravings and exultations of love as immature sufferings. Yet the reality of the world does not allow for a total extinguishing of cravings. We deal with bosses who expect us to have certain desires

We need to give happiness a chance.

(e.g., for money or fame), and bit of consumerism is good for keeping the economy going; the very high savings rate in the East is seen as problematic as well. Without love and sex, there is no humanity. Buddhism also includes ethical prescripts that emphasize compassion and nonviolence, which are intended to invoke positive feelings. The point is that in the modern world, people do well to be aware of the suffering that they invite for themselves, as some suffering is inevitable. In the words of the famous contemporary Taiwan artist Ju Ming, "There is hell and heaven on earth. It is only a matter of mindset."[24] This is surely a widely held belief in East Asia.

The folklore of Buddhism also recognizes patterns (or realms) of suffering that occur. The "hungry ghost" realm is characterized by people who seek external gratifications for internal needs, which inevitably fails to satisfy (hence a person remains hungry). The "hell" realm is represented by people who quickly lose their temper; in doing so, they drive even kind and generous people away. The "animal" realm is marked by ignorance and, hence, the inability to overcome one's sufferings. The "God" realm[25] is marked by great wealth and power, yet one is unable to connect with the suffering of others, hence causing a lack of wisdom and compassion. The realm of "titans" is marked by great and fierce beings who are given to hate and jealousy. The "human" realm is characterized by desires and doubt but contains the possibility of one overcoming one's suffering. Surely, being this way at work increases one's suffering. As one persons writes, "Our only hope of cutting of [suffering] is not through more exploration, theorizing or partying, but through learning to see just how we're chronically confused."[26] These realms project some of the ways in which people become confused.

The experience of people's suffering being widespread and enduring shows that it is not easy for people to either recognize or resist their cravings, aversions, and confusions. The expression "We have seen the enemy, and it is us" reflects this. Yet there is a problem of getting to know what thoughts cause sufferings. The challenge is well known in Western psychotherapy. As Blackman writes, "The human mind has an amazing capacity to invent mechanisms that shield a person from becoming aware of unpleasant emotions."[27] The mind is strongly predisposed to avoiding (not dealing with) unpleasantness. By way of further example, some readers may be doubtful that positive emotions can indeed be a source of suffering. If it feels good, how can it be bad? Is it not good to live life with love and something to struggle for? Isn't it normal to want to feel good? In both Buddhism and Western psychology, such questions can be viewed as defenses of the mind that shut it off from further inquiry. Strong cravings for love and career are associated with strong sufferings (such as contracting sexually transmitted diseases and sacrificing sanity), but the mind does not want to go there.

To get to know one's thoughts and to pierce through such defenses and games of the mind, one can practice observing what thoughts come up in one's mind. People often find their mind wandering to the past or future, producing thoughts that evoke anger or resentment over things in the past or anxiety and dread over things in the future. Such thoughts include cravings and aversions that are then further examined as regarding one's perception of the nature of things, such as how they cause other sufferings (dependent arising), whether one is assuming a fixed, nontransient view of things, whether one ascribes a meaning to something that has invited one's grasping or aversion, and so on. Upon closer examination, it may be possible to extinguish some of one's cravings and aversions and thus avoid some sufferings of the above realms. (This often is a moment of happiness too!)

Another exercise is to focus on the here and now. Many of people's anxieties occur because people are overly focused on events in the future or past, causing cravings and aversions. A basic premise is that all that one needs to feel good is occurring right here and now; the challenge is to know what it is and to appreciate it. The best-selling book *Power of Now* focuses just on that and provides a few techniques for doing so.[28] In the present, there is no fear of the future or upset about the past. There is air that we are breathing, a house that gives shelter, a job that provides food and other resources for our family, a seat that may be comfortable, and work that engages our skills and abilities. The focus on now strongly cultivates the skill of appreciation and, in doing so, produces positive feelings of fulfill-ment. Surely there is reason for visiting the future and taking care of what needs to be done, but after that, one should return to the present and enjoy that. The cultivation of appreciation is very simi-lar to that of positive psychology, though the latter also focuses on empowering reinterpretations of events. Perhaps it is no coincidence that both positive psychology and Eastern philosophy gained broad interest at roughly the same time.

It should be noted that beyond a certain point, self-help progress becomes difficult. Some thoughts and patterns may not be known to people, and even in meditation they do not become fully known. People are unconscious of some ways in which they sabotage them-selves. This is why getting feedback and input from others often is essential too. In addition, people often hold beliefs that produce repeated patterns of suffering but about which they are unclear. Examples include beliefs that people do not deserve to be happy, that they do not deserve to be liked, that bad things will surely happen when good things happen, that they are not smart enough, and that the world is highly uncertain and needs to be controlled.[29] We can-not fully agree with Ju Ming, however. Acting according to these beliefs about which people are not fully aware inevitably produces suffering. Almost everyone has a few of these, but the mind does not want to acknowledge these. Instead, the mind produces other thoughts related to the present, which appear as being more urgent but that inevitably leave people puzzled by their repeated poor for-tune and suffering. Some of these beliefs also lie in childhood events of which people are no longer conscious. In psychology, the term *defense mechanism* refers to specific patterns through which the mind deflects attention and keeps problematic behaviors intact, hence promulgating repeated suffering (see Box 16.1). There are some things that require the help from others.

Being aware of and reducing one's own suffering is the first step toward happiness. There may be limits to self-help, but people should do what they can. Happiness cannot live in a mind that is full of crav-ings and aversions. What goes for happiness in such a mind often is a series of adrenaline rushes with attendant letdowns. A better way

BOX 16.1 DEFENSE MECHANISMS

People have ways of acting in the face of negative feelings that are designed to make them feel better or even avoid pain. Many of these behaviors are also seen at work. The following are some defense mechanisms. The problematic nature of these mechanisms is that while they avoid difficult issues and feelings in the immediate short run, they seldom address the underlying problem giving rise to them. Consider the following:

- *Projection:* Being upset with one's own failure for a project under one's responsibility, a person blames events or others for the failings instead.
- *Denial:* A person denies that a problem exists, for example, by using words that obfuscate the matter ("The result is excellent based on past achievements.").
- *Idealization:* People consider others to have more positive qualities than they actually have as a way to avoid working harder or taking on more responsibility themselves.
- *Negativism or hostility:* People are negative or hostile to others as a way to avoid getting involved with something or others.
- *Humor:* One makes light of more serious failings.
- *Identification:* One models oneself as someone else to ward off negative images of oneself ("I am just as good as Jane.").
- *Socialization:* People become socially active to avoid or distract from unpleasant tasks.
- *Reaction formation:* People feel positive to avoid experiencing negative emotions.
- *Somatization:* People become sick as a way to avoid working or confronting unpleasantness.
- *Repression:* People forget things to avoid dealing with negative events.
- *Splitting:* People see someone as exceptionally positive or in an exceptionally negative light.

to find happiness is to arrest our own creation of negative feelings; we need to give happiness a chance. However one regards the Dalai Lama, no one has ever accused him of being dour and unhappy, despite losing a home and kingdom and leading the diaspora of millions. It is time to assess the thoughts that come up and to carefully examine the reality and needs expressed by those thoughts. We need to assess the various tasks that we set for ourselves and ask whether they really contribute to our happiness in the present and future. Einstein is quoted as saying, "Insanity is doing the same thing over and over again, and expecting a different result."[30] It is time to rethink what we are thinking, and many of the techniques used in doing so contribute to experiencing happiness and fulfillment.

At present, our understanding of happiness and fulfillment is a bit fragmented and incomplete, but it contains many useful pointers. First, all people want to experience happiness and fulfillment. They are prone to seeking it in many places, including work. Second, the evidence suggests that people have varying experiences of happiness and that people's "set point" of happiness varies. Third, negative emotions drive out (or kill off) positive feelings such as happiness and fulfillment, and the workplace provides ample opportunity for experiences of negative emotions. Fourth, because of the previous pointer, it is essential to reduce negative emotions and increase our production of happy feelings. Fifth, because all emotions are fleeting, it is necessary to be skilled in frequently creating happy feelings for oneself. Thoughts are antecedents of feelings, and so what we think matters. Sixth, positive psychology shows that people can learn to produce thoughts that increase happiness by focusing on appreciation and increased opportunities for action. They can also learn to acknowledge and take negative thoughts less seriously. Seven, Eastern philosophy also focuses on the cessation of suffering by careful examination of one's cravings and aversions. It also includes meditative techniques for increasing appreciation and happiness. People need to carefully consider what goals they take on, as they inevitably produce some suffering. Thus, people can reduce their suffering and increase their happiness and fulfillment at work, even though it is not possible to totally reduce suffering.

There are limitations, however, to what people can do for themselves. Many drives that cause suffering are unconscious. In addition, people may experience low (and variable) set points of happiness that may point to problems that involve medical attention. The next chapter discusses some of these challenges.

17
Mental Health

The privilege of a lifetime is to become who you truly are.

—**Carl Gustav Jung**[1]

Everyone sometimes get angry, upset, or nervous at work. People become irritable, angry, withdrawn, impulsive, worried, and nervous and are given to flights of fancy. Such responses affect people's relations and performance. Becoming angry or irritable can cause people to interrupt others or use a tone of voice that is typically taken as showing a lack of courtesy and respect. Being withdrawn leads to a lack of social interaction that others may interpret as unwelcoming or even disrespectful. Being angry or worried and having flights of fancy and grandiosity can also cause others to question one's capability; a professional person is usually taken to be someone who stays calm and has things under control. While everyone is sometimes given to such behaviors, habitual behaviors will certainly affect one's ability to get along and be effective. Even demonstrating such behaviors toward strangers may leave quite unfavorable first impressions.

Previous chapters described the importance of avoiding these behaviors as part of having social manners (Chapter 2) and getting along (Chapter 4) and also noted their relevance to professional commitment (Chapter 8), expectations (Chapter 10), and ethics

(Chapter 11). However, it is not always useful to consider these as separate or disconnected behaviors. For many people, the above behaviors form patterns of recognizable behavior and thought processes. The above are also manifestations of proclivities of the mind that many people experience as being resistant to even their own efforts. Even when people know that something is not good or proper for themselves and others, they still may not always be able to change it on their own. The forces are sometimes quite strong that drive people to experience and interpret the world in certain ways. We need to know the machine that we are so that we can better deal with it.

The topic of this chapter is mental health, which has made great strides in recent years. People should not be surprised about a topic of medical significance in this book. Medical expenditures are about 6 to 10 percent of the gross domestic product in most countries (about 16 percent in the United States);[2] people have many medical issues, and some of these relate to behavioral health and the mind, which affect work. We should not be surprised that the complexity of the human mind and consciousness sometimes gives rise to problems. Mental health is defined as emotional and cognitive well-being that is characterized by the absence of a mental disorder or illness, but the latter often is only a matter of degree. It is estimated that about 26 percent of Americans age eighteen years and older suffer from a diagnosable mental disorder every year, of which one-quarter (6 percent of the population) suffers a serious degree.[3] This figure includes various degrees and types of anxiety, mood disturbance, impulse (and attention) control, and substance abuse problems.[4] Table 17.1 shows general U.S. prevalence rates.[5] Major depression is thought to be the leading cause of disability in the United States for people ages fifteen to forty-four.[6] Mental health is a widespread problem that is hard to ignore and, according to many, deserves far more discussion and integration with models of workplace functioning.[7]

The subject of mental health is sometimes given to stigma, fear, and a lack of informed opinion. The ancient Greeks coined such words as *melancholy*, *hysteria*, and *phobia*, but for much of human history, knowledge has often been very basic, and treatment more palliative than curative. Modern mental health care dates back to

Table 17.1 Prevalence of Mental Disorders in the United States (Annual)

Disorder	Rate (%)
Anxiety disorders	18.1
Mood disorders total (major depression, dysthymia, bipolar)	9.5
Personality disorders	9.1
Social phobias	6.8
Major depression	6.7
Eating disorder (lifetime rate)	4.4
Attention deficit disorder	4.1
Post-traumatic stress disorder	3.5
Generalized anxiety	3.1
Bipolar disorder	2.6
Dysthymic disorder	1.5
Schizophrenia	1.1
Obsessive-compulsive disorder	1.0

Source: Adapted from U.S. National Institute of Mental Health, *The Numbers Count: Mental Disorders in America*, U.S. National Institute of Mental Health, Washington, DC, 2010.

the late nineteenth century, but therapy and medicine have made enormous advances of diagnosis and treatment in just the past thirty years; the availability of new treatments has now made mental health the second-fastest-growing cause of all medical health costs.[8] Still, textbooks and schools seldom teach much about mental health. Much of what most people know comes from family members experiencing mental conditions or from talk shows. However, the tide of ignorance may be slowly changing, at least in the United States. In a recent survey of one thousand randomly selected Americans between ages eighteen and sixty-four, 48 percent of those polled reported a visit to a mental health professional by someone in their household this year, and 91 percent said that they would recommend a mental health professional if they or a family member experienced a problem.[9] In the United States, antidepressants are now the most prescribed drugs, according to the U.S. Center for Disease Control.[10] Anecdotally, older generations seem most out of touch with recent advances, which may explain why so little still shows up in textbooks and teaching materials in many fields. There is a lot of knowledge diffusion that has yet to occur, and anecdotally the United States seems far ahead of other countries on this matter.[11]

This chapter focuses on tendencies of anxiety and depression, and we also note hyperactivity; these problems are widely seen at work and account for about 38 percent of mental health problems. The next chapter discusses personality dysfunctions and other difficult behaviors. These chapters include one of the authors' extensive experiences in clinical practice in the United States. Though we focus on manifestations at work, the current state of knowledge is far more advanced in the clinical area; sometimes a focus on more extreme cases does bring less severe conditions into perspective too. Although the information presented here is deemed reliable and consistent with professional practice, the following is not provided for diagnosis and treatment, and readers should always contact their mental health professional for any such purposes. Finally, we do not aim to do justice to the vast body of research and knowledge; we provide essentials only. Readers seeking to go beyond this material can readily find information online (see notes).

Anxiety at work. Everyone experiences occasional apprehension and concerns about challenges of life and future events. Being concerned about current conditions and future events is part of the human experience and is to some functional, helpful, and necessary. We need to be concerned that program goals are met, that subordinates and contractors are on schedule and meet quality standards, that we get along with others, that our career goals are set, and so on. Work brings much to think about. Anxiety involves a state of worry (fear) and physiological symptoms that go beyond this. Worry can be defined as intrusive thoughts that distract or interrupt existing activity. Physiological symptoms that may accompany worry include sweating, feeling jittery, having an accelerated heart rate, and feeling tightness in the chest or throat. For example, many students have a pinch of anxiety before or during tests. People get a bit anxious when their boss asks to speak with them.

Such physiological responses are the body's normal reaction to danger. Work exposes people to their strong and weak sides, and people are naturally concerned with the possibility of failure. People get nervous because they care, but how much caring about something is too much? It is important to periodically visit the future, but it is also important that people not get caught up in it and are able to return to the present and enjoy that, as described in the previous chapter. However, the mind has a way of grasping on to problems and then finding more. Anxiety varies in level, frequency, and duration. Some people continually worry about many things, such as whether they will be able to meet deadlines, whether they will be able to keep their job, whether they are sufficiently liked by others, whether work will be completed on time, whether their car will start on time, and so on.

Unhappily, persistent anxiety can feed on itself and become its own cause of people and performance problems. People may become overly controlling and give others less space, hence becoming less liked; they are seen as too demanding. Their mind jumps quickly, and they are prone to interrupting others and being a bit impulsive, which can cause them to appear less than courteous, patient, or attentive to the needs of others. Some judgments may indeed be ill considered and wrong, hence causing others to question their suitability for promotion. Paradoxically, the desire, perhaps a bit too strong, to keep things under control or on track may suggest to others that they do not have things on track or under control. Anxiety may exacerbate physical symptoms, giving rise to stuttering (choking up in social situations), extreme or uncontrolled sweating, problems with digestion and bowel movement, lower backache, frequent headaches, and so on. These physiological symptoms affect performance and others' perception of performance (e.g., "Don't let them see you sweat."). In short, the worries that drive people to act sometimes also make them less successful.

> **The worries that drive people to act sometimes also make them less successful.**

Anxiety is widespread and common. Table 17.1 shows the annual incidence of anxiety disorders as 18.1 percent, but the lifetime incidence is 28.8 percent.[12] People vary in their level and degree, but even casual observation of people suggests that many people at work are given to anxiety of some kind. Symptoms of anxiety that people may experience include feeling jumpy, thinking about bad or worst outcomes, being irritable, and having trouble concentrating, and physical symptoms include frequent headaches, sleeplessness, twitches, sweating, shortness of breath, stomach pain, or frequent toilet visits. People's physical symptoms of anxiety vary. Part of knowing oneself is to know one's manifestation to anxiety. Others observe not these symptoms, of course, but rather the experience of others' jitteriness, lack of courtesy, cutting them off, impulsive judgment, not taking their needs into consideration, and sometimes excessive working, concern, and focus.

The widespread prevalence of anxiety suggests that anxiety is a problem not only of the mind but also of physiology and genetics. Clinical studies show that about half of patients with panic disorders also have an affected relative.[13] People with first-degree relatives who have panic disorders (see below) are themselves up to eight times more likely to develop a panic disorder themselves.[14] Studies of twins suggest a genetic contribution to generalized anxiety disorder (GAD; see below). Anxiety sometimes has a strong family connection. Physiological studies show that people with anxiety disorder often have greater sensitivity and responsiveness of their nervous system to external stimuli.[15] Strong physiological reactions to external events prompt thinking about them, hence furthering propensity for worrying. Three neurotransmitters (norepinephrine, serotonin, and gamma-aminobutyric acid) in the brain are found to be implicated in causing increased sensitivity. Hence anxiety is mental problem that has not only mental roots but physiological and genetic conditions too.

A variety of specific anxiety conditions can be distinguished. Diagnosis of mental health disorders in the United States is based on the *Diagnostic and Statistical Manual of Mental Disorders*, text revision (*DSM-IV-TR*), which is consistent with the *International Statistical Classification of Diseases and Related Health Problems*, tenth edition (ICD-10), published by the World Health Organization.[16] The *DSM-IV-TR* is the basis for classifying mental disorders, and we refer to it for authoritative description (see also Box 17.1). GAD

BOX 17.1   WHAT IS *DSM*?

The *Diagnostic and Statistical Manual of Mental Disorders* (*DSM*) provides guidelines and criteria for diagnosing mental health disorders. The *DSM* grew out of World War II, when the Army developed a taxonomy and guidelines for diagnosing mental health disorders among military personnel, called "War Department Technical Bulletin, Medical 203." The first civilian version, *DSM-I*, was released in 1952 and contained 130 pages and 106 disorders. The current fourth edition, *DSM-IV-TR* (text revision), contains 886 pages and 297 disorders and was released in 2000. A fifth edition is set for release in 2013, and a preview (beta version) is available online.[17] The *DSM* is produced by the American Psychiatric Association and used by federal agencies, insurance companies, mental health providers, policy makers, and others.

Though use of the *DSM* is intended for individuals with appropriate training and experience in diagnosis,[18] it is nonetheless useful for others to get a sense of how mental health diagnosis is defined and made. Terms such as *anxiety, depression, bipolar disorder, borderline personality,* and so on have entered the popular lexicon, and people do well to know the definitions of such terms and the criteria for diagnosing the disorders. A mental health disorder is defined as "a clinically significant behavior or psychological syndrome or pattern that occurs in an individual and that is associated with present distress or disability or with significantly increased risk of suffering death, pain, disability or an important loss of freedom."[19]

The *DSM-IV-TR* distinguishes between clinical disorders (e.g., developmental disorders, anxiety, depression, eating and sleep disorders, adjustment, sexual and learning disorders), personality disorders (e.g., antisocial, borderline, paranoid, narcissistic, etc.; see Chapter 18), and retardation. In addition, diagnoses include assessment of medication conditions, psychosocial and environmental problems that contribute to a problem (e.g., housing, educational economic problems), and an assessment of overall functioning. The assessment of disorders is based on observing signs and symptoms as indicating the underlying condition. While the approach has been criticized at times for being insufficiently theoretical or research based, it is a practical approach that is useful. The classification and diagnosis system is now widely used and forms a basic system of what is often found, in abbreviated form, on many reputable Web sites such as that of the Mayo Clinic. The time is not far off when managers will be expected to be familiar with a wide range of common mental health problems that are defined in *DSM*.

involves excessive worrying that the individual finds difficult to control for at least six months about a number of activities or events and at least three of the following symptoms: restlessness, fatigue, difficulty concentrating, irritability, muscle tension, and disturbed sleep. Associated with muscle tension are trembling, twitching, shakiness, and muscle aches. In GAD, these symptoms should not occur exclusively with mood disorders (see further), substance (medication or drug) abuse, and a few other situations. GAD is a description of frequent or constant worry and anxiety over many different activities and events that has become characteristic or pervasive in one's life.[20a]

Some anxieties are given to discrete events. Social phobia concerns fear of social and performance situations (e.g., public speaking) where there are concerns about sharp evaluation of others (being rejected or perceived as stupid or anxious etc.). Some people have anxieties for certain animals, blood, or flying, which sometimes interfere with work responsibilities. Agoraphobia concerns fear of places or situations from which escape may be difficult and in which a person may experience panic-attack-like symptoms. Post-traumatic stress disorder concerns people's reliving traumatic events (e.g., disasters, accidents, molestation) brought on by stressors that cause people to reexperience these in some way. Traumatic events can also cause acute stress disorder, which can include features similar to those of panic attacks (see below). Obsessive-compulsive disorder (OCD) involves recurrent highly intrusive thoughts, impulses, and compulsions (ritualistic behaviors that aim to reduce anxieties caused by one's thoughts or impulses). OCD was made famous in the movie *As Good as It Gets* (1997). Common triggers of OCD are contaminations (germs), doubts, disorderliness, morality, and sexual images, all of which the workplace provides plenty of. Anxiety disorders come in many shapes and forms.

People are often well aware of situations that are stressors for them, and they usually try to avoid them or cope with them in some way. There is wisdom to intervening at an early stage of signals and manifestations, but this is not always the case, and it is not uncommon for people to experience one or more significant crises that they are unable to avoid before treatment or help is sought. Anxiety often is integrated into a person's repertoire, and people may not be aware of behaviors that cause them problems with others such as their being overly controlling or impulsive or exercising questionable judgment.[20] Crises induced by anxiety occur because people underestimate or don't see the impact of their anxiety on their human relations. At worst, this can include their being fired or let go for failure to get along. It can also include panic and anxiety attacks in which physical sensations (e.g., shortness of breath, tingling, palpitations, nausea, etc.), along with frequent mental fears, become overwhelming and temporarily disable people from continuing their work.[21] Some people experience only modest symptoms of anxiety, which are readily hidden from others at work (e.g., through sick leave, toilet breaks, etc.). For people with anxiety, the fear of experiencing anxiety is typically an ongoing and powerful concern.

As an aside, the notion of "functional dysfunctionality" suggests that some (low) degree of anxiety may have positive outcomes and even be rewarded and encouraged by organizations. This is indeed the case. People who experience modest amounts of anxiety are likely seen as being responsible and productive organizational citizens. They proactively ensure that things happen. They engage others but are not overly controlling or unintentionally inconsiderate. They can hurry up, but they also know how and when to relax in the presence of others. A little but not too much anxiety is what seems to be valued in many workplaces. But the problem is knowing how much is enough. It is easy to get caught up in anxiety. Prevalence rates suggest that some people operate at clinical levels; at those levels people not only experience personal discomfort but may also see their growth opportunities hindered. People with a proclivity to anxiety have the challenge of putting on the brakes. Not surprisingly, people with a proclivity for anxiety often exhibit clinical symptoms of anxiety at one or more points in their life.

As an example of a rather modest level of anxiety, "Mary" is responsible for screening and ensuring that applications for new pharmaceuticals are complete. Her role is important to the success of new pharmaceutical drugs, which could improve the lives of sometimes millions of people, as well as the fortunes of companies. Mary is very good at meeting deadlines and target dates, ensures that requests for additional information are met, and obtains good experts in a timely manner for review processes. Because she is on the ball, she carries a relatively high caseload of applications. But her work causes her to come in contact with very distinguished and influential people, and there have been times when she rubbed people the wrong way. She is sometimes less cordial or polite than she might be or than some people would like to experience. She is also a bit quick to be critical of her coworkers' work, who therefore keep their distance from her. She sometimes also says things that might best not be said. Her boss is concerned about her promotion potential, which would require greater interaction with people. She is sometimes perceived as hyper and a bit overachieving. It is now time to recommend employees for rewards, and it may be better to give a reward to someone who is more suitable for promotion, despite Mary's otherwise excellent performance. This example shows some of the symptoms that anxiety can produce.

Though the above example is a modest case (one can easily think of more serious cases from colleagues or movies), there is much that can be done to reduce anxiety, and such treatments may be helpful for Mary as well. Research shows that treatment is often most effective when it involves both (1) medicine and (2) cognitive-behavioral (talk) therapy. Self-help alone is inadequate in the cases that constitute the 28 percent of clinically diagnosed lifetime anxiety incidence. Anxiety often is not only a mind-set, and pharmacology reduces sensitivity to stimuli and restores bodily calm. (Indeed, Mary is seen as being physically hyper.) A variety of medications have become increasingly popular in recent years, especially relating to serotonin. Insofar as the exact dosage and type of medication cannot be exactly known in advance, patients often go through a trial or testing period of a few months in which different dosages and drugs are tried, usually smaller doses that are increased as needed. Medicine often is continued six months or several years beyond the initial treatment phase. Studies suggest that medicine provides considerable short-term improvements, and therapy provides considerable long-term improvement.[22] There often are genetic, physiological, and medical factors that need to be addressed.

Talk therapy is needed as many problems involve ingrained behaviors and assumptions. Often a mental health professional is needed to deal with compulsively and intrusive thoughts and when symptoms are long lasting or are interfering with performance or quality of life (e.g., sleeping). The focus of therapy often is to examine unrealistic thoughts and increase management of work situations. As regarding work, assumptions about others' responses and the need for worrying about them or specific work processes are often brought into question. Anxiety is about fear, but some level of uncertainty needs to be accepted. Not everything can be controlled, and people can learn to deal with some imperfections. People increase confidence in their abilities. Some self-help approaches are to create a "worry period" during the day, while leaving other times for just doing one's work and not worrying about worrying or postponing worrying for some later time.[23] One could also use the strategy of a psychological contract to periodically revisit and clarify job expectations and performance. However, often a mental health professional is needed to deal with compulsive and intrusive thoughts or long-lasting or interfering symptoms. Anecdotally, for individuals, the effectiveness of their provider is an additional and perhaps the most important factor of treatment success.

Everyone experiences moments of anxiety, but for some it has become a way of life in certain areas. Anxiety often has genetic elements. A little bit of anxiety may be functional (and even rewarded by organizations), but it is important to be able to bring the mind to the present, enjoy the present, and relax the body and mind. When these things are not possible, people are at risk for having or developing anxiety problems. Then the worries that drive people to act will, paradoxically, also cause them to be less successful in the workplace.

Depression. A very common class of mental conditions is depression. Depression is also called a mood disorder, because depression affects how people feel about themselves.[24] A person's mood can be normal, depressed, or elevated. The depressed mood is a sense of sadness and helplessness and, in more extreme manifestations, hopelessness. Very elevated moods give rise to expansiveness and heightened self-esteem, as well as thoughts of grandiosity and flights of fancy. People with mood disorders experience rather significant levels of depression or elevation and, unlikely healthy people, are unable to sufficiently regulate their moods. People with a depressive disorder may feel stuck in a gloomy or negative outlook for several weeks or months. People with depression typically hold on to negative thoughts that further reinforce and give justification for the depressed mood. As regarding work, people with depression experience strong diminished pleasure in various activities, including work. "Depression drains a person's energy," states Haznedar, an administrative director for behavioral health services at New York City's Saint Vincent Catholic Medical Centers.[25] It is estimated that major depression is the leading cause of disability in the United States for people ages fifteen to forty-four.[26]

> **"Depression drains a person's energy."**

People with depression often express their gloomy outlook at work, such as through generalization ("Management is always looking out for itself."), injustice ("It is always unfair here."), and self-blame

("I am not able to …"). Depression often furthers negative outlooks: "Researchers have known for years that depressed people have a selective recall bias for unhappy events in their lives; it is not that they are fabricating negative stories so much as forgetting the good ones. In that sense, their negative views and perceptions can be depressingly accurate, albeit slanted and incomplete."[27] There are also patterns of low energy, indecision, and inability to execute and follow up on orders. Depression often leads to withdrawal accompanied by irritability and episodic blowups among those who make demands on them (which may be experienced as stressful or unfair in some way). People with depression sometimes respond to demands with episodic bouts of anger or passive-aggressiveness. Blowups keep others at a distance and hence minimize future demands. Whereas anxiety is future oriented, depression is past oriented; examining the past often causes people to perceive injustices which in turn provides further justification for withdrawal or opposition. People with depression may also find it difficult to achieve happiness, as discussed in the previous chapter; strategies such as expressing appreciation and creating choices may be experienced as mentally draining and, hence, not be done or continued to effectiveness.[28] Thus, like anxiety, depression is characterized by distinctively patterned thought, perception, and behavior.

The *DSM-IV-TR* distinguishes a variety of depressive disorders. Dysthymic disorder is defined as a depressed mood for at least two years that occurs on most days and that has at least two of the following features: (1) the inability to concentrate or indecisiveness, (2) insomnia or sleepiness during the day, (3) feelings of worthlessness or guilt, (4) body movements that are agitated or retarded, (5) recurrent thoughts of death or suicide, (6) significant weight gain or loss, and (7) fatigue or loss of energy. Dysthymia is often seen as low-grade ongoing depression (sometimes also called "subclinical" depression). A major depressive episode is defined as a depressed mood (feeling sad, lacking energy, etc.) or loss of pleasure in all or most activities for most of every day during a consecutive two-week period not caused by other conditions such as bereavement or substances and with at least four of the above features.[29] Dysthymia additionally requires that no major depressive episode has occurred in the two-year period. It is obvious that many of these conditions affect one's work. Disinterest, profound sadness, lack of concentration, and indecisiveness are sure to diminish what work one is willing to take on (withdrawal); even work requiring only modest degrees of responsibility and decision may be seen as overwhelming and hence be avoided. Additional workplace symptoms are unfinished projects and irritability. It is estimated that about 10 to 25 percent of women and 5 to 12 percent of men suffer from a major depressive episode in their lifetime.[30] Fifty-eight percent of those with a lifetime incidence of depression also have an anxiety disorder (most often GAD, panic disorder, or post-traumatic stress disorder).[31]

Diagnosis of other depressive disorders reflects patterns or variations of this assessment. For example, a minor depressive episode involves a depressed mood or loss of interest plus up to four of the above symptoms. A major depressive disorder can also involve several major depressive episodes without manic or mixed episodes. Bipolar disorders are those where depressive episodes are interspersed with episodes of manic (elevated) moods. Bipolar disorder (historically called manic depression) is a very complex and ongoing disorder in which the level and cycles of mania and manifest behaviors can vary greatly. Depression comes in many degrees and variations, and it is useful to consider these divisions as reflecting a range of different ways depression manifests itself. Many people also suffer from lower levels of depression in which only some of these symptoms are present. As with anxiety, depression encompasses a range of forms and manifestations.

As with anxiety, there is "functional dysfunctionality." Some very mild degree of depression is sometimes helpful and actually sought by society in some circumstances. Lincoln and Churchill were known for their depressive and melancholic outlooks. Obviously some people learn to manage their symptoms and perform in satisfactory ways. Some people develop especially good skills at social interaction, taking the time to read and understand others. Anecdotally, we have observed that some people with minor characteristics of depression often appear as "uncle-like," and because they appear nonthreatening, they are often promoted to higher positions when their performance and social interactions are consistent enough. Their Type B personalities put others at ease. They are easy to like and seem to be a frequent choice of upper managers and governing boards. Everybody likes a supportive and friendly boss. As regarding energy deficits, people with low levels of depression may actually find that work demands produce adrenaline that lifts their mood up. Also, episodic prickly behaviors are useful in organizational politics.

By way of a modest example, consider "Fred," who is a senior HR staff person in a large organization. He is the compensation specialist and is responsible for working with departments when they hire new employees. Fred has a casual demeanor and appearance, which puts people at ease. Fred often discusses the importance of professional norms and often states that he feels it is important that the organization maintains compliance and integrity in its hiring processes. Recently, Fred's supervisor is (again) hearing increasing concerns that Fred has been slow to get back to managers (not answering e-mail for five days), and in two or three cases, this delay caused good employee prospects to be lost. When confronted about his performance, Fred justifies his actions as being in the best interest of the organization: "You wouldn't want any lawsuits, would you?" When pressed whether he could be a bit more timely and flexible in helping other managers to recruit bright employee prospects, he responds that he really doesn't care what others thought about his performance. If his boss wanted to replace him, that would be fine by him, but he is unwilling to lower his standards. It is easy to see how this situation can lead to intransience and deteriorating performance. This example also shows that many cases have a reasonable side to them as well. Everybody wants to avoid lawsuits, but it also matters that work is done in a timely way.

But being more than just a little depressive can be problematic, as it quickly affects work performance, social interaction, and enthusiasm. When people cannot get along with others or fail to perform at their tasks, they risk stagnating and in extreme cases being let go. Though by law people are protected from termination because of mental health conditions, in practice "courts overwhelmingly side with the employers," says Deirdre Smith, the director of a legal aid clinic at the University of Maine.[32] People need to get along, and they can be let go for not doing so, independent of mental health concerns. Cruelly for those with depression, such episodes hurt their self-esteem, which can further cause depression.

As with anxiety, physiology and genetics also play a role in depression. A possible neurochemical cause of depression is insufficient serotonin, a neurotransmitter that many common antidepressant drugs target in different ways. Some drugs also target norepinephrine, another neurotransmitter. As with anxiety, drugs usually take a few weeks to take effect and often require some trial. Serotonin is targeted in anxiety as well; though medicines for these disorders differ, a common purpose is to decrease hypersensitivity that causes mood swings and depression; as already noted, anxiety and depression sometimes go together (comorbidity). As in anxiety, cognitive-behavioral therapy in conjunction with medicine is a recommended therapy that often greatly alleviates the extent of depression and its symptoms. Often, psychoanalytic therapy is also effective, as many depressive thoughts and response patterns originate in childhood and other past activities. However, anecdotally, people with depression are often resistant to seeking therapy and many hit the bottom before realizing the need for it. The mind often does not want to be there and denies that there is a problem (a defense mechanism). The challenge is getting people with depression to take care of their depression.

Dealing with people with depression at work is not resolved by cajoling, threatening, or otherwise pushing them into action. Prospects of increased stress outweigh any rewards that others might offer and can itself bring on depression. Threats are often returned with assertions of one's rights, foot-dragging, and barely acceptable performance. A better approach may be the use of periodic performance contracts (or psychological contracts in writing; see Chapter 10), ensuring agreement and limiting the frequency of making new work requests. In addition, managers and colleagues will frequently need to address negative assertions, defeatism, and generalizations with questions and suggestions of specifics. "I don't think this can be done" might be met with "I think this can be done; I will show you how." "This is an injustice" might be met with "People are within their rights, but we are still trying to also improve outcomes," and so on.

Mental health ailments are many, though anxiety and depression are among the most prevalent. Some mental health conditions are far more severe and limiting than those discussed above, for example, schizophrenia and developmental disorders, which often limit professional and even routine work activities and need to be managed by a professional to maximize a person's potential for social interaction and work performance. Other disorders such as gender identity and eating disorders seem to only tangentially affect the workplace, but they also affect performance and social interactions, and people with eating disorders may experience extended periods of absence because of hospitalization. Sleeping disorders are also understood as a mental health problem that clearly affects performance and safety. A major category of personality disorders is discussed in the next chapter. Medical and behavioral interventions in these areas vary and do not always sufficiently relieve symptoms to meet workplace expectations.

In addition to the above-mentioned disorders, we briefly note attention-deficit/hyperactivity disorder (ADHD). Though this is regarded as a childhood disorder, about 60 percent of children diagnosed with ADHD continue to display symptoms in adulthood. The worldwide prevalence of ADHD is estimated at 5 percent of the population.[33] We mention ADHD because, anecdotally, this form is sometimes readily observed at work. Characteristics in adults vary, with some forms focusing on inattentiveness and others on hyperactivity. Hyperactivity (which is also called impulsive-type) often causes people to seek stimulating activity, avoid work that is sedentary or requires long periods of concentration, pursue constant activity, be easily bored, be irritated or impatient, often make snap decisions, and sometimes rather easily lose their temper or get angry. Though some of these features are also present in other disorders, the constellation of these characteristics does paint a picture, as well as its onset and diagnosis in childhood. Though ADHD is not fully understood, neurochemical and neurophysiological factors play a role. Regardless of diagnosis difficulties (and some controversy exists over diagnosing ADHD in adults who have not been previously diagnosed with childhood ADHD), the pattern is indeed common among some people at work. Anecdotally, we have observed that some people with these problems sometimes rise high in organizations when the degree is not too severe, when they can find others who can ensure performance in activities that require organization and concentration, and when the organization places them in jobs where these attributes are assets rather than liabilities. Sometimes minor degrees of a mental health disorder produce advantageous conditions for people in their organizations.

People need to know the machine that they are and take care of it accordingly. People are responsible for achieving a modicum of reasonable performance. Even moderate levels of anxiety, depression, or ADHD make well-being and performance far more difficult to achieve. The lifetime incidences of anxiety, depression, and ADHD alone affect almost 38 percent of the population,[34] and many people have mild manifestations of these disorders. Many symptoms are overlapping and comorbid; for example, it is common for some people to experience both anxiety and depression at different times. People tend to underestimate the impact of their behaviors, which include irritability, worry, social avoidance, poor judgment, and distraction. Moreover, anxiety and depression have a tendency to feed on themselves, and research shows that self-help often is insufficient; there are genetic and physiological factors in the background. Mental health is increasingly sought, and millions of people use such conventional strategies as exercise, morality, religion, and group belonging, which bring insufficient relief. The human condition is that people need to know their proclivities and take care of them.

18

The Little Tyrant … and Other Problems

The best political, social, and spiritual work we can do is to withdraw the projection of our shadow onto others.

—**Carl Gustav Jung**[1]

We are apt to come across some people at work who are difficult at best and evil at worst. Personality is commonly defined as a person's characteristic qualities, and some people have these qualities in an abundance of distinctive ways that upset others greatly. There are those whose ingrained patterns defy strategies of getting along (Chapter 4) or even psychological contracts (Chapter 10). This chapter looks at a selection of difficult behavior and personality disorders that often involves others in situations that cause stress and harm. Many personality disorders involve difficult behaviors, but not all difficult behaviors are part of personality problems, of course. Though, clinically, the prevalence of different personality problems (or disorders) in the general population is each fairly small (1 to 2 percent), Table 17.1 shows that they are found among 9.1 percent of the population.[2] The implication is that most work teams (of say ten to twelve people) are likely to have one person who is significantly difficult (or even odd) in some way, and about 20 to 30 percent of such teams will have a person who is highly disruptive, manipulative, and a source of great distress. This, too, is the human condition at work. Anecdotally, this accords well with our experience.

Almost all people will come across a few very disruptive and upsetting individuals in the course of their careers, and it is worthwhile to be prepared. Difficult behaviors come in many different shapes and sizes. Some people are masters at dividing groups. Some people are highly manipulative and a source of high drama in the office. Some people want to be the center of attention. Some people are bullies that engage in persistent, offensive, abusive, intimidating, and malicious or insulting behavior; they make people feel threatened, angry, and insecure over the future. Some people see conspiracies and power plays in everything and are quick to blow up. Some routinely break rules and conventions, pushing boundaries and decorum, but somehow they are able to keep their jobs; some are upper managers' favorites, even though they produce little. Some manipulate others into working for them and blame others for their failures. Some are thin-skinned and quick to blow up, which has others walking on eggshells. Still others are persistently negative and waffling and have an endless range of reasons for not supporting new and needed ideas. Some never delegate and hold back information.

Many people have known people with one or more of the above characteristics. Not all of the above are disorders; some are just difficult behaviors. People with difficult behaviors are found at all levels of society and among all races, genders, and age groups. They include presidents, professors, politicians, lawyers, and doctors. The range of difficult behavior is vast but finite. The workplace offers many sources of negative emotions, and these persons are some. It should be noted that organizations do a very poor job at screening for these problems in the hiring process. Candidates with the above features often are quite charming and do exceedingly well in interviews. Sometimes the deceit of candidates is very thorough, and they fabricate achievements that would be hard to detect in any case. Few managers are skilled in detecting the personality problems discussed below. References are not always thoroughly checked, sometimes because people doing the hiring do not want to see a consensus candidate disqualified. Also, the people discussed below usually show adequate if not exceedingly proper conduct for the duration of the probationary period. Difficult behaviors start thereafter, but people often are difficult to fire as they avoid many such offenses, and they are quick to compromise those who might do so or speak up against them. In short, people with difficult personalities and behaviors are a fact of the workplace.

> **About 20 to 30 percent of work teams will have a person who is highly disruptive.**

Happiness and fulfillment are nearly impossible to come by when one's mind is preoccupied with the behaviors of others that cause concern and distress. Avoiding those people and setting clear boundaries are about as good as can be done, but it is difficult to avoid getting caught up in the disturbances that go on. In truth, many good workers decide to move on, when they can. The fact that one can talk about what follows does not mean that some of the worst cases always have happy outcomes. Good intentions are surely not enough in dealing with the following cases; dealing with difficult people requires exceptionally good people skills. There are snakes in the grass.

There is no one best way to describe the range of difficult behaviors that people may show. The management literature is at best casual in its description, while the clinical literature is highly defined but focused on personality disorders. Many personality disorders surely give rise to difficult behaviors at work, but not all difficult behaviors are evidence of mental pathology; some may reflect proclivities that are bit overdone. Clinically, ten different types of personality disorders are distinguished (*Diagnostic and Statistical Manual of Mental Disorders*, text revision; *DSM-IV-TR*), though in practice some people have traits that overlap (or borrow) from two or more types. Our approach is to begin by examining some of the most challenging personality disorders and then move on to those that have only some of these features.

Antisocial personality. The antisocial personality is behaviorally defined as a pervasive disregard for the rights and dignity of others, along with remorseless manipulation of others for the purpose (or emphasis) of getting ahead at any cost. It involves repeated lying (deceitfulness) and conning of others for pleasure or profit, with no sense of remorse, guilt, or any feelings toward their victims.[3] Typical expressions that characterize this mentality at work are "It's a dog-eat-dog world" and "We are not a charity" to justify actions that are insensitive to the needs of others. People with antisocial personality disorder often use others to achieve their goals and then drop allegiance to them, causing others to eventually feel duped and used. According to Lester,[4] diagnostic qualities include being manipulative, deceitful, charming, or self-centered; having temper tantrums; and being contemptuous and untrustworthy. This disorder has an onset in adolescence and continues thereafter.

Well-known "big-time" examples of those with antisocial personality disorder are Saddam Hussein, John Gotti, Idi Amin, Joseph Stalin, and Slobodan Milošević (though not everyone with antisocial personality disorder gets this far, of course). People around them typically experience fear, betrayal, and anger, to which some respond with avoidance or denial. According to some estimates, about 3 percent of men and 1 percent of women exhibit antisocial personality traits, though the prevalence of antisocial personality among women is likely underestimated.[5] About 40 percent of those diagnosed with antisocial personality disorder also experience alcoholism at some point in their life. Because people with antisocial personality disorder tend to break rules, some have interactions with the law; according to the *DSM-IV-TR*, the prevalence of antisocial behavior in forensic settings (prisons, etc.) may be as high as 30 percent. Manipulation and disregard for the dignity of others are key features.

Borderline personality. The borderline personality is characterized by an unstable mood, unstable relationships, an unstable self-image (or lack of sense of self), marked impulsivity that brings excitement, a thin skin, high demands, and a tendency to see others as all good or all bad. Examples include Alex Forrest (Glenn Close's character) in *Fatal Attraction* (1987), Susanna Kaysen (Winona Ryder's character) in *Girl, Interrupted* (1999), Adolf Hitler, and Marilyn Monroe (suspected). Diagnostic criteria further include feelings of emptiness, fits of rage, possible suicidal thoughts, and a high level of self-damaging behaviors and acts of impulsivity in at least two of the following areas: spending, sex, substance abuse, driving, binge eating, and shoplifting. People with this disorder are easily bored, and impulsivity in these areas brings excitement ("Let's do something wild!"). Early abandonment and insomnia are additional defining characteristics, and people with a borderline personality seldom apologize for their actions, except when facing abandonment. Because of these many instabilities, work performance often is erratic, and sometimes performance is not possible. Some of the above qualities are likely to spill over into the workplace, which often make these people a cause of general disturbance. Indeed, they experience a lot of problems, and while some people may feel sorry for them, others who have been used by them report feeling angry (vengeful), fearful, and as if they are walking on eggshells. Borderline personality disorder is more commonly diagnosed in women: 3 percent versus 1 percent among men. A lack of consideration and empathy is common, and people with borderline personality may be given to tactics very similar to those associated with antisocial personality behaviors and can be charming and manipulatively scheming for getting what they want.[6]

Antisocial and borderline personality disorders often occur (i.e., are comorbid) with other problems. For example, some people with borderline personality also have bipolar mood disorders and alcohol abuse. People with the above features are likely to exhibit one or more of the following problems as well. The combined prevalence of antisocial personality and borderline personality is about 4 percent of the population, making it quite common and accounting for about half of the most serious, disruptive behavior. Hence about 20 to 30 percent of teams consisting of ten to twelve people would be expected to have their own Joseph Stalin or Marilyn Monroe. These individuals are highly disruptive at work. The people described below usually lack one or more features of those with antisocial or borderline personality disorder, but they are very difficult and also bring out negative emotions.

Paranoid. Paranoid people are given to distrust and suspiciousness of others' motives, which they see as malevolent. People assume that others will "exploit, harm or deceive them, even if no evidence exists to support this expectation."[7] A famous paranoid was J. Edgar Hoover (FBI director), but many dictators with antisocial personality come to develop paranoid behaviors too (e.g., Idi Amin, Saddam Hussein, etc.). At work, some people see conspiracies against them, their projects, or their office even when others might see the glass as half full. Because they see threats everywhere, loyalty is held in high regard, and they have a "with me or against me" attitude. However, they are apt to distrust even their closest associates and even compliments for their work are distrusted ("What does she want from me?"). They are quick to become angry and take things very personally and are likely to fiercely attack opponents, perhaps because they overexaggerate the severity of threats. They hold grudges, tend to be angry, and are loath to confide in others for fear that any information might be used against them. People around them often feel scared of them. Ironically, their hypervigilance and suspiciousness cause others to also not confide in them, which gives them less access to information and hence makes them more susceptible to attacks and schemes by others.

Narcissist. People with a narcissistic personality see themselves as all-important and above others. They have a sense of self-entitlement and being somehow special or unique. They are grandiose, arrogant, and self-righteous and when confronted with criticism, they may become enraged. Narcissistic people are inconsiderate and demeaning to subordinates. In the presence of superiors they are deferential but often derogatory behind their back. Narcissistic people crave admiration and often have fantasies of grandiose successes for themselves. Those around them often feel fearful and hateful; they try to avoid, resist, or placate them. Though self-confidence and the ability to enjoy power are positive qualities, narcissists are over the top and demonstrate many of the above qualities, as well as a lack of remorse and concern for others. Some people distinguish between "situational" narcissism, which is acquired (e.g., a job title that has gone to one's head), and narcissism as ingrained in one's personality. The prevalence of the latter is less than 1 percent of the population. Narcissism is sometimes confused with antisocial personality, and people with the latter are apt to have some narcissistic behavior, but narcissism lacks the aggressiveness, impulsivity, and deceit of the latter.[8] Some famous narcissists are said to include Napoleon and General George Patton, though many celebrities also believe that they are special and act with disdain toward others.

Histrionic personality. People with this attention-seeking personality want to be at the middle of the attention: "Often lively and dramatic, they draw attention to themselves and may initially charm new acquaintances by their enthusiasm, apparent openness or flirtatiousness. These qualities wear thin, however, as these individuals continually demand to be at the center of attention."[9] When they are not at the center of attention, they do something dramatic such as make up stories, be seductive, or get caught up in problems of some kind (which may require them to be rescued). They tend to dress well in ways that draw attention or cause compliments. They may be given to dramatic expressiveness ("drama queen"), but they lack depth and substance; there is a marked shallowness and superficiality about them. They may get involved in projects but then quickly lose interest in the face of mundane and routine tasks. Some people may become overly trusting of authority figures. Many people exhibit histrionic traits, but in some people they are maladaptive and excessive. While people with borderline personality are also given to histrionic attention seeking, those with histrionic personality are not given to the many instabilities of moods and relationships and the self-destructive behaviors that are common with borderline personality. About 2 to 3 percent of the general population exhibits this trait.

At this time, the proposed revision of the *DSM* for 2013 (*DSM-5*) includes the new trait domain "antagonism," defined as "manifestations of antipathy toward others, and a correspondingly exaggerated sense of self-importance," with the following trait facets: callousness, manipulativeness, narcissism, histrionism, hostility, aggression, oppositionality, and deceitfulness. While the above classifications are to be retained, a common trait of antagonism will likely be introduced, though the trait model is still in the process of empirical validation.[10] The *DSM-IV-TR* lists other personality disorders as well, but we think the above types, along with those mentioned below, adequately describe those that people should be familiar with. In addition to the above, the management and self-help literature mentions other behaviors that are problematic, sometimes describing these as personality types at work. What follows are not considered mental health disorders (unlike those above), but they include behaviors that are likely to cause problems at work; among these, bullying is common in borderline and antisocial personality types. But because what follows are not considered mental health problems, consequently less research and statistics are available about them.

Codependents. Codependency is not a recognized mental disorder, though numerous books are written about it and talk shows are replete with such cases.[11] Codependency is about (only) feeling good when others feel good. (Clinically, codependency is more, namely, an addiction to relationships.) At work, codependents are described as people who listen well and make others feel liked and appreciated but who withhold critical information or fail to make hard decisions when these are needed. As Bramson notes, "They collude with your wish that all will come out right, and thus sweetly blind you to pitfalls."[12] They are able to make decisions but don't do so when it upsets someone else; hence decisions get endlessly postponed. When orders are given, they are often passed on as unavoidable directors from their own boss. But when subordinates want to complain to their boss's boss, they are rebuked as being out of order. Codependent bosses want to maintain their relationship with their own boss above all else; that often is their key relationship. Codependent people excel at projecting an air of friendliness, but underneath they are rigid and inflexible; they do not want to rock the boat. When pushed, they become angry, which may show as a blow up or passive-aggressiveness. Everyone likes a codependent boss for the first few years, but after that disappointment and even conflict are unavoidable between codependent managers and employees who want to grow. Sometimes codependent bosses experience cycles of good workers leaving: "He's a fine man, but things are going nowhere here." The nature of the problem described here is very different from those in the above clinical cases.

Bullies. Bullying is a common tactic in antisocial personality, borderline personality, paranoid, and narcissistic personality disorders; perhaps that is why it is so widely mentioned in the management literature. It is sometimes referred to as a "hostile-aggressive" personality type. Bullying is sometimes used to describe "persistent, offensive, abusive, intimidating, malicious or insulting behavior, abuse of power or unfair penal sanctions, all of which makes the recipient feel upset, threatened, humiliated or vulnerable, which undermines their self-confidence and which may cause them to suffer stress."[13] It is easy to instill fear in humans, and bullies take advantage of that fact. Their objective is to get others to do what they want of them in a reliable and compliant way through psychological and other distress and threats thereof. Bullying includes making threats to professional status and development, personal standing, and relations with others at work. Bullies are tyrants. Bullying tactics at work include hovering over people, overmonitoring people's efforts, constantly undervaluing effort, being persistently critical, having explosive outbursts, belittling people (cutting them down), spreading malicious rumors, having temper tantrums directed at others, withholding information, taking credit for others' ideas, ignoring or excluding an individual, setting impossible objectives or deadlines, giving too many or unachievable tasks, and humiliating people in front of others.[14] Many people with *DSM-IV-TR* personality disorders use bullying tactics, but not all bullies have these other features as well or to a clinical degree.

Control freaks. Control freaks are those who hold on to everything and do not delegate. They may be very nice and charming, be highly knowledgeable in their area, and have a marked record of accomplishment, but they do not allow those under them to act with the independence and command that are expected. Control freaks hold on to resources, decisions, people, plans, and so on. Even when they delegate these to others, they in fact will insist on making final decisions. They tell others what to do, and they are micromanagers. Those who try to circumvent them at first are rebuked, and the control freak will seek to prevent reoccurrence through daily interactions. Bramson notes that control freaks lack confidence and trust, have an irrational search for perfection, and an overly strong wish to be in charge.[15] They have a strong sense of responsibility, and the need for control may be born from previous experiences or failures. Though paranoid and antisocial personalities are also controlling, control freaks may lack "evil intent" or distrust in the malicious motives of others. Bullies may also use control tactics, but the control freak is not out to humiliate or demean others.

Indecisives. Some people are just given to not making decisions usually because of problems with responsibility. Manifestations of indecisiveness are overly delegating (shifting decision-making responsibilities to others), being supernegative (giving reasons why decisions should be postponed or not made), and being avoidant (missing meetings where important decisions are expected to be made). These people usually don't go very far in an organization, as their persistent inability to act is problematic for their superiors as well, but they may be highly knowledgeable and able to talk a great shop, hence landing themselves jobs. For people working with indecisives, frustration is likely to surface and will occur sooner than when working with codependents. It should be noted that indecisiveness is associated with many types of mental health. Making decisions is also difficult for people with depression, as decisions bear uncertain and likely some negative outcomes, as well as the need for new energy and efforts. Many of the above types may also show indecisiveness as a tactic, such as codependents (to avoid upsetting others), histrionics (to get attention: "Please help me."), control freaks (to study the issue a bit more before telling others what decision to make), bullies (to ask for opinions of others and then belittle them), and even antisocials (to see how others act and then take advantage of them in some way). Thus, indecisiveness is a behavior that usually requires a bit more observation in order to paint a more complete picture of which it is part.

While we do not deal with alcohol and substance abuse problems in this book, it is clear that these also affect people skills, and many of the more serious personality disorders often exhibit a good deal of alcohol and substance use too. Substance abuse is usually a process of gradual build up, and different degrees of substance abuse are associated with increasing severity of problems. Typical signs and behaviors include having unexplained absences, missing deadlines, avoiding colleagues and coworkers, borrowing money from coworkers, lacking concentration, overreacting to criticism, having unreasonable resentments, and having above average absences for medical reasons. Higher degrees of substance abuse may include loss of ethical judgment and values, grandiosity or exaggeration of performance, legal issues, refusal to discuss problems, being undependable, high frequency of domestic problems, and poor performance. Some of these symptoms and behaviors are also similar or identical to those in the above personality disorders. In our experience, coworkers usually observe one or more of these signs. One does not always observe substance abuse on the job or signs such as alcohol on the breath, slurred speech, or unusual gait, of course.[16]

The self-help literature mentions many others types too. For example, there are hot heads (people who are given to episodic or explosive tantrums or impulsive decisions), know-it-alls (people who think they don't need to hear from others), and superagreeables (people who always agree but as employees often produce wrong products).[17] We think that many other behaviors, when not part of those discussed above, can often be addressed with conventional approaches already mentioned in previous chapters (e.g., Chapters 4, 7, and 10). It is not only a single behavior that matters but the intent and constellation of other behaviors too.

Though the above types point to behaviors that are difficult in some way, some of the clinical cases are characterized by a pattern of strategic behaviors that rises far above that of specific tactics. Our reason for including the following section about psychopaths is the potential for them to cause career-ending damage for others. Babiak and Hare describe the strategic pattern followed by psychopaths, on which the following section is based.[18] The term *psychopath* often is loosely used, such as signaling criminally deviant behavior, existing concurrently with antisocial personality disorder, or referring to someone who meets the criteria defined by various tests (e.g., *Hare Psychopathy Checklist–Revised*).[19] Anecdotally, we think the following descriptions fit some or all workplace patterns of some other known or suspected types, including some with borderline personality and bullies. The strategic pattern incorporates many of the above specific behaviors.

The basic actors in the drama of workplace psychopaths are patrons, pawns, detractors, and patsies.[20] Psychopaths define others according to the labels, which they change as the need arises. Patrons are superiors who can be helpful in some way (including protecting psychopaths from those who might complain about them), and pawns are helpful subordinates and coworkers. Patrons and pawns are befriended but used and even compromised when possible. Detractors are people who complain to others about workplace psychopaths; they are to be removed or at least neutralized in some way. The organizational police (e.g., auditors) are always a potential detractor. Patsies are those who serve no purpose in the plans and who have been removed as a detractor.

The drama has four acts: entry, assessment, manipulation (or ascension), and confrontation. The purpose of the entry phase is for the psychopath to get hired by an organization or department that has something to be gained. Psychopaths may be convincing liars and charmers who are readily hired. They often have very good or even excellent credentials and set of achievements and references to match. Psychopaths are very good at using the professional commitment statement (Chapter 8). Some achievements may belong to others, but there is no flag that alerts others to that. Though sometimes there are rumors of prior workplace issues, there is no corroborating or hard evidence. When asked, psychopaths offer persuasive explanations ("Oh, that was just sour grapes by one coworker."). Managers and HR people are seldom trained or asked to dig deeply, and quite simply, they are no match for the psychopath.

The second phase is assessment, in which psychopaths assess others for utility, power, and access. A befriending period is used in which they get to know others—what they can offer, what they need or seek, and what their weaknesses might be. Psychopaths continue to be very charming and often get people to say things about themselves that they have told few others. The third phase is manipulation. During this phase, psychopaths begin to cast doubt and spread rumors about those they wish to turn into victims or patsies. They cast rumors that question the quality and integrity of others' work, the conduct and ethics of others, and whether others in fact even do their own work. Barr and O'Connor said, "To look for psychopaths in the workplace, look for the commotion and disruption around them," but it is a commotion that is often known to only a few.[21] They preemptively make informal complaints and let others know that they will file complaints or even seek legal action if anyone questions them.

With top managers, psychopaths engage in highly ethical and useful ways that earn them their interest and, later, support. They come up with good ideas and make good presentations about them, though they are often based on borrowed work of others. Their direct superiors may appreciate the effort to put their office in a good light. Access to top managers is secured at "impromptu" chance encounters (cocktail parties, elevators, etc.) in which appointments are made for further follow-up ("Can I talk with you about a plan for … ? It would really help the agency."). To an outsider, this behavior is acceptable, and psychopaths might bring their boss further credibility and legitimacy. Eventually, they establish their own relationship of utility with the patron.

Their behavior is markedly different towards coworkers and subordinates. Different people get different behavior. To get what they want and to ensure loyalty and control, psychopaths give too many or too stressful assignments or assign demeaning work to some subordinates who question them or report being bullied. (The message is "If you talk or don't do what I tell you to, I will make your life miserable.") Young subordinates often cry or experience extreme distress when working for those who bully, and some quit after just a few weeks or months. Regarding coworkers who have something to offer, they will try to team up and use their work. To control pawn coworkers, they create situations that make coworkers accomplice to potentially career-ending or even criminal acts, involving fraud or other inappropriate acts that may involve alcohol, drugs, or sex. For example, they may have someone else give the unsuspecting coworker fraudulent data that the coworker then presents or signs off on. They may initiate an exchange of risqué e-mail and come into the coworkers' office and engage in inappropriate conduct and later threaten to sue the person (for sexual harassment) or to inform his or her spouse. They create minicrises (e.g., misplacing key data or having a drink) that lead to secret alliances ("We don't need to tell anyone about this, OK?"), which are later used to blackmail coworkers into silence. Coworkers dealing with such people are surely the victims of workplace psychopathy.

However, toward others, psychopaths behave with a markedly professional demeanor. Any coworkers or subordinates who do speak up (confrontation phase) are apt to be met with incredulity by others who have known the person in only professional ways ("She must have had an off day."), even leading to questioning the motives of those making any allegations ("Why would he speak so badly about him?"). High-ranking patrons are especially apt to defend psychopaths. Anecdotally, this does seem to be the case. They often play into the power games of psychopaths by giving support to their projects or even participating in them, without knowing really who these psychopaths are or what they have done to others in their organization ("They have such good ideas! Real leadership material."). CEOs, top managers, and others who only infrequently deal with these people are easily duped and will often support them even in the face of some evidence of rule-breaking and unusual behavior ("You don't have firm evidence, and this project is in the interest of the organization.").

The Hollywood fantasy of justice coming to those who deserve it is not suggested by any author, and we have not anecdotally observed that. Though systematic data are lacking, we see psychopaths being routinely promoted at work, as those who have evidence against them are unable to speak out or get acceptance for the information they do have. Barr and O'Connor perceptively note, "Selected anti-social traits or behaviors may not seem particularly problematic or serious when viewed in isolation, but their overall constellation can be problematic."[22] But others often do not want to see the pattern in the absence of evidence of specific laws being broken, which is seldom available. It is sometimes difficult for others to want to see the pattern. Also, psychopaths usually network well and get good references that help them get a next job. People at psychopaths' current job are happy to see them go and are unlikely to give a poor recommendation, sometimes also for fear of litigation. Psychopaths do have troublesome personal lives that sometimes get them in serious trouble, but that does not always have workplace implications.

The above story line is real and often observed and shows how many tactics of bullying, deceit, and manipulation can come together. For psychopaths, the workplace is a veritable playground for getting excitement and gain at the expense of others. We have seen this played out in offices of hospitals, universities, law practices, churches, and state governments. Not all psychopaths are smart and clever, for sure, but many with higher education degrees and political ambition are. A small number of people are sufficiently prevalent to do a great deal of harm to others. There is likely a psychopath in your midst.

Of course, not all difficult behaviors are as complex and strategic as those just described. Many difficult behaviors are separate and distinct patterns of behavior that are not associated with antisocial or malicious intent. Still, the question is how people can best deal with difficult behaviors.

First, many authors suggest that assessment is the first step, but it often takes some time for patterns to become clear. Bullies engage in a broad range of behaviors, and they often are very charming too. It can take one or two years on the job before the pattern of, say, a codependent becomes clear. Usually, one does not even know that one is dealing with a psychopath until it is too late. How many times does one have to witness abuse before a diagnosis of "bully" can be reliably made? Three areas of behaviors to be alert for are questionable, unusual, or inappropriate (1) behavior or interactions, (2) supervision styles, and (3) work outcomes. In each of these areas, the critical part is to be clear on the standards of normality that people are willing to put up with. People need to know when something does not look quite right or right at all. Often it helps to triangulate with coworkers; unanimity of opinion is not required, but it may help to more quickly assess and verify initial impressions.

Second, people develop very negative emotions toward people who cause them distress. Emotional behavior often arises. One's negative emotions arise that reflect fear, anger, and resentment caused by being bullied, subjected to overly controlling behavior, manipulated or lied to. The recommendation is to cool down, walk it off, assess the situation, get confirmation, and make a plan. Emotional reactions and responses are often labeled by others as immature and inappropriate, and what people say can be and is used against them. It often is said that one's attitude is often something one can control.[23] The decision to cool down and make a plan is often the first step toward dealing with the situation.

Third, none of the above types are easily able to fundamentally change who they are. At best, one can hope for some modest accommodation in narrowly targeted behaviors. If the problem is dealing with people who are control freaks or paranoid, it may be useful to show them that a person can be trusted to do the work. People can discuss what steps they will take and how they make decisions and the nature of any contingency plan. If the matter is one of loyalty, people can state and show their loyalty and ask why someone might question it. If the problem is with codependents or indecisives, it may be useful to begin the conversation with a personal appeal and appreciation for the work done. Codependents like decisions that are compromises and that keep everyone happy, and indecisives like others to take the responsibility for their decisions. People may insist on being told of decisions rather than hearing about them later through others. If the problem is dealing with bullies, people might state their right to speak up and to be treated as a professional. Since we can't change the person, the target is *specific behavior.*

Fourth, in the spirit of progressive discipline, the first approach or interaction is a friendly one, the second is a bit more stern, the third interaction is a formal or informal but written notification, and the fourth one involves one's supervisor (who may have been notified long before) or other formal approach. While the general objective is to stop the behavior at every encounter (say "no"), different types do suggest some differentiated responses, requiring some specification of the above points. When one of the above situations is at hand, it inevitably requires a custom-tailored approach. As these kinds of situations could end up in a lawyer's office, it is wise to record incidents and note responses. If the problem is with the borderlines and antisocials, then the time has come to set very clear boundaries, avoid or severely restrict interactions, and expose everything into the open through widely copied e-mail in the office. Eventually, they will go away when they have nothing to gain from you. They will search for another victim.

Some of the above responses can be stated in the following ways (these suggestions have bosses in mind, though they could be recast to deal with others):

- *To the bully:* "Please sit down, and let's all understand the details of what you are asking." Or "We agreed that it would be done at 6 p.m., and I will give it to you by then."
- *To the control freak:* "I am sorry, but it is my responsibility to sign off on this. But you can check it before it gets processed."
- *To the paranoid:* "Let me know what you need from me—I am loyal and yours."
- *To the narcissist:* "That's an interesting idea, but let's check with others to see what they say before we run with it."
- *To the codependent or indecisive:* "I appreciate your hard work and thinking on this. We have spoken with others, and there is agreement to move forward. We can do it in this way ... . And we would make everyone very unhappy if after all this work nothing happened, and I think even your boss would be."
- *To the psychopath or borderline:* "No, I will not do that—it is not appropriate conduct."

Usually it is unclear in advance which approach might work and what tack to take. Several trials may be necessary until the right chord is found that resonates, and the tools of diplomacy may be useful too (see Table 4.1). Berman's Rule of Three (Chapter 3) suggests that it will need to be often repeated and that it may be useful for the target to get similar suggestions from different people. Thus, a few interactions may in fact define each step in progressive discipline.

Fifth, in dealing with difficult behavior, it is important to remember the basics too. Emotions do get high. Little is gained from rushing into dealing with the above types without taking care of the following (see Chapter 4):

- *Doing your own job well:* Little is gained from being fired or opening oneself up to complaints.
- *Being pleasant:* Little is gained by being unpleasant or unprofessional.
- *Supporting others doing their job:* Some friends are now needed more than ever.
- *Avoiding hot buttons:* One is to pick one's fights and battles intentionally, not unintentionally.
- *Going gently with excellence:* This has little to do with matters here (except, possibly, for the control freaks).
- *Dealing well with difficult situations without making many waves:* This is the point here.

There is no doubt that dealing with such people is not the highlight of one's career. Most people experience dealing with difficult people as enraging. In response, many people temporarily disconnect from the workplace and dial back their involvement. They find other things to get involved with. Others begin to look for another job or transfer, but others just wait it out. Eventually, such people may turn their attention to others when they get no satisfaction or benefit. All bad things come to an end.

In the end, we need to accept the reality of the above forms of behavior at work. The Dalai Lama speaks of the need for showing compassion and developing one's sense of that through daily practice, but as the above shows, some people have very little or close to none of such feelings to share or develop. If compassion is like a muscle to be exercised so it develops, then some people lack that muscle or have it severely atrophied, which lies at the root of the above types. No known medicine exists that can make people more caring or remorseful or otherwise better at connecting with others; brain research is nascent, and perhaps one day such medicine might come to be—but not now. In addition, organizations do a poor job of screening for these problems. Managers are untrained and a poor match for the finely developed skills of many manipulators. Thus, we cannot wish away the above patterns of behavior. If 9 percent of the population has clinically diagnosable personality dysfunctions, then perhaps 15 to 20 percent or more of people at work have one or more of the above difficult problems too. While these are not all severe cases, they include proclivities that show in people's daily work and judgment. This helps explain why the workplace often is a difficult place. It is not only about management systems and task problems but also about having such people operating with considerable free reign and a lack of consequences. We are reminded of GE's concern, discussed in Chapter 4, to select people who also get along well— while that exercise of building Lego helicopters surely cannot and does not prevent all of the above problems, just avoiding some bad hires is already progress worth having.

Everybody knows that what is in management textbooks is not exactly the reality of the workplace. But it is impossible to be happy at work if one cannot deal with the above situations. States one person, "I get so disillusioned with people at work. Half are with anxiety or depression—clinical or subclinical—and we have one borderline and a few bullies, too. Some people chat all day long about their nieces and nephews, or about their plans for the weekend. They get by on mediocre work, and management thinks it's just fine. How can I be happy? Some days it is really tough. My workplace is just one big dysfunctional family." By analogy, if people are to organizations what construction materials are to buildings, then the quality of elements of organizations is very imperfect. It is the nature of the human condition. People develop coping mechanisms in response to this, such as accepting that some matters are not their problem, focusing on doing their job, finding satisfaction in helping some clients, and having an office friend to whom one can air one's frustrations. In addition, the previous chapters also suggest the following:

- Take care of your own problems first (anxiety, depression, or other).
- Practice seeing the glass as half full.
- Stay out of traps of people with personality problems (above).
- Practice getting along with others (Chapter 4, see all six points).
- Make a few friends at work (Chapter 5).
- Focus on your own career objectives (professional commitment statement).

The failure of management theory to deal with the above problems is one the big oversights of our time. What is to be expected of teamwork in the presence of a psychopath? What is to be made of loyalty in the face of layoffs, a bullying boss, or even a mortgage to be paid? What is to be expected of civility and trust in the face of uncaring and deceitful employees? People's responses to difficult behaviors, uncertain futures, their own limitations, and responsibility to their family may be a good deal more rational (or understandable) than the management fantasy of people working with great commitment and trust toward common objectives. The human condition is to navigate many limitations and constraints in the workplace. If it is not to make things better, then it is at least to make them bearable and not worse. It is the master engineer who despite all the challenges keeps both the machines going and the people at the factory happy.

19
Transitions

If it doesn't kill you, it makes you stronger.

—Popular expression

L ife has its moments of major transition. People graduate from college and take on new jobs and careers—this is not just a physical change, such as moving to a new city or buying a new wardrobe, but also a psychological one. We leave one set of identities and roles behind and adopt a new set that often is yet to be defined. Old behaviors that have become ingrained are now no longer acceptable, and new behaviors are needed that are still in the process of development. People also experience transition when they leave one organization and job and accept employment at another organization. One's old colleagues and support networks are gone, but new ones are not yet in place. Such transitions into new organizations also involve an assessment phase that is usually challenging and surprising, and the transition is even bigger when the job is a new one of some kind, such as a promotion. Transitions often are defining moments in one's career development, and it is useful and beneficial to handle transitions well.

Transitions point to the inevitability of change. Change is everywhere, not only around us but also in us. We change and get new ideas. Other people also change and formulate new objectives. The organizations we work for and deal with also change, and sometimes things come to a boil, reaching a defining point. Change is inevitable. This chapter is about transitions—the big changes that seem to involve the end of one chapter and the beginning of a new one.

Transitions are characterized by three phases: (1) ending, (2) accommodation and exploration, and (3) beginning.[1] Whether it concerns a job, an organization, or a group of people, every transition begins with an ending. There is something that we need to say good-bye to—including any part of our identity, relationships, and security that may have been wrapped up with that. The loss of the latter can lead to major suffering and is why transitions are often quite personal. The accommodation and exploration phase is about accepting one's situation and the presence of a temporary existence whose purpose is to explore new beginnings. The final, beginning stage occurs when one has secured a new job or task that provides for a new set of circumstances that fulfills one's economic, security, and identity needs. In sum, a transition is like a book in reverse—a transition begins with an ending and ends with a beginning.

The topic of this chapter strikes a personal chord for us. As survivors of both Hurricane Katrina (New Orleans 2005) and Hurricane Andrew (Miami 1992), we have experienced some endings and new beginnings, for sure. We have seen our car in a tree, and a tree in our house. In such moments, it is hard to see a satisfactory way out. People often feel that the world, or at least their world, has come to an end in some way. The first part is true—a part of one's world has ended, but the second part remains to be seen. As the chapter vignette shows, change does not always have a bad outcome.

Although this chapter has much to say about involuntary transitions, voluntary transitions also often involve concerns about endings—people are often surprised how much in their new job or situation people miss something about their former self or environment. Some transitions involve moving into long sought promotions—transitions occur for happy reasons, too. The pattern of ending and beginning often is the same, even as the magnitude is less.

> A transition begins with an ending and ends with a beginning.

✳

Endings. Work entails endings. Involuntary endings are often sudden and dramatic, involving a sense of crisis. They often give people at work a little time, but not too much, to deal with the ending that is about to come. Examples include cases where people lose a job, lose a contract, lose a coworker, or lose an employee—lose a favorable situation of some kind. Typically, losses are announced ahead of time, or people see them coming. But not all losses are only dreaded. One of the most celebrated losses was the end of the Apollo space program—a humongously successful public effort that first put a man on the moon. The achievement was celebrated many times over and still stands as a monument of what the human spirit and the public sector can do. Yet the end of the Apollo program also caused one-quarter of all jobs in Brevard County, home to the Kennedy Space Center, to evaporate—it was both success and loss together.

As one person states, "Consider how often we have to deal with endings all our lives, most of us handle them very badly."[3] This is hardly a surprise, as endings usually involve negative emotions that are hard to deal with. Indeed, even endings with positive achievements often leave people with a sense of emptiness or void. Completions cause a person to lose a sense of purpose and occupation of the mind. People with major achievements often experience a letdown that is more than postadrenaline. People commonly celebrate success by having a drink with friends, and many rush headlong into the next project—all of which help deal with or avoid emptiness. It is said that the gods have two ways of dealing with people: by refusing them their wish and by granting them their wish. The latter produces the eventual recognition "Is that all there is?" A popular commercial asks an Olympic gold medalist, "Congratulations! What are you going to do next?" The answer, "I am going to Disney World!" They might have well added "for distracting my mind." All endings have pain to some extent. It is the nature of the phenomenon.

Of course, involuntary endings at work often bring a good deal more additional pain. Anger is quite common, as people may feel let down or betrayed by others who had implicitly or otherwise promised that things would work out or that they would not be let go. Projects and employments are complex and long enough for things to have happened about which others can take umbrage. Anger often is directed at both people and the organization, and this is one reason why people who are terminated are immediately escorted out of the building by security guards. It is also why terminations often happen on Friday, so that people might cool off over the weekend.

Additional emotions are guilt and shame. People are apt to second-guess whether they could have somehow prevented the negative outcome: "If only I would not have said that." While this may reflect a desire for more control than actually existed, feelings of guilt (and thoughts of stupidity) are not uncommon. People may also be ashamed that they ended up in their situation, such as being unemployed, or that someone "as good as I am" has now had some misfortune occur. The movie *The Company Men* (2010) portrays managers who are laid off during a recession; one of these men is not allowed to return home by his wife during business hours in order that the neighbors do not know that he has become unemployed.[4] There is personal and social embarrassment.

The above emotions are often punctuated by fear and anxiety about the future. There is economic fear or heightened concern about paying bills in the future, as well as the possible impact of involuntary endings on one's reputation: "How will I explain this in job interviews?" The latter may begin to point to psychological angst, the existential concern that one's identity is diminished or is soon to be diminished in the eyes of others. It is hard to find much happiness and relief when one's mind is engaged in an ongoing stream of anger, guilt, fear, shame, anxiety (worry), anger, and so on.

One smart piece of advice in dealing with the above is to minimize or avoid it to the extent possible. Negative emotions are never easy to deal with—an ounce of prevention is better than a pound of cure. A good ending often is defined as one that (1) brings the current project or phase to a successful close, then provides (2) a little time off for reenergizing and "finding oneself" again and (3) a date when a new activity is to be started that is consistent with one's career objectives. This sequence greatly minimizes, if not largely avoids, many negative emotions. For example, consultants usually try to have six to nine months of salary earnings in reserve to ensure time to obtain their next project contract.[5] Many people also try to take a few short holidays during the year, preferably coinciding with the lull between projects. Even when working conditions are extremely upsetting, it is still best to produce a happy ending to be able to leave on one's own terms, that is, when a new job has been lined up. The tools of diplomacy and getting along (Chapter 4) may be useful to postpone separation and ensure a better ending, even if an ending cannot be eventually avoided. A good ending also helps to ensure one has helpful references.

Involuntary endings have many different patterns but almost always deviate from the above good ending. Young people who are fired for lack of people skills may have things come up to a boil and be given only two weeks' notice. Typically, their boss has not been happy with their performance for some time, and a record of dissatisfaction may also exist about interactions. In the above-mentioned movie *The Company Men*, another manager is given three months of severance pay and is unable to secure a new job before having to sell his car and family's home after about three months. Increased competition from new college graduates during the recession makes it difficult to find another a job.[6] The obvious point is to avoid such outcomes as much as possible. There is wisdom in trying to secure the best possible good ending that minimizes anger, anxiety, self-recrimination, and emptiness.

Of course, negative emotion is not totally avoidable; it is the nature of most endings. It is now common to consider great pain (involving loss of identity, income, security, etc.) as requiring a grieving process through which it slowly fades away. Kübler-Ross's research in the late 1960s on dying and catastrophic loss suggested that grief over loss of life involves five stages:[7] denial ("This can't be happening to me!"), anger ("Who caused this?!"), bargaining ("What can I do to get out of this mess?"), depression ("My life is just so sad."), and, finally, acceptance ("If this is the way it is going to be, I might as well as enjoy the ride."). Some people question the sequencing and number of steps, and even Kübler-Ross noted that they can occur

302 • People Skills at Work

in different order.[8] People who go through painful episodes often recognize the above steps.

Dealing with negative emotions is seen as a management process. It is very common to experience temporary relief that is punctuated by flare-ups—situations that trigger memories of the past that cause a reliving of the pain. Most people revisit the above steps a few times. The point of management is to help people get pain out of their system, to get on with their life in ways that build up new positive experiences and emotions that eventually replace the older ones. There are three key management strategies for dealing with negative emotions: (1) hope and faith, (2) reframing, and (3) depth psychology. Having hope about a positive future surely reduces pain in the present by putting more focus on the future. Faith involves putting one's emotions, and responsibility for dealing with them, in the hands of others and letting them take care of it; some people turn to their religious faith for this purpose. Hope and faith surely allow people to reduce the sharp impact of the present pain. Being positive and having hope are very essential qualities in dealing with endings.

People often feel a sense of victimization ("Poor me!") and injustice, and some engage in generalization ("All companies are like that!") and "catastrophizing" ("I will surely lose my house now!"). Reframing is about looking at things in a different light, which can help people avoid these negative and disempowering interpretations of the facts. Most generally, the point about painful feelings is that they push people into action, and that is surely most needed here. Victimization and injustice may point to taking things a bit too personally or, if they are personal, not recognizing one's own role in the negative outcome. Fallacies in generalization and catastrophizing are easily pointed out. It is important to adopt some revision in one's outlook and feelings. If one is still angry, it may show up in interviews. If one feels stupid or guilty, that will show up too. Some people may sense that something is not quite right, even if they can't put their finger on it.

Depth psychology is about going back to one's childhood and earlier formative experiences to help explain why a person adopts a certain response to the ending. Not everyone reacts in the same way to the same event. Helping to understand one's sensitivity to, say, rejection, abandonment, and uncertainty can go a long way to better understanding one's response. As we said before, people need to know the machine that they are (Chapter 17). Doing so allows people to put more distance between them and their response ("Oh, this is just me going off again. I know this response well. Let me ignore this for now and get on with something else."). In addition, crying over something can help bring momentary relief and also help people get more quickly to this point: "I already cried three times about it. I have no more tears left!" (In the Kübler-Ross model, this is about getting over depression and moving toward acceptance.)

Beyond this, exercise can also help people feel better, as does yoga and other physical activity, though negative emotions do require some of the above mental work. People vary greatly in what they experience (some experience a little, some experience a lot) and what works best for them, but knowing how they deal with such matters is essential. Negative emotions are surely part of life, and work brings out the need to deal with hurt and losses of various kinds. There is good reason to aim to have good endings.

Accommodation and exploration. The second transition phase occurs when a person acknowledges the finality or certainty of the previous ending. For some people this coincides with a physical departure, but for others this realization may have come long before or after. Some have mentally checked out and moved on to searching for a new job long before they hand in their resignation; they have accommodated the reality of an ending. Others accept the ending only weeks or months after they physically left: "I still cannot believe that they fired me!" People may hope that a situation will be undone or that one of their contacts will quickly provide another job. At some point, they realize that a situation has ended and that no quick solutions will be forthcoming.

The accommodation and exploration phase is by nature a temporary phase whose main objectives are (1) dealing with negative emotions so that they no longer are the only or most important focus of a person, (2) creating a new situation that is comfortable and provides positive (happy) experiences, and (3) exploring a person's possible new purposes by considering both lessons of the past and actual new opportunities. The latter should eventually result in a new activity (e.g., contract or job) that effectively ends the temporary nature of this phase as a person looks forward to and starts a new beginning. (Some people also call this second phase "transitional," but we try to avoid confusion by not calling both the overall process and a specific phase by the same name.)

The accommodation and exploration phase usually begins with a heavy dose of the emotional work described above. Negative emotions usually surface during the ending phase but are often more strongly experienced thereafter. The postending situation usually contains many reminders that cause negative emotions to surface (flare up), such as receiving e-mail from past clients, hearing about awards, not going to work, getting bills, canceling trips, and so on. People not only lost their job or contract or other physically evident circumstances but also, equally important, lost some emotional well-being and predictability. People need to also accept that the negative emotions that they are experiencing are going to be a main part of their life and focus for some time.

Creating a new situation that is comfortable and provides positive (happy) experiences is therefore key. There is no need to add discomfort to the already long list (see Table 15.1). As a general matter, people do well to define "being comfortable" relative to their new situation, as this is a new experience, and some objectivity is useful and needed in view of many negative emotions.[9] The following is a checklist of things to do to create a more comfortable situation depending on the gravity of one's situation: (1) schedule daily exercise, (2) reduce financial pressure (expenses), (3) schedule a social life, (4) take on new activities that give pleasure or meaning, (5) see a doctor to relieve symptoms (e.g., sleep, depression, anxiety), and (6) see a counselor (to work through negative feelings). Undoubtedly, some of these are things that people have always wanted to do; being able to now do them really is a silver lining of one's present circumstances. Having some comfort can also be helpful for focusing on work through the past.

People vary greatly in their general approach to this transition phase. Many people want it over as soon as possible. People often have financial obligations that push them to quickly find a new source of income; they often have a family to take care of. People who are additionally strongly in pursuit of identity and professional recognition (e.g., being a successful broker or scientist) may not want to delay or digress from their career development path. These circumstances often push people to quickly want to find another job. There is a tendency to also just do "something" to bring the transition period to a close. Several authors caution against taking action too quickly. One has to be ready to face one's old contacts and put oneself in the best possible light. If one is still very angry or sad, it may show up in some way. While there is a tendency to take a job, any suitable job, that may not be the best action and involves additional stress in some way. There are moments in one's life when a bit of time is needed. If there are still lessons to be articulated or digested, it may be necessary to first do that. In light of this, some people suggest taking a temporary job or engaging in some consulting work to reduce financial pressures while giving oneself a bit more time.

But there is another road too, one of deliberately taking some time off. The temporary situation does not need to be an altogether unpleasant or unproductive one; it is an opportunity for some personal recalibration. Theoretically, whereas success is about achievement and accumulation, ending is about shedding: the shedding of responsibility and a task; the shedding of perceived needs for security, fame, accomplishment, and so on; the shedding of illusions about what was supposed to make one happy; and the shedding of pent-up emotions that were developed in pursuit of the previous objective. Now, in this phase, people are required to live and be happy with much less than what they had before. People often experience or see the nature of things without all the trappings and distractions. Endings are an opportunity for fundamental and existential reflection that brings a modicum of enlightenment about one's human condition and what really matters. The suffering of

> ## The temporary situation does not need to be an unpleasant or unproductive one.

en*lighten*ment is about the shedding of material and psychological baggage and getting closer to some essential truths. Anecdotally, people who gain insight during this phase often regard it as one of their more rewarding life experiences— "If doesn't kill you, it makes you stronger." People sometimes do not want to go back to their exact former life; they opt for a simpler and more balanced life.

However, conditions do not always favor this approach. People are often tied up with family planning and development that bring financial pressures. Some people get very nervous in the face of uncertainty and cannot focus on much else but finding a job. Also, wise people can help one find existential insight and enlightenment, but one often has to search hard for the right people (e.g., a counselor or faith-based person). Beyond this, existential insight does not always lead to major changes in one's career, though it may affect how one looks at one's career. Job markets emphasize competitive advantages that reflect prior investments in education and skills; while some people can modify what they want to do next, they still need to find a version of some generally accepted pattern. Some find a middle approach, such as taking a brief holiday ("I need a break from all of this!") for reflecting and relaxing, before returning back to the task of finding a new job or contract. In short, people vary in their approach to this period.

Regardless of whether a short or a long accommodation phase is realized, at some point a next job or contract is sought. This exploration aspect is, for the most part, a direct application of the information presented in Part 2 of this book. To quote, "Successful people often have an enduring commitment to a cause or skill set that they enjoy." At some point, the time comes for people to redefine their professional commitment statement (Chapter 8) and restate or rediscover what they enjoy doing, why they are good at it, and what specific kinds of work they would like to do that involve that skill. At some point, the pleasure of doing one's job needs to return and be communicated to others. A stepping-stone is usually to talk with about twenty people about where their organizations are going and what needs they think they may have. Introductions to these people usually come from former contacts.

As mentioned in Chapter 9, the professional commitment statement is central to addressing many questions that come up. In this context, some additional questions usually involve reasons for having left their prior employer and whether, eventually, they can contact the former employer.

- *"Can you tell me about why you left your former employer?"* Different answers are possible, depending on one's situation: (1) "I want to grow and have more and different experiences." (2) "They were going through some reorganizations that would make future promotion very difficult." (3) "I wanted to strike out on my own (be my own boss)." (4) "There was a lot of turnover and shifts in direction, and it was just not the kind of place to stay." (5) "I had worked very hard for six years but wanted a break and was able to take it." Some of these answers might be used in conjunction.
- *"Can I contact your former employer?"* "Sure, please contact Mr. Jones. He was a coworker (or supervisor) who will gladly tell you about me, the office, and anything else you want to know."
- *"I see that your résumé has a gap in your employment."* "That is correct. I worked very hard for many years, and this was a great opportunity to take some time off. I planned to find new work after about six months, and that seems about right. I might expect to sign a contract for some consulting work, but I am still looking around and my ambition is to do … ."

As is often the case, the point is to turn back to one's professional commitment statement. The questions are what people and their organizations are doing and what needs they might have. It is important to end conversations with other names of people who can be contacted, as well as with ways to touch base and follow up in the future again. As appropriate, you may also ask them whom they use as their contractor for the work you would like to do or whether they accept any proposal or bids for the work you would like to do.

New jobs often come by accident, but creating a lot of contacts and favorable impressions increases the chances of good accidents happening. We increase the odds of good things happening. Having a few well-regarded influential supports help, but people also need a good professional commitment statement, résumé, and professional appearance and an enthusiastic positive demeanor.

Eventually, a new job or contract arises that a person looks forward to and that effectively ends the second phase; the third phase of beginning a new beginning arises. Earlier chapters in this book provide ample guidance and tips for getting off on the right foot—such as the importance of social skills, getting along and assessment of peoples' work styles. The chapters on happiness, mental health and psychopathy provide additional information for keeping one's balanced mind and avoiding potentially compromising behaviors. We think it is wise to write down whatever lessons one has learned from one's transition experience, as it is often useful to remind oneself of them in the future.

Change is inevitable, and it is sometimes necessary to go with the flow and reinvent oneself. It is not always necessary to go through major crises and transitions to change. People take out time to reflect on where their work has taken them and where they are apt to go to next. Sometimes people make their change:

> Change is good. This is what I admire about you. You are giving me the inspiration to learn from you, it is your courage not to be static in any shape or form and to remain dynamic, fluid and on the go to always expand your horizons. The rest of us become too complacent in accepting the status quo despite its limitation because we are afraid of change, so we seek stationary in sake of stability, only to chock us in our potentials and kill whatever possibility we

may actualize. This is sad because it make us limited, unimaginative, noncreative and fearful. Life is short and needs to be explored to the fullest. Stationary life style is boring and misses life itself. I salute you my friend for grabbing life by the horn and allowing yourself to always reinvent yourself.[10]

Life is a journey no matter how it is played out.

Five

Epilogue

20

Knowledge Is Power?

Only through our connectedness to others can we really know and enhance the self. And only through working on the self can we begin to enhance our connectedness to others.

—**Harriet Goldhor Lerner**[1]

How can people better manage their interactions and be successful at work? How can the knowledge and information of the previous pages help people? It often is said that "knowledge is power," but is that really true? While we intend and hope that the preceding will help people in some way be more effective at work and experience greater satisfaction from what they do, we know that the subject matter of people skills and human relations is highly multifaceted and complex. How can the knowledge of the preceding pages best be put into practice? Much of what we read or learn seems to fall by the roadside; it is not much used. Will the same happen to the material in this book?

Though the terms *information* and *knowledge* are often used as synonyms, they can be used in ways that clarify a useful difference. Information is sometimes defined as the set of facts and data that describes a situation or phenomenon (e.g., having information about flying). Knowledge is a broader concept that includes information as well as, at times, deeper or learned information about a topic, including know-how, methods, and perspectives that are relevant to handling a situation (e.g., having knowledge of flying). Wisdom is that part of knowledge that is about judgment—the interpretation of a situation, the judicious selection of goals, the selection and implementation of strategies in the face of situations. Information becomes knowledge when it is applied effectively. The point about knowledge is that it is to be put into practice.

One of several critiques of education today is that it insufficiently promotes creativity and competitiveness. Traditional education often empathizes rote learning, which has the virtues of instilling discipline, patience, diligence, and obedience. Teaching people how to apply information is in many ways more difficult. It requires the ability to define new problems from complex situations, find new uses for existing information, and sometimes recall information that has long been forgotten. A criticism of American education, with the exception of graduate education at some elite institutions, is that it no longer sufficiently emphasizes these learning objectives; it has also become test oriented, not excellent, manipulated by those who work the system, and overly expensive. The mantra from Korea to Singapore is to foster creative abilities and emphasize application and innovation. Today requires a greater emphasis on the creative application of knowledge.

Reading often stimulates the mind and imagination. But reactions of the mind to new material and teachings show proclivities that do not always bring useful applications. For example, some people will read phrases or passages in the book and use certain phrases or arguments to justify their own actions or beliefs ("See, I knew it!"). Some people will like the book if it makes them feel good about themselves in some way. Other people like to play intellectual games and find holes, incomplete or inconsistent treatment, incidental erroneous facts, and other problems that, for them, invalidate the material in some way, in whole or in part. Whatever merit, it obviously does little for increasing powerful applications for the reader. Not all agitations of the mind are equal. (Indeed, these approaches may actually point to defense mechanisms of the reader!)

Rather, the challenge of application is to use the information in this book in future situations, when a person has the need for it. We need to be able to imagine situations in which this material is to be used and then develop in our mind scenarios and responses. Perhaps a person already has a need, such as dealing with a boss or difficult person today, or perhaps one is facing a job interview in the very near future. Other people may have needs to better understand something from the past—a desire to understand how they could have done better in handling a situation, such as getting along in the workplace or having been too trusting of another. None of this is about rote memory, except for being able to recall some of the situations for which this material has relevance. It is very likely that working through a problem increases one's skills, which, typically, remains with a person for the next time. Skills often become ingrained as part of one's abilities, and important, hands-on lessons are usually not soon forgotten. To facilitate application, consider the following:

1. *Having problems getting along with someone?* See Chapter 4; for example, competence is not enough; we need the right attitude and performance too.
2. *Starting a new job? Just hired someone new?* See Chapter 7 on assessment and some ways of working that are important styles to be in sync with; also see Chapter 10 on psychological contracts.
3. *Feeling like you are losing your sanity or balance?* See Chapter 16 on happiness and perhaps also Chapter 17 on mental health.
4. *Working with a young person who looks and talks unprofessionally?* See Chapter 1, or just give him or her this book.
5. *Feeling a bit down or anxious?* See Chapter 15 on stress or Chapter 17 on mental health.
6. *Not sure what to do next in your career?* See Chapter 8 on how to develop a professional commitment statement.
7. *Having time management problems?* See Chapter 15.

8. *Have a really bad boss or coworker who plays dirty?* See Chapter 18 on personality dysfunctions and difficult behaviors.
9. *Got fired?* See Chapter 19 on transition.
10. *Looking for a new job, or have a job interview coming up?* See Chapter 8 on the professional commitment statement and Chapter 9 on dealing with specific interviewing questions.

People skills and human relations are complex, and they have many variations. We harbor no illusion or hope that readers will find in this or any other book sufficient information to help with each and every situation that they might encounter. Rather, it is the nature of the phenomenon that people skills usually involve an interaction, a back-and-forth, a meeting of the minds, a give-and-take. It is almost impossible to script these out—you never know what another person is going say. The permutations and variations are considerable and usually quite large. In these kinds of situations, a flexible, adaptive response is needed, where outcomes are greatly affected by the following:

- one's attitudes and intentions;
- criteria and goals by which one judges the final outcome (and that are shared with others);
- flexibility to adapt one's attitude, criteria, or goals in dealing with others; and
- the ability to genuinely connect with others on some matters.

The four matters are often key to getting alignment and agreement. They often challenge people in essential ways. Some "other" people may be highly demanding and have high standards, though often the problem is that people have low or no standards and merely want to maintain some status quo. Sometimes the environment in which one finds oneself has limitations and constraints that must be accepted. Some people spend hours and days talking with others about how they will handle this or that situation, but in the end dialog and improvisation are needed to improve one's assessment and reach an accommodation about the matters above.

As we learn to deal better with others, the lessons of doing that transform us. We learn to be more flexible in some areas and more assertive in others. Assumptions about others and ourselves are changed. We begin to see ourselves in a different way. The application of knowledge is nothing less than, by definition, the creation of new knowledge itself. The above quote is on target: "Only through our connectedness to others can we really know and enhance the self. And only through working on the self can we begin to enhance our connectedness to others." Though there may be other avenues to self-change, this is surely a highway. Ironically, those who set out to manipulate others often end up deceiving themselves in some essential way, too. Those who set out to just get by and survive, end up having lived their life in such a way too. By connecting with others, people also connect more with themselves.

If knowledge is to lead to power, then in many situations it must be about keeping some simple but important pointers in mind that can guide one to good outcomes in a broad but manageable range of situations that typically come up in the workplace. People in business and public administration often talk at length about systems and structures, but the quality and ability of people matter who make these systems work. Both professional orientations and a personality for getting along are needed. Everybody knows of leaders and employees who moved things forward, and others who were like sand in the gears that kept things back. People skills at work cannot be ignored. It seems a bit ironic to us that such important things in this book are seldom taught and that the workplace often does little to promote more sharing of the knowledge about people skills.

Life is a journey, one that includes learning and improving one's people skills. We hope this book helps.

Appendix A: A Short Primer on Emotions

Feelings are such real things, and they change and change and change.

—Carol Hall, *Sesame Street*

Emotions are commonly understood as feelings (physiological sensations) that are associated with a state of mind (or consciousness). Typical human examples include joy, fear, anger, and love. Scientists vary in their definitions, and the Merriam-Webster dictionary defines *emotion* as "the affective aspect of consciousness" or "a conscious mental reaction such as anger or fear that is subjectively experienced as a strong feeling that is usually directed toward a specific object and typically accompanied by physiological and behavioral changes in the body." However, while conscious experiences surely trigger emotions (e.g., an interaction with someone that causes affinity or aversion), the mental activity a person is not (yet) fully conscious: "I am feeling a dislike about this, but I don't know why."

Emotions are basic forces that shape human actions and interaction. The word *emotion* is based on the French word *émouvoir*, which, in turn, is based on the Latin *emovere*, which means to "move out." It is long held that the purpose of emotions is to move people. Emotions are distinguished by intensity, duration, and the nature (direction) of attraction. Some emotions are short (e.g., surprise), whereas others may last for years (love). Some emotions pull people toward things (positive or pleasurable emotions), whereas others repel people (negative emotions). People are moved to experience pleasant (positive) sensations such as joy (happiness) and love (acceptance), and they seek things and people out that provide these for them. People are also moved to avoid experiencing unpleasant (negative) emotions such as fear, anger, and sadness, and they work to avoid situations that trigger these emotions.

No definitive list of emotions exists. Feelings exist in many intensities and gradations that involve a combination or mixing of different feelings. By analogy, the color wheel shows an ever-finer gradation of colors based on mixing of primary colors; emotions arise from a similar mixing of basic or primary feelings. To illustrate, a popular conceptualization is that of Robert Plutchik (1927–2006), who identified eight basic emotions—joy, trust, anticipation, fear, surprise, sadness, disgust, and anger—and eight composite emotions that are derived from a mixing of them (see Table A.1).[1]

Table A.1 Emotions

Emotion Type	Basic Emotion	Composite Emotion	
Positive	Joy	Love	(joy + trust)
	Trust	Submission	(trust + fear)
	Anticipation	Optimism	(anticipation + joy)
Negative	Fear	Awe	(fear + surprise)
	Surprise	Disappointment	(surprise + sadness)
	Sadness	Remorse	(sadness + disgust)
	Disgust	Contempt	(disgust + anger)
	Anger	Aggression	(anticipation + anger)

Source: Author, based on Plutchik, R., *Emotions and Life: Perspectives from Psychology, Biology, and Evolution*, American Psychological Association, Washington, DC, 2002.

Thus, love is seen as a combination of the primary feelings of joy and trust. A more elaborate scheme is that of Parrott,[2] who distinguishes between primary, secondary, and tertiary emotions. Parrott's primary emotions are love, joy, surprise, anger, sadness, and fear. For example, the secondary emotions of love are affection, lust (sexual desire), and longing. The tertiary emotions of affection are adoration, fondness, liking, attraction, caring, tenderness, compassion, and sentimentality. In this manner, there are about as many emotions as one's language distinguishes. Parrott's scheme has 6 primary emotions, 25 secondary emotions, and 136 tertiary emotions. The term *emotional literacy* is used to describe one's knowledge of different emotions, specifically, being able to name and describe emotions. For example, people are asked to name and define such emotions as joy, trust, anger, and fear. (In a subsequent activity, they are then taught to identify actions that cause these feelings to arise.)

It is noteworthy that almost all authors note a preponderance of negative emotion types (e.g., Parrott's scheme has 2.8 times more negative emotions), though this does not imply that people necessarily experience more negative emotions than positive ones in the course of their day. A recent study, across several countries, shows that people experience 1.4 to 1.7 times more positive emotions than negative emotions weekly.[3] Various theories exist that explain why and how emotions arise (i.e., origination). Evolutionary theories posit that positive emotions further reproduction and child-rearing functions and that negative emotions exist to warn us about and repel us from myriad dangers and, hence, keep us safe. Cognitive theories focus on the role of thoughts and perceptions in causing emotions. Perceptual theories see emotions as ways of perceiving the world along with sensory inputs such as sight, smell, and touch. Though many different theories exist, in recent times neurobiological theories of the brain have gained great popularity. Among other things, these theories help explain why conscious thought sometimes lags behind the feeling of emotions (feeling before thought) and also points to specific brain activities that can be targeted by medicine.

Succinctly, neuroscientists distinguish between functions of the limbic system (in particular, the +dala) and the cortex (in particular, the amygdala) in generating emotions. First, the limbic system is an inner part of the brain that resides above the brain stem, which is located at the end of the spine. Neurological signals are immediately evaluated and translated by the amygdala into strong emotions of fear and surprise and bodily responses of fright and defensive posture. They are evaluated against memories that reside in the hippocampus, located close to the amygdala. These are automatic evaluations and reactions and evaluations that involve no conscious mental activity; bodily reactions of fright and defensiveness often occur before one is even aware of what is going on. Second, the prefrontal cortex, located behind the forehead, is associated with distinctively human emotions of pride, guilt, envy, resentment, and so on, as well as a mentally conscious assessment of neurological stimuli.[4] The origination of these emotions is a much slower process than evaluation and reaction in the limbic system; they often involve activity of which a person is conscious. The slower prefrontal cortex processes explain why a person first undergoes a response through the limbic system, then becomes aware of it, and then creates additional responses and emotions.

The interplay of different parts of the brain in the origin and cessation of emotion is not well understood at this time. Knowledge exists of only certain processes. Processes of fear (a primary emotion) have been especially well studied in recent years and further specify generally accepted understanding. For example, Niccolo Machiavelli (1469–1527) long noted that fear was readily and successfully used by kings and princes in governing; one can round up a few innocent citizens and punish them in a public square as reminder of the princes' power. Neurobiology concurs that under such conditions, inducing negative states is not very difficult, as it is an autonomous response. Analyzing history, Machiavelli concluded that rulers do well to occasionally cause subjects some pain as a reminder of greater pain and that doing so was helpful in maintaining their power and achieving their aims. The fear of pain causes people to obey authority, and surprise also stops people from doing whatever they are doing. Machiavelli also noted that rulers who use fear arbitrarily and cruelly come to be seen as despotic tyrants against which people eventually rise up and also that tyrants often live in fear of their subjects.[5] (We are emphatically not advocating fear-based and cruel management but pointing out how neurobiology furthers understanding of these phenomena.)

Medical research also specifies the harmful impact of negative emotions and beneficial impacts of positive emotions. Negative emotions, such as anger, anxiety, and depression, are important risk factors for coronary heart disease.[6] These emotions trigger specific substances (e.g., epinephrine, norepinephrine) and processes (e.g., hypertension) associated with heart disease. Negative emotions also compromise the immune system, such as a release of the antibody immunoglobulin A (sIgA), considered the first line of defense against the common cold. Stress reduces other abilities to fight disease too.[7] Suppression of negative emotional states is also hypothesized to be related to the development of coronary heart disease, as well as the progression of cancer.[8] Studies also find that people who frequently experience positive emotions live longer and are less prone to illness; positive emotions may help slow the heart rate, lower blood pressure, reduce stress hormones, and improve sleep.[9] While being happy may not prevent illness, people have many good reasons to not like people who cause them grief.

The cessation of negative emotion is an important topic, especially for those who are experiencing emotional suffering. Traditionally, psychotherapy and philosophical systems within religions such as Buddhism are most strongly associated with the cessation of negative emotion. Buddhism focuses on the tendencies of human beings to create and experience suffering for themselves and offers an eightfold path for ceasing suffering. Other religions also offer spiritual guidance for those suffering. In modern times, psychotherapy documents mental health pathologies and offers a variety of cognitive behavioral and depth-analysis approaches. In recent years, pharmaceutical companies have done much to alleviate medical conditions associated with suffering, providing numerous medicines for anxiety, depression, psychosis, and bipolar disorders, for example. The avoidance and cessation of negative emotions is an important topic.

Generally, appreciation for the role of emotions in human behavior is increasing and coming full circle. From the enlightenment period onward, emotions have had a long history of being buried and suppressed in the modern world. The enlightenment period was about using reason to set people free from false beliefs and superstition and to use science to create new possibilities. Descartes (1595–1650) said, "I think, therefore I am." He did not say, "I feel, therefore I am." The bias against emotions in contemporary culture has long been strong. For example, in the United States, many baby boomers prefer not to talk about emotions, and to act professionally is to follow a script that is devoid of emotional expression. To show emotion is to be weak, though every culture has its contradictions and exceptions (e.g., sport celebrations). But the tide against emotions is slowly turning, perhaps suggesting a course correction of the scientific rationalism of the twentieth century. At work, people are expected to be mindful of others' feelings. Getting along well is surely a criterion in hiring and promotion, and it is OK to be liked. Managers are encouraged to bring the joy back in for workers and to make them feel appreciated and supported. Emotions also serve a useful purpose of warning us against danger ("Something he said just doesn't feel right, I don't know what …").[10] Many young workers have been taught to talk about their feelings in school, and many are comfortable discussing the above matters. Having feelings is what tells people that they are alive; "I feel, therefore I am" is also part of the human experience.

In recent years, the term *emotional intelligence* has been used by Goleman to describe one's ability to identify, assess, and manage emotions of oneself, of others, and in groups.[11] Theories of emotional intelligence focus on four domains: (1) self-awareness (which includes emotional literacy, as well as accurate self-assessment and awareness of the impact of one's emotions on one's actions), (2) self-management (the ability to control one's emotions, such as evidenced by, for example, being able to delay gratification, putting up with some stress, dealing with hunger, and thinking clearly under pressure), (3) social awareness (being attuned to the feelings of others, and responding appropriately to them in the face of their conditions such as anxiety, apprehension, grief, joy, etc.), and (4) relationship management (such as being skilled at teamwork and conflict management, getting people to produce results and be committed to group goals, communicating information in clear and timely ways, etc.).

Appendix B: Essential Social Manners for the Workplace

The following is a list of forty social manners one can use for getting along with others at work, based on those mentioned in the text. No list is exhaustive, yet few will likely disagree that these are among the essentials.

GREETING AND ACKNOWLEDGING OTHERS

1. Say hello to people, especially those we have met before.
2. Occasionally bring small gifts and tokens.
3. Make small talk with colleagues (but not too much).
4. Remember birthdays and significant occasions.
5. Congratulate others on their achievements.
6. Allow others to get on and off the elevator first.
7. Thank others for their contributions.
8. Acknowledge the positions and roles of others.

9. Be mindful of others' difficult moments in life.
10. Be polite and helpful to people in subordinate positions.

SPEAKING AND LISTENING

11. Use language that is respectful.
12. Listen to others with full and complete attention.
13. Be precise but not abrupt.
14. Avoid derogatory remarks.
15. Avoid making inciting comments.
16. Be accessible to others (e.g., open door).
17. Be polite and factual when confronting poor performance and inaccurate opinions.
18. Speak favorably about your group to those outside the group.
19. Be approachable for conversation.
20. Do not say bad things about others.

WORK PERFORMANCE

21. Do your job well.
22. Be mindful of the consequences of your work to others.
23. Help others doing their job well.
24. Apologize when you have done or said something wrong.
25. Correct what you did wrong.
26. Be mindful of another's time.
27. Project a professional demeanor.
28. Be open to the suggestions of other effective people.
29. Dress professionally (or not more casually than others).
30. Avoid suggestive comments or dress at work.

RESPECTING BOUNDARIES

31. Do not bring strong-smelling foods to work.
32. Do not wear strong perfume or cologne.
33. Avoid body odors, and regularly change clothes.
34. Avoid flirtatious or sexually revealing clothing or behavior.

35. Do not speak loudly, have the radio on, or otherwise distract others.
36. Wash your hands.
37. Stay away when you are sick.
38. Contribute to keeping office spaces organized, hygienic, and safe.
39. Do not hover around others.
40. Do not read others' e-mail or computers without permission.

Appendix C: Sample Professional Commitment Statements

Below are some annotated examples of Personal Commitment Statements (PCS). They were developed by students in my classes, and I have edited and revised them. Each is as different as the person making it; there is no standard language, of course. However, some are better than others, and I show where some improvement opportunities might lie. Hope these examples help. (As this is based on what we developed, no further reading is available about these, but you can email us for more.)

EXAMPLE 1

This is a good example that shows the individual's career path, commitment, past commitments and reasons for choosing the commitment, and sense of successes. By the way, this is a posting from a student who does not have much prior work experience.

> I would like to utilize my background in economics, along with the managerial and analytical skills obtained by my current course work in public administration, to aid in the delivery of quality health care services to individuals of all ages and income levels. In my concentration courses in health care administration, I wish to develop the skills necessary to meaningfully contribute to the efficiency and effectiveness of an organization aiming to provide affordable and accessible health care to individuals. I will commit myself to continuous self-education of current health care trends and policy issues in order to perform my professional duties as diligently as possible.
>
> I wish to bring the same high levels of leadership and commitment to an organization as I have displayed in previous course work, past organizational memberships, and past places of employment. In order to get some valuable exposure to and experience within the health care field, I have recently accepted an internship at The John Smith Hospital here in my city. I will be exposed to functional areas of the hospital such as quality management, human resources, accounting, and outpatient services. I will also have the opportunity to work on a project involving state hospital accreditation and will be able to sit in on many internal operational meetings with top administrators in order gain personal insight into emerging issues facing this hospital as well as many others within the state system.
>
> After completing this current internship, I will seek employment either at a hospital or within a different type of health care setting, such as an assisted living facility, home health care service, or state health department. In order to help me, an administrator could take the time to talk to me in order to give me advice on what steps I need to take right now in order to achieve my ultimate career goals. In addition, fellow MPA students, faculty members, or full-time employees at my current place of employment can let me know of available job opportunities or place me in contact with individuals who may be able to give me further advice about the health care field or otherwise direct me in my career path.

EXAMPLE 2

Here's another good example (Chapter 8 shows a shorter version). It clearly shows the individual's career path and commitment, as well as the reasons for choosing the commitment and sense of past successes.

> Throughout my life, I have been privileged with the opportunity to mentor several individuals from various backgrounds. As a result of these opportunities, I am committed to assisting disadvantaged and underprivileged young men reach high levels of success. I want to continue mentoring young men that may have single parents, uninvolved parents, low economic statuses, and/or poor educational systems available. My near-term goal is to begin a program that mentors male high school juniors and seniors as well as college undergraduates, who will in turn mentor younger boys. Mentoring will consist of being and providing examples of strong, educated, ambitious men that will cause the student to reach and surpass his potential. My distant goal is to develop and further an effective mentoring method and program that would extend throughout the nation and to females as well.
>
> Since I have been in the same situation as these types of young men, I feel confident that I can accomplish this commitment successfully. I believe I have done an excellent job in my life, overcoming many odds and not becoming "just another statistic." As a result, through my experiences (successes and failures) I can help young men make a difference in their communities, provide encouragement to others, support each other, and develop into effective leaders of today and tomorrow.
>
> I also believe I am qualified to fulfill my commitment because I've been mentoring younger individuals since I was in middle school. I have served and continue to serve in my church as an unofficial mentor by helping various individuals reach for higher heights in their lives and teaching them to be (more) ambitious. I have also served in many leadership capacities in school and believe mentoring is often included in leadership. I, in recent years, have continued to mentor several family members, friends, and university athletes. Some successes I have had in mentoring include helping young men graduate high school and go to college, encouraging young men to overcome transition from high school to college, encouraging athletes to strive for better academic performances and to understand life is about more than

football, and encouraging young men not to give up when life throws them a curve ball or because of past and current negative situations.

I am currently researching information about the operation and organization of nonprofit organizations to initiate a mentoring program of my own. If anyone knows of any information and/or individuals that could be an asset to my ambitious attempt, please feel free to inform me. This will greatly help me continue the pursuit of my commitment to restoring our communities by mentoring underprivileged and disadvantaged youth, especially young men.

EXAMPLE 3

Another good example.

I am pursuing my career in urban planning and economic development. I would like to both be involved in the physical comprehensive planning for communities and provide economic development services. Ultimately, I hope to assist particularly rural communities with the implementation of up-to-date planning principles and help those communities find creative ways to finance the implementation of such principles. I am also interested in development and would like to assist such communities with venture capital through development projects, for which I, or someone I'm associated with, has been involved. Although this might not be classified as "working in the public sector," the public (communities) would certainly be my clients, and thus I would be working for the public.

My undergraduate education, pursued graduate education, and professional experience complement this professional commitment statement. During and after my undergraduate studies in landscape architecture and urban planning, I held a variety of internships that have provided several opportunities to gain valuable experience in both the public and the private sectors. A previous internship with an urban planning consulting firm in Oklahoma provided a great deal of experience in dealing with rural and depressed communities; an internship with a local landscape design and build firm helped to strengthen my design background and familiarize myself with the professional design and construction processes; and an internship with the Downtown Development District has provided a wealth of knowledge in both planning and economic development, as well as physical development. I have recently accepted a position as "grants coordinator" for a college at this university. This position should provide a wealth of experience in seeking and procuring grant monies to fund programs and familiarize me with different funding resources.

Past successes that demonstrate my ability to succeed include helping successfully acquire grant monies to fund projects in rural Arkansas, participating in several planning and design projects throughout the country, and organizing a young people's nonprofit to assist in attracting new businesses to our downtown. I also believe that my ability to gain a variety of experiences through internships and education also displays my ability to succeed. Others can help me succeed by sharing information that relates to my career goals and by creating a network environment that can be beneficial to all of us as we eventually gain positions in the public sector.

EXAMPLE 4

The following example is from an international student.

I am from a Latin American country, and I believe that trade and good business strategies can benefit and develop countries' economies, improving the living standards of their citizens. For this reason, I would like to use my background and practice in business law and international trade, along with the classes I took in the master's program in business law and master's program in Taiwan studies, and the courses I am planning to take in the PhD program in international business and elective courses from the PhD program in Asia Pacific studies (IDAS) at National Chengchi University (NCCU), to help the business community of Latin America have a better understanding of Asian business culture and the legal framework within the region and vice versa in order that they could develop business ventures together and open their markets in an effective and efficient way. My goal is to be a channel between Latin America and Asia, working in a law firm, in a consulting division, or in a trade company or being a part-time professor in a Latin American or Asian university.

In the summer of July 2006, I joined an international conference about leadership in Colombia. There were three hundred talented participants from Latin America, Spain, and Portugal, who are expected to change the world and be competent leaders. For my surprise, I was the only one studying in Asia; most of them were pursing master's or PhD degrees in the USA, Europe, or Latin America. Therefore, when I presented my paper about competition policy in

East Asia, I realized there was much interest and questioning in this matter because they did not know much. They discussed that China's economic development could be a threat for Latin America, but no one there was making research about how to transform this into an advantage. At the end, I was very satisfied with the results because my purpose was to motivate and bring some consciousness about Asian countries' development, their impact in today's world economy, and how their markets could bring great opportunities if you are ready to deal with and study them.

As well, last summer I was invited by a Nicaraguan university to make a presentation about business culture in Taiwan (ten-hours class) to the business community that is trading with Taiwan through a free trade agreement (FTA). I felt very committed to this task because I was contributing for the better understanding of the cultures and the trade development. The comments were very positive, and they recognized that it is not just about doing business per se but also about understanding the environment, which would result in better business relations, improve their marketing and public relations areas, and avoid mistakes in the future. However, there is still much to do.

With this motivation to help the business community of both regions, I commit myself to the continued learning of the Asia Pacific area and direct my research in the fields of business law and international trade. In the short term, I am planning to do an internship in the Central American Trade Office in Taiwan (CATO) or in the Taiwan External Trade Development Council (TAITRA), with the objective to get more experience and practical knowledge of how trade is being promoted and developed in the area. Also, I will take advantage of any opportunity to join and contribute in an active way in international conferences and exhibitions related to this topic.

Lately I have been participating in trade shows promoted by TAITRA, making some market research and contacts for businessmen in Central America, which inspired me to set up this year my own trading company in Nicaragua. For this reason, in the long term, I am planning to work and develop this trading company and a law firm that would provide legal advice to the business community dedicated to trade between Latin America and Asia. I also would like to contribute to the academia, teaching as a part-time professor at a law or business school in subjects related to international trade, business law, regional development of East Asia, competition law, or labor law.

I believe that a PhD in international business and the courses of the IDAS program would help me to improve my research skills to become a professor and would give me valuable insights into the environment in which companies operate in the Asia Pacific region and their trade performance. With my research and work I hope to contribute to the Latin American and Asian business community.

EXAMPLE 5

Here's another example, now with some opportunity for improvement. It clearly shows the individual's career path and commitment, but it needs to show a bit more of the reasons for choosing the commitment and sense of past successes too.

> I would like to help the city with establishing and implementing policies that will create better living standards for those who need public housing assistance. I am committed to helping these individuals and families; this is the reason I have returned to school to earn a MPA.
>
> I would like to help people who, for whatever reason, must live with substandard housing conditions. One summer, when I was an undergraduate pursuing a degree in international business, I realized that there must be more to life than making money. That same summer, there was a massive earthquake in Turkey. I watched the news for hours and saw repeatedly how lives were destroyed because the apartment buildings they lived in were not earthquake proof. These buildings were designed by corrupt architects and approved by corrupt government officials, and it was allowed because no one was there to speak up for the people who had to live in these shabby conditions. It was then that I realized that the poor should not suffer because they are poor.
>
> That is why I have committed my focus in my MPA degree on housing policy. I also plan on interning in a capacity that will further my ability to help those in need. I would be interested in meeting leaders in the housing and community development area to possibly volunteer, intern, or work for them.

EXAMPLE 6

The following professional commitment statement has many good elements, but it is a bit too autobiographical. It is important to get to the point directly, as is often required in professional introductions and settings. What career is being pursued here?

I developed an interest in public service while working as a congressional page in Washington during my junior year of high school. This ten-month experience compelled me to stay involved in politics when I returned home to Michigan and volunteered on my congressman's reelection campaign. Volunteering turned into summers of working as a paid campaign staff on various campaigns. Working on these campaigns fostered my interest in the public sector and politics, motivating me to participate in a D.C. university's semester program in economic policy. During this semester, I interned for a policy research and advocacy organization, and wrote a research paper on child care policy. My internship included a project on economic security for women and children in which I gathered helpful resources on the topic for the organization's Web site. It was in this semester that I realized that I am more interested in the nuts and bolts of policy than the game of politics. This is also the point where I became interested in public policy affecting low-income families.

After the semester, I stayed in Washington to intern for the Senate Finance Committee. There, a welfare analyst knew of my interest and invited me to a few meetings preparing for the reauthorization debate. One of my primary projects at the Finance Committee was to help one of the tax counsels with the oversight of implementation of the refundable child tax credit by putting together information on the administration of the EITC. The purpose of this project was to see how implementation of a refundable tax credit could be improved. During the fall of 2001, I studied social policy in Scotland at the University of Edinburgh. Although my classes focused on social policy in Europe, it was only natural to compare American policies to European policies. I think I learned as much about social policy in the United States during that semester as I did about social policy in Europe. When I returned for my last three semesters of undergrad, I took an economics class on poverty and also completed an independent study on the economics of welfare policy, which I later presented at an academic conference.

I am currently a research intern at a public affairs research organization. In this position, I am learning that there are other policy issues in which I am interested, specifically, health care reform and public retirement systems. Upon completion of a dual degree in public administration and economics, I would like to continue in the field of policy research and analysis. While I am most interested in welfare policy, I am open to exploring other policy areas, as I have unexpectedly become interested in issues through work-related experiences. Most important to me in a future position is the ability to continue learning while still using my education and experience to help my organization or agency positively contribute to the policy-making process.

EXAMPLE 7

Sometimes a professional commitment statement contains a lot of language about traits, such as being "energetic and confident." Others have used such terms as *dynamic*, *outgoing*, and *enthusiastic*. This is not necessary, and besides, talk is cheap. It is better to let the facts speak for your past commitments and accomplishments. Try to reduce the trait language a bit. In addition, the "concurrent career" information could work against you; it may show insufficient commitment to the primary career.

Motivation, work performance, and, most important, teamwork are strengths displayed in order for one to secure a successful work environment. I am a very energetic and confident person, and I welcome and embrace a challenging position. I have over fifteen years of work experience with state government in the field of technical information and human resource documentation. Concurrently, I am an entrepreneur engaging in the operation and performance of a commercial carrier service.

I currently supervise three employees within the technical field of gaming with State Police. I have developed internal managerial policies by creating written instructions and manuals as a means of training and performing daily job tasks and duties. I also conduct technical training and seminars internally and externally.

In addition to weekly employment, my husband and I developed and created a small business. It is a professional commercial carrier service, assisting major chemical plants in transporting needed materials and substances. Through creativity and organization, this business was forged from the ground up and is currently a success. With the ability to multitask, network, and utilize learned experiences and knowledge into other areas of concern, It continues to flourish.

My past work experience and initiative to take charge of a small business by succeeding as an owner and operator proves that I am dependable, knowledgeable, and able to jump into a task with confidence and control. I have consistently set high standards of efficiency and effort. I would like to assist your agency by developing internal managerial procedures, policies, and training within the technical realm of government, facilitating an effort to stay abreast of current and changing technology.

Given the opportunity, I can show you how I can put my successful experience to work for your agency by exerting a positive effort for future growth.

Appendix D: Sample Psychological Contract

Many psychological contracts are informal, but some can be more structured, following the model shown in Figure 10.1. They need not be, but they can. The following contract is between a midlevel employee and her supervisor. The contract was adapted from one made by a student in one of our classes. Names are omitted for anonymity. Psychological contracts are, of course, as unique as the interests and concerns of the parties making them.

I expect to get:

- Flexible scheduling for my schooling and other professional commitments that provide me opportunities for personal growth and networking with other agencies in an overall effort to promote the organization
- Travel opportunities to represent the organization at national meetings and to interact with the national headquarters staff in DC whom I work closely with by phone but rarely get to see face-to-face

- Assistance with and access to some of the information he discusses on the director's teleconferences, enabling me to understand the current politics and trends in conservation
- Time each week to bounce ideas off one another because botany is not my background, and I often need to pick my supervisor's brain about scientific information to do my job well
- An open door to ask questions of him and staff members
- An open communication policy allowing me to provide honest feedback on the project and other existing and new commutations
- Representation from the director in dealing with university policy and personnel affairs

I expect to give:

- Creative and innovative marketing ideas for the organization
- Up-to-date information of current agricultural and conservation marketing trends, evaluation of their use, and potential implementation at the organization
- The design of an overall marketing plan for the organization, and the implementation of all components in a timely manner, even if this means working late; I accept this responsibility with the flextime option
- Representation of the organization at any and all of my official and other professional travel relating to conservation
- Regular communication about current projects, accomplishments, and future plans
- Open feedback on documents that my supervisor requests to review

My supervisor expects to get:

- National marketing initiatives for the organization to be implemented in creative, professional, and innovative ways
- My effort to keep him aware of current projects, accomplishments, and future plans
- Timely completion of tasks

- Relationship and partnership marketing efforts
- Establishment of new contacts through travel that could benefit the organization
- Open feedback on his work

My supervisor is willing to give:

- Support of and opportunities for official travel, and time for other professional travel that can mutually benefit me and the organization
- Flextime as long as work is completed
- Regular communication about current conservation politics and trends
- Representation to the university regarding personnel affairs
- Flexible scheduling to allow for graduate school studies
- An open-door policy to answer questions and receive honest feedback

Appendix E:
Further Readings

We recommend the following books and online resources that advance issues or matters discussed in the text. These are among our favorites, though no doubt many readers have their own.

FOR FURTHER SELF-EXPLORATION

We think that these five books will provide a nice and meaningful extension of the subject matter that gives people much to think about and share with others.

1. David Keirsey, *Please Understand Me II* (Del Mar, CA: Prometheus Nemesis, 1998). This is a popular version of the classic *Myers-Briggs* test. The first version of this book sold over two million copies. As mentioned in Chapter 14, this self-test consists of seventy items that result in sixteen personality types. This book approach relates not only to different occupations or activities but also to mating, parenting, and leadership preferences. This book is a must read for anyone who is undertaking a career choice or dating. The lack of a

more recent book simply points to the excellence of this book, and more recent information is available at www.keirsey.com. After reading this book, one will find a relevant application to workplace problems in R. Bolton and D. Bolton, *People Styles at Work* (New York: AMACOM, 1996). Though using a slightly different typology, this book brings attention to the overuse of one's strengths and the need to use a bit more of one's weaknesses in dealing with different types of people.

2. James Hollis, *Finding Meaning in the Second Half of Life* (New York: Gotham Books, 2005). This book was written in the Jungian tradition and is an excellent sample of work in this genre. While the title will strike a chord with anyone over age forty, we have also given it to students who are in their early twenties. It shows the importance of dealing with not only one's issues but also, equally important, the issues one needs to focus on and why. Hollis deals with perennially existential issues such as becoming an adult and loneliness that are timeless and ageless and are a potent reminder to anyone who is caught in the rat race of work. Hollis asks, what does it really mean to be grown-up in today's world? When is having it all just not enough? A second book from Hollis, *Why Good People Do Bad Things* (New York: Gotham Books, 2007) focuses more narrowly.

3. Dan Baker, *What Happy People Know* (New York: St. Martin's Press, 2003). We have our reservations about positive psychology, but, as we note in Chapter 16, "positive psychology has a point about seeing the glass as half full." This book gives in great detail the twelve qualities (elements) of happiness and six tools of happiness. This book is clear about practices that cause people to be happy. It also discusses traps that keep people from finding happiness, some of which are associated with the defense mechanisms mentioned in this book. While more is needed than just these tools to be happy at work, they will surely amplify the practices described in Chapter 16. There are other books in this genre too, such as the best seller Stefan Klein, *The Science of Happiness* (Philadelphia: Perseus Books, 2006).

4. Steve Hagan, *Buddhism Plain and Simple* (New York: Random House, 1997). A current trend in psychology and research in recent decades continues to be the rationalism of Buddhism. We mean Buddhism not as a religion but as a philosophical orientation. This book is a short (150 pages) well-written introduction that is stimulating, in depth, and not dumbed down. Hagan clearly shows how this perspective drives a new way of looking at the world and of shaping one's experience in it. He provides a contemporary treatment of main Buddhist concepts such as the art of seeing, the nature of wisdom, and the causes of suffering. This is an excellent book for a rainy Sunday. For readers who want a deeper introduction, with an orientation toward psychology, we suggest Mark Epstein, *Thoughts without a Thinker* (New York: Basic Books, 2004).

5. Daniel Goleman, *Emotional Intelligence: Why It Can Matter More Than IQ* (New York: Bantam Books, 1995). This best seller sparked a renewed interest in the topic of emotion in everyday life. Goleman is a *New York Times* journalist who brought in-depth reporting to this area and work. Though now it is about twenty years old, this book still does an admirable job discussing research in the area of the brain and emotion and how emotions are a central part in one's functioning and key to success. It has a separate chapter on application to work, family, and education. This is a must read for anyone interested in this topic. This book sparked a stream of research; see www.eiconsortium.org, some of which is applied to the workplace. See D. Goleman and R. Boyatzis, *Primal Leadership* (Boston: Harvard Business School, 2002).

FOR PRACTICAL USE

Hundreds of books exist that profess to provide practical advice for the matters under discussion here. We doubt anyone has read them all or would even want to. We identify a few books that nicely advance some of the issues discussed here.

The strength of these books is that they are practical, but the weakness is that they lack psychological depth, which explains why people are not doing these things to begin with and what issues these practices may involve. People use from them what they can.

1. Paul Falcone, *101 Tough Conversations to Have with Employees* (New York: AMACOM, 2009). The title says it all. This book deals with a huge range of issues such as cultural intolerance, inadequate job skills, policy violations, substandard communication skills, lack of skills, personality style issues, and so on.

2. Bob Wall, *Working Relationships*, 2nd ed. (Mountain View, CA: Davies-Black, 2008). Bob Wall has written a few books on working with others. This book deals with common wrong assumptions of wrong behaviors of people at work. Though basic, it is to the point.

3. Adele Lynn, *The EQ Interview: Finding Employees with High Emotional Intelligence* (New York: AMACOM, 2008). The book contains over 250 questions to ask during interviewing and some guidance on interpreting responses.

4. Kenneth Ashworth, *Caught between the Dog and the Fireplug (or How to Survive Public Service)* (Washington, DC: CQ Press, 2001). This book has seventeen chapters on different topics in which an older mentor gives advice to a new incumbent. Chapter titles include " 'Walking with Kings,' " "Ethics and Morality in Public Service," "Working with the Press," "Dealing with Difficult and Unpleasant People," "Taking the Initiative, or Risk Taking Inside Government," "The Kinds of Pressures and Influence Used on You," and "Learning from Your Boss." Whereas we focus on people skills, Ashworth takes a broader perspective. The bibliography also includes some books by Stewart Liff that are also practical and useful for managing careers and employees in government.

5. Richard Bolles, *What Color Is Your Parachute?* (New York: Random House, 2010). This is the perennial favorite job-hunting book, loaded with practical advice.

Notes

PREFACE NOTES

1. E. Berman and J. West, "Managing Emotional Intelligence in U.S. Cities: A Study of Public Managers," *Public Administration Review* 68, no. 4 (2008): 742–58.
2. In public administration, notably the excellent work of R. Hummel, *The Bureaucratic Experience*, 5th ed. (Armonk, NY: M. E. Sharpe, 2007).

CHAPTER 1 NOTES

1. The term *common sense* is subject to varying definitions. Here, it is used as general knowledge or guidelines that are considered as valid by a group and therefore adopted by its group members, usually in rather unreflected ways.
2. An adage is a condensed but memorable saying embodying some important fact of experience that is taken as true by many people. An axiom is a saying that is widely accepted on its own merits. Presumably, common sense knowledge that guides people reflects experience.
3. R. Hollinger, National Retail Security Survey (Gainesville: University of Florida, 2005). In C. Dugas, "More Consumers, Workers Shoplift as Economy Slows," USA Today, June 19, 2008, p. 1B.

4. Much of the surfing is for shopping, travel, auctions, investment, news, and sports, but 24 percent of employees also visited Web sites with live music, 15 percent with games, and 4 percent with porn. Another survey estimates that workers spend over an hour each day on personal business, costing about $8,800 per worker per year. C. D'Abate and E. Eddy, "Engaging in Personal Business on the Job: Extending the Presenteeism Construct," Human Resource Development Quarterly 18, no. 3 (2007): 361–84. Also E. Palmer, "The Work Force Is Surfing," iMedia Connection, October 28, 2005, http://www.imediaconnection.com/content/7068.asp; "Vault Survey of Internet Use in the Workplace" (Fall 2000) reported in "26% of Employees Use Instant Message at Work," Business Wire, October 13, 2000, http://www.allbusiness.com/labor-employment/human-resources-personnel/6572446-1.html.

5. There are some excellent blogs about work gripes and rants: http://www.weeklygripe.co.uk/links.asp, http://www.workrant.com, and http://www.disgruntledworkforce.com/blog.

6. N. Mooney, I Can't Believe She Did That! Why Women Betray Other Women at Work (New York: St. Martin's Press, 2006).

7. Interview quote in authors' research.

8. J. Scott, "Do Attractive People Get Better Treatment Than Others?" Jet 100, no. 12 (2001): 52–54.

9. "Randstad USA Survey Identifies Biggest Office Flirts: Westerners and Men," Business Wire, February 6, 2007, http://findarticles.com/p/articles/mi_m0EIN/is_2007_Feb_6/ai_n27138934.

10. "Workplace Dating: 44% of Office Romances Led to Marriage, AMA Survey Shows," February 10, 2003, http://www.amanet.org/training/articles/2003-Survey-on-Workplace-Dating-32.aspx.

11. Many other data sources are online surveys whose results should be treated with caution because of possible self-reporting bias. Vault's 2008 online Office Romance Survey reported that 47 percent of workers in the United States and 43 percent of workers in the United Kingdom have had an office romance. Consistent with the AMA ("Workplace Dating"), 50 percent stated that they have worked with a couple who was having an office romance and went on to get married ("Love Is Blooming by the Watercooler," http://www.vault.com/wps/portal/usa/vcm/detail?id=5119). Another online survey reports that nearly 40 percent of workers have had a workplace romance ("Be My Valentine? Nearly 40 Percent of Workers Have Had a Workplace Romance," Spherion Survey, January 29, 2007, http://www.spherion.com/press/releases/2007/workplace-romance.jsp). Vault's 2008 survey finds that 56 percent of U.S. employees had dated a coworker during their careers, and 25 percent of those surveyed admitted to dating a

superior. Another online survey, participated by 31,207 people and reported on MSNBC and Elle.com "Office Sex and Romance Survey" (by Janet Lever, California State University at Los Angeles), reports that roughly half of women and 20 percent of men have had an affair with a superior; for 28 percent of women and 10 percent of men, it was with their boss. Only 7 percent of women have dated a subordinate, compared with 25 percent of men (http://www.msnbc.com/news/748467.asp, no longer available).

12. While the text makes the point that sex at work occurs, one obvious question is why it occurs so often. One reason is that people with similar interests spend a lot of time with each other and also that Americans have an increasingly poor social life with fewer friends who traditionally provide such introductions; hence, work is a convenient place to meet someone. Another reason is that sex is used for career advantage. Data on this are scarce, but one online survey reports that 25 percent of men say that dating the boss helped boost their careers (MSNBC and Elle.com "Office Sex and Romance Survey," by Janet Lever). One article reports, "A recent study of 475 University of Michigan undergraduates ages 17 to 26 found that 27 percent of the men and 14 percent of the women who weren't in a committed relationship had offered someone favors or gifts—help prepping for a test, laundry washing, tickets to a college football game—in exchange for sex" (reported in M. Goodman, "Bartering Sex for Stuff or Services," CNN.com, August 25, 2008, http://www.cnn.com/2008/LIVING/personal/08/25/sex.for.stuff/index.html?iref=mpstoryview). A third reason is that some people report that flirting or having an affair makes the workplace better, more fun, or exciting. Finally, the downside risk is modest at best. While many articles warn that office romance complicates one's workplace situation and can lead to termination, Vault's 2008 romance survey ("Love Is Blooming by the Watercooler") finds that only 13 percent of those involved in an office romance experienced one or both people leaving the company because of awkwardness (voluntary) or company policy. Negative consequences are far from certain, though firing is obviously very severe; K. Davis, "Date Your Boss, Boost Your Career," *Kansas City Daily News*, February 12, 2006, http://findarticles.com/p/articles/mi_qn4181/is_20060212/ai_n16058270. Some articles in 2010, during the economic recession, suggest that employers are tightening up and are more quick to let such workers go.

13. M. Frone, "Prevalence and Distribution of Alcohol Use and Impairment in the Workplace: A U.S. National Survey," *Journal of Studies on Alcohol 76, no.* 1 (2006): 147–56: "Illicit drug use in the workplace

involved an estimated 3.1% of employed adults (3.9 million workers)." See also U.S. Department of Health and Human Services, "Workplace Substance Abuse Statistics," n.d., http://www.drugfreeworkplace.gov/WPWorkit/pdf/workplace_substance_abuse_statistics_fs.pdf.

14. H. Gensler, "The Golden Rule," http://www.jcu.edu/philosophy/gensler/goldrule.htm.

15. One study compares a sample of these value statements that for-profit, nonprofit, and public organizations have adopted. Among companies, 70 percent most often mention integrity, which often is discussed in terms of truthfulness, honesty, candor, trust, and good faith. Second most common are statements about respecting the law (54 percent). Among public and nonprofit organizations, concerns of confidentiality are most common (72 percent and 71 percent, respectively), followed by integrity (52 percent and 69 percent, respectively) and avoiding conflicts of interest (56 percent and 57 percent, respectively). G. Grobman, "An Analysis of Codes of Ethics of Nonprofit, Tax-Exempt Membership Associations," *Public Integrity* 9, no. 3 (2007): 245–63.

16. J. O'Donell, "10 Career Realities: Helping Grads Transition from College to Career," May 5, 2008, http://www.brazencareerist.com/2008/05/05/10-career-realities-helping-grads-transition-from-college-to-career (accessed September 1, 2010).

17. For a list of common text messaging abbreviations, see "Text Messaging & Chat Abbreviations: A Guide to Understanding Online Chat Acronyms & Smiley Faces," http://www.webopedia.com/quick_ref/textmessageabbreviations.asp.

18. See P. O'Connell, "Generational Tension," *Bloomberg Businessweek*, June 9, 2008, http://www.businessweek.com/business_at_work/generation_gap/archives/2008/06/generation_gap.html.

19. Stated by Lawrence Peter in L. Peter and R. Hull, *The Peter Principle* (New York: William Morrow, 1969).

20. We first heard this expression in Louisiana. It matches well with the roux sauces there.

21. O'Connell, "Generational Tension."

22. For a discussion of the cultural features of these generations, see much later in this book or the following: C. Marston, *Motivating the "What's in It for Me?" Workforce* (New York: Wiley, 2007) or J. Twenge, *Generation Me* (New York: Free Press, 2006). The nomenclature refers to *millennials*, also Generation Y or Gen Y, born after 1979 (under thirty years of age) and who are now in school or recently joining the workforce as new entrants. Millennials make up about 20 percent of

the workforce; *Generation Xers*, also called Gen X, born between 1965 and 1979 (thirty to forty-five years old), make up about 30 percent of the workforce; *baby boomers*, born between 1945 and 1964 (forty-five to sixty-five years old), make up 45 percent of the workforce, but this percentage will dramatically decline in upcoming years due to retirement; and *matures*, born before 1945 (now 65 years and over), now constitute only about 5 percent of the workforce.

23. For example, Marston, *Motivating the "What's in It for Me?" Workforce.*
24. "Nurture Rising Talent: The 'Lucky to Have a Job' Feeling Is Fading," InformationWeek, April 30, 2007.
25. "Death by Overwork in Japan," *The Economist*, December 19, 2007. Also, the entry "Karochi" on Wikipedia (http://en.wikipedia.org http://en.wikipedia.org/wiki/Kar%C5%8Dshi).
26. National Institutes of Mental Health, "The Numbers Count: Mental Disorders in America," 2008, http://www.nimh.nih.gov/health/ publications/the-numbers-count-mental-disorders-in-america/ index.shtml. See also U.S. SAMHSA, *Special Report: Improving Mental Health Insurance Benefits without Increasing Costs* (Washington, DC: U.S. Department of Health and Human Services Substance Abuse and Mental Health Services Administration, 2001), http://store. samhsa.gov/shin/content/SMA01-3542/SMA01-3542.pdf. See also U.S. Department of Health and Human Services, "Mental Health: A Report of the Surgeon General—Executive Summary," 1999, http:// www.surgeongeneral.gov/library/mentalhealth/chapter2/sec2_1. html#epidemiology.
27. U.S. HHS, *Results from the 2009 National Survey on Drug Use and Health: Volume I. Summary of National Findings* (Washington, DC: U.S. Department of Health and Human Services, Office of Applied Studies, NSDUH Series H-38A, HHS Publication No. SMA 10-4586, 2010), http://www.oas.samhsa.gov/NSDUH/2k9NSDUH/2k9ResultsP.pdf.
28. E. Cohen, "CDC: Antidepressants Most Prescribed Drugs in U.S.," *CNNhealth.com*, July 9, 2007, http://www.cnn.com/2007/HEALTH/ 07/09/antidepressants/index.html.
29. While younger workers would like their bosses to know about their abilities as well as their limitations (e.g., "don't push me!"), their bosses want to know only about the former. Younger workers correctly perceive that telling older workers about their stress, especially in conjunction with other afflictions, will have repercussions later, such as being denied rewarding assignments. For more information see Chapter 17. The Internet is also full of self-help Web sites, such as that of the Mayo Clinic (www.mayoclinic.com).

CHAPTER 2 NOTES

1. HRVoice.org, "NFI Research Survey Results: Good Manners at Work," June 12, 2007, http://www.hrvoice.org/story.aspx?regionid= 10&storyid=3841&issueid=870&pagemode=displaystory (accessed September 1, 2010).

2. R. McFall, "A Review and Reformulation of the Concept of Social Skills," *Behavioral Assessment* 4, no. 1 (1982): 1–33; K. Merrell and G. Gimpel, *Social Skills of Children and Adolescents: Conceptualization, Assessment and Treatment* (Mahwah, NJ: Lawrence Erlbaum, 1998); J. Greene and B. Burleson, *Handbook of Communication and Social Interaction Skills* (London: Routledge, 2003).

3. F. Robinson, "Poll: Americans Are Becoming More Rude," *Deseret News*, September 22, 2009, http://www.deseretnews.com/article/705331806/ Poll-Americans-becoming-more-rude.html.

4. Voice of America, "Poll Finds America's Image Still Negative Abroad," June 24, 2005, http://www1.voanews.com/english/news/a-13-2005-06-24-voa1-67392542.html. Anecdotally, Americans are sometimes perceived as having friendly ways, but they do not interact and support each other and others well. They are also perceived as being rude and unpolished in grace and good manners too.

5. See, for example, K. Kavanagh and P. Nailon, *Excellence in the Workplace: Legal and Life Skills* (St. Paul, MN: Thomson/West, 2007). It should be noted that research on social manners at work is very scarce; today's research on social manners deals mostly with deficiencies among school-age children and those with mental health conditions. The ways of teaching these populations social skills are scarcely relevant to adults, and the social skills they are concerned with are only naively relevant to the workplace. Some research in business settings exists, but it is far from encompassing, dealing with only a few values or behaviors (e.g., regarding bribery or styles of supervisory relations). Many books have a chapter or two that talk about these matters, such as S. Liff, *Managing Your Government Career* (New York: AMACOM, 2009).

6. Most general use definitions are based on http://www.merriam-webster. com/dictionary/. Those definitions shown are adapted by the authors.

7. Various books make this point, but here are two relevant to the public service: S. Liff, *Managing Government Employees* (New York: AMACOM, 2007) (e.g., Chapter 3); K. Ashworth, *Caught between the Dog and the Fireplug (or How to Survive Public Service)* (Washington, DC: CQ Press, 2001).

8. Blog posting on October 15, 2005, on http://www.freerepublic.com/
focus/f-news/1502967/posts (accessed September 1, 2010; no longer
available). Also see the video "Weatherman Flings Ringing Cell Phone
on Air," July 6, 2008, http://www.cnn.com/video/#/video/us/2008/
07/05/levs.cell.phone.etiquette.cnn.

9. By mutual agreement, people can agree that attending to interruptions should not be perceived as rude, but, as this quote shows, interruptions are often perceived as rude by strangers and others who are
not part of this understanding. Socially, we may even say, "Oh, that's
OK," because we want to maintain our working relationship, but we
are thinking how rude the other person actually is.

10. Survey listed on http://www.workrant.com/archive/archive.php
(accessed September 1, 2010). Other responses are *incompetent*, 32
percent; *egotistic*, 27 percent; and *micromanaging*, 18 percent. There are
not many polls and scientific surveys on this matter. One author states
that only 25 percent of listeners grasp the central ideas of communication; see C. McNamara, "Habits to Differentiate Good from Poor
Listening," *Free Management Library*, http://www.managementhelp.
org/commskls/listen/gd_vs_pr.htm.

11. A popular expression is that "First impressions are often the truest."
Well, first impressions are sometimes wrong, but people are expected
to be on their best behavior, as failure to conduct oneself in socially
acceptable ways often is taken as a sign of possible trouble (disrespect)
down the road (http://thinkexist.com/quotation/first_impressions_
are_often_the_truest-as_we_find/298161.html). Another expression
is "You never get a second chance to make a first impression," which
also tacitly acknowledges the importance of first impressions.

12. W. Lowther, "Blundering Bush Makes ANOTHER Gaffe as He Winks
at the Queen," *Mail Online*, May 8, 2007, http://www.dailymail.co.uk/
news/article-453199/Blundering-Bush-makes-ANOTHER-gaffe-
winks-Queen.html; S. Stolberg and J. Rutenberg, "Bush to Get Etiq
uette Tips before He Receives the Queen," *New York Times*, May 4,
2007, http://www.nytimes.com/2007/05/04/world/americas/04iht-
04queen.5573127.html.

13. Adapted from "Am I Glad to Have a Colleague Like This," http://
drkumaresh.blogspot.com/2010/01/am-i-glad-to-have-colleague-
like-this.html.

14. In our earlier studies, we often find association between ethics and
social skills, and performance and performance management strategies. E. Berman and J. West, "Managing Emotional Intelligence in U.S.
Cities: A Study of Public Managers," *Public Administration Review* 68,
no. 4 (2008): 742–58.

15. Authors increasingly find among those entering work and college not only a lack of respect and courtesy but also a lack of work ethic, which is associated with reduced U.S. competitiveness relative to competing labor forces in East Asia and India. In a different context, Pulitzer Prize–winning columnist Thomas Friedman argued, "In a flat world where everyone has access to everything, values matter more than ever. Right now the Hindus and Confucians have more Protestant ethics than we do, and as long as that is the case we'll be No. 11!" "We're Number 1(1)!" *New York Times*, September 11, 2010, http://www.nytimes.com/2010/09/12/opinion/12friedman.html?ref=thomaslfriedman.

CHAPTER 3 NOTES

1. E. Berman, *Performance and Productivity for Public and Nonprofit Organizations*, 2nd ed. (New York: M. E. Sharpe, 2006).
2. S. Gillinson and D. O'Leary, *Working Progress: How to Reconnect Young People and Organizations* (London: Demos, 2006), http://www.demos.co.uk/files/workingprogress1.pdf, p. 39. S. Leitsch, *Review of Skills, Interim Report Chapter 6: The Increasing Importance of Skills* (London: HM Treasury, 2006), http://www.hm-treasury.gov.uk/media/4/A/pbr05_leitchreviewchapters_619.pdf, p. 46 (full report available at http://www.hm-treasury.gov.uk/independent_reviews/leitch_review/review_leitch_index.cfm). About half of the employers also note shortfalls in technical skills, practical skills, and problem-solving skills. In the United States a 2008 survey shows that baby boomers say only 16 percent and 25 percent of Generation Yers and Generation Xers, respectively, have good communication skills. Randstad/Harris Poll, *2008 World of Work*, http://www.us.randstad.com/2008WorldofWork.pdf (accessed September 1, 2010).
3. "Survey by Newsweek and Princeton Survey Research Associates, July 12–July 15, 1996" (Princeton, NJ). Dissatisfaction with bosses and coworkers typically rate low in polls, but while being helpful and sympathetic in some ways, bosses often are unhelpful and unavailable too.
4. E. Cordin, P. Odgers, R. Redgate, L. Rowan, and A. Barnes, "*$37 Billion: Counting the Cost of Employee Misunderstanding*" (White Paper, IDC, London, 2008), http://www.cognisco.com/downloads/white-paper/us_exec_summary.pdf.

5. Numerous organizational behavior textbooks make this point, such as J. Osland, D. Kolb, and I. Rubin, *Organizational Behavior: An Experiential Approach* (New York: Prentice Hall, 2006) and dedicated books on this topic. The model is also widely found on the Internet, such as B. Bulleit, *Four Key Elements of Effective Business Communication* (Cary, NC: Global Knowledge Training, 2008), http://images.globalknowledge.com/wwwimages/whitepaperpdf/WP_Bulleit_BusCommunication_P.pdf. Also http://findarticles.com/p/articles/mi_qa5331/is_200001/ai_n21450611?tag=untagged.

6. See http://en.wikipedia.org/wiki/Tenerife_disaster#Safety_response.

7. A. Gheytanchi, L. Joseph, E. Gierlach, S. Kimpara, J. Housley, Z. Franco, and L. Beutler, "The Dirty Dozen: Twelve Failures of the Hurricane Katrina Response and How Psychology Can Help," *American Psychologist* 62, no. 2 (2007): 118–30.

8. For example, M. Liberman, "Sex on the Brain: Women Use 20,000 Words a Day, Men Only 7,000—Or So Says a New Bestseller. Fact-checking 'The Female Brain,' " *Boston.com*, September 24, 2006, http://www.boston.com/news/globe/ideas/articles/2006/09/24/sex_on_the_brain.

9. A third problem causing the accident was mentioned in the introduction. The KLM copilot questioned the KLM pilot about whether in fact they had clearance for take-off but was rebuffed. Tension in the cockpit, respect for authority, and concern that they were already at the very end of their allowable duty hours all caused the copilot to not question further.

10. See homonyms at http://www.cooper.com/alan/homonym_list.html.

11. Doing so may also be used to communicate standing within a group. Some people also use references that are unknown to other to dominate, suggesting that someone is not in the know and therefore not worthy of as much esteem as others.

12. M. Zouhali-Worrall, "Found in Translation: Avoiding Multilingual Gaffes," *CNN.com*, July 14, 2008, http://money.cnn.com/2008/07/07/smallbusiness/language_translation.fsb/index.htm; and M. Zouhali-Worrall, "How Not to Sell Abroad," *CNN.com*, September 30, 2008, http://money.cnn.com/galleries/2008/fsb/0807/gallery.bad_translations.fsb/index.html.

13. English speakers, who might be perplexed by this, can realize that each of these sounds involve a similar tightening of the lips and releasing of a small puff of air from the mouth.

14. T. Chambers, "Misunderstandings Mar Workplace," *Korea Times*, October 13, 2005, http://www.scribd.com/doc/267098/misunderstandings.

15. M. Knapp and J. Hall, *Nonverbal Communication in Human Interaction*, 6th ed. (Belmont, CA: Wadsworth, 2006), 22.
16. "One of the worst culprits for creating the potential for misunderstanding is our increasing dependency on email as our primary communication channel," writes a columnist. M. Moriarty, "Workplace Coach: Be Clear: Conflict Thrives in Confusing Situations," *Seattle PI Business*, November 18, 2007, http://seattlepi.nwsource.com/business/340156_workcoach19.html. In a related matter, recall also that deleted e-mail can be recovered later, such as in the trial of Oliver North. See "Deleted Files Can Be Recovered," http://www.akdart.com/priv9.html.
17. M. Gladwell, *Outliers: The Story of Success* (New York: Little, Brown, 2008), 184.
18. See http://thinkexist.com/quotation/if_you_have_ten_thousand_regulations_you_destroy/150122.html.
19. M. Knapp and A. Vangelisti, *Interpersonal Communication and Human Relationships*, 5th ed. (New York: Allyn & Bacon, 2006), 425.
20. For example, at this time, Internet-based calls to China landlines are about $0.02 a minute; PC-to-PC calls are free, worldwide.
21. Young people who use Facebook and other social networking tools extensively may tend to underestimate these problems of precision in communication at work. The overuse of e-mail and texting creates problems that some younger workers are now beginning to encounter.
22. A. Malcolm, "Did You Hear What Michelle Said?" *Los Angeles Times*, August 22, 2007, http://latimesblogs.latimes.com/washington/2007/08/did-you-hear-wh.html.
23. "Escalation," *Confessions of a Community College Dean*, May 9, 2007, http://suburbdad.blogspot.com.
24. D. Tannen, *You Just Don't Understand—Women and Men in Conversation* (New York: William Morrow, 1990).
25. N. Mooney, *I Can't Believe She Did That! Why Women Betray Other Women at Work* (New York: St. Martin's Press, 2006).
26. L. Brizendine, *The Female Brain* (New York: Morgan Road Books, 2006). This book received a good deal of press, but some claims are also sharply contested. See S. Baron-Cohen, *The Essential Difference: The Truth about the Male and Female Brain* (New York: Basic Books, 2003); K. Simpson, "The Role of Testosterone in Aggression," *McGill Journal of Medicine* 6 (2001): 32–40. Some comments by Brizendine about the male brain are made at "Love, Sex and the Male Brain," *CNN.com*, March 25, 2010, http://edition.cnn.com/2010/OPINION/03/23/brizendine.male.brain/index.html.
27. It is also said that women speak about 20,000 words a day, compared to 7,000 by men.

CHAPTER 4 NOTES

1. This is one of several pieces of advice widely given. For this and others, see http://www.net-temps.com/careerdev/career-tools/view-article. html?type=topics&id=3159.
2. *Collins English Dictionary: Complete and Unabridged*, 2003, http://www. thefreedictionary.com/_/misc/HarperCollinsProducts.aspx?English.
3. "Survey by Gallup Organization, December 5–December 8, 2002." A report by the U.S. National Institute for Occupational Safety and Health (NIOSH) cites other surveys that report dissatisfaction with stress in between 26 percent and 40 percent among surveyed workers; U.S. NIOSH, *Stress at Work*, Publication Number 99-101 (Washington, DC: U.S. NIOSH, 1999). In another survey, 48 percent of adults stated that they had made a voluntary change in their life in the past few years that resulted in their making *less* money. When asked why they did so, 47 percent stated that they wanted a less stressful life, and 36 percent stated that they wanted a more balanced life; "Survey by Center for a New American Dream and Widmeyer Communications, August 4–August 9, 2004." See also http://www.stress.org/job.htm.
4. As regarding the sources of stress, when asked, "Which of the following causes you the most stress in your job?" 54 percent of respondents (employed adults) stated the demands of the job itself, 20 percent stated the people whom they work with, 10 percent stated their boss, and 8 percent stated the fear of being laid off; "Survey by UBS and Gallup Organization, September 5–September 26, 2002." A survey by the American Psychological Association found that 44 percent of respondents stated that too heavy a workload is a very significant or somewhat significant factor affecting stress levels in their work; "Survey by American Psychological Association, National Women's Health Resource Center, and iVillage and Greenberg Quinlan Rosner Research, January 12–January 24, 2006."
5. Randstad/Harris Poll, *2008 World of Work* (Amsterdam, the Netherlands: Randstad/Harris, 2008), us.randstad.com/2008WorldofWork.pdf.
6. Add to this a tendency of some people to sue for discrimination or hostile working environments when confronted with unsatisfactory job evaluations. This makes addressing excuses for underperformance that much harder.
7. Shana Alexander (1925–2005), http://thinkexist.com/quotation/the_ sad_truth_is_that_excellence_makes_people/219904.html (accessed September 1, 2010).

8. Resentment is sometimes described as a secondary emotion, that is, one that follows other emotions. Indeed, someone who is helped may at first experience being happy, before resentment later builds up. Resentment is the emotion that warns people of the need to take responsibility for something. For more on resentment, see also http://eqi.org/resent1.htm.

9. Adding to this problem is that those who pursue technical excellence sometimes have weakly developed people skills; they may be a bit blind of how they rub people the wrong way.

10. For example, E. Berman and J. West, "What Is Managerial Mediocrity? Definition, Prevalence and Negative Impact (Part 1)," *Public Performance and Management Review* 27, no. 2 (2003): 7–27.

11. S. Lohr, "G.E. Goes with What It Knows: Making Stuff," *New York Times*, December 5, 2010, http://www.nytimes.com/2010/12/05/business/05ge.html?hp=&pagewanted=all.

12. "Survey by Newsweek and Princeton Survey Research Associates, July 12–July 15, 1996."

13. E. Bender, "Personality Disorder Prevalence Surprises Researchers," *Psychiatric News* 39, no. 17 (2004): 12. "Almost 15 percent of Americans, or 30.8 million adults, meet diagnostic criteria for at least one personality disorder, according to the results of the 2001–02 National Epidemiologic Survey on Alcohol and Related Conditions (NESARC)," http://pn.psychiatryonline.org/cgi/content/full/39/17/12, but a lower estimate is about 9 percent in the U.S. population, according to National Institute of Mental Health; see Table 17.1 in this book and NIMH, "National Survey Tracks Prevalence of Personality Disorders in U.S. Population," *Science Update*, October 18, 2007, http://www.nimh.nih.gov/science-news/2007/national-survey-tracks-prevalence-of-personality-disorders-in-us-population.shtml. Estimates vary widely; for example, antisocial personality makes up 0.6 percent to 3.6 percent. Not all personality disorders cause the above problems, but not all people with low levels of these problems meet diagnosable criteria, either. Hence, 5 to 15 percent seems reasonable and consistent with many people's experiences.

14. J.-P. Sartre, *Huis Clos* (Paris: Gallimard, 1944). To follow up, an interesting online article is Clayton Morgareidge, "Hell Is Other People, but Must Other People Be Hell?" 2005, http://www.lclark.edu/~clayton/commentaries/hell.html. This also deals with some themes explored later in this book.

15. "Meeting spelers na incident Oranje" [Players meet after incident], *De Telegraaf*, June 29, 2010 (in Dutch), http://www.telegraaf.nl/telesport/wk2010/7066000/__Meeting_spelers_na_incident_Oranje__.html?sn=wkvoetbal2010.

16. A variety of books give general advice about careers, often dealing with some of these matters. As regarding those in government, see K. Ashworth, *Caught between the Dog and the Fireplug (or How to Survive Public Service)* (Washington, DC: CQ Press, 2001); and S. Liff, *Managing Your Government Career* (New York: AMACOM, 2009).

17. As a further example, sometimes it feels difficult to say "no" to someone without creating social distance. For example, we may be asked to fill in or cover for someone, once too often. Advances in the office can be this way too. A tactful way may be to point to one's own limitations: "I'd really like to, but I really just can't."

18. Surely, in dealing with difficult situations there are times when trouble needs to be raised in order to get action, but such instances should be few, well thought out, and accompanied by cogent argumentation. The topic of dealing with tough situations is also taken up in Chapters 6 and 16.

19. D. McKay, "Toward a More Civil Work Place: Avoiding Offensive Behavior on the Job," http://careerplanning.about.com/od/bosscoworkers/a/respect.htm.

20. N. Feig, "Mind Your Manners: Etiquette in the Workplace," January 1, 2005, http://www.allbusiness.com/human-resources/careers/937464-1.html (accessed September 1, 2010); A. Humphries, "Saying the Unsayable to Your Co-worker," *CNN.com*, March 26, 2001, http://archives.cnn.com/2001/CAREER/corporateclass/03/22/etiquette/index.html; S. Kanga, "Workplace Etiquette: Mind Your Manners!" *Rediff News*, August 25, 2008, http://www.rediff.com/getahead/2008/aug/25work.htm. The latter article (in India) and its date show the diffusion of these concerns in the global workplace.

21. For example, many people like Korean kimchi, which is fermented cabbage with hot chili peppers. Some Indian curries can also be quite smelly.

22. S. Lucas, "Too Dressed Up," June 18, 2008, http://evilhrlady.blogspot.com.

23. Randstad, "New Randstad Work Watch Survey Reveals What Really Irks Employees," May 5, 2010, http://us.randstad.com/content/aboutrandstad/news-and-press-releases/press-releases/2010/20100505003.xml.

24. Ibid.

28. Also, oxytocin levels are lower in men than women. Empirical research about the roles of oxytocin in men and women is still under development at this time, and many studies are done on animals, not humans; for example, "Aggression as Rewarding as Sex, Food and Drugs, New Research Shows," which studies mice (January 15, 2008,

http://biopsychiatry.com/aggression/rewarding.html). Note also that effects of oxytocin are also modulated by other hormones not mentioned in this discussion. For readers seeking more, consider the Web sites http://www.merck.com/mmpe/sec12/ch150/ch150a. html and http://en.wikipedia.org/wiki/Oxytocin or a poplar account at http://www.hugthemonkey.com/2007/03/paul_zak_oxytoc.html.

29. See, for example, "Michael Gurian on Teens, Sex and Love," January 26, 2007, http://www.hugthemonkey.com/2007/01/michael_gurian_. html. It might also be noted that men have lower oxytocin levels than women. Also see "Gender Responses to Stress," http://www.fi.edu/ learn/brain/stress.html#genderresponses.

30. For example, C. Fine, *Delusions of Gender* (New York: W. W. Norton, 2010). A discussion of this book is found at K. Bouton, "Peeling Away Theories on Gender and the Brain," *New York Times*, August 23, 2010, http://www.nytimes.com/2010/08/24/science/24scibks.html?8dpc.

31. These differences do indeed lie at the basis of misunderstandings. See the previously mentioned online resource by Bulleit, p. 4, http:// images.globalknowledge.com/wwwimages/whitepaperpdf/WP_ Bulleit_BusCommunication_P.pdf.

32. Psychologically, this may embody a desire for everyone to be just like us. Keirsey and Bates (1984) call this is the "Pygmalion Project." In Greek mythology, Pygmalion is a sculptor who falls in love with a statue he made. The term "Pygmalion Project" is used to describe the effort of people to sculpt someone into the person they want him or her to be: "If only everyone would just speak and think like me, how easy the world be." It is not to be.

33. For example, G. Chapman, *Five Languages of Love* (Chicago: Northfield, 1992), www.5lovelanguages.com.

34. Ironically, it is sometimes said that women have a more action-oriented style of caring than men. In a traditional world, women need to feed their children, and so on, whereas men need to convince women that they make for good providers, which is more word based and less action based.

35. R. Curnow, "Knowing When 'Yes' Means 'No' in Business," *CNN. com*, June 24, 2010, http://business.blogs.cnn.com/2010/06/24/ knowing-when-yes-means-no-in-business/?hpt=C2.

36. For an interesting look, see, for example, B. Broyard, *My Father's Secret*, CNN video, July 10, 2008, http://www.cnn.com/video/#/video/ living/2008/07/10/bia.bliss.broyard.cnn; http://blissbroyard.com.

CHAPTER 5 NOTES

1. See http://www.brainyquote.com/quotes/topics/topic_friendship.html.
2. This statement does not imply that competence is irrelevant, as it is popularly often taken. We need competent people, and incompetent people often are an embarrassment to those who support them, reflecting poorly on their judgment and commitments.
3. T. Rath, *Vital Friends* (New York: Gallup Press, 2006); cited from http://www.jonathanfields.com/blog/friends-at-work-divine-or-disaster/. In addition, people with at least three close friends at work were 46 percent more likely to be extremely satisfied with their job and 88 percent more likely to be satisfied with their life.
4. E. Berman, J. West, and M. Richter, "Workplace Relations: Friendship Patterns and Consequences (According to Managers)," *Public Administration Review* 62, no. 2 (2002): 155–68.
5. Also, nearly two-thirds of employees believe that office productivity improves when coworkers are friendly outside of the office, according to a recent study by Accountemps, a staffing company for financial services professionals. Cited on http://www.fastcompany.com/blog/rusty-weston/job-world/careers-do-you-working-friends.
6. Organizations can do much to acknowledge these risks. In many cases, the matter is managed by formulating and insisting on professional standards and conduct such as not having known friends serve on the same committees or be in charge of decisions that would affect each other. Office romance has also been much discussed. For example, experts agree that when love strikes, it is best to be smart by knowing the organization's policy, keeping a low profile, and not using office e-mail for sending private messages. Among those who have had an office romance, 19 percent of respondents said that they or the romantic partner eventually left the organization: 9 percent because the company had a policy forbidding office romance, 6 percent because the couple didn't want to work together after they became a couple (too much closeness), and 4 percent because it was too awkward after the breakup. Vault, "Office Romance Survey," 2008, http://www.vault.com/wps/portal/usa/vcm/detail?id=5119 (accessed September 1, 2010).
7. J. Kornblum, "Study: 25% of Americans Have No One to Confide In," *USA Today*, June 22, 2006, http://www.usatoday.com/news/nation/2006-06-22-friendship_x.htm.
8. M. Mehta, "NY Jets' Dustin Keller Grateful for Lessons Learned under Mentor Brett Favre," *NJ.com*, September 18, 2009, http://www.nj.com/jets/index.ssf/2009/09/ny_jets_dustin_keller_grateful.html.

9. D. Berger, *Clinical Empathy* (Northvale: Jason Aronson, 1987). Compassion is a bit stronger than empathy and focused on the desire to alleviate another's suffering. Compassion is thought to be emotion, though Buddhism sees it as a state of mind, a desire to alleviate another's suffering. In a broader context, caring is also seen to build up networks and success in stakeholder relations. A book that makes the case in business is D. Patnaik and P. Mortensen, *Wired to Care: How Companies Prosper When They Create Widespread Empathy* (Upper Saddle River, NJ: FT Press, 2009).

10. See http://en.wikipedia.org/wiki/Laurence_J._Peter.

11. Many Web sites give the same kind of practical-oriented advice. For example, S. Jones, "How to Make Friends at Work: Ten Super Sensible Ideas," *AssociatedContent*, May 30, 2007, http://www.associatedcontent.com/article/257209/how_to_make_friends_at_work_ten_super; "How to Make Friends," http://www.wikihow.com/Make-Friends.

12. J. Berman and V. Murphy-Brown, "Sex Differences in Friendship Patterns in India and the United States," *Basic and Applied Social Psychology* 9, no. 1 (1998): 61–71.

13. M. Cavell, "Valuing Emotions" (paper presented at the annual meeting of the Rapaport-Klein Study Group, June 11, 2004), http://www.psychomedia.it/rapaport-klein/cavell04.htm.

14. "Friends at Work," June 16, 2005, http://monster.typepad.com/monsterblog/2005/06/friends_at_work.html.

15. See http://www.brainyquote.com/quotes/topics/topic_friendship.html.

16. Useful books are L. Lowndes, *How to Talk to Anyone: 92 Little Tricks for Big Success in Relationships* (New York: McGraw-Hill, 2003); and S. Deep and L. Sussman, *What to Say to Get What You Want: Strong Words for 44 Challenging Types of Bosses, Employees, Coworkers, and Customers* (Reading, MA: Addison-Wesley, 1992). For a broader background on connecting, see M. Knapp and J. Hall, *Nonverbal Communication in Human Interaction*, 6th ed. (Belmont, CA: Thomson Wadsworth, 2006). Often, the matter does go beyond tips and tactics and concerns matters of personality and mental health (discussed in Part 4).

17. Some people reject this, as in the following blog post: "I really believe 'friends at work' is not necessarily appropriate. Friendly at work is better. I am friendly with all my co-workers. I would rather have 10 people who do their job and work as a team than one 'friend' who expects me to cover for them when they make a mistake or don't feel like working. Expecting friends at work is when there is subtle prejudice in hiring, saying a certain kind of person would be a good fit. … I much prefer to work with people who are good at their job. I add that people who are good at their job generally know that

being cordial in the work place adds to productivity"; http://monster. typepad.com/monsterblog/2005/06/friends_at_work.html. We think that both friendly relations with coworkers and a few close friends are beneficial.

18. R. Westonand, "Is It Risky to Work with Friends?" July 10, 2010, http:// www.myglobalcareer.com/2010/07/05/is-it-risky-to-work-with-friends.

CHAPTER 6 NOTES

1. See http://en.wikipedia.org/wiki/Rodney_King.

2. There are many definitions of *conflict* in managerial or organizational settings, many of which go back some years. See, for example, J. Pfeffer, *Power in Organizations* (Marshfield, MA: Pitman, 1981); L. Bolman and T. Deal, *Modern Approaches to Understanding and Managing Organizations* (San Francisco: Jossey-Bass, 1984). See also the general definition in Merriam-Webster: http://www.merriam-webster.com/ dictionary/conflict.

3. S. Greenhouse, "Flex Time Flourishes in Accounting Industry," *New York Times*, January 8, 2011, http://www.nytimes.com/2011/01/08/ business/08perks.html?hp.

4. Centre for Conflict Resolution International, "The Cost of Conflict," http://www.conflictatwork.com/conflict/cost_e.cfm; Mediating Solutions, "Cost of Conflict," http://mediatingsolutions.com/cost_ of_conflict.htm; P. Forte, "The High Cost of Conflict," *Nursing Economics* 15, no. 3 (1997): 119–23, http://findarticles.com/p/articles/ mi_m0FSW/is_n3_v15/ai_n18607389; B. Amble, "Poor Conflict Management Costs Business Billions," *Management Issues*, May 26, 2006, http://www.management-issues.com/2006/8/24/research/ poor-conflict-management-costs-business-billions.asp.

5. As one bumper sticker has it, "He who has the most toys, wins."

6. L. Kubzansky and I. Kawachi, "Going to the Heart of the Matter: Do Negative Emotions Cause Coronary Heart Disease?" *Journal of Psychosomatic Research* 48, nos. 4–5 (2000): 323–37. Also L. Gallo and K. Matthews, "Understanding the Association between Socioeconomic Status and Physical Health: Do Negative Emotions Play a Role?" *Psychological Bulletin* 129, no. 1 (2003): 10–51, http:// www.uic.edu/classes/psych/Health/Readings/Gallo,%20SES,%20 health,%20emotions,%20PsyBull,%202003.pdf.

7. P. Salovey, "Emotional States and Physical Health," *American Psychologist* 55, no. 1 (2000): 110–21. Also L. Temoshok, "Personality, Coping Style, Emotion and Cancer: Towards an Integrative Model," *Cancer Surveys* 6 (1987): 545–67; J. Gross, "Emotional Expression in

Cancer Onset and Progression," *Social Science Medicine* 28 (1989): 1239–48; M. Jensen, "Psychobiological Factors Predicting the Course of Breast Cancer," *Journal of Personality* 55 (1987): 317–42.

8. For practical advice on firing people, from a management perspective, see S. Liff, *The Complete Guide to Hiring and Firing Government Employees* (New York: AMACOM, 2010).

9. Being able to show that one has done so is also relevant to any subsequent employment or disciplinary action. Doing so also increases communication, which is often essential to avoiding litigation and spiteful responses. For example, even if someone is fired, the way in which that is done and the way in which a consensual solution is reached make a difference. Being concerned is also important to reducing the risk of later lawsuits. The best-selling book *Blink: The Power of Thinking without Thinking* (New York: Little, Brown, 2005) by Malcolm Gladwell notes, "Doctors do not get sued for the mistakes they make. Analyses of malpractice lawsuits show that some highly skilled doctors get sued a lot while other doctors who make many mistakes are never sued. The overwhelming number of people who suffer an injury due to the negligence of a doctor do not seem to file a malpractice suit at all. In other words, patients don't file lawsuits because they've been harmed by shoddy medical care. They do so because they perceive they've been treated, badly on a personal level, by their doctor. Patients file suits often because they are rushed or ignored or treated poorly."

10. The foundational book is R. Fisher and W. Ury, *Getting to Yes: Negotiating Agreement without Giving In* (New York: Penguin Books, 1983). Despite the date, it remains relevant. It is the basis of that which is now on many Web sites such as E. Brahm, "Conflict Stages," BeyondIntractability. org, September 2003, http://www.beyondintractability.org/essay/conflict_stages; Newberger, "The Escalating Stages of Church Conflict," Hartford Institute for Religion Research, http://www.resolvechurchconflict.com/the_stages_of_unresolved_church_conflict.htm; A. Kjerulf, "5 Essential Steps to Resolve Conflict at Work," *Chief Happiness Officer*, 2006, http://positivesharing.com/2006/07/5-essential-steps-to-resolve-a-conflict-at-work.

11. These tactics may also be useful in interoffice conflict. It is not uncommon for two or more departments to be at odds with each other. Memos are written attacking the position of the other, and favors are sought of those who can provide leverage. In these situations, having other departments, sometimes higher departments, establish some boundaries on the attacks is useful, as is ensuring that they collaborate in other ways.

12. As an example of this, when Sarah cries in the face of criticism, her character reflects a lack of fortitude rather than inexperience that is overcome in time. An inexact variation is "We judge ourselves by our intentions and others by their impact."

13. A Dutch expression states, "Soft doctors create stinking wounds."

14. A variety of Web sites provides information on devious political tactics in organizations, such as Chaco Canyon Consulting, http://www.chacocanyon.com/cgi-bin/search.pl?Range=All&Format=Standard &Terms=devious+political+tactics&　FormVersion=%5BPage%5D+ SearchForm+05%2F05%2F2007+09%3A04%3A54&Submit=Go.

15. These tactics should be distinguished from teasing or giving someone a tough time as a rite of passage. There is something to be said for taking a small amount of teasing in stride; it shows others one's ability to put up with difficult circumstances and stay out of fights, while being graceful or playful about it and also taking the opportunity to set limits as to what one is willing to endure ("OK, but now it is enough."). Teasing of new employees is an outdated ritual of an older generation that still exists. But the text is not about "breaking someone in" but about "kicking someone out." It is a game that is played at a different level; it aims to destroy.

16. Quoted in: Guy Spier, My $650,100 Lunch with Warren Buffet, Time, June 30, 2008. http://www.time.com/time/business/article/ 0,8599,1819293,00.html

CHAPTER 7 NOTES

1. See, for example, http://en.wikipedia.org/wiki/Lisa_Nowak.

2. National Institute of Mental Health, "The Numbers Count: Mental Disorders in America," 2008, http://wwwapps.nimh.nih.gov/health/ publications/the-numbers-count-mental-disorders-in-america. shtml; National Institute of Mental Health, "National Survey Tracks Prevalence of Personality Disorders in U.S. Population," *Science Upd ate*, October 18, 2007, http://www.nimh.nih.gov/science-news/2007/ national-survey-tracks-prevalence-of-personality-disorders-in-us-population.shtml.

3. NIMH, "The Numbers Count"; NIMH, "National Survey Tracks Prevalence of Personality Disorders in U.S. Population."

4. U.S. Department of Health and Human Services, "Workplace Substance Abuse Statistics," n.d., http://www.drugfreeworkplace.gov/ WPWorkit/pdf/workplace_substance_abuse_statistics_fs.pdf.

5. This is the 25-50-25 rule reported in E. Berman, *Performance and Productivity for Public and Nonprofit Organizations*, 2nd ed. (New York: M. E. Sharpe, 2006, p. 48). Berman said, "The 25-50-25 rule states that when a new idea is suggested, about 25% of the manager's audience will embrace it (with varying degrees of enthusiasm), 25% of the manager's audience will reject it (with varying degrees of enthusiasm), and 50% will be indifferent; they may come to support it in time, if and when it works out and becomes a fait accompli. They are 'fence sitters.' The 25-50-25 rule has not been rigorously validated by scientific research, but many managers feel that it more or less accurately represents their experience when they propose any new idea."

6. E. Berman and J. West, "What Is Managerial Mediocrity? Definition, Prevalence and Negative Impact (Part 1)," *Public Performance and Management Review* 27, no. 2 (2003): 7–27.

7. For example, L. Miller, *From Difficult to Disturbed* (New York: AMACOM, 2008); R. Yandrick, *Behavioral Risk Management* (San Francisco: Jossey-Bass, 1996). Some books focus only on drug and alcohol addiction at work: J. Fearing, *Workplace Intervention* (Center City, MN: Hazeldon, 2000). In recent years, the risk management literature has focused more on matters of terrorism, but many books still note this aspect too; for example, J. Turner, J. Mccann, and M. Gelles, *Threat Assessment: A Risk Management Approach* (London: Routledge, 2003).

8. P. Tetlock, "Accountability and the Perseverance of First Impressions," *Social Psychology Quarterly* 46, no. 4 (1983): 285–92; M. Rabin and J. Schrag, "First Impressions Matter: A Model of Confirmatory Bias," *Quarterly Journal of Economics* 114, no. 1 (1999): 37–82.

9. Selection is one the poorest skills in all of human resource management, and many people feel that hiring is akin to flipping a coin with a 50 percent chance.

10. G. de Becker, *The Gift of Fear and Other Survival Signals that Protect Us from Violence* (Beverly Hills, CA: Phoenix Books, 1997).

11. M. Gladwell, *Blink: The Power of Thinking without Thinking* (New York: Little, Brown, 2005).

12. P. Ekman, *Telling Lies* (New York: W. W. Norton, 1985). See also http://www.paulekman.com/.

13. R. Bolton and D. Bolton, *People Styles at Work* (New York: AMACOM, 1996).

14. Ibid.

CHAPTER 8 NOTES

1. D. Rey, *1001 Ways to get promoted* (Pompton Plains, NJ: Career Press, 2000), www.scribd.com/doc/41796636/1-001-Ways-to-Get-promoted.

2. For a broader perspective on career development, see J. Greenhaus, G. Callanan, and V. Godshalk, *Career Management*, 4th ed. (Thousand Oaks, CA: Sage, 2010); D. Brown, *Career Choice and Development* (San Francisco: Jossey-Bass, 2002); J. Draper and J. O'Brien, *Induction: Fostering Career Development at All Stages* (Edinburgh: Dunedin Academic Press, 2006); M. London, *Career Barriers: How People Experience, Overcome, and Avoid Failure* (Mahwah, NJ: Lawrence Erlbaum, 1998); S. G. Niles and J. Harris-Bowlsbey, *Career Development Interventions in the 21st Century* (Englewood Cliffs, NJ: Prentice Hall, 2008); J. Swanson and N. Fouad, *Career Theory and Practice: Learning through Case Studies* (Thousand Oaks, CA: Sage, 2009).

3. U.S. Bureau of Labor Statistics, *Number of Jobs Held, Labor Market Activity, and Earnings Growth among the Youngest Baby Boomers: Results from a Longitudinal Survey* (Washington, DC: U.S. Bureau of Labor Statistics, 2010), news release, September 10, 2010, http://www.bls.gov/news.release/pdf/nlsoy.pdf and http://www.bls.gov/nls/nlsfaqs.htm#anch41.

4. This estimate is based on the estimated decline in number of jobs as people get older. Younger workers, ages eighteen to twenty-two have 4.4 jobs, whereas workers ages thirty-nine to forty-four have had 2 jobs. Our assumption of about 5 jobs for those between ages forty-four and sixty-five is a conservative one.

5. S. Polachek and W. Robert, *The Economics of Earnings* (London: Cambridge University Press, 1993).

6. A recent survey in Australia of undergraduates shows that they expect to work for five employers in their lifetime; that is likely a great underestimate. Gradient, "Gen Y 'Hopelessly Devoted' to Employers," November 26, 2008, www.daemongroup.com/pagesys/docview.aspx?documentid=168.

7. Estimates are very rough. According to one study, 26 percent of the U.S. population thinks of themselves as chronic procrastinators. P. Steel, "The Nature of Procrastination: A Meta-Analytic and Theoretical Review of Quintessential Self-Regulatory Failure," *Psychological Bulletin* 133, no. 1 (2007): 65–94. Procrastination is increasing in the general population and also sharply higher among college students, but procrastination is not a mental health condition,

so statistics are not authoritative. Three types of procrastinators are those who wait to the last minute for the euphoric rush they get, those who don't act because of fear of either success or failure, and people who cannot make decisions. Various self-help books are available, such as J. Ferrari, *Still Procrastinating: The No Regrets Guide to Getting It Done* (New York: Wiley, 2010); M. E. Bernard, *Procrastinate Later* (Melbourne: Schwartz & Wilkinson, 1991). However, many procrastination behaviors are also symptoms of mental health problems mentioned in Part 4 of this book for which self-help may not work.

8. M. Gladwell, *Outliers: The Story of Success* (New York: Little, Brown, 2008), Chapter 2. The point about passion and choosing something you like is also made in L. Boldt, *How to Find the Work You Love* (New York: Penguin Group, 1996).

9. G. Colvin, *Talent Is Overrated: What Really Separates World-Class Performers from Everybody Else* (New York: Portfolio Trade, 2010).

10. For example, K. Inkson, *Understanding Careers: The Metaphors of Working Lives* (Thousand Oaks, CA: Sage, 2006), Chapter 8. In broader context, see also N. Christakis and J. Fowler, *Connected: The Amazing Power of Social Networks and How They Shape Our Lives* (London: Harper Press, 2009).

11. While a full discussion of identity is beyond the scope of this book, two points can be made. First, identity is dynamic and changes over time. As Shakespeare famously states, "All the world's a stage, and all the men and women merely players: They have their exits and their entrances; And one man in his time plays many parts." Holding on to one's "identity" in the face of change leads to suffering (Chapter 16). Second, identity requires balance and alignment between who we are (see Chapter 14) and want to do, and what is expected or required of us. Too much emphasis on the latter (i.e. living someone else's script) is associated with significant psychological stress and generalized dissatisfaction -- it is easy to feel inadequate for not living up to someone's or society's expectations. It is also a tough job trying to do so which can lead to extreme restlessness, anxiety or depression (Chapter 17).

Yet, while these problems are increasingly recognized, a focus on adopting occupational identities is still persists. We ask people what they *are*, such as being a dentist, manager, etc, rather than what they do, contribute to, or enjoy doing. Young people sometimes voluntarily organizational identities or self-script their self-image, but few people have adequate self-knowledge to fully foresee what identity is good for them. But people have ideas about their role in society, and so developing a notion of identity is unavoidable. Then, it may suffice to simply define one's identity as "*being a person who can make and enjoy fulfilling commitments.*" Such a construct does not narrow oneself, has little additional baggage for causing stress, is consistent with a positive self-image, and is readily adapted to specific contexts.

To further illustrate the danger of taking identity too seriously, an early draft added "*being a person who can make and enjoy fulfilling commitments in ethical and professional ways*," but even that seems too much. What is the use of defining oneself too strongly as an ethical and professional person when everyone is apt to have a lapse of judgment? What is the benefit of adopting a negative self-image when the inevitable finally happens? Consistent with Chapter 6, the focus should be on correcting the activity, rather than on blaming the person. Is someone a bad person for having done something wrong? Usually not (though there are cases of psychopathy. See Chapter 18, and Hollis, J. 2007. *Why Good People Do Bad Things*. New York: Gotham.) In short, we do well to tread lightly in the matter of identity, which is this book's stance. It might also be noted that peoples' ideas about their role in society causing notions of identity is an example of dependent arising, discussed in Chapter 16.

12. L. Petak, "Young Lawyers Turn to Public Service," *New York Times*, August 19, 2010.

13. This is often in the eye of the beholder. For professors in public administration, teaching quantitative methods and finance is appropriate, but for those in business schools, those subjects would be thought to be taught by professors in different departments, with different specializations.

14. For example, J. Perry, "Measuring Public Service Motivation: An Assessment of Construct Reliability and Validity," *Journal of Public Administration Research and Theory* 6, no. 1 (1996): 5–22; D. Moynihan and S. Pandey, "The Role of Organizations in Fostering Public Service Motivation," *Public Administration Review* 67, no. 1 (2007): 40–53.

15. For example, some direct market or future market speculation. However, people in financial services do well only when their services are demanded. Only few money-orientated activities make a lot of money.

16. Generally, studies of working in jobs with predominantly technical skills (e.g., budgeting, information technology, evaluation), working for quasi-government agencies, and being a manager rather than a senior employee are each associated with a $10,000 to $12,000 annual salary increase; "Compensation for Graduate Degrees in Public Affairs and Administration," in E. Berman, J. Bowman, J. West, and M. Van Wart, *Human Resource Management in Public Service* (Thousand Oaks, CA: Sage, 2010), 228–30. While there are some very well-paying private sector jobs (especially in high-growth sectors

that offer bonuses), generally people find that pay differences are offset by sharply reduced job security and reduced working conditions (longer hours, more off-site travel). People do well to examine these matters for their specific situation. To learn more about salaries in public administration, visit http://www.naspaa.org/students/careers/salary.asp. For a more thorough look at salaries in public and nonprofit organizations, see http://www.bls.gov/oes/current/oessrci.htm (for government, scroll down and select sector 92; for nonprofits, select NAICS 712100, museums, or NAICS 813300 and then the subgroup "community and social services"). For an interesting look at public sector careers, see http://www.naspaa.org/students/careers/careers.asp and especially the profiles of alumni. There is also a link to job resources. For information on federal jobs, see also http://www.calltoserve.org. This site has information about federal jobs and how to find them, as well as links to sites with jobs. Also, the federal government has a program designed to attract top MPA graduates into federal service. This two-year program, through which MPA graduates are rotated through management assignments at different agencies, is called the Presidential Management Fellows program (previously called the Presidential Management Intern program). To learn more about this program, visit http://www.pmi.opm.gov/. Some people go for MBA or law degrees in the hopes of high fortunes, but the market is well saturated too. For a cautious take, see D. Segal, "Is Law School a Losing Game?" *New York Times*, January 8, 2011, http://www.nytimes.com/2011/01/09/business/09law.html?src=me&ref=general.

CHAPTER 9 NOTES

1. The Internet has many examples of good-looking résumés. See also M. Yate, *Resumes That Knock 'em Dead* (Holbrook, MA: Adams Media, 2006).
2. Jack Handy quote, http://en.thinkexist.com/search/searchquotation.asp?search=job+interview.
3. There are many books on job interviews, such as P. Falcone, *96 Great Interview Questions to Ask Before You Hire*, 2nd ed. (New York: AMACOM, 2009); V. Oliver, *301 Smart Answers to Tough Interview Questions* (Naperville, IL: Sourcebooks, 2005). Our approach is a bit different, focusing on the PCS, which we find works excellently.
4. Personal communication to author.
5. Also, any people who already know you at the organization also know you wear earrings, and yet they still invited you for the interview. However, they will surely appreciate your taking the earring out to

make their job easier of selling you to others who do not know you. Why make their job of helping you more difficult?

6. See also "Hiring Managers Reveal Top Five Biggest Mistakes Candidates Make During Job Interviews in CareerBuilder.com Survey," http://findarticles.com/p/articles/mi_pwwi/is_20050229/ai_mark3882102963/.

7. These problems are sometimes also mentioned for candidates whom we do not want to hire but are overlooked for those we do want to hire.

8. Of course, there are many job search books. See R. Bolles, *What Color Is Your Parachute?* (New York: Random House, 2010); M. Yate, *Knock 'em Dead 2009: The Ultimate Job Search Guide* (Holbrook, MA: Adams Media, 2008).

9. For example, P. Barada, "Five Reference-Checking Mistakes," *Monster. com*, http://hiring.monster.com/hr/hr-best-practices/recruiting-hiring-advice/job-screening-techniques/Reference-Checking-Mistakes.aspx.

10. A. Bryant, "Meetings, Version 2.0, at Microsoft," *New York Times*, May 16, 2009, http://www.nytimes.com/2009/05/17/business/17corner.html.

11. He adds, "And I try to figure out sort of a combination of I.Q. and passion. I just ask somebody to tell me what they've done that they are really proud of and tell me about it. And if it's something you are proud of, you should be able to answer any question I can come up with, at least at a level that would satisfy my interest. I ought to be able to see your passion. It might be quiet passion; it might be bubbly passion. But I should be able to sense that you are one of those people who just sort of throws themselves into things."

12. A. Doyle, "Reference Check Questions," *About.com*, http://jobsearch.about.com/od/referencesrecommendations/a/refercheck.htm (accessed January 25, 2011).

13. Employers may call reference checks before bringing candidates in for an interview. While doing so takes time, bringing in candidates who are not appropriate also takes time. They then also follow up with references after the interview to address issues or questions that may have surfaced. Interviewees may also be asked for additional references during the interview.

14. R. McFadden, "Army Doctor Held in Ft. Hood Rampage," *New York Times*, November 6, 2009; J. McKinley and J. Dao, "Fort Hood Gunman Gave Signals Before His Rampage," *New York Times*, November 9, 2009; E. Buhmiller and S. Shane, "Pentagon Report on Fort Hood Details Failures," *New York Times*, January 16, 2010.

15. A second particularly challenging example of assessing performance and detecting exaggerations is the case of Bernard Madoff,

stockbroker, who was convicted in 2009 of operating the largest Ponzi scheme in history of about $65 billion but causing losses to investors of about $11 billion. Madoff falsified books and records to show his returns to investors, which included prominent and well-educated leaders, including famous people such as Steven Spielberg. Madoff had many fine degrees, titles, and connections. He was a prominent Jewish philanthropist who served on boards of nonprofit institutions, many of which entrusted his firm with their endowments. He also served as chairman of the board of directors of the Sy Syms School of Business at Yeshiva University. He had longstanding, high-level ties to the Securities Industry and Financial Markets Association (SIFMA), the primary securities industry organization. He had excellent social skills and quickly made people at ease. He provided investors with above average returns. It is unclear how people, who did not work in the financial securities industry, could have detected the sophisticated fraud.

16. This often causes people to ask how this is possible. Well, the call starts with this: "I am of the XYZ University and a student in the public administration program. As part of my class, I am exploring careers in XYZ field. I expect to graduate in about X months (or one year). Do you have ten to fifteen minutes to talk with me?" Students say they have a 95 percent success rate in lining up interviews and that most people spend about twenty to forty minutes with them, using the questions in the text.

CHAPTER 10 NOTES

1. See http://leadership.uoregon.edu/resources/quotes.
2. See E. Berman and J. West, "Psychological Contracts in Local Government: A Preliminary Survey," *Review of Public Personnel Administration* 23, no. 4 (2003): 267–85.
3. In another example, an HRM class listed the following responses to the statement "What I want to get out of this class": (1) applications of HRM theory, (2) share and contribute situations that work, (3) learn about HR as a discipline, (4) how to deal with organizational change and resistance, (5) how to motivate people, (6) how to diplomatically reprimand and discipline personnel, (7) how salaries and wages are determined, (8) interviewing techniques and confidence building, (9) understanding HR laws, (10) realistic assessment of careers and recruiting strategies, (11) money worth, and (12) opportunity to earn an A grade. The responses to the statement "What I expect to

give" are as follows: (1) time, (2) honest and constructive criticism, (3) advanced preparation, (4) participation, (5) do everything possible to get an A grade, (6) sacrifice other aspects of one's life, (7) attentiveness, and (8) time to other students.

4. G. Odiorne, "MBO in State Government," *Public Administration Review* 36, no. 1 (1976): 28–33. Reprinted in R. Kearney and E. Berman, eds., *Public Sector Performance: Management, Motivation and Measurement*, ASPA Classics Series (Boulder, CO: Westview, 1999).

5. E. Berman, *Performance and Productivity for Public and Nonprofit Organizations*, 2nd ed. (New York: M. E. Sharpe, 2006), 133. Also see Berman and West, "Psychological Contracts in Local Government."

6. We also give the psychological contract as an assignment to students. Those who work are expected to make one with their boss, subordinates, or coworkers. Those who do report significant improvement in relations and expectations. Those who do not work are allowed to make one with their roommate or study mate. These too are shown to be productive. A few mature students choose to make it with their teenage children, and they report significant progress in getting them, for example, to clean up their room!

7. Survey by author, Berman, E., D-Y. Chen, C-Y Jan and T-Y Huang. (*forthcoming*). "Public Agency Leadership: The Impact of Informal Understandings with Political Appointees On Perceived Agency Innovation in Taiwan." *Public Administration.*

8. We do not focus on career development efforts, but we do suggest the following for readers interested in that: W. B. Walsh and M. Savickas, *Handbook of Vocational Psychology: Theory, Research, and Practice*, 3rd ed. (Mahwah, NJ: Lawrence Erlbaum, 2005).

9. B. Wall, *Working Relationships: The Simple Truth about Getting Along with Friends and Foes at Work* (Palo Alto, CA: Davies-Black, 1999), 35.

CHAPTER 11 NOTES

1. See http://en.thinkexist.com/quotation/a_man_without_ethics_is_a_wild_beast_loosed_upon/221809.html.

2. For example, D. Menzel, *Ethics Moments in Government* (New York: Taylor & Francis, 2010).

2a. See Chapter 9, note 15.

3. See http://en.thinkexist.com/quotation/the_first_step_in_the_evolution_of_ethics_is_a/146835.html.

4. Menzel, *Ethics Moments in Government*. See also J. Hyatt, "Unethical Behavior: Largely Unreported in Offices and Justified by Teens," *Corporate Responsibility Magazine*, 2008, http://www.thecro.com/node/612 (accessed January 25, 2011).

5. J. Bowman, J. West, E. Berman, and M. Van Wart, *The Professional Edge: Competencies for Public Service* (New York: M. E. Sharpe, 2004), 60–86.

6. T. Schwartz, "Dope, Dopes, and Dopamine: The Problem with Money," *Harvard Business Review*, October 26, 2010, http://blogs.hbr.org/schwartz/2010/10/dopes-and-dopamine-the-problem.html (accessed January 25, 2011).

7. P. Northouse, *Leadership Ethics* (Thousand Oaks, CA: Sage, 2004).

8. J. Dobel, "Political Prudence and the Ethics of Leadership," *Public Administration Review* 58, no. 1 (1998): 74–81.

CHAPTER 12 NOTES

1. See http://en.thinkexist.com/quotation/he-had-a-knack-for-getting-things-out-of-people/1335519.html.

2. By L. Gullick and L. Urwick, *Papers on the Science of Administration* (New York: Institute of Public Administration, 1937). See http://en.wikipedia.org/wiki/POSDCORB.

3. The need for increased leadership is increasingly noted. See also J. Raffel, "What We Have Learned from the NASPAA Standards Review Process," *Journal of Public Affairs Education* 16, no. 1 (2009): 5–12, http://www.naspaa.org/JPAEMessenger/Article/jpae-v16n1/raffel.pdf.

4. Some people from hierarchical and authoritarian cultures may be more willing to interpret orders in a positive ways, for example, as someone who has likely cleared matters with superiors and is implementing a plan that will lead to success. That set of assumptions is often unlikely in the West, with exception of military and paramilitary organizations.

5. See http://leadership.uoregon.edu/resources/quotes.

6. See http://en.thinkexist.com/quotation/true-leadership-lies-in-guiding-others-to-success/369839.html.

7. See http://leadership.uoregon.edu/resources/quotes.

8. See http://en.thinkexist.com/quotes/David_Cooper.

9. See http://leadership.uoregon.edu/resources/quotes.

10. See http://www.scribd.com/doc/233002/1001-Ways-to-Get-Promoted-David-E-Rye.

11. See "Making Yourself Dispensable," June 24, 2010, http://suburbdad. blogspot.com/search?q=Making+Yourself+Dispensable.

12. It might be noted that the literature is full of styles that are seen as very problematic, which contrasts with what is described here. We are saying that what is in the text is not always reality but rather an approach to leading that is helpful at work. A simplified version is in G. Gaynor, *What Every New Manager Needs to Know* (New York: AMACOM, 2004), 147–48. There are autocrats with varying degrees of capricious action and disregard for the professional development of their members. There are also wishy-washy folks and airheads or "cheerleaders" who lack direction, backbone, and professional judgment. There are also power brokers: "I've seen administrators try to make themselves indispensable by hoarding information or by constructing elaborate networks of side deals in which they fancy themselves key nodes. It never ends well. Moving people around like chess pieces creates an illusion of control, but then the chess pieces start moving on their own and the entire scheme crashes. Worse, someone eventually catches wind of some little side deal you were hoping to keep quiet, takes offense, calls in a third party, and makes your life hell. Not worth it." From http://suburbdad.blogspot.com/.

13. A useful book is E. Becker and J. Wortman, *Mastering Communication at Work* (New York: McGraw-Hill, 2009).

14. A key rub against authoritarian leadership is that it is thoughtless and arrogant in these ways.

15. See http://leadership.uoregon.edu/resources/quotes.

16. E. Berman, *Performance and Productivity for Public and Nonprofit Organizations*, 2nd ed. (New York: M. E. Sharpe, 2006), 55.

17. Ibid., 48.

CHAPTER 13 NOTES

1. See http://en.thinkexist.com/quotation/mentor-someone_whose_ hindsight_can_become_your/192457.html.

2. D. Jones, "Often, Men Help Women Get to the Corner Office," *USA Today*, August 5, 2009, http://www.usatoday.com/money/companies/ management/2009-08-04-female-executives-male-mentors_N.htm.

3. K. Ivie, "Millennials and Mentoring: Making It Work," *Social Citizens*, August 17, 2010, http://www.socialcitizens.org/blog/millennials-and- mentoring-making-it-work (accessed January 25, 2011).

4. J. Greenhaus, G. Callanan, and V. Godshalk, *Career Management*, 4th ed. (Thousand Oaks, CA: Sage, 2010).

5. B. Bozeman and M. Feeney, "Public Management Mentoring: What Affects Outcomes?" *Journal of Public Administration Research and Theory* 19, no. 2 (2009): 427–52.

6. For example, E. Schein, *Career Anchors* (San Francisco: Pfeiffer, 1979).

7. R. Davis Jr. and P. Garrison, "Mentoring: In Search of a Typology" (master's thesis, MIT Sloan, 1979).

8. Greenhaus, Callanan, and Godshalk, *Career Management*, 212.

9. M. Lankau and T. Scandura, "An Investigation of Personal Learning in Mentoring Relationships: Content, Antecedents, and Consequences," *Academy of Management Journal* 45, no. 4 (2002): 779–90. See also M. Higgins and K. Kram, "Reconceptualizing Mentoring at Work: A Developmental Network Perspective," *The Academy of Management Review* 26, no. 1 (2001): 264–88.

10. D. Clutterback and D. Megginson, *Making Coaching Work* (London: Chartered Institute for Personnel and Development, 2005), 7.

11. J. Hunt and J. Weintraub, *The Coaching Manager*, 2nd ed. (Thousand Oaks, CA: Sage, 2011), 12.

12. M. Kraft, "Mentoring in Knowledge Work," August 23, 2010, http://www.bpmnforum.net/blog27/bpm/mentoring-in-knowledge-work (accessed January 25, 2011).

13. For example, S. Tonidandel, D. Avery, and M. Phillips, "Maximizing Returns on Mentoring: Factors Affecting Subsequent Protégé Performance," *Journal of Organizational Behavior* 28, no. 1 (2007): 89–110.

14. S. Payne, "Longitudinal Examination of the Influence of Mentoring on Organizational Commitment and Turnover," *Academy of Management Journal* 48, no. 1 (2005): 158–68.

15. Ivie, "Millennials and Mentoring." See also D. Clutterbuck, *Everyone Needs a Mentor: Fostering Talent in Your Organisation*, 4th ed. (London: Chartered Institute of Personnel and Development, 2004); L. A. Daloz, *Mentor: Guiding the Journey of Adult Learners* (San Francisco: Jossey-Bass, 1999); T. J. Delong, J. Gabarro, and R. Lees, "Why Mentoring Matters in a Hypercompetitive World," *Harvard Business Review* 86, no. 1 (2008): 115–21.

16. For example, B. Raabe and T. Beehr, "Formal Mentoring versus Supervisor and Coworker Relationships: Differences in Perceptions and Impact," *Journal of Organizational Behavior* 24, no. 3 (2003): 271–93.

17. D. Zmorenski, "Developing Your Leadership Skills through Mentoring," August 6, 2010, http://blogs.reliableplant.com/1211/developing-leadership-skills-mentoring/. Reported as an excerpt from a *Wall Street Journal* report in collaboration with *MIT Sloan Management Review*, dated May 24, 2010.

18. For a distinction on coaching and mentoring and a review of coaching, see Chartered Institute for Personnel and Development, "Coaching and Mentoring," June 2010, http://www.cipd.co.uk/subjects/lrnanddev/coachmntor/coaching.htm (accessed January 25, 2011).
19. Adapted from an interview.

CHAPTER 14 NOTES

1. In Dutch: "Je moet roejen met de riemen die je heb."
2. The phrase *passages* is taken from G. Sheehy, *Passages* (New York: Ballantine Books, 1996). This books examines difference life phases rather than work phases.
3. Though the stage model is well accepted and found in most books on career development, all stage models invite academic debate on when stages end and begin, how long each stage is, and whether people can skip a stage or do them in another order. Levinson's model was well debated in the 1980s. Levinson sees stages as "periods in the development of the adult life structure" that are not set in any fixed time, and some people do go through some stages faster or slower; D. Levinson, *The Seasons of a Woman's Life* (New York: Knopf, 1996), 6. One criticism at the time was that the model is devoid of social context; for example, D. Dannefer, "Adult Development and Social Theory: A Paradigmatic Reappraisal," *American Sociological Review* 49, no. 1 (1984): 100–16. Current research on the younger generation may well lead to adjustments of this model going forward.
4. This is sometimes called the "protean career," which is self-directed rather than determined by others, such as the organization. See D. Hall, *Careers in Organizations* (Glenview, IL: Scott Foresman, 1976). As the date of the Hall book indicates, the distinction drew attention of emerging discussion in society about the need for greater individual action, but in practice while people take a decisive hand in deciding what they want to do, it is surely not in isolation of organizations and family, for example. The treatment in the text tries to get that.
5. D. Keirsey, *Please Understand Me II* (Del Mar, CA: Prometheus Nemesis, 1998).
6. J. Arnold, *Managing Careers into the 21st Century* (London: Paul Chapman, 1997). See also Keirsey, *Please Understand Me*, and D. F. Alwin, "Aging, Personality and Change: The Stability of Individual Differences over the Adult Life Span," in *Life-Span Development and Behaviour*, ed. D. L. Featherman, R. M. Learner, and M. Perlmutter, vol. 12 (Hillsdale, NJ: Lawrence Erlbaum, 1994).

7. By one estimate, about 38 percent of people fall into this category (Keirsey, *Please Understand Me*, 39). By contrast, scientists may make up less than 1.5 percent of personality profiles in society.

8. A different but similar instrument can be found in J. Osland, D. Kolb, and I. Rubin, *Organizational Behavior: An Experiential Approach*, 8th ed. (New York: Prentice Hall, 2006), chap. 3.

9. The test is sometimes also referred to as the Jung-based personality test. At the time of writing, the test is free available at http://www.humanmetrics.com/cgi-win/JTypes2.asp. The Keirsey Web site charges a small fee: http://keirsey.com/sorter/instruments2.aspx?partid=0.

10. E. Schein, *Career Anchors*, 3rd ed. (San Francisco: Pfeiffer, 2006).

11. This is a commercial test with a small fee: www.cpp.com.

12. Available at http://online.onetcenter.org/skills.

13. See U.S. Bureau of Labor Statistics, "National Industry-Specific Occupational Employment and Wage Estimates," http://www.bls.gov/oes/current/oessrci.htm.

14. For example, "Big Five Personality Traits," http://en.wikipedia.org/wiki/Big_Five_personality_traits. See also L. R. Goldberg, "An Alternative Description of Personality: The Big-Five Factor Structure," *Journal of Personality and Social Psychology* 59 (1990): 1216–29.

15. See J. Greenhaus, G. Callanan, and V. Godshalk, *Career Management*, 4th ed. (Thousand Oaks, CA: Sage, 2010), 122–23.

16. Those with the problem of indecision described in the text are different from those who have shallow interests or a lack of inquisitiveness. Many people do not have great interests and, hence, inner motivations. They lack inquisitiveness. Anecdotally, some students in business schools seem to fit this profile; for them, the prospect of making money provides clear and ample motivation.

17. G. Hofstede, *Culture's Consequences* (London: Sage, 1980).

18. The opposite of being too assertive is being too shy or too nice. While this will seldom get people in trouble, the lack of initiative and assertiveness spells risk for subsequent career development. People do need to occasionally speak up, take a stand, and show their worth to others, and they usually have a few bad experiences. Worse, bullies and others may run over them or take advantage of them in ways that are unprofessional or unethical. But allowing oneself to be victimized and then playing the victim role may not be enough; people do catch on to a lack of assertiveness and performance. We need to avoid the extreme behaviors of too much and too little assertiveness.

19. P. Trunk, "Positive Psychology Exhausts Me: Requires So Much Self-Discipline," February 12, 2008, http://blog.penelopetrunk.com/2008/02/12/the-big-secret-about-happiness-its-really-about-self-discipline (accessed January 25, 2011).
20. This refers to the Pleasure Principle (Chapter 5) as well as the problem of defense mechanisms, discussed in Chapter 16.
21. D. Goleman, *Emotional Intelligence: Why It Can Matter More than IQ* (New York: Bantam Books, 1995).
22. Ibid.
23. C. Cherniss and D. Goleman, *The Emotionally Intelligent Workplace: How to Select for, Measure, and Improve Emotional Intelligence in Individuals, Groups, and Organizations* (San Francisco: Jossey-Bass, 2001); U. Druskat and S. Wolff, "Building the Emotional Intelligence of Groups," *Harvard Business Review* 79, no. 3 (2001): 80–90; L. Gardenswartz, J. Cherbosque, and A. Rowe, *Emotional Intelligence for Managing Results in a Diverse World* (Mountain View, CA: Davies-Black, 2008).
24. E. Berman and J. West, "Managing Emotional Intelligence in U.S. Cities: A Study of Public Managers," *Public Administration Review* 68, no. 4 (2008): 742–58.
25. For example, http://www.eiconsortium.org/reports/emotional_competence_framework.html or http://www.eiconsortium.org/measures/eqi.html.
26. A variety of online tests exist, but most charge a small fee, such as http://testyourself.psychtests.com/testid/2092.
27. For example, A. Lynn, *The EQ Interview: Finding Employees with High Emotional Intelligence* (New York: AMACOM, 2008). See also B. Wall, *Working Relationships: Using Emotional Intelligence to Enhance Your Effectiveness with Others* (Mountain View, CA: Davies-Black, 2008).
28. The religious expression is "Everyone has a cross to bear."

CHAPTER 15 NOTES

1. For example, B. Harrington and D. Hall, *Career Management and Work-Life Integration* (Thousand Oaks, CA: Sage, 2007), chap. 6; D. S. Burden and B. Googins, *Balancing Job and Homelife Study: Managing Work and Family Stress in Corporations* (Boston: Boston University Center on Work and Family, 1987); R. Rapport, L. Bailyn, J. Fletcher, and B. Pruitt, *Beyond Work-Family Balance: Advancing Gender Equity and Workplace Performance* (San Francisco: Jossey-Bass, 2001).

2. Mental Health America, "Americans Reveal Top Stressors, How They Cope," 2006, http://www.nmha.org/index.cfm?objectid= ABD3DC4E-1372-4D20-C8274399C9476E26.

3. L.-S. Hwai, "Taiwan's Fertility Rate at Record Low," *Asian News Network*, August 18, 2010, http://www.asianewsnet.net/home/news. php?id=13705 (accessed January 25, 2011). The U.S. fertility rate is just at the replenishment level of 2.1; R. Rubin, "CDC: U.S. Birth Rate Falls, but Not among Moms 40 and Up," *USA Today*, April 6, 2010, http://www.usatoday.com/news/health/2010-04-06-birth-rate_N. htm.

4. B. Seward, *Managing Stress* (Sudbury, MA: Jones-Bartlett, 2006). For an overview of stress theory, see M. O'Driscoll and C. Cooper, "Job-Related Stress and Burnout," in *Psychology at Work*, 5th ed., ed. P. Warr (London: Penguin Books, 2002), 203–30.

5. T. Holmes and R. Rahe, "Social Adjustment Rating Scale," *Journal of Psychosomatic Research* 11, no. 2 (1967): 213–21.

6. Gallup, "Attitudes in the American Workplace VI," American Institute of Stress, 2000, http://www.stress.org/job.htm (accessed January 25, 2011). Also, according to a U.K. survey, the top five reasons for job stress are workload (50 percent); feeling undervalued or a lack of job satisfaction (35 percent); not enough hours in the day (34 percent); frustration with environment, culture, and polices (30 percent); and lack of control over the day (23 percent). Skillsoft, *Research into UK Workers Stress Levels* (Camberley, UK: Compass House, 2008), http:// www.skillsoft.com/infocenter/whitepapers/documents/research-into-uk-workers-stress-levels.pdf.

7. F. Landy, *The Psychology of Work Behavior* (Belmont, CA: Wadsworth, 1989), chap. 14.

8. Numerous texts exist on the distinction between Type A and Type B personalities. See Wikipedia, http://en.wikipedia.org/wiki/Type_A_and_Type_B_personality_theory.

9. See also R. Washer, "Job and Workplace Stress," December 19, 2010, http://doctorwascher.blogspot.com/2010/12/job-and-workplace-stress.html.

10. Mayo Clinic, "Exercise: 7 Benefits of Regular Physical Activity," December 21, 2010, http://www.mayoclinic.com/health/exercise/ HQ01676. See also http://en.wikipedia.org/wiki/Physical_exercise.

11. Sometimes organizations even help employees in this matter by offering job "series" (e.g., engineer or accountant I, II, and III) and personnel appraisal discussions so people are able to envision a path toward higher achievements.

12. J. Hollis, *Finding Meaning in the Second Half of Life* (New York: Gotham Books, 2005), 86.

13. As one example, a fifty-seven-year accountant with Boeing was let go and unable to find a new job. "As an auditor, Ms. Reid loved figuring out the kinks in a manufacturing or parts delivery process. But after more than 20 years of commuting across Puget Sound to Boeing, Ms. Reid was exhausted when she was let go from her $80,000-a-year job." Since then she has sent out hundreds of résumés and taken classes to retool to help provide general personal income tax return services. M. Rich, "For the Unemployed over 50, Fears of Never Working Again," *New York Times*, September 19, 2010.
14. Bill Werther, personal communication.

CHAPTER 16 NOTES

1. See http://www.wisdomquotes.com/topics/connections/index2.html.
2. As concerning flow, see M. Csikszentmihalyim, *Flow: The Psychology of Optimal Experience* (New York: Harper and Row, 1990).
3. P. Warr, *Work, Happiness and Unhappiness* (New York: Lawrence Erlbaum, 2007).
4. P. Howard, *The Brain (An Owner's Manual)* (Austin, TX: Bard Press, 2006), 813. For a general discussion of well-being, see T. Rath and J. Harter, *Wellbeing: The Five Essential Elements* (New York: Gallup Press, 2010). They examine five factors affecting well-being: career, social, financial, physical, and community. Of these, two are directly linked to work.
5. For example, D. Rock, *Your Brain at Work* (New York: Harper Business Press, 2009), 108.
6. D. Lykken and A. Tellegen, "Happiness Is a Stochastic Phenomenon," *Psychological Science* 7, no. 3 (1996): 186–89, http://www.psych.umn.edu/psylabs/happness/happy.htm; S. Lyubomirsky, D. Schkade, and K. Sheldon, "Pursuing Happiness: The Architecture of Sustainable Change," *Review of General Psychology* 9, no. 2 (2005): 111–31.
7. See http://www.indianchild.com/Quotes/happy_quotes.htm.
8. J. McManamy, "Lincoln and His Depressions," *McMan's Depression and Bipolar Web*, November 10, 2005, http://www.mcmanweb.com/lincoln_depression.html (accessed January 25, 2011).
9. For example, F. Murphy, I. Nimmo-Smith, and A. D. Lawrence, "Functional Neuroanatomy of Emotions: A Meta-analysis," *Cognitive, Affective, and Behavioral Neuroscience* 3, no. 3 (2003): 207–33; N. L. Sin and S. Lyubomirsky, "Enhancing Well-being and Alleviating Depressive Symptoms with Positive Psychology Interventions: A Practice-Friendly Meta-analysis," *Journal of Clinical Psychology* 65 (2009): 467–87; P. Ekamn, W. Friessen, and D. Davidson, "The

Duchenne Smile: Emotional Expression and Brain Physiology II," *Journal of Personality and Social Psychology* 58, no. 2 (1990): 342–53.

10. M. Seligman, *Authentic Happiness* (New York: Free Press, 2004). Also http://www.happylifeu.com/Elements_of_Happiness.html. Sometimes people go for shortcuts and simplifications. An example is "the cure for unhappiness is happiness." Happiness can alleviate some suffering temporarily, but a mind that is given to producing a lot of suffering will not be alleviated by more happiness alone. People need to know how to both create happiness and reduce unhappiness.

11. Warr, *Work, Happiness and Unhappiness*, 82.

12. People get positive feelings when things occur as they anticipate.

13. These are well known and stated by Maslow as meeting physiological needs, safety, belonging (including love and friendship), self-esteem (including confidence, achievement, respect from others), and self-actualization (including creativity, spontaneity, problem solving). A. Maslow, *Towards a Psychology of Being* (New York: Wiley, 1998).

14. D. Kahneman and A. Deaton, "High Income Improves Evaluation of Life but Not Emotional Well-Being," *Proceedings of the National Academy of Sciences* 107, no. 38 (2010): 16489–93, http://www.pnas.org/content/107/38/16489.full.

15. D. Baker, *What Happy People Know* (New York: St. Martin's Press, 2003), 37. Also S. Lyubomirsky, *The How of Happiness* (New York: Penguin Press, 2007); M. Seligman, *What You Can Change and What You Can't: The Complete Guide to Successful Self-Improvement* (New York: Ballantine Books, 1993).

16. R. Friedman, "When Self-Knowledge Is Only the Beginning," *New York Times*, January 17, 2011, http://www.nytimes.com/2011/01/18/health/views/18mind.html?_r=2&src=me&ref=homepage.

17. V. Frankl, *Man's Search for Meaning* (1946; repr. Boston: Beacon Press, 2006). From this book, two quotes: "In Nietzsche's words, 'He who has a why to live can bear with almost any how.' " "We can discover this meaning in life in three different ways: (1) by creating a work or doing a deed; (2) by experiencing something or encountering someone; and (3) by the attitude we take toward unavoidable suffering." Well, work is always number 1 and may include numbers two and three too. Of course, most people's experiences at work are nowhere near those of Frankl's Nazi concentration camp on which these quotes are based. Also, "When we are no longer able to change a situation—just think of an incurable disease such as inoperable cancer—we are challenged to change ourselves."

18. A. Pattakos, *Prisoners of Our Thoughts* (San Francisco: Berrett-Koehler, 2008), 1.

19. This is a generally true statement, but if one's "happiness set point" is low (such as due to depression), then one might not experience such an effect. This statement is also consistent with cognitive psychology and other schools of psychology.

20. See C. R. Colvin and J. Block, "Do Positive Illusions Foster Mental Health? An Examination of the Taylor and Brown Formulation," *Psychological Bulletin* 116, no. 1 (1994): 3–20. This takes issue with the illusion thesis described in S. Taylor and J. Brown, "Illusion and Well-Being: A Social Psychological Perspective on Mental Health," *Psychological Bulletin* 103 (1988): 193–210.

21. For example, traditional routines of blaming others or circumstances, operating on the basis of fear, thinking in terms of rights and entitlement, feeling better by demeaning others, doing nothing for fear of failure, assuming a lack of options, and so on.

22. See http://www.quotationvault.com/author/_Voltaire.

23. For a great basic introduction, see S. Hagan, *Buddhism Plain and Simple* (New York: Random House, 1997). Also D. Lama, *The Art of Happiness* (New York: Riverhead Books, 1998).

24. Quote from J. Ming, "A Restless Mind," *Discover Taiwan* 13 (2010): 45–48.

25. The name refers to powerful people, not God in the Judeo-Christian sense, for example.

26. Hagen, *Buddhism Plain and Simple*, 125.

27. J. Blackman, *101 Defenses: How the Mind Shields Itself* (New York: Brunner-Routledge, 2004), ix.

28. E. Tolle, *Power of Now* (Novato, CA: New World Library, 1999).

29. S. Rosner and P. Hermes, *The Self-Sabotage Cycle* (Westport, CT: Praeger, 2006).

30. See http://www.brainyquote.com/quotes/quotes/a/alberteins133991.html.

CHAPTER 17 NOTES

1. See http://www.goodreads.com/author/quotes/38285.Carl_Gustav_Jung. A related quote from Jung is "One does not become enlightened by imagining figures of light, but by making the darkness conscious." A further quote is "Where there is ruin, there is hope for a treasure," Mawlana Jalal-al-Din Rumi (1207–1273), celebrated Persian poet, jurist, theologian, and Sufi mystic; http://www.goodreads.com/quotes/show/8521.

2. Organization for Economic Cooperation and Development, *Health Statistics: Total Expenditure as % of GDP (Most Recent) by Country* (Paris: Organization for Economic Cooperation and Development, 2010), http://www.oecd.org/document/16/0,2340,en_2649_34631_2085200_1_1_1_1,00.html.

3. R. Kessler, W. Chiu, O. Demler, and E. Walters, "Prevalence, Severity, and Comorbidity of Twelve-Month *DSM-IV* Disorders in the National Comorbidity Survey Replication (NCS-R)," *Archives of General Psychiatry* 62, no. 6 (2005): 617–27. Also cited in National Institute of Mental Health, "The Numbers Count: Mental Disorders in America," 2008, http://wwwapps.nimh.nih.gov/health/publications/the-numbers-count-mental-disorders-in-america.shtml.

4. The *DSM-IV-TR* criteria focus on "a maladaptive pattern of substance use leading to clinically significant impairment or distress," which is far more restrictive than merely use. It includes criteria that require "recurrent substance use resulting in a failure to fulfill major role obligations at work, school, or home" or "use in situations in which it is physically hazardous" or "causing legal problems" or "recurrent social or interpersonal problems caused or exacerbated by the effects of the substance (e.g., arguments with spouse about consequences of intoxication, physical fights)."

5. The rates in Table 17.1 add up to well over the above-mentioned 26 percent rate, as about 45 percent of people are diagnosed with multiple disorders; people with severe problems often have multiple disorders.

6. National Institute of Mental Health, "The Numbers Count: Mental Disorders in America."

7. See also J. Kahn and A. Langlieb, eds., *Mental Health and Productivity in the Workplace* (San Francisco: Jossey-Bass, 2003); D. Kemp, *Mental Health in the Workplace: An Employer's and Manager's Guide* (Westport, CT: Quorum Books, 1994).

8. Mental health now ranks second (only behind heart disease) among the conditions accounting for rising health care costs between 1987 and 2000, accounting for 7.4 percent of health care cost increases. M. Moran, "Many More People Seeking MH Treatment Since 1980s," *Psychiatric News* 39, no. 19 (2004): 15, http://pn.psychiatryonline.org/content/39/19/15.full.

9. American Psychological Association, "Survey Says: More Americans Are Seeking Mental Health Treatment," *Monitor on Psychology* 35, no. 7 (2004): 17, http://www.apa.org/monitor/julaug04/survey.aspx (accessed January 25, 2011).

10. E. Cohen, "CDC: Antidepressants Most Prescribed Drugs in the U.S.," *CNNhealth.com*, July 9, 2007, http://articles.cnn.com/2007-07-09/health/antidepressants_1_antidepressants-high-blood-pressure-

drugs-psychotropic-drugs?_s=PM:HEALTH. For a list of best-selling drugs, see http://en.wikipedia.org/wiki/List_of_bestselling_drugs (see "Depression, Anxiety Disorders").

11. A recent book claims that the United States is "exporting" its mental health problems: E. Watters, *Crazy Like Us: The Globalization in American Psyche* (New York: Free Press, 2010). Despite its provocative title and thesis, we think that other countries are just now improving their diagnosis and treatment.

12. Among 9,282 participants in the *National Comorbidity Survey Replication*. See also Anxiety Disorders Association of America, http://www.adaa.org/resources-professionals/conference/overview. Lifetime prevalence rates are 4.7 percent for panic disorder, 12.5 percent for specific phobias, 12.1 percent for social anxiety disorder, 5.7 percent for GAD, 6.8 percent for post-traumatic stress disorder, and 1.6 percent for OCD. Although most patients do not seek treatment until adulthood, more than 75 percent experience their first symptoms before age twenty-two, with eleven as the average age for the onset.

13. H. Kaplan and B. Sadock, *Synopsis of Psychiatry*, 10th ed. (Baltimore, MD: Lippencott, Williams & Wilkins, 2007), 586.

14. American Psychiatric Association, *Diagnostic and Statistical Manual of Mental Disorders*, text rev. (Washington, DC: American Psychiatric Association, 2000), 437.

15. Kaplan and Sadock, *Synopsis of Psychiatry*.

16. American Psychiatric Association, *DSM-IV-TR*. The *DSM* is now consistent with the *International Statistical Classification of Diseases and Related Health Problems* (ICD-10), published by the World Health Organization. For more information on *DSM*, see http://en.wikipedia.org/wiki/Diagnostic_and_Statistical_Manual_of_Mental_Disorders.

17. See http://www.dsm5.org/Pages/Default.aspx.

18. American Psychiatric Association, *DSM-IV-TR*, xxxvii.

19. Ibid., xxxi.

20. Feedback may be indirect, and in any event people have rationalizations for their behavior. Anxiety is also associated with successful performance (e.g., concern with test results might make one a better test taker, if the level of anxiety is not overwhelming), hence causing mixed signals at best about the need for change.

20a. See also: National Institutes of Health. "Generalized anxiety disorder." Source: http://www.ncbi.nlm.nih.gov/pubmedhealth/PMH0001915

21. A panic attack is defined as a discrete period of intense fear or discomfort with four or more of the following symptoms that develop abruptly and reach a peak within ten minutes: (1) palpitations, pounding heart, or accelerated heart rate; (2) sweating; (3) trembling

or shaking; (4) sensations of shortness of breath or smothering; (5) feeling of choking; (6) chest pain or discomfort; (7) nausea or abdominal distress; (8) feeling dizzy, unsteady, lightheaded, or faint; (9) "derealization" (feelings of unreality) or depersonalization (being detached from oneself); (10) fear of losing control or going crazy; (11) fear of dying; (12) numbness or tingling sensations (paresthesias); and (13) chills or hot flushes. An anxiety attack occurs in response to a specific stressor, though panic attacks also involve situations in which no apparent stressor is present or of which the person is conscious. American Psychiatric Association, *DSM-IV TR*, 432.

22. J. Thomas and M. Hersen, *Psychopathology in the Workplace* (London: Routledge, 2004), 109.

23. For example, A. Smith, R. Segal, and J. Segal, "How to Stop Worrying: Self-Help Strategies for Anxiety Relief," *Helpguide.org*, December 2010, http://helpguide.org/mental/anxiety_self_help.htm (accessed January 25, 2011). For a general overview of some treatment strategies, see S. Johnson, *Therapist's Guide to Clinical Intervention* (San Diego: Academic Press, 1997). Another useful book is R. Leider, *Life Skills: Taking Charge of Your Personal and Professional Growth* (San Diego: Pfeiffer, 1994). Though this is an older book, we find it very useful.

24. A mood is defined as a pervasive and sustained emotion that colors the person's perception of the world. Kaplan and Sadock, *Synopsis of Psychiatry*, 252.

25. "How to Recognize the Symptoms of Depression," *Health.com*, May 6, 2008, http://www.health.com/health/condition-article/ 0,,20187939,00.html?cnn=yes (accessed January 25, 2011).

26. National Institute of Mental Health, "The Numbers Count: Mental Disorders in America."

27. R. Friedman, "When Self-Knowledge Is Only the Beginning," *New York Times*, January 17, 2011, http://www.nytimes.com/2011/01/18/ health/views/18mind.html?_r=2&src=me&ref=homepage.

28. Clinically, one problem facing people with depression is that their gloomy outlook also extends to their willingness to acknowledge and seek treatment. Statements such as "but I am happy the way I am" or "this is just how I always am" are commonly heard. It is quite common for people to consider treatment only when events become overwhelming.

29. If both a depressed mood and loss of interests are present, then only three of the following must be present. A total of five symptoms of the entire list must be present.

30. P. Truax and T. McDonald, "Depression in the Workplace," in *Handbook of Mental Health in the Workplace*, ed. J. Thomas and M. Herson (Thousand Oaks, CA: Sage, 2002).

31. A. Sullivan, "Diagnosing Depression," Public Health Detailers' Training, NYC Department of Health and Mental Hygiene, *www.nyc.gov/html/doh/downloads/ppt/…/dmh-depression-04.ppt*. Based on *National Comorbidity Survey Replication* (NCS-R), 1999. Other sources state the lifetime incidence of depression as 12 percent for men and 20 percent for women. T. King and M. Brucker, *Pharmacology for Women's Health* (San Francisco: Jones & Bartlett, 2009), 759.

32. See http://www.health.com/health/condition-article/0,,20189151,00.html?cnn=yes.

33. G. Polanczyk, M. Silva de Lima, B. Lessa Horta, et al. "The Worldwide Prevalence of ADHD: A Systematic Review and Metaregression Analysis," *American Journal of Psychiatry* 164 (2007): 942–48.

34. Based on data reported in this chapter. ADHD: 60 percent of 5 percent = 3 percent; anxiety: 28.8 percent; mood disorders where one does not also experience a life incident of anxiety: (100 percent – 58 percent) of (12 + 20/2 =) 16 percent = 6.7 percent. The total (3 + 28.8 + 6.7) is 38.5 percent.

CHAPTER 18 NOTES

1. See http://www.goodreads.com/author/quotes/38285.Carl_Gustav_Jung.

2. Table 17.1 shows this as 9.1 percent, but some authors have suggested as much as 15 percent. There is a tendency among practitioners to underdiagnosis these disorders as they are considered harsh diagnoses that are largely untreatable. Bender reports, "Almost 15 percent of Americans, or 30.8 million adults, meet diagnostic criteria for at least one personality disorder, according to the results of the 2001–02 National Epidemiologic Survey on Alcohol and Related Conditions (NESARC)." E. Bender, "Personality Disorder Prevalence Surprises Researchers," *Psychiatric News* 39, no. 17 (2004): 12.

3. As always, we refer to the *DSM-IV-TR* for authoritative diagnostic criteria. American Psychiatric Association, *Diagnostic and Statistical Manual of Mental Disorders*, text rev. (Washington, DC: American Psychiatric Association, 2000).

4. G. Lester, *Personality Disorders in Social Work Practice* (Denver, CO: G. Lester, 2001). Course materials.

5. American Psychiatric Association, *DSM-IV-TR*, 704. See also M. Stout, *The Sociopath Next Door* (New York: Broadway Books, 2005).

6. R. Friedel, *Borderline Personality Disorder Demystified* (New York: Marlowe & Co., 2004). Few books deal only with borderline personalities at work; most are more general and have only a chapter or more; for example, L. Miller, *From Difficult to Disturbed* (New York: AMACOM, 2008), chap. 3, or B. Goff, "Borderline Personality Disorder," in *Handbook of Mental Health in the Workplace*, ed. J. Thomas and M. Hersen (Thousand Oaks, CA: Sage, 2002), 241–310. But the issue is important, and some Web sites provide cases and examples: M. Unterberg, "Personality Disorders in the Workplace: The Impulsive, Divisive Employee," *Business and Health*, September 1, 2003, http://managedhealthcareexecutive.modernmedicine.com/mhe/Psychology/Personality-Disorders-in-the-Workplace-The-Impulsi/ArticleStandard/Article/detail/134262.

7. American Psychiatric Association, *DSM-IV-TR*, 690.

8. Ibid., 705.

9. Ibid., 711.

10. See http://www.dsm5.org/ProposedRevisions/pages/proposedrevision.aspx?rid=470.

11. The *DSM-IV-TR* recognizes a dependent personality as a disorder but not a codependent personality. This is not projected to change in the *DSM-5*.

12. Op. cit., 50.

13. R. Hadikin and M. O'Driscoll, *The Bullying Culture* (Oxford, UK: Books for Midwives, 2000), 15.

14. Ibid., 16. See also M. Sartwell, *Bosses from Hell* (New York: Plume/Penguin Books, 1994).

15. R. Bramson, *Coping with Difficult Bosses* (New York: Fireside/Simon & Schuster, 1992), 71. Also R. Branson, *Coping with Difficult People* (Garden City, NY: Doubleday, 1981).

16. Virginia Commonwealth University, *Recognizing Substance Abuse in the Workplace: A Guide for Faculty and Staff Managers* (Richmond: Virginia Commonwealth University, Human Resource Division, 2005).

17. For example, S. Deep and L. Sussman, *What to Say to Get What You Want: Strong Words for 44 Challenging Types of Bosses, Employees, Coworkers, and Customers* (Reading, MA: Addison-Wesley, 1992).

18. P. Babiak and R. Hare, *Snakes in Suits: When Psychopaths Go to Work* (New York: HarperCollins, 2006). Also Stout, *The Sociopath Next Door*.

19. The *Hare Psychopath Checklist–Revised*, http://www.minddisorders.com/Flu-Inv/Hare-Psychopathy-Checklist.html.

20. K. Barr and B. O'Connor, "Antisocial Personality Disorder," in *Handbook of Mental Health in the Workplace*, ed. J. Thomas and M. Herson (Thousand Oaks, CA: Sage, 2002).

21. Ibid., 275.

22. Ibid., 273. They cite B. O'Connor and J. Dyce, "Personality Disorders," in *Advanced Abnormal Psychology*, ed. M. Herson and V. Van Hasselt (New York: Kluwer, 2001), 399–417.

23. S. Liff, *Managing Your Government Career* (New York: AMACOM, 2009).

CHAPTER 19 NOTES

1. The title of this chapter is taken from the book W. Bridges, *Transitions: Making Sense of Life's Changes* (Reading, MA: Addison-Wesley, 1980). A related book is J. D. Adams, J. Hayes, and B. Hopson, *Transition: Understanding and Managing Personal Change* (London: Martin Robertson, 1976).

2. Any number of possible people may suffer this. Planning: a compulsive person (e.g., executive)? Security: a child of divorced parents? Past: someone suffering from depression?

3. Bridges, *Transitions*, 90.

4. An older manager about sixty years old (Phil Woodward), played by Chris Cooper.

5. Employees do well to have about four to six months of extra salary in the bank, given the limits of unemployment benefits and separation payments. Many observers have long suggested that American families get back to basics; the fact that few have this amount does not bode well and likely increases anxiety.

6. The role of Bobby Walker, played by Ben Affleck.

7. E. Kübler-Ross, *On Death and Dying* (New York: Routledge, 1973).

8. For example, R. Friedman and J. W. James, "The Myth of the Stages of Dying, Death and Grief," *Skeptic Magazine* 14, no. 2 (2008): 37–42; P. Maciejewski, B. Zhang, S. Block, H. Prigerson, "An Empirical Examination of the Stage Theory of Grief," *Journal of the American Medical Association* 297, no. 7 (2007): 716–23. Others have questioned the number of stages; some suggest seven stages that include shock along with denial and an upward turn before acceptance in which people deal with mundane practical issues before experiencing acceptance. See "7 Stages of Grief," *Recover-from-grief.com*, 2011, http://www.recover-from-grief.com/7-stages-of-grief.html.

9. This is an exercise in reframing. People are apt to experience feeling bad and then look for reasons or conditions that justify these feelings. Some of these feelings may lie in the imperfections of one's present state, of course.
10. Personal communication.

CHAPTER 20 NOTE

http://www.wisdomquotes.com/topics/connections.

APPENDIX A NOTES

1. Plutchik does not classify these eight emotions, but joy, acceptance, and anticipation can be considered positive emotions. Another distinction is between primary and secondary emotions. Primary emotions are what we feel first; secondary emotions are what they lead to and what we may be aware of most. R. Plutchik, *Emotions and Life: Perspectives from Psychology, Biology, and Evolution* (Washington, DC: American Psychological Association, 2002). See also Wikipedia entry, "List of Emotions," http://en.wikipedia.org/wiki/List_of_emotions#Plutchik.27s_wheel_of_emotions.
2. W. Parrott, *Emotions in Social Psychology* (Philadelphia: Psychology Press, 2001).
3. P. Kuppens, A. Realo, and E. Diener, "The Role of Positive and Negative Emotions in Life Satisfaction Judgment across Nations," *Journal of Personality and Social Psychology* 95, no. 1 (2008): 66–75.
4. H. Kaplan and B. Sadock, *Synopsis of Psychiatry*, 8th ed. (Baltimore: Lippencott Williams & Wilkins, 1998), 93; see also R. Pally, *The Mind–Brain Relationship* (London: Karnac Books, 2000).
5. Similarly, frequent or arbitrary use of fear and statements causing fear is deeply resented by employees and is ultimately self-defeating for managers.
6. L. Kubzansky and I. Kawachi, "Going to the Heart of the Matter: Do Negative Emotions Cause Coronary Heart Disease?" *Journal of Psychosomatic Research* 48, nos. 4–5 (2000): 323–37. See also L. Gallo and K. Matthews, "Understanding the Association between Socioeconomic Status and Physical Health: Do Negative Emotions Play a Role?" *Psychological Bulletin* 129, no. 1 (2003): 10–51.
7. P. Salovey, "Emotional States and Physical Health," *American Psychologist* 55, no. 1 (2000): 110–21.

8. J. Gross, "Emotional Expression in Cancer Onset and Progression," *Social Science Medicine* 28 (1989): 1239–48; M. Jensen, "Psychobiological Factors Predicting the Course of Breast Cancer," *Journal of Personality* 55 (1987): 317–42; L. Temoshok, "Personality, Coping Style, Emotion and Cancer: Towards an Integrative Model," *Cancer Surveys* 6 (1987): 545–67.
9. For example, J. LaPool, "Do Happy People Live Longer?" *CBSNews.com*, March 4, 2010, http://www.cbsnews.com/stories/2010/03/04/health/cbsdoc/main6266646.shtml (accessed January 25, 2011).
10. And it is also not wise to ignore or suppress our feelings, as doing so causes somatizations such as stomach ulcers, depression, and muscle aches.
11. D. Goleman, *Emotional Intelligence: Why It Can Matter More Than IQ* (New York: Bantam Books, 1995). See also http://en.wikipedia.org/wiki/Emotional_intelligence.

Bibliography

Adams, J. D., J. Hayes, and B. Hopson. *Transition: Understanding and Managing Personal Change.* London: Martin Robertson, 1976.

Alwin, D. F. "Aging, Personality and Change: The Stability of Individual Differences over the Adult Life Span." In *Life-Span Development and Behaviour,* edited by D. L. Featherman, R. M. Learner, and M. Perlmutter, vol. 12. Hillsdale, NJ: Lawrence Erlbaum, 1994.

Amble, B. "Poor Conflict Management Costs Business Billions." *Management Issues,* May 26, 2006, http://www.management-issues. com/2006/8/24/research/poor-conflict-management-costs-business-billions.asp.

American Management Association. "Workplace Dating: 44% of Office Romances Lead to Marriage, AMA Survey Shows." 2003. http:// www.amanet.org/press/amanews/ workplace_dating.htm (accessed September 1, 2010).

American Psychiatric Association. *Diagnostic and Statistical Manual of Mental Disorders,* text rev. Washington, DC: American Psychiatric Association, 2000.

———. "Survey Says: More Americans Are Seeking Mental Health Treatment." *Monitor on Psychology* 35, no. 7 (2004): 17.

Arnold, J. *Managing Careers into the 21st Century.* London: Paul Chapman, 1997.

Ashworth, K. *Caught between the Dog and the Fireplug (or How to Survive Public Service).* Washington, DC: CQ Press, 2001.

Babiak, P., and R. Hare. *Snakes in Suits: When Psychopaths Go to Work.* New York: HarperCollins, 2006.

Baker, D. *What Happy People Know*. New York: St. Martin's Press, 2003.

Baron-Cohen, S. *The Essential Difference: The Truth about the Male and Female Brain*. New York: Basic Books, 2003.

Barr, K., and B. O'Connor. "Antisocial Personality Disorder." In *Handbook of Mental Health in the Workplace*, edited by J. Thomas and M. Herson. Thousand Oaks, CA: Sage, 2002.

Becker, E., and J. Wortman. *Mastering Communication at Work*. New York: McGraw-Hill, 2009.

Bender, E. "Personality Disorder Prevalence Surprises Researchers." *Psychiatric News* 39, no. 17 (2004): 12.

Berger, D. *Clinical Empathy*. Northvale, NJ: Jason Aronson, 1987.

Berman, E. *Performance and Productivity for Public and Nonprofit Organizations*. 2nd ed. New York: M. E. Sharpe, 2006.

Berman, E., and J. West. "Psychological Contracts in Local Government: A Preliminary Survey." *Review of Public Personnel Administration* 23, no. 4 (2003): 267–85.

———. "What Is Managerial Mediocrity? Definition, Prevalence and Negative Impact (Part 1)." *Public Performance and Management Review* 27, no. 2 (2003): 7–27.

———. "Managing Emotional Intelligence in U.S. Cities: A Study of Public Managers." *Public Administration Review* 68, no. 4 (2008): 742–58.

Berman, E., J. Bowman, J. West, and M. Van Wart. *Human Resource Management in Public Service*. Thousand Oaks, CA: Sage, 2010.

Berman, E., J. West, and M. Richter. "Workplace Relations: Friendship Patterns and Consequences (According to Managers)." *Public Administration Review* 62, no. 2 (2002): 155–68.

Berman, J., and V. Murphy-Brown. "Sex Differences in Friendship Patterns in India and the United States." *Basic and Applied Social Psychology* 9, no. 1 (1998): 61–71.

Bernard, M. E. *Procrastinate Later*. Melbourne: Schwartz & Wilkinson, 1991.

Blackman, J. *101 Defenses: How the Mind Shields Itself*. New York: Brunner-Routledge, 2004.

Bogdanich, W. "As Technology Surges, Radiation Safeguards Lag." *New York Times*. January 26 2010.

Boldt, L. *How to Find the Work You Love*. New York: Penguin Group, 1996.

Bolles, R. *What Color Is Your Parachute?* New York: Random House, 2010.

Bolman, L., and T. Deal. *Modern Approaches to Understanding and Managing Organizations*. San Francisco: Jossey-Bass, 1984.

Bolton, R., and D. Bolton. *People Styles at Work*. New York: AMACOM, 1996.

Bouton, K. "Peeling Away Theories on Gender and the Brain." *New York Times*. August 23, 2010. http://www.nytimes.com/2010/08/24/science/24scibks.html?8dpc.

Bowman, J., J. West, E. Berman, and M. Van Wart. *The Professional Edge: Competencies for Public Service.* New York: M. E. Sharpe, 2004.

Bozeman, B., and M. Feeney. "Public Management Mentoring: What Affects Outcomes?" *Journal of Public Administration Research and Theory* 19, no. 2 (2009): 427–52.

Bramson, R. *Coping with Difficult People.* Garden City, NY: Doubleday, 1981.

———. *Coping with Difficult Bosses.* New York: Fireside/Simon & Schuster, 1992.

Bridges, W. *Transitions: Making Sense of Life's Changes.* Reading, MA: Addison-Wesley, 1980.

Brizendine, L. *The Female Brain.* New York: Morgan Road Books, 2006.

Brown, D. *Career Choice and Development.* San Francisco: Jossey-Bass, 2002.

Broyard, B. *My Father's Secret.* CNN video. July 10, 2008. http://www.cnn.com/video/#/video/living/2008/07/10/bia.bliss.broyard.cnn; http://blissbroyard.com.

Bryant, A. "Meetings, Version 2.0, at Microsoft." *New York Times.* May 16, 2009.

Buhmiller, E., and S. Shane. "Pentagon Report on Fort Hood Details Failures." *New York Times.* January 16, 2010.

Bulleit, B. *Four Key Elements of Effective Business Communication.* Cary, NC: Global Knowledge Training, 2008. http://images.globalknowledge.com/wwwimages/whitepaperpdf/WP_Bulleit_BusCommunication_P.pdf.

Bunkley, N. "Prosecutor Tries to Kill Himself after Arrest in Pedophile Case." *New York Times.* September 21, 2007.

Burden, D. S., and B. Googins. *Balancing Job and Homelife Study: Managing Work and Family Stress in Corporations.* Boston: Boston University Center on Work and Family, 1987.

Cavell, M. "Valuing Emotions." Paper presented at the Annual Meeting of the Rapaport-Klein Study Group. June 11, 2004. http://www.psychomedia.it/rapaport-klein/cavell04.htm.

Chambers, T. "Misunderstandings Mar Workplace." *Korea Times.* October 13, 2005.

Chapman, G. *Five Languages of Love.* Chicago: Northfield, 1992.

Cherniss, C., and D. Goleman. *The Emotionally Intelligent Workplace: How to Select for, Measure, and Improve Emotional Intelligence in Individuals, Groups, and Organizations.* San Francisco: Jossey-Bass, 2001.

Christakis, N., and J. Fowler. *Connected: The Amazing Power of Social Networks and How They Shape Our Lives.* London: Harper Press, 2009.

Clutterbuck, D. *Everyone Needs a Mentor: Fostering Talent in Your Organisation.* 4th ed. London: Chartered Institute of Personnel and Development, 2004.

Clutterback, D., and D. Megginson. *Making Coaching Work.* London: Chartered Institute for Personnel and Development, 2005.

Cohen, E. "CDC: Antidepressants Most Prescribed Drugs in U.S." *CNNhealth.com.* July 9, 2007. http://www.cnn.com/2007/HEALTH/07/09/antidepressants/index.html.

Colvin, C. R., and J. Block. "Do Positive Illusions Foster Mental Health? An Examination of the Taylor and Brown Formulation." *Psychological Bulletin* 116, no. 1 (1994): 3–20.

Colvin, G. *Talent Is Overrated: What Really Separates World-Class Performers from Everybody Else.* New York: Portfolio Trade, 2010.

Cordin, E., P. Odgers, R. Redgate, L. Rowan, and A. Barnes. "$37 Billion: Counting the Cost of Employee Misunderstanding." White Paper. London: IDC, 2008.

Csikszentmihalyim, M. *Flow: The Psychology of Optimal Experience.* New York: Harper and Row, 1990.

Curnow, R. "Knowing When 'Yes' Means 'No' in Business." *CNN. com.* June 24, 2010. http://business.blogs.cnn.com/2010/06/24/knowing-when-yes-means-no-in-business/?hpt=C2.

D'Abate, C., and E. Eddy. "Engaging in Personal Business on the Job: Extending the Presenteeism Construct." *Human Resource Development Quarterly* 18, no. 3 (2007): 361–84.

Daloz, L. A. *Mentor: Guiding the Journey of Adult Learners.* San Francisco: Jossey-Bass, 1999.

Dannefer, D. "Adult Development and Social Theory: A Paradigmatic Reappraisal." *American Sociological Review* 49, no. 1 (1984): 100–16.

Davis, K. "Date Your Boss, Boost Your Career." *Kansas City Daily News.* February 12, 2006. http://findarticles.com/p/articles/mi_qn4181/is_20060212/ai_n16058270.

Davis Jr., R., and P. Garrison. "Mentoring: In Search of a Typology." Master's thesis, MIT Sloan, 1979.

De Becker, G. *The Gift of Fear and Other Survival Signals that Protect Us from Violence.* Beverly Hills, CA: Phoenix Books, 1997.

Deep, S., and L. Sussman. *What to Say to Get What You Want: Strong Words for 44 Challenging Types of Bosses, Employees, Coworkers, and Customers.* Reading, MA: Addison-Wesley, 1992.

Delong, T. J., J. Gabarro, and R. Lees. "Why Mentoring Matters in a Hypercompetitive World." *Harvard Business Review* 86, no. 1 (2008): 115–21.

Dobel, J. "Political Prudence and the Ethics of Leadership." *Public Administration Review* 58, no. 1 (1998): 74–81.

Doyle, A. "Reference Check Questions." *About.com.* n.d. http://jobsearch.about.com/od/referencesrecommendations/a/refercheck.htm.

Draper, J., and J. O'Brien. *Induction: Fostering Career Development at All Stages.* Edinburgh: Dunedin Academic Press, 2006.

Druskat, U., and S. Wolff. "Building the Emotional Intelligence of Groups." *Harvard Business Review* 79, no. 3 (2001): 80–90.

Dugas, C. "More Consumers, Workers Shoplift as Economy Slows." *USA Today*. June 19, 2008, 1B.

Ekman, P. *Telling Lies*. New York: W. W. Norton, 1985.

Ekman, P., W. Friessen, and D. Davidson. "The Duchenne Smile: Emotional Expression and Brain Physiology II." *Journal of Personality and Social Psychology* 58, no. 2 (1990): 342–53.

Epstein, M. *Thoughts without a Thinker*. New York: Basic Books, 2004.

Falcone, P. *96 Great Interview Questions to Ask Before You Hire*. 2nd ed. New York: AMACOM, 2009.

———. *101 Tough Conversations to Have with Employees*. New York: AMACOM, 2009.

Fearing, J. *Workplace Intervention*. Center City, MN: Hazeldon, 2000.

Ferrari, J. *Still Procrastinating: The No Regrets Guide to Getting It Done*. New York: Wiley, 2010.

Fine, C. *Delusions of Gender*. New York: W. W. Norton, 2010.

Fisher, R., and W. Ury. *Getting to Yes: Negotiating Agreement without Giving In*. New York: Penguin Books, 1983.

Forte, P. "The High Cost of Conflict." *Nursing Economics* 15, no. 3 (1997): 119–23.

Frankl, V. *Man's Search for Meaning*. Boston: Beacon Press, 2006. First published 1946.

Friedel, R. *Borderline Personality Disorder Demystified*. New York: Marlowe & Co., 2004.

Friedman, R. "When Self-Knowledge Is Only the Beginning." *New York Times*. January 17, 2011. http://www.nytimes.com/2011/01/18/health/views/18mind.html?_r=2&src=me&ref=homepage.

Friedman, R., and J. W. James. "The Myth of the Stages of Dying, Death and Grief." *Skeptic Magazine* 14, no. 2 (2008): 37–42.

Friedman, T. "No. 11! We're Number 1(1)!" *New York Times*. September 11, 2010.

Frone, M. "Prevalence and Distribution of Alcohol Use and Impairment in the Workplace: A U.S. National Survey." *Journal of Studies on Alcohol* 76, no. 1 (2006): 147–56.

Gallo, L., and K. Matthews. "Understanding the Association between Socioeconomic Status and Physical Health: Do Negative Emotions Play a Role?" *Psychological Bulletin* 129, no. 1 (2003): 10–51.

Gallup. "Attitudes in the American Workplace VI." American Institute of Stress. 2000. http://www.stress.org/job.htm (accessed January 25, 2011).

Gardenswartz, L., J. Cherbosque, and A. Rowe. *Emotional Intelligence for Managing Results in a Diverse World*. Mountain View, CA: Davies-Black, 2008.

Gaynor, G. *What Every New Manager Needs to Know.* New York: AMACOM, 2004.

Gheytanchi, A., L. Joseph, E. Gierlach, S. Kimpara, J. Housley, Z. Franco, and L. Beutler. "The Dirty Dozen: Twelve Failures of the Hurricane Katrina Response and How Psychology Can Help." *American Psychologist* 62, no. 2 (2007): 118–30.

Gillinson, S., and D. O'Leary. *Working Progress: How to Reconnect Young People and Organizations.* London: Demos, 2006.

Gladwell, M. *Blink: The Power of Thinking without Thinking.* New York: Little, Brown, 2005.

———. *Outliers: The Story of Success.* New York: Little, Brown, 2008.

Goff, B. "Borderline Personality Disorder." In *Handbook of Mental Health in the Workplace*, edited by J. Thomas and M. Hersen, 241–310. Thousand Oaks, CA: Sage, 2002.

Goldberg, L. R. "An Alternative Description of Personality: The Big-Five Factor Structure." *Journal of Personality and Social Psychology* 59 (1990): 1216–29.

Goleman, D. *Emotional Intelligence: Why It Can Matter More Than IQ.* New York: Bantam Books, 1995.

Goleman, D., and R. Boyatzis. *Primal Leadership.* Boston: Harvard Business School, 2002.

Goodman, M. "Bartering Sex for Stuff or Services." *CNN.com.* August 25, 2008. http://www.cnn.com/2008/LIVING/personal/08/25/sex.for. stuff/index.html?iref=mpstoryview.

Greene, J., and B. Burleson. *Handbook of Communication and Social Interaction Skills.* London: Routledge, 2003.

Greenhaus, J., G. Callanan, and V. Godshalk. *Career Management.* 4th ed. Thousand Oaks, CA: Sage, 2010.

Greenhouse, S. "Flex Time Flourishes in Accounting Industry." *New York Times.* January 8, 2011.

Grobman, G. "An Analysis of Codes of Ethics of Nonprofit, Tax-Exempt Membership Associations." *Public Integrity* 9, no. 3 (2007): 245–63.

Gross, J. "Emotional Expression in Cancer Onset and Progression." *Social Science Medicine* 28 (1989): 1239–48.

Gullick, L., and L. Urwick. *Papers on the Science of Administration.* New York: Institute of Public Administration, 1937.

Hadikin, R., and M. O'Driscoll. *The Bullying Culture.* Oxford, UK: Books for Midwives, 2000.

Hagan, S. *Buddhism Plain and Simple.* New York: Random House, 1997.

Hall, D. *Careers in Organizations.* Glenview, IL: Scott Foresman, 1976.

Harrington, B., and D. Hall. *Career Management and Work-Life Integration.* Thousand Oaks, CA: Sage, 2007.

Higgins, M., and K. Kram. "Reconceptualizing Mentoring at Work: A Developmental Network Perspective." *The Academy of Management Review* 26, no. 1 (2001): 264–88.

Hofstede, G. *Culture's Consequences*. London: Sage, 1980.

Hollinger, R. *National Retail Security Survey*. Gainesville: University of Florida, 2005.

Hollis, J. *Finding Meaning in the Second Half of Life*. New York: Gotham Books, 2005.

———. *Why Good People Do Bad Things*. New York: Gotham Books, 2007.

Holmes, T., and R. Rahe. "Social Adjustment Rating Scale." *Journal of Psychosomatic Research* 11, no. 2 (1967): 213–21.

"How to Recognize the Symptoms of Depression," *Health.com*. May 6, 2008. http://www.health.com/health/condition-article/0,,20187939,00.html?cnn=yes (accessed January 25, 2011).

Howard, P. *The Brain (an Owner's Manual)*. Austin, TX: Bard Press, 2006.

Hummel, R. *The Bureaucratic Experience*. 5th ed. Armonk, NY: M. E. Sharpe, 2007.

Humphries, A. "Saying the Unsayable to Your Co-Worker." *CNN.com*. March 26, 2001. http://archives.cnn.com/2001/CAREER/corporateclass/03/22/etiquette/index.html.

Hunt, J., and J. Weintraub. *The Coaching Manager*. 2nd ed. Thousand Oaks, CA: Sage, 2011.

Hwai, L.-S. "Taiwan's Fertility Rate at Record Low." *Asian News Network*. August 18, 2010. http://www.asianewsnet.net/home/news.php?id=13705 (accessed January 25, 2011).

Hyatt, J. "Unethical Behavior: Largely Unreported in Offices and Justified by Teens." *Corporate Responsibility Magazine*. 2008. http://www.thecro.com/node/612 (accessed January 25, 2011).

Inkson, K. *Understanding Careers: The Metaphors of Working Lives*. Thousand Oaks, CA: Sage, 2006.

Ivie, K. "Millennials and Mentoring: Making It Work." *Social Citizens*. August 17, 2010. http://www.socialcitizens.org/blog/millennials-and-mentoring-making-it-work (accessed January 25, 2011).

"Japanese Employees Are Working Themselves to Death." *The Economist*. December 19, 2007. http://www.economist.com/world/asia/story_id=10329261.

Jensen, M. "Psychobiological Factors Predicting the Course of Breast Cancer." *Journal of Personality* 55 (1987): 317–42.

Johnson, S. *Therapist's Guide to Clinical Intervention*. San Diego: Academic Press, 1997.

Jones, D. "Often, Men Help Women Get to the Corner Office." *USA Today*. August 5, 2009.

Jones, S. "How to Make Friends at Work: Ten Super Sensible Ideas." *AssociatedContent*. May 30, 2007. http://www.associatedcontent.com/article/257209/how_to_make_friends_at_work_ten_super.

Kahn, J., and A. Langlieb, eds. *Mental Health and Productivity in the Workplace*. San Francisco: Jossey-Bass, 2003.

Kahneman, D., and A. Deaton. "High Income Improves Evaluation of Life but Not Emotional Well-Being." *Proceedings of the National Academy of Sciences* 107, no. 38 (2010): 16489–93.

Kanga, S. "Workplace Etiquette: Mind Your Manners!" *Rediff News*. August 25, 2008. http://www.rediff.com/getahead/2008/aug/25work.htm.

Kaplan, H., and B. Sadock. *Synopsis of Psychiatry*. 8th ed. Baltimore: Lippencott Williams & Wilkins, 1998.

———. *Synopsis of Psychiatry*. 10th ed. Baltimore: Lippencott Williams & Wilkins, 2007.

Kavanagh, K., and P. Nailon. *Excellence in the Workplace: Legal and Life Skills*. St. Paul, MN: Thomson/West, 2007.

Kearney, R., and E. Berman, eds. *Public Sector Performance: Management, Motivation and Measurement*. ASPA Classics Series. Boulder, CO: Westview, 1999.

Keirsey, D. *Please Understand Me II*. Del Mar, CA: Prometheus Nemesis, 1998.

Kemp, D. *Mental Health in the Workplace: An Employer's and Manager's Guide*. Westport, CT: Quorum Books, 1994.

Kessler, R., W. Chiu, O. Demler, and E. Walters. "Prevalence, Severity, and Comorbidity of Twelve-Month *DSM-IV* Disorders in the National Comorbidity Survey Replication (NCS-R)." *Archives of General Psychiatry* 62, no. 6 (2005): 617–27.

King, T., and M. Brucker. *Pharmacology for Women's Health*. San Francisco: Jones & Bartlett, 2009.

Klein, S. *The Science of Happiness*. Philadelphia: Perseus Books, 2006.

Knapp, M., and J. Hall. *Nonverbal Communication in Human Interaction*. 6th ed. Belmont, CA: Wadsworth, 2006.

Knapp, M., and A. Vangelisti. *Interpersonal Communication and Human Relationships*. 5th ed. New York: Allyn & Bacon, 2006.

Kolb, D. A. *Learning Style Inventory*. Boston: McBer, 1985.

Kornblum, J. "Study: 25% of Americans Have No One to Confide In." *USA Today*. June 22, 2006. http://www.usatoday.com/news/nation/2006-06-22-friendship_x.htm.

Kraft, M. "Mentoring in Knowledge Work." August 23, 2010. http://www.bpmnforum.net/blog27/bpm/mentoring-in-knowledge-work (accessed January 25, 2011).

Kübler-Ross, E. *On Death and Dying*. London: Routledge, 1973.

Kubzansky, L., and I. Kawachi. "Going to the Heart of the Matter: Do Negative Emotions Cause Coronary Heart Disease?" *Journal of Psychosomatic Research* 48, nos. 4–5 (2000): 323–37.

Kuppens, P., A. Realo, and E. Diener. "The Role of Positive and Negative Emotions in Life Satisfaction Judgment across Nations." *Journal of Personality and Social Psychology* 95, no. 1 (2008): 66–75.

Lama, D. *The Art of Happiness.* New York: Riverhead Books, 1998.

Landy, F. *The Psychology of Work Behavior.* Belmont, CA: Wadsworth, 1989.

Lankau, M., and T. Scandura. "An Investigation of Personal Learning in Mentoring Relationships: Content, Antecedents, and Consequences." *Academy of Management Journal* 45, no. 4 (2002): 779–90.

LaPool, J. "Do Happy People Live Longer?" *CBSNews.com.* March 4, 2010. http://www.cbsnews.com/stories/2010/03/04/health/cbsdoc/main6266646.shtml (accessed January 25, 2011).

Leider, R. *Life Skills: Taking Charge of Your Personal and Professional Growth.* San Diego: Pfeiffer, 1994.

Leitsch, S. *Review of Skills, Interim Report Chapter 6: The Increasing Importance of Skills.* London: HM Treasury, 2006.

Lester, G. *Personality Disorders in Social Work Practice.* Denver, CO: G. Lester, 2001.

Levinson, D. *The Seasons of a Man's Life.* New York: Knopf, 1978.

———. *The Seasons of a Woman's Life.* New York: Knopf, 1996.

Liberman, M. "Sex on the Brain: Women Use 20,000 Words a Day, Men Only 7,000—Or So Says a New Bestseller. Fact-checking 'The Female Brain.' " *Boston.com.* September 24, 2006. http://www.boston.com/news/globe/ideas/articles/2006/09/24/sex_on_the_brain.

Liff, S. *Managing Government Employees.* New York: AMACOM, 2007.

———. *Managing Your Government Career.* New York: AMACOM, 2009.

———. *The Complete Guide to Hiring and Firing Government Employees.* New York: AMACOM, 2010.

Lohr, S. "G.E. Goes with What It Knows: Making Stuff." *New York Times.* December 5, 2010.

London, M. *Career Barriers: How People Experience, Overcome, and Avoid Failure.* Mahwah, NJ: Lawrence Erlbaum, 1998.

Lowndes, L. *How to Talk to Anyone: 92 Little Tricks for Big Success in Relationships.* New York: McGraw-Hill, 2003.

Lowther, W. "Blundering Bush Makes Another Gaffe as He Winks at the Queen." *Mail Online.* May 8, 2007. http://www.dailymail.co.uk/news/article-453199/Blundering-Bush-makes-ANOTHER-gaffe-winks-Queen.html (accessed January 25, 2011).

Lykken, D., and A. Tellegen. "Happiness Is a Stochastic Phenomenon." *Psychological Science* 7, no. 3 (1996): 186–89.

Lynn, A. *The EQ Interview: Finding Employees with High Emotional Intelligence*. New York: AMACOM, 2008.

Lyubomirsky, S. *The How of Happiness*. New York: Penguin Press, 2007.

Lyubomirsky, S., D. Schkade, and K. Sheldon. "Pursuing Happiness: The Architecture of Sustainable Change." *Review of General Psychology* 9, no. 2 (2005): 111–31.

Maciejewski, P., B. Zhang, S. Block, and H. Prigerson. "An Empirical Examination of the Stage Theory of Grief." *Journal of the American Medical Association* 297, no. 7 (2007): 716–23.

Malcolm, A. "Did You Hear What Michelle Said?" *Los Angeles Times*. August 22, 2007.

Marston, C. *Motivating the "What's in It for Me?" Workforce*. New York: Wiley, 2007.

Maslow, A. *Towards a Psychology of Being*. New York: Wiley, 1998.

McFadden, R. "Army Doctor Held in Ft. Hood Rampage." *New York Times*. November 6, 2009.

McFall, R. "A Review and Reformulation of the Concept of Social Skills." *Behavioral Assessment* 4, no. 1 (1982): 1–33.

McKinley, J., and J. Dao. "Fort Hood Gunman Gave Signals Before His Rampage." *New York Times*. November 9, 2009.

McManamy, J. "Lincoln and His Depressions." *McMan's Depression and Bipolar Web*. November 10, 2005. http://www.mcmanweb.com/lincoln_depression.html (accessed January 25, 2011).

"Meeting spelers na incident Oranje." [Players meet after incident.] *De Telegraaf* (Dutch). June 29, 2010.

Mehta, M. "NY Jets' Dustin Keller Grateful for Lessons Learned under Mentor Brett Favre." *NJ.com*. September 18, 2009. http://www.nj.com/jets/index.ssf/2009/09/ny_jets_dustin_keller_grateful.html.

Menzel, D. *Ethics Moments in Government*. New York: Taylor & Francis, 2010.

Merrell, K., and G. Gimpel. *Social Skills of Children and Adolescents: Conceptualization, Assessment and Treatment*. Mahwah, NJ: Lawrence Erlbaum, 1998.

Miller, L. *From Difficult to Disturbed*. New York: AMACOM, 2008.

Ming, J. "A Restless Mind." *Discover Taiwan* 13 (2010): 45–48.

Mooney, N. *I Can't Believe She Did That! Why Women Betray Other Women at Work*. New York: St. Martin's Press, 2006.

Moran, M. "Many More People Seeking MH Treatment since 1980s." *Psychiatric News* 39, no. 19 (2004): 15.

Moriarty, M. "Workplace Coach: Be Clear: Conflict Thrives in Confusing Situations." *Seattle PI Business*. November 18, 2007.

Moynihan, D., and S. Pandey. "The Role of Organizations in Fostering Public Service Motivation." *Public Administration Review* 67, no. 1 (2007): 40–53.

Murphy, F., I. Nimmo-Smith, and A. D. Lawrence. "Functional Neuroanatomy of Emotions: A Meta-analysis." *Cognitive, Affective, and Behavioral Neuroscience* 3, no. 3 (2003): 207–33.

National Institute of Mental Health. "National Survey Tracks Prevalence of Personality Disorders in U.S. Population." *Science Update*. October 18, 2007. http://www.nimh.nih.gov/science-news/2007/national-survey-tracks-prevalence-of-personality-disorders-in-us-population.shtml.

———. "The Numbers Count: Mental Disorders in America." 2008. http://wwwapps.nimh.nih.gov/health/publications/the-numbers-count-mental-disorders-in-america.shtml.

Niles, S. G., and J. Harris-Bowlsbey. *Career Development Interventions in the 21st Century*. Englewood Cliffs, NJ: Prentice Hall, 2008.

Northouse, P. *Leadership Ethics*. Thousand Oaks, CA: Sage, 2004.

O'Connell, P. "Generational Tension." *Bloomberg Businessweek*. June 9, 2008. http://www.businessweek.com/business_at_work/generation_gap/archives/2008/06/generation_gap.html (accessed January 25, 2011).

O'Connor, B., and J. Dyce. "Personality Disorders." In *Advanced Abnormal Psychology*, edited by M. Herson and V. Van Hasselt, 399–417. New York: Kluwer, 2001.

Odiorne, G. "MBO in State Government." *Public Administration Review* 36, no. 1 (1976): 28–33.

O'Driscoll, M., and C. Cooper. "Job-Related Stress and Burnout." In *Psychology at Work*, edited by P. Warr, 203–30. 5th ed. London: Penguin Books, 2002.

Oliver, V. *301 Smart Answers to Tough Interview Questions*. Naperville, IL: Sourcebooks, 2005.

Organization for Economic Cooperation and Development. *Health Statistics: Total Expenditure as % of GDP (Most Recent) by Country*. Paris: Organization for Economic Cooperation and Development, 2010.

Osland, J., D. Kolb, and I. Rubin. *Organizational Behavior: An Experiential Approach*. 8th ed. New York: Prentice Hall, 2006.

Pally, R. *The Mind–Brain Relationship*. London: Karnac Books, 2000.

Parrott, W. *Emotions in Social Psychology*. Philadelphia: Psychology Press, 2001.

Patnaik, D., and P. Mortensen. *Wired to Care: How Companies Prosper When They Create Widespread Empathy*. Upper Saddle River, NJ: FT Press, 2009.

Pattakos, A. *Prisoners of Our Thoughts*. San Francisco: Berrett-Koehler, 2008.

Payne, S. "Longitudinal Examination of the Influence of Mentoring on Organizational Commitment and Turnover." *Academy of Management Journal* 48, no. 1 (2005): 158–68.

Perry, J. "Measuring Public Service Motivation: An Assessment of Construct Reliability and Validity." *Journal of Public Administration Research and Theory* 6, no. 1 (1996): 5–22.

Petak, L. "Young Lawyers Turn to Public Service." *New York Times*. August 19, 2010.

Peter, L., and R. Hull. *The Peter Principle*. New York: William Morrow, 1969.

Pfeffer, J. *Power in Organizations*. Marshfield, MA: Pitman, 1981.

Plutchik, R. *Emotions and Life: Perspectives from Psychology, Biology, and Evolution*. Washington, DC: American Psychological Association, 2002.

Polachek, S., and W. Robert. *The Economics of Earnings*. London: Cambridge University Press, 1993.

Polanczyk, G., M. Silva de Lima, B. Lessa Horta, et al. "The Worldwide Prevalence of ADHD: A Systematic Review and Metaregression Analysis." *American Journal of Psychiatry* 164 (June 2007): 942–48.

Raabe, B., and T. Beehr. "Formal Mentoring versus Supervisor and Coworker Relationships: Differences in Perceptions and Impact." *Journal of Organizational Behavior* 24, no. 3 (2003): 271–93.

Rabin, M., and J. Schrag. "First Impressions Matter: A Model of Confirmatory Bias." *Quarterly Journal of Economics* 114, no. 1 (1999): 37–82.

Raffel, J. "What We Have Learned from the NASPAA Standards Review Process." *Journal of Public Affairs Education* 16, no. 1 (2009): 5–12.

Randstad. "New Randstad Work Watch Survey Reveals What Really Irks Employees." May 5, 2010, http://us.randstad.com/content/aboutrandstad/news-and-press-releases/press-releases/2010/20100505003.xml.

Randstad/Harris Poll. *2008 World of Work*. Amsterdam, the Netherlands: Randstad/Harris, 2008.

"Randstad USA Survey Identifies Biggest Office Flirts: Westerners and Men." *Business Wire*. February 6, 2007. http://findarticles.com/p/articles/mi_m0EIN/is_2007_Feb_6/ai_n27138934 (accessed January 25, 2011).

Rapport, R., L. Bailyn, J. Fletcher, and B. Pruitt. *Beyond Work–Family Balance: Advancing Gender Equity and Workplace Performance*. San Francisco: Jossey-Bass, 2001.

Rath, T. *Vital Friends*. New York: Gallup Press, 2006.

Rath, T., and J. Harter. *Wellbeing: The Five Essential Elements*. New York: Gallup Press, 2010.

Rey, D. *1001 Ways to Get Promoted*. Pompton Plains, NJ: Career Press, 2000.

Rich, M. "For the Unemployed over 50, Fears of Never Working Again." *New York Times*. September 19, 2010.

Robinson, F. "Poll: Americans Are Becoming More Rude." *Deseret News*. September 22, 2009.

Rock, D. *Your Brain at Work*. New York: Harper Business Press, 2009.

Rosner, S., and P. Hermes. *The Self-Sabotage Cycle*. Westport, CT: Praeger, 2006.

Rubin, R. "CDC: U.S. Birth Rate Falls, but Not among Moms 40 and Up." *USA Today*. April 6, 2010. http://www.usatoday.com/news/health/2010-04-06-birth-rate_N.htm.

Salovey, P. "Emotional States and Physical Health." *American Psychologist* 55, no. 1 (2000): 110–21.

Sartre, J.-P. *Huis Clos*. Paris: Gallimard, 1944.

Sartwell, M. *Bosses from Hell*. New York: Plume/Penguin Books, 1994.

Schein, E. *Career Anchors*. San Francisco: Pfeiffer, 1979.

———. *Career Anchors*. 3rd ed. San Francisco: Pfeiffer, 2006.

Schwartz, T. "Dope, Dopes, and Dopamine: The Problem with Money." *Harvard Business Review*. October 26, 2010. http://blogs.hbr.org/schwartz/2010/10/dopes-and-dopamine-the-problem.html (accessed January 25, 2011).

Scott, J. "Do Attractive People Get Better Treatment Than Others?" *Jet* 100, no. 12 (2001): 52–54.

Segal, D. "Is Law School a Losing Game?" *New York Times*. January 8, 2011.

Seligman, M. *What You Can Change and What You Can't: The Complete Guide to Successful Self-Improvement*. New York: Ballantine Books, 1993.

———. *Authentic Happiness*. New York: Free Press, 2004.

Seward, B. *Managing Stress*. Sudbury, MA: Jones-Bartlett, 2006.

Sheehy, G. *Passages*. New York: Ballantine Books, 1996.

Simpson, K. "The Role of Testosterone in Aggression." *McGill Journal of Medicine* 6 (2001): 32–40.

Sin, N., and S. Lyubomirsky. "Enhancing Well-Being and Alleviating Depressive Symptoms with Positive Psychology Interventions: A Practice-Friendly Meta-analysis." *Journal of Clinical Psychology* 65 (2009): 467–87.

Skillsoft. *Research into UK Workers Stress Levels*. Camberley, UK: Compass House, 2008. http://www.skillsoft.com/infocenter/whitepapers/documents/research-into-uk-workers-stress-levels.pdf.

Smith, A., R. Segal, and J. Segal. "How to Stop Worrying: Self-Help Strategies for Anxiety Relief." *Helpguide.org*. December 2010. http://helpguide.org/mental/anxiety_self_help.htm (accessed January 25, 2011).

Steel, P. "The Nature of Procrastination: A Meta-analytic and Theoretical Review of Quintessential Self-Regulatory Failure." *Psychological Bulletin* 133, no. 1 (2007): 65–94.

Stolberg, S., and J. Rutenberg. "Bush to Get Etiquette Tips before He Receives the Queen." *New York Times*. May 4, 2007. http://www.nytimes.com/2007/05/04/world/americas/04iht-04queen.5573127.html.

Stout, M. *The Sociopath Next Door*. New York: Broadway Books, 2005.

Swanson, J., and N. Fouad. *Career Theory and Practice: Learning through Case Studies*. Thousand Oaks, CA: Sage, 2009.

Tannen, D. *You Just Don't Understand: Women and Men in Conversation*. New York: William Morrow, 1990.

Taylor, S., and J. Brown. "Illusion and Well-Being: A Social Psychological Perspective on Mental Health." *Psychological Bulletin* 103 (1988): 193–210.

Temoshok, L. "Personality, Coping Style, Emotion and Cancer: Towards an Integrative Model." *Cancer Surveys* 6 (1987): 545–67.

Tetlock, P. "Accountability and the Perseverance of First Impressions." *Social Psychology Quarterly* 46, no. 4 (1983): 285–92.

Thomas, J., and M. Hersen, eds. *Handbook of Mental Health in the Workplace*. Thousand Oaks, CA: Sage, 2002.

———. *Psychopathology in the Workplace*. London: Routledge, 2004.

Tolle, E. *Power of Now*. Novato, CA: New World Library, 1999.

Tonidandel, S., D. Avery, and M. Phillips. "Maximizing Returns on Mentoring: Factors Affecting Subsequent Protégé Performance." *Journal of Organizational Behavior* 28, no. 1 (2007): 89–110.

Truax, P., and T. McDonald. "Depression in the Workplace." In *Handbook of Mental Health in the Workplace*, edited by J. Thomas and M. Herson. Thousand Oaks, CA: Sage, 2002.

Trunk, P. "Positive Psychology Exhausts Me: Requires So Much Self-Discipline." February 12, 2008. http://blog.penelopetrunk.com/2008/02/12/the-big-secret-about-happiness-its-really-about-self-discipline (accessed January 25, 2011).

Turner, J., J. Mccann, and M. Gelles. *Threat Assessment: A Risk Management Approach*. London: Routledge, 2003.

Twenge, J. *Generation Me*. New York: Free Press, 2006.

Unterberg, M. "Personality Disorders in the Workplace: The Impulsive, Divisive Employee." *Business and Health*. September 1, 2003. http://managedhealthcareexecutive.modernmedicine.com/mhe/Psychology/Personality-Disorders-in-the-Workplace-The-Impulsi/ArticleStandard/Article/detail/134262.

U.S. Bureau of Labor Statistics. *Number of Jobs Held, Labor Market Activity, and Earnings Growth among the Youngest Baby Boomers: Results from a Longitudinal Survey*. Washington, DC: U.S. Bureau of Labor Statistics, 2010.

U.S. Department of Health and Human Services. "Workplace Substance Abuse Statistics." n.d. http://www.drugfreeworkplace.gov/WPWorkit/pdf/workplace_substance_abuse_statistics_fs.pdf (accessed January 25, 2011).

———. "Mental Health: A Report of the Surgeon General—Executive Summary." 1999. http://www.surgeongeneral.gov/library/mentalhealth/chapter2/sec2_1.html#epidemiology.

———. *Results from the 2009 National Survey on Drug Use and Health: Volume I. Summary of National Findings.* NSDUH Series H-38A, HHS Publication No. SMA 10–4586. Washington, DC: U.S. Department of Health and Human Services, Office of Applied Studies, 2010.

U.S. National Institute for Occupational Safety and Health. *Stress at Work.* DHHS (NIOSH) Publication No. 99–101. Washington, DC: U.S. National Institute for Occupational Safety and Health, 1999.

U.S. SAMHSA. *Special Report: Improving Mental Health Insurance Benefits without Increasing Costs.* Washington, DC: U.S. Department of Health and Human Services Substance Abuse and Mental Health Services Administration, 2001.

Virginia Commonwealth University. *Recognizing Substance Abuse in the Workplace: A Guide for Faculty and Staff Managers.* Richmond: Virginia Commonwealth University, Human Resource Division, 2005.

Voice of America. "Poll Finds America's Image Still Negative Abroad." June 24, 2005. http://www1.voanews.com/english/news/a-13-2005-06-24-voa1-67392542.html (accessed January 25, 2011).

Wall, B. *Working Relationships: The Simple Truth about Getting along with Friends and Foes at Work.* Palo Alto, CA: Davies-Black, 1999.

———. *Working Relationships: Using Emotional Intelligence to Enhance Your Effectiveness with Others.* Mountain View, CA: Davies-Black, 2008.

Walsh, W. B., and M. Savickas. *Handbook of Vocational Psychology: Theory, Research, and Practice.* 3rd ed. Mahwah, NJ: Lawrence Erlbaum, 2005.

Warr, P., ed. *Psychology at Work.* 5th ed. London: Penguin Books, 2002.

———. *Work, Happiness and Unhappiness.* New York: Lawrence Erlbaum, 2007.

Watters, E. *Crazy Like Us: The Globalization in American Psyche.* New York: Free Press, 2010.

Yandrick, R. *Behavioral Risk Management.* San Francisco: Jossey-Bass, 1996.

Yate, M. *Resumes That Knock' em Dead.* Holbrook, MA: Adams Media, 2006.

———. *Knock 'em Dead 2009: The Ultimate Job Search Guide.* Holbrook, MA: Adams Media, 2008.

Zouhali-Worrall, M. "Found in Translation: Avoiding Multilingual Gaffes." *CNN.com.* July 14, 2008.

———. "How Not to Sell Abroad." *CNN.com.* September 30, 2008. http://money.cnn.com/galleries/2008/fsb/0807/gallery.bad_translations.fsb/index.html.

Index